SEASON OF THE WITCH

SEASON OF THE WITCH

THE BOOK OF GOTH

CATHI UNSWORTH

NINE EIGHT BOOKS

NINE EIGHT BOOKS
NEB 016

First published in the UK in 2023 by Nine Eight Books
An imprint of Bonnier Books UK
4th Floor, Victoria House, Bloomsbury Square, London, WC1B 4DA
Owned by Bonnier Books, Sveavägen 56, Stockholm, Sweden

@nineeightbooks

@nineeightbooks

Hardback ISBN: 978-1-7887-0624-7
eBook ISBN: 978-1-7887-0625-4

A CIP catalogue record for this book is available from the British Library.

Publishing director: Pete Selby
Senior editor: Melissa Bond

Typeset by IDSUK (Data Connection) Ltd
Printed and bound in Great Britain by Clays Ltd, Elcograf S.p.A

1 3 5 7 9 10 8 6 4 2

Nine Eight Books is an imprint of Bonnier Books UK
www.bonnierbooks.co.uk

FSC
www.fsc.org
MIX
Paper from responsible sources
FSC® C018072

For my dear friends, Joe McNally and Pete Woodhead

Film Club Forever!

'In the old days, the Devil was often referred to as the Lord of Misrule. The object of these high-up Satanists is to deliver the world to him and the only way they can do that is to cause the breakdown of good rule so that misrule may take its place. With that as their goal, they do everything they can to foment wars, class hatred, strikes and famine; and to foster perversions, moral laxity and the taking of drugs.'

– Dennis Wheatley, *To the Devil a Daughter* (1953)

CONTENTS

PROLOGUE

In the flat field

I turned from a child into a teenager during the first four years of our first woman prime minister's reign. Even from the distance of four decades, I can still feel a shadow stealing across the happy, sunlit days of my '70s childhood – coinciding with the onset of puberty, transition to high school and all the embarrassment and alienation that came with that. I felt the wind change in 1979, though I scarcely comprehended the forces behind it.

Shocking events flashed before my eyes via the BBC News, *Top of the Pops* and *Nationwide*. The strikes by rail and public workers they called the Winter of Discontent that left the dead unburied and rubbish rotting in the streets. The death of king punk rocker Sid Vicious, on bail for the murder of his girlfriend Nancy Spungen in New York, from a hotshot of heroin purchased by his mother, Anne Beverley. The assassination of Airey Neave by the Irish National Liberation Army. The murder of Blair Peach on an anti-Nazi demo in Southall. And the Ripper still running wild in Yorkshire, claiming his eleventh murder victim – a girl of just nineteen.

I didn't have many friends in school and lived miles apart from them anyway, in a rambling old house set in the 20 acres of arable east Norfolk land farmed by our only neighbours, a thirty-minute bike ride from the nearest village. My parents were both teachers and wanted my brother and me to grow up in rural idyll – they had spent their childhoods in cities that were being Blitzed during the Second World War. Great Yarmouth, the seaside town where they worked and we went to school, had many social problems caused by poverty and unemployment – it was ranked the fourth most deprived town in Europe.[1] My parents' desire to keep us at a safe distance from our peers was, I'm sure, born of concern that we didn't get to experience too many of these problems first-hand. But you know what kids are like. Curious about the things you wish to shield them from, they want instead to try to understand why they seem to be so different from everyone else they know. My fumbling search for enlightenment turned me to the dark side.

Books and music were both my solace and the source of all the information I wasn't getting at school. At home, our abundant shelves were stacked with high and popular literature; local, modern and ancient history; geography and the arts. Two of my childhood favourites were Beverley Nichols' tale of suburban sorcery, *The Wickedest Witch in the World* and Dodie Smith's *The Hundred and One Dalmatians*, which I read at least as many times. I was also a big fan of Oscar Wilde, Sherlock Holmes and Rosemary Sutcliff's stories about ancient Britain and Rome. So perhaps I had already made my start down a certain path when, from a corner of the spare room, a cluster of pulp paperbacks beckoned me away from their more worthy literary companions.

Thick black typeface spelled out their sinister subject matter against sulphurous yellow spines: *The Satanist. The Devil Rides Out. To the Devil a Daughter.* Their presence here was a riddle in itself – though we didn't go to church regularly, my parents were definitely God-fearing Christians, so what the devil were they doing with these?

I picked one out. On its front cover a young woman, her body entwined by snakes, stood on the brink of an abyss, surrounded by fire-breathing demons. An Author's Note preceded the first chapter. Dennis Wheatley explained that, during his research into the subject, 'I found ample evidence that Black Magic is still practised in London, and other cities at the present day.' He went on to warn any readers tempted to make a more serious study of the 'Secret Art' that 'to do so would bring them into dangers of a very real and concrete nature'.

This was something I had heard about. Rumours circulated by kids in the village, warnings muttered darkly as we sat about the Belton bus shelter of an evening. Not to spend too long staring into mirrors, through which the Devil could come and snatch your soul. Not to sit up trees in the graveyard at midnight in an attempt to summon Norfolk's notorious hellhound, the demon dog Old Shuck. One would-be young Magus had tried it and been sent to an exorcist as a result.

But temptation soon overcame fear. I lifted *To the Devil a Daughter* from the shelf and carried it over the threshold of my bedroom, digesting its contents over long winter nights when sleep never did come easily – not once the sun had gone down and the old house began to clank its pipes, the wind moaning back across the flat fields and whistling through the roof tiles to the accompanying lament of the fog horn from Yarmouth harbour and the gnarled fingers of the old willow tree behind my bedroom tap-tap-tapping on the window pane.

The novel was engrossing enough to hold such terrors at bay. The heroine, Molly Fountain, was a stylish woman of about the same age as my Grandma Joan and possessed of similar qualities of nosiness and self-assurance. She also lived by the sea – but in the slightly more glamorous surrounds of the French Riviera. In the opening chapter, Molly's curiosity is piqued by Christina, the young woman who has just moved in next door, but only comes out at night. Molly – who worked for the secret services during the Second World War – goes on to discover that Christina's father has sold her to a cabal of Satanists, to be sacrificed in an important ritual.

It was as I came to understand the ethos of these devil worshippers that it all became clear. With its nurturing of the individual and overriding aim to disrupt ordered society, this must be the same philosophy as Margaret Thatcher's government. Devil worship was indeed still being practised in London – behind the doors of 10 Downing Street! That explained why my mother became so cold with rage every time the PM came on TV, repeating the words: 'That woman is a traitor – to her class, to her sex, to her country,' over and over, like a curse.

Disembodied voices accompanied my reading, summoned through the transistor radio by my bed by a medium called John Peel. This was my second line of defence against the noises of the house, the night and the fields – sounds that were scarier than they were. A certain number of the discerning DJ's favourite bands resonated louder than others. Their hallmarks were slasher guitars, swirling fairground keyboards, loping basslines and percussion that recalled either the echo of jackhammers or the march of insect feet. Science fiction and horror themes swirled around satirical social commentary, delivered by singers whose voices distilled a generation's alienation and disdain – Joy Division's Ian Curtis, Magazine's Howard Devoto, the Cure's Robert Smith – and, iciest and most alluring of all, Siouxsie Sioux, who, with her band the Banshees, had a song about a mysterious girl called Christine.

Could she be the same person as Molly Fountain's neighbour? Had Siouxsie made a serious study of the Secret Art? Her appearance certainly suggested so. Did she know what Margaret Thatcher was up to and was she going to stop her from serving up Britain as a sacrifice in a diabolical ritual? If anyone looked like they could stand up for their class, their sex and their country, it was her.

It was Siouxsie who led me through the abyss of the '80s, the imaginary cool-and-hard best friend I didn't have in real life. Siouxsie and a subsequent coven of women – and androgynous, unconventional men – who wore their hair in spiked shards or ringed coils in shades of raven black or flaming red and looked to the future through kohl-ringed eyes. The unique strand of music they made and the glamour they cast about themselves brought me and many other little misfits solace, intrigue, kinship and inspiration on the journey from child to adult, bringing with it the enlightenment that being different was, in fact, a good thing. Thanks to them, I became part of a society so secret its name could not be spoken, not even by its highest adepts.

I became a Goth.

CHAPTER 1

The Rebel Alliance

How the '70s reaped the Winter of Discontent

If there is any one word that sums up '80s Britain, it is Individualism. Independent thinkers who challenged consensus and defied acceptable social norms both shaped the politics of, and wrote the soundtrack to, the profound societal shift instigated by the general election of 3 May 1979. In both cases, these individualistic entities were the result of unlikely alliances made by outsiders who had struck their allegiances in the mid-'70s and, sensing opportunity in those volatile days of strikes, bombs and three-day weeks, worked their shock doctrines into the mainstream using methods nobody had anticipated. Feeding on the dissent of the nation throughout the last, bitter winter of the old decade, by the time the new dawn of 1979 faded into storm clouds of impending financial disaster and mounds of uncollected household waste, their eye-catching female figureheads were ready to take centre stage:

Margaret Thatcher, a glowing, Harrods-helmeted Britannia in a neat tweed suit with a pussy-bow tied around her trident.

Siouxsie Sioux, glowering in fishnets and thigh-high vinyl boots, hair like ravens' wings and the eyes of Cleopatra.

What I didn't know then was that the PM and the most enduring icon of Gothic music had one major thing in common: they had both been inspired into their roles – conjured into being, you might say – by a sort of magus; in each case, a single-minded, ideas-driven outsider determined to break up the status quo.

Margaret Thatcher's political guru Alfred Sherman was memorably described by the cultural commentator Peter York as 'a man who made a profession of thinking the unthinkable and then trying it out on the first person he could find, to see what effect it had.' He could equally have been talking about Malcolm McLaren, whose boutique on the King's Road began the incubation of punk in 1974, when he changed its name from Too Fast to Live Too Young to Die to the bluntly provocative SEX and gathered beneath its rubber skirts all of the alienated youth who would go forth and deliver his great ideas.

Sherman's life story takes in almost every sociopolitical extreme of the twentieth century. Born in 1919, to a family who had fled Russian pogroms for the East End of London, he joined the Communist Party as a teenager: 'To be a Jew in 1930s Britain was to be alienated. The world proletariat offered us a home.'

At the age of seventeen, he volunteered to fight for the International Brigades in the Spanish Civil War and during the Second World War saw action in the Middle East. On his return, he studied at the London School of Economics, where he became president of his student branch of the party, but became disillusioned with the Left and switched to strident advocacy of free market economics.

To coin a phrase he invented, there was no 'middle ground' with Sherman, a man who detested consensus and loved conflict. As the '70s began, he was writing speeches for Tory baronet Sir Keith Joseph, extolling monetarist policies as the solution to Britain's problems. Which included the Oil Crisis of 1973 and miners' strikes of 1973–74, that left the country in a darkness of power cuts and three-day weeks, toppling Edward Heath's government in the general election of 28 February 1974 and ushering old adversary Harold Wilson's Labour back in to power. Sherman capitalised on this chaos when he joined forces with a provincial shopkeeper's daughter.

The secretary of state for education and science, Margaret Hilda Thatcher, was not from a typical Tory background. Born in 1925, the daughter of greengrocer Alf Roberts (no relation to the *Coronation Street* character), a Liberal alderman and lay Methodist preacher from Grantham in Lincolnshire, she evinced upwardly mobile ambitions from an early age.

Young Margaret was sceptical of her father's Wesleyan faith. According to her biographer Charles Moore, she did not believe in angels as she had calculated they would need at least a six-foot breastbone to support their wings. Instead she put her faith in hard graft and self-improvement, working her way through successive scholarships from Kesteven and Grantham grammar school, where she was head girl, to Somerville College Oxford, where she took a Bachelor of Science degree in chemistry, becoming president of the Oxford University Conservative Association while she was about it. It was here she first began reading the work of economist philosopher Friedrich Hayek, whose *Road to Serfdom* (1944) condemned government control of the economy through centralised planning – such as the entire Post-War Consensus had been founded on – as illiberal and oppressive. His repudiation of classical Marxist thinking was one that had caught on with reformed Commie Sherman, too. Hayek's ideas would become the wellspring of the policy they crafted together.

After graduating, Miss Roberts applied for a job at ICI. The personnel department found her to be 'headstrong, obstinate and dangerously self-opinionated', so she increased her efforts in politics instead, joining the Tory grassroots Vermin Club[1] and seducing the Dartford Conservative Association into selecting her on their candidates list in 1950. Here, she met her Prince Charming, wealthy businessman Denis Thatcher (1915–2003), whom she married in 1951. Now comfortably off, with Denis able to fund further studies as a barrister specialising in taxation, her trajectory continued upwards. She landed her first cabinet position after the 1970 election and fell in with Joseph and Sherman.

The trio founded the Centre for Policy Studies (CPS) think tank in 1974, with the aim, as Sherman put it, 'to influence the climate of opinion from the top.' There was yet another election that year, Wilson maintaining office in October with a majority of three. Though Labour were teetering – Wilson stood down in March 1976, succeeded by his foreign secretary, James Callaghan – Thatcher was by no means the natural successor to Heath and was still in need of a makeover. Throughout the classrooms of the land, she was better known as 'Milk Snatcher' after she stopped junior school children getting their free bottle a day, prompting headlines in *The Sun* to identify her as the Most Unpopular Woman in Britain.

But never mind the kids – and never underestimate the power of the Tory Party's dissatisfaction with itself either. Heath's chief whip, the decorated Second World War veteran and Colditz escapee Airey Neave, urged him to stand down as leader after the loss of two elections. When Ted proved unwilling, Neave persuaded his three greatest rivals – William Whitelaw, Edward du Cann and Sir Keith Joseph – to stand against him instead. His preferred candidate Joseph demurred, pushing his more eye-catching and confident CPS colleague out front instead. Neave, a man who had also worked deep inside the secret services during the War, became Thatcher's campaign manager.

With Sherman as her scriptwriter and the legendary actor Laurence Olivier arranging voice coaching via the National Theatre, the Grantham bombshell seized her hour. She was voted Conservative leader on 11 February 1975 with 146 votes, William Whitelaw trailing behind on a meagre seventy-nine.

'She is a trim and comely woman,' ran *The Times*' assessment, 'quintessentially English in her features and manner. Her face is fine-boned, her eyes grey-blue, frank and alive. She was wearing a pinhead black-and-white Donegal tweed dress and jacket, the lapels and pockets braided, with black leather buttons and sensible black shoes . . .

'"Phwooar!" You can imagine the 1922 Committee collectively drooling as those shoes tapped their way down the corridors of power. "Here comes Nanny Whip!"'

Whip It

Elsewhere in 1974–75, dominatrices were being catered for in a new boutique on the King's Road, London's premiere youth fashion thoroughfare since the Swinging Sixties. SEX, its name provocatively displayed in pink inflatable letters above the door, sold a specialised mix of fetish clothing and outré new designs – T-shirts embossed with images and slogans that could, and did, get their wearers arrested. It was the brainchild of former art student Malcolm McLaren, perfectly described by visiting journalist David Mays as 'a psychotic visionary in the ephemeral sub-culture of the fashion underworld'.[2]

McLaren wanted to disrupt the Establishment and spread his influence through the land every bit as much as Alfred Sherman. Born in 1945 in Stoke Newington, north London, he had an unconventional childhood, raised largely by his Jewish grandmother, Rose Corré Isaacs, onto whom his feckless mother Emily had dumped him and his brother Stuart when, exhausted by her serial infidelities, their Scottish father Peter deserted. Rose neglected Stuart and nurtured Malcolm, letting him sleep in her bed and teaching him her mantra: 'To be bad is good, because to be good is simply boring.' Advice he took to heart, getting thrown out of school and more than half a dozen art colleges as he grew up. He found a role model in a book written by one of Sherman's contemporaries, Alexander Baron (born Joseph Alec Bernstein, 1917–99). *The Lowlife* (1963), set in the same Stokey streets where McLaren grew up, tells the story of Harryboy Boas, a Second World War veteran who lives on his wits and winnings at the dog tracks, lavishing gelt on nineteenth-century French novels, fine living and dandy outfits. When on his uppers, Harryboy goes back to his former profession in the rag trade, operating a Hoffman press in the sweatshops of Whitechapel. Like Sherman, two years his junior, the book's author had been a committed Communist Party member as a teenager and saw action during the Second World War – writing *The Lowlife* for Baron was partly a way of coming to terms with the fallout of the War and the

Holocaust. Something that McLaren – who would make use of the swastika on his future fashion creations and remodel SEX as Seditionaries after being inspired by photographs of the 1945 bombing of Dresden – may not have picked up on.

He did, however, discover his own political creed at Croydon College of Art in the inflammatory year of 1968. Situationism, a counter-cultural, anti-authoritarian critique of capitalism co-founded by the French philosopher Guy Debord, was also a rejection of classical Marxist thinking. Inspired by rioting students in Paris and assisted by his future artistic collaborator Jamie Reid – the man who would put a safety pin through the Queen's nose – Malcolm staged his own sit-in and enjoyed a brief foundation course in local press notoriety. In response, the college governors attempted to have him committed.

Malcolm's own greengrocer's daughter, from Tintwistle in the Peak District, was Vivienne Isabel Westwood (1941–2022). A former schoolteacher, she had only limited training in silversmithing when the couple first met in 1971, going on to learn pattern-cutting at Malcolm's insistence. But she possessed the instinctive creative flair to translate his ideas and slogans into fashion durables, manufacturing outrage from their base at 430 King's Road, in Chelsea's World's End.

When the pair first arrived there, the shop was Paradise Garage, a simulated '50s surfing shack with a bamboo frontage and a vintage jukebox. Owner Trevor Myles rented them space to sell rock 'n' roll records and ephemera – McLaren's enthusiasm for the Situationists was equalled, if not exceeded, by his admiration of '50s Brit Beat Svengali Larry Parnes, the man who discovered Billy Fury and Marty Wilde. When Myles left Britain at the end of 1971, McLaren took possession of the lease and turned the shop into Teddy Boy emporium Let It Rock. The interior resembled a Modernist front room, with film posters and guitar-shaped mirrors. Tellingly, the jukebox remained.

It stayed exactly where it was as the shop evolved into Too Fast to Live Too Young to Die in 1973. Outsider American youth culture was the theme – bikers' leather jackets and zoot suits – along with Westwood's customised leather mini-skirts and mohair jumpers, whose production was outsourced to housewives in Bromley and collected each week at Victoria Station by Vivienne, to be transported to the shop in bin bags. No previous King's Road hipsters had ever conducted their business in quite this way before.

The skull-and-crossbones flag that hung from the World's End corner attracted a generation of malcontents and misfits. Some would become the biggest pop stars of the '80s: Adam Ant, his guitarist Marco Pirroni and one Susan Janet Ballion – also from Bromley, but not herself a noted knitter – who would become Siouxsie Sioux. Crucial to McLaren's place in history were teenage reprobates Steve Jones and Paul Cook, who had started a band and turned to Malcolm for managerial advice.

The Sex Pistols evolved out of McLaren's aim to sell clothes and desire to become the next Larry Parnes, their name intrinsically brand-linked to the shop's next, and pivotal, incarnation. Once he had the perfect line-up assembled – Saturday shop boy Glen Matlock on bass, frequent customer and auto-clothes customiser Johnny Rotten (real name: John Joseph Lydon) on vocals – he dressed the band in T-shirts that combined his preferred philosophy with pornography. Doing their best to foster perversion and moral laxity, these variously featured bare breasts, two well-endowed cowboys naked from the waist down and the mask worn by a terrifying real-life felon, the Cambridge Rapist[3] – who was not only still at large but also, SEX managers Jordan and Michael Collins suspected, one of their actual customers.

During his attacks on students in the university city, this fiend wore a full-face leather bondage mask with a zipper mouth, onto which he had painted a pair of eyes and the word RAPIST. Malcolm's first thought on hearing his staff's concerns that he had purchased said item from his boutique was *not* to inform the police immediately, but rather to wait until he had turned this potential association into a T-shirt he could sell.

Still, the boys in blue would find out about McLaren soon enough – another former SEX staffer, Alan Jones, was arrested in Piccadilly Circus for wearing the gay cowboys number in August 1975. He and the boutique were subsequently prosecuted for obscenity. Undeterred, Malcolm and Vivienne went on to create the Destroy T-shirt – featuring Karl Marx text alongside swastikas – while the Pistols engendered nationwide outrage with the fallout from their 1976 appearance on Thames Television's *Today* show, swearing along with drunken host Bill Grundy. Queen-baiting Silver Jubilee singles (wrapped in Jamie Reid's iconoclastic artwork), police-raided Thames boat trips, multiple rock 'n' roll swindles and the replacing of Glen Matlock by a swaggering Sid Vicious – a close friend of Rotten's, who Vivienne thought Malcolm should have cast as his singer originally – swiftly followed.

By the time of Margaret Thatcher's election, the inferno of the Pistols' brief existence had ignited in the minds of kids across the country the urge to pick up any instrument that came to hand and play. Crucially to this story, the foundation bands of Goth owed their very existences to Malcolm's vision. Magazine frontman Howard Devoto formed his first band Buzzcocks with fellow Bolton Institute of Technology student Pete Shelley after driving down to see the Sex Pistols in High Wycombe on 19 February 1976. Chatting with Malcolm afterwards, they arranged to bring the band to Manchester, booking a gig at the Lesser Free Trade Hall on 4 June. This – and a subsequent Pistols' return date on 20 July when Buzzcocks made their debut – was attended by the future members of Joy Division, who promptly decided this was something they could do, too.

Exactly two months later, Grundy veteran Siouxsie (the 'Punk Shocker' of *Daily Mirror* headline fame) put together the first incarnation of the Banshees for the Punk Rock Festival at the 100 Club, another McLaren brainchild. Her then boyfriend Steven Severin (née Bailey) played the bass he had first picked up twenty-four hours earlier, while fellow SEX shopper and comparative musical veteran Marco Pirroni took lead guitar. On drums was Sid Vicious. 'He said he had absolutely no ability,' Severin would later reacall. 'That sounded absolutely brilliant to us.' Their set consisted of a twenty-minute version of 'The Lord's Prayer'.

Along with all these musical upstarts grew an attendant network of independent record companies, fanzine writers, photographers, fashion designers, graphic artists and outlandish hair stylists. Like the heads of a sort of Open Art College, Malcolm and Vivienne offered their 'students' – who may not have made it through the 11-plus – another way out of the dead-end jobs they might otherwise have been expected to take.

But in the bleak mid-Winter of Discontent, the flames were guttering around McLaren. Sid's presence in the Pistols helped accelerate the band's demise, largely because his fatal attraction to the American Nancy Spungen and her drug of choice, heroin, alienated everyone close to him. With life in London becoming increasingly intolerable for the young couple, they moved to New York in August 1978. Nancy had plans to manage Sid's career on her home turf – but, after only three months, on 12 October, she was stabbed to death in the room they were sharing at the Chelsea Hotel with a knife she had bought for her beau. Arrested at the scene, Sid admitted responsibility and was remanded in Rikers Island prison. Malcolm managed to raise his bail and get him treatment in Bellevue psychiatric hospital. But he couldn't stop Sid's mother, Anne Beverley, from flying out to greet him and supplying him with the drugs that would cause his death on 2 February 1979.

Setting the tone for the decade to come, Sid managed to have a hit from beyond the grave. Rush-released by Virgin Records only a week after their bail money had gone to waste, 'Something Else' was a song originally recorded by American rocker Eddie Cochran – himself only one year older than Sid when he was killed in a car crash while headlining a Larry Parnes rock 'n' roll package tour in 1960. The Pistols' disc sold twice as many copies as 'God Save the Queen' had managed to shift when it was held off the number-one position at the height of HM the Queen's 1977 Silver Jubilee.

James Callaghan's Labour lost a vote of no confidence in the Commons on 28 March 1979. Two days later, Airey Neave – who had been rewarded for his efforts with Thatcher by being given the role of shadow Northern Ireland secretary – was blown up by an INLA bomb, planted on his Vauxhall Cavalier in the MPs' underground car park outside the Palace of Westminster.

Murder, magic and bad psychic weather: must be the Season of the Witch.

CHAPTER 2

The Clock Strikes Thirteen

Northern soul and suburban subversion: Joy Division, Magazine, Siouxsie and the Banshees, the Cure

'Where there is despair . . .' Margaret Thatcher entered 10 Downing Street on 4 May 1979, with the prayer of St Francis of Assisi on her lips. One of those voters who believed she had come to deliver the spring was Ian Curtis, the then 22-year-old singer of Joy Division, new father to Natalie and charismatic focus of 'the cult with no name', as the seers on the weekly music press had dubbed his band's intense following. More than anyone else in this chapter, the music Joy Division made in their brief existence encapsulates the despair that Thatcher spoke of, as disillusioned survivors of the worn-out, bashed-up, dirty old '70s ditched the last tattered vestiges of the Post-War Consensus and put their faith in her and a gleaming new '80s to come.

Curtis might well be the only person in this book who voted for Thatcher – and he didn't just give her his ballot; he insisted his wife Deborah did the same in order not to 'cancel his vote'. He's certainly the only person still revered as an icon by everyone who didn't – which testifies to the contradiction at the core of this most charismatic and troubled young man. Ian Curtis struggled to contain so many conflicting identities within him that he would end up bringing his own life to a brutal conclusion in just over a year's time.

In the immediate future, though, it seemed as if he'd got everything right. Joy Division had determinedly been making their presence felt since 20 July 1976, when Curtis, guitarist Bernard Sumner and bassist Peter Hook had attended the second of the Sex Pistols' Lesser Free Trade Hall gigs organised by Pete Shelley and Howard Devoto. Forming a band they called Warsaw, initially with Terry Mason on drums, their first ever gig captured the attention of young music journalist Paul Morley, who would bring them to a much wider audience through the pages of the *NME*. After Mason was replaced by Stephen Morris, the band changed their name to Joy Division, self-financed their first EP *An Ideal for Living* and recorded it at Pennine Sound Studios, Oldham, Lancashire, in December 1977.

With this artefact in hand, Curtis used a Battle of the Bands competition staged by punk labels Stiff and Chiswick at Manchester nightclub Rafters to catch up with local TV star Tony Wilson, whose 'What's On' music slot on evening magazine programme *Granada Reports* was the showcase every new Manchester band vied for. Ian was not shy about stating his case.

'You fucking cunt, why the fuck haven't you played us yet?' he enquired.

Wilson liked the cut of his jib and rewarded the band with a moment of TV history when Joy Division played the sparse and sinister 'Shadowplay'. Morris's motorik drums, Hook's propulsive bass and Sumner's sheet metal guitar perfectly matched the footage of desolate inner-city landscape, culled from a *World in Action* programme about the CIA, that the band's performance was noirishly transposed over. In a chilling baritone, Curtis delivered his mantra-like lyrics, 'To the centre of the city where all roads meet, waiting for you,' with saucer eyes fixed to the camera, while his tall, thin body jerked as if being struck with electrodes.

Shortly after, a deeply enamoured Wilson would use a family inheritance to set up Factory Records, a northern song manufacturer that operated in defiance of the London-centric music industry. The name could be seen as a nod to Manchester's industrial past, or in homage to Andy Warhol's New York studios – the artwork and cataloguing of all its various releases, from records to gig tickets to office cats, very much in the premier Pop Artist's taste – or indeed to the slang word for a police station then currently employed by Jack Regan and George Carter of *The Sweeney* (ITV). He signed Joy Division and put them in Strawberry Studios, Stockport, with Martin Hannett, aka Martin Zero – a veteran producer and psychonaut who had produced the Buzzcocks' debut *Spiral Scratch* EP and ghosted as the Invisible Girls, in-house band for the recordings of Salford's barbed bard John Cooper Clarke, whom he also managed.

The band had their doubts about this acid-fried, shaggy-haired wild man but Hannett transformed their sound from the ferocious live performance they had been honing. He used unconventional means and state-of-the-art technology to sculpt Joy Division's songs into what he called 'sonic holograms', which gave him the same feeling as 'deserted public places, empty office blocks' – an epic scope of desolation. Like the BBC's Radiophonic workshop, he also recorded foley sounds to drop into the mix, such as the clanking of an antique lift on 'Insight' and smashing glass on 'I Remember Nothing'. He routinely tortured Stephen Morris by making him play each of his drum parts separately for the 'cleanliness' of their sound and delighted in turning the studio's air conditioning up to the max to stop the band from hanging around to argue.

Unknown Pleasures, Joy Division's debut LP, arrived on 15 June 1979. Its glacial soundscapes, psychogeographic rendering of the brutalised landscape of its construction and unnerving conduit of both personal and political despair chanelled the Winter of Discontent into a slab of black vinyl. Packaged without a photograph of the band and minimal information, its Peter Saville-designed front cover instead offered a graphic image of a pulsar: the emissions of a dying sun.

The record was hailed by the most perceptive voices in the three weekly music papers – then reaching a combined readership of over 2 million – as the most significant release since the Sex Pistols' *Never Mind the Bollocks*. Reviewers marvelled at how acutely the band tapped into the generational malaise: 'Investigate these confined spaces, these insides of cages, this outside of insanity,' wrote Max Bell in *NME*. 'They all bring to mind endless corridors where doors clank open and shut on an infinite emotional obstacle course.' *Sounds*' Dave McCullough reviewed the album as a Gothic horror story pastiche about a murderous young man named Andrew, who perceives his entire life mirrored within its grooves and eventually slashes his throat 'ecstatically' to 'She's Lost Control'. *Melody Maker*'s Mary Harron's expounded on this theme: 'Nineteenth-century Gothic tales used ruined castles and vampires as symbols of vague subconscious terrors. Joy Division are twentieth-century Gothic, and their images of assassins, imprisonment, pursuit, draw off the modern nightmare.' *Unknown Pleasures* is an album that sounds like it was recorded entirely at night, in the cavernous atrium of a disused factory that has fallen into a clanging, dripping, vermin-riddled state of disrepair.

What none of the critics could have known was that, while writing and recording these songs, Curtis had experienced a series of life-changing traumas. With his heavily pregnant wife waiting at home, he suffered his first epileptic fit on the journey back from a gig in London on 27 December 1978. Increasingly violent episodes would rapidly follow and while he waited to get specialist help, the singer was prescribed a succession of psychiatric drugs that had devastating effects on his physical and mental health.

Only the year before, while working as an assistant disablement resettlement officer at the Employment Exchange in Macclesfield, Curtis had been specially trained to recognise the symptoms of and support sufferers of epilepsy. He had become attached to one in particular, a young woman who came into the day centre where he worked. His conversations with her, and his shock at her subsequent sudden death from a grand mal seizure, informed his lyrics for 'She's Lost Control' – 'And she turned around and took me by the hand and said, "I've lost control again"' – which, as

Melody Maker's Mary Harron noted, 'has the mysterious feeling of tenderness and loss you find in dreams'.

During the first three months of 1979, Curtis would suffer a succession of grand mal attacks himself. But despite having an electroencephalogram (EEG) at Macclesfield Hospital, his medical records stated no abnormalities were found. After Natalie was born, on Easter Monday, 16 April, he was too scared to hold his new baby daughter in case he had a seizure while she lay vulnerable in his arms. Deborah Curtis, in her 1995 memoir *Touching from a Distance*, writes affectingly of the shocking indifference shown to her husband by every medical professional he came into contact with after his first fit; and of her disbelief that Ian, with no family history of epilepsy, could have been stricken with the condition so soon after making a study of it. It was almost as if, she seems to suggest, he was so empathetic that he developed the condition via contact with it. As if he literally was, as Martin Hannett would later put it, 'a lightning rod'.

Hell Is a City

Certainly, Ian Curtis always was an outsider. Fittingly, for someone who would come to symbolise the rainy city of Manchester, he was born on St Swithin's Day, 15 July 1956, in Memorial Hospital, Old Trafford.[1] He was brought up in the village of Hurdsfield, on the outskirts of Macclesfield, where he lived with his father Kevin, a detective in the Transport Commission Police, mother Doreen and younger sister Carole. The area is an interzone between the Dark Satanic Mills and the wild ancient landscape of the Peak District; the same side of those hills that gave birth to visionary authors Alan Garner and Hilary Mantel and, further to the north up on Saddleworth Moor, the unholy burial grounds of the victims of child killers Ian Brady and Myra Hindley, whose unspeakable crimes haunted the landscape of Ian's childhood.[2]

A bright lad, cheeky and sensitive in equal measure – especially when it came to his looks – Ian passed his 11-plus and was sent to the King's School, Macclesfield, where the year-younger Stephen Morris was also a pupil. Perhaps significantly, the Curtis family moved house around the same time.

Throughout the '60s, town-planning officials across the land had been busy tearing down terraces of pre-war housing – regardless of any actual bomb damage – calling it 'slum clearance' and putting up tower blocks instead. The Curtis family was typical of those lured into the mod con of the high-rise with their wonderful indoor toilets. They left their house with its garden at the back of the old railway station in 1967 for a flat in new development Victoria Park, close to Macclesfield town centre.

Bernard Sumner, who hailed from the Salford suburb of Lower Broughton, would later pinpoint a sense of irretrievable loss for childhood community as a primary source of the darkness within Joy Division's music: 'I remember the summer holidays when I was a kid: we could stay up late and play in the street, and 12 o'clock at night there would be old ladies outside the houses, talking to each other,' he told Jon Savage in 1994.[3] Then: 'We were moved over the river into a tower block. The place where I used to live, where I had my happiest memories, all that had gone. All that was left was a chemical factory.'

Solace would come in musical form. The teenage Curtis devoured alienated Americana: New York's Velvet Underground with their picaresque tales of drag queens, junkies, prostitutes and runaways; Michigan's sonic brothers-in-arms the Stooges and MC5; and the band Joy Division would most often be compared to, California's darkest dreamers, the Doors, whose shamanic singer Jim Morrison had died in mysterious circumstances in July 1971. Closer to home, the arthouse glitterburst of Roxy Music's 1972 eponymous debut album came as a revelation in a world of beige and grey, and – standing betwixt the Americans' weird scenes and Roxy's reinvention of glamour – David Bowie. By the same year, and with the help of Hull bovver boys Mick Ronson, Trevor Bolder and Woody Woodmansey, Bowie was toughening up the still rather fey, whimsical androgyny of *Hunky Dory* into the full-on Technicolor platform boot stomp of *Ziggy Stardust*. As part of the emerging Ziggy narrative in his live set, he replaced 'Amsterdam', one of two Jacques Brel songs he had first heard on Scott Walker's 1967 *Scott* album, with the other, 'My Death'. According to Deborah Curtis, it was a song that fascinated Ian.[4]

Under this glittery influence, Curtis began to wear eyeliner and nail varnish. He scoured secondhand shops for clothes he considered to be in the worst possible taste and used his greatcoat – the standard issue Army & Navy stores purchase for moody teenage boys in the early '70s – as handy cover for stealing records from Macclesfield's indoor market. The impact of Roxy and Bowie on Manchester's club culture cannot be overstated: a whole, clandestine proto-punk scene began to grow around a few gay clubs in Manchester – Pips, the Ranch Bar – where cabaret, chicken-in-a-basket and faux '40s film stars mingled in 'Bowie Rooms' exchanging ideas and exploring identities, safe from the city's marauding boot boys.[5]

Later, after another family move to New Moston in Manchester, Ian would abandon his A-levels and take a job instead at the Rare Records Shop, where he could fuel his true passion. Here, he made plenty of gay friends and followed his Lou Reed muse through them to clubs like the Rembrandt, Napoleons, Union and the Bier Keller – portals into the taboo parallel worlds of Manchester's outsider communities that really inspired him.

Yet, at the same time, he was bound by the rules of a working-class northern man's existence: anxious to get married and buy a house, which would lead to him taking more secure employment as a civil servant at the Manpower Services Commission. Nevertheless, his impulse to know what went on behind the green door would continue. After his wedding to Deborah on 23 August 1975, and while they waited for the mortgage on their new home to go through, the couple stayed with Ian's grandparents in Moss Side, where a lot of the *Windrush* generation of Manchester's West Indian migrants had settled. Here, Ian soon developed an interest in reggae, particularly Toots and the Maytals and Bob Marley and the Wailers, the Jamaican heavyweights who were having their own golden years in another parallel universe of the mid-'70s.

Ian began experimenting with drugs while he was still at school. Despite being a model pupil academically – he scored seven O-levels and won prizes for his two favourite subjects, History and Divinity – Curtis was furtively rebellious. King's School ran a scheme intended to instill kindness and selflessness in its older boys, whereby they would visit elderly people and do chores for them. This policeman's son used these visits to raid their bathroom cabinets for all the prescription drugs he could lay his hands on. He managed to take his first overdose by the age of fifteen, on three tablets of stolen Largactil (chlorpromazine hydrochloride), a drug prescribed for schizophrenia. This was in the same year he met Deborah, who records in her memoir his further self-destructive impulses, including self-harming with the countless cigarettes he smoked and hitting himself with a spiked running shoe. While Jim Morrison drove out into the Californian desert to take peyote and commune with his totem animals, Ian walked into the graveyard of St Michael's church in Macclesfield and sniffed dry cleaning fluid. He told his teenage sweetheart he had no interest in living beyond twenty-five.

Though Curtis was possessive and controlling with Deborah, she had fallen in love with the sensitive teenage poet who 'cried like a baby' while reading her copy of Oscar Wilde's *The Happy Prince*, a story all about selflessness and sacrifice. In it, the titular jewel-encrusted, gold-plated statue, who can see into all the poor places of the city he stands over, persuades a migrating swallow to put off his flight to Egypt until he has dismantled all these rich trappings and distributed them to the needy. After which the swallow dies of cold and the statue's lead heart breaks. Deemed ugly and worthless now by the local dignitaries, both characters are thrown onto the scrap heap, but taken up to Heaven by an angel who recognises them as the two most precious things in the city.

'There is no mystery so great as misery,' as the Happy Prince tells the swallow.

New Dawn Fades

Between the recording of *Unknown Pleasures* and its follow-up, *Closer*, Ian met a young Belgian journalist and music promoter called Annik Honoré at the Nashville Club in West Kensington, London. In the wee small hours after Joy Division's gig there, while listening to David Bowie's *Low*, he fell for a fellow policeman's child.[6] It was the start of an intensely cerebral relationship that, according to Honoré, was never physically consummated. But from the time Joy Division played the club where she worked as a booker, Plan K in Brussels, on its opening night, on 16 October 1979, the pair were rarely apart.

Honoré devoted herself to promoting Joy Division and likeminded British bands dubbed 'Cold Wave' in French-speaking Europe. She founded the label Disques du Crépuscule (Records of the Twilight) with her business partner Michel Duval, through which she planned to release a Joy Division album and did issue an impressive catalogue of discs by artists as diverse as John Foxx, Harold Budd, Michael Nyman and Brian Eno. Discs du Crépuscule would subsequently merge with Factory Records to become Factory Benelux, a gateway into Europe for the Manchester label's bands. By which time, Annik had got herself a job at the Belgian Embassy in London. She stayed by Ian's side throughout Joy Division's European tour of January 1980, breaking manager Rob Gretton's strict rule barring wives or girlfriends from travelling with the band. But it wouldn't be long before those women found out about her.

The night Ian returned home from the tour, Deborah found him in the blue-painted room of their house in Macclesfield, where he did all his writing. He had passed out from emptying a bottle of Pernod down his throat and carving weals into his back with a knife. Beside him was his Bible, opened at Chapter 2 of *Revelation*, St John the Divine:

20 Notwithstanding I have a few things against thee, because thou sufferest that woman Jezebel, which calleth herself a

prophetess, to teach and to seduce my servants to commit fornication, and to eat things sacrificed unto idols.
21 And I gave her space to repent of her fornication; and she repented not.
22 Behold, I will cast her into a bed, and them that commit adultery with her into great tribulation, except they repent of their deeds.

Still unaware of Annik, Deborah saw this as 'a cry for help', but it was one that seemingly went unheard by anyone else close – other than the more perceptive critics following his career. In a *Melody Maker* review of Joy Division's University of London Union gig, on 16 February 1980, Biba Kopf wrote: 'Less colourful now, they're getting closer to the despair that has been the core of their work so far.'

By the time recording of *Closer* began at Britannia Row Studios, London, in March 1980, Deborah had found out about the affair and Ian had promised her that he would break things off with Annik. Far from this being the case, he was sharing a flat with the Belgian in London, rented at Factory's expense. His despair at living this double life burst to the surface at the band's residency at the Moonlight Club in West Hampstead on 2–4 April, when he suffered epileptic fits onstage. This was a rare occurrence – his fits normally came when he was at home, although his audience had become used to his wild, jerky dancing as an integral part of the show.

The differing attitudes of the women in Ian's life to his epilepsy couldn't have been starker. While Deborah – struggling to bring up a baby and earn enough money working as a barmaid to make up for her husband's lack of income – had desperately sought to get him treatment, Annik seemed to see something rather more romantic in his seizures.

'When he has his attacks, it makes him surreal, terribly frightening,' she told Philippe Cornet in 2010.[7] 'I have seen him practically airborne. But it's also something magical as a contact between the conscious and unconscious. Suddenly, he would enter a world with no relation to reality.' As if he was like Jim Morrison, breaking on through to the other side.

Like Morrison, Ian didn't have much more time left to convey what he had found there. Returning home on Easter Sunday, 7 April, he took an overdose of his prescription drug Phenobarbitone, leaving a note saying there was 'no need to fight now' and to 'give my love to Annik'. Deborah got him to hospital in time to have his stomach pumped, but the bewildering downward spiral of his final days had begun.

Ian was somehow judged by a psychiatrist not to be suicidal and also managed to persuade his epilepsy specialist that he was sorting his life out. Tony Wilson – who had taken the suicide note from Deborah and given her a lecture about the inevitability of her husband's infidelity in return – took him home from hospital to recover at his house. He had his protégé back on stage at Derby Hall, Bury, on 8 April, but Ian could only manage to sing two numbers. This sparked a riot in the audience, which Wilson thought was wonderful, comparing it to an infamous Lou Reed gig at the Free Trade Hall that had ended the same way.

Joy Division did go on to play one final time on 2 May 1980 at Birmingham University, before which they made the video to accompany the new album's prophetic first single 'Love Will Tear Us Apart' on 25 April 1980. Ian went back to live with his parents, Doreen and Kevin Curtis, who had been told about Annik by Deborah, as she began to instigate divorce proceedings.

As far as his manager, bandmates and record company were concerned, Ian was flying high on the brilliance of the music Joy Division had been creating and was eager to travel to America on 18 May to begin a tour. Nor did Annik feel that his life was in any danger, though she reportedly hated the lyrics he had been writing for *Closer* because she could feel the guilt in each line.

A few days before the planned trip, he paid a visit to his wife and daughter, insisting on having his photo taken with Natalie. Then, on Saturday 17 May, he returned, while Deborah was out at work. He told his manager Rob Gretton it was because he wanted to watch a film on TV that his parents wouldn't have liked – Werner Herzog's *Stroszek*. It's not hard to imagine how he might identify with this intensely strange, bleak satire, written by the director and cast with a bunch of non-actor misfits worthy of the cover of the Doors' *Strange Days*. The lead character is played by Bruno S, a man who had been abused as a child and spent time in a mental institution, who routinely prepared for his scenes by screaming for hours on end. The film ends with Bruno at an old-fashioned Wisconsin sideshow, feeding coins into a slot to watch chickens dancing on a hot plate. On the DVD sleeve notes, Herzog says this is 'a great metaphor' – for what, he doesn't go on to elucidate. But the peerless film critic Roger Ebert makes a good guess: 'A force we cannot comprehend puts some money in the slot, and we dance until the money runs out.'[8]

'Watching the reel as it comes to a close, brutally taking its time,' go Curtis's lyrics to *Closer*'s 'Passover', 'Can I go on with this train of events?'

When Deborah came home from her bar job that day, Ian had finished watching the film and, wired from drinking pots of coffee, begged her to drop the divorce proceedings. Worried he was working himself up to a fit, she offered for him to stay the night, but he turned cold on her. Exhausted, she went to her parents' house – they were babysitting Natalie that night. Ian made her promise not to come back before 10 a.m., when he was due to catch his train.

Just before she awoke the next morning, Deborah dreamt she could hear the Doors 'The End' playing on the radio. When she returned home, she found Ian had hanged himself from the ceiling-mounted clothes drying rack in their kitchen.

'Ian would have made a gifted actor,' she surmised from a fifteen-year distance.[9] 'He convinced us all that the conflicts in his life were caused by outside influences and that the stress he was suffering was a direct result of the lifestyle he was leading. Truly, as his own judge and gaoler, he had engineered his own hell and planned his own downfall. The people around him were only minor characters in his play.'

Joy Division's music press champions could not disguise their shock and grief. As Biba Kopf so poignantly put it: 'Ian Curtis's death didn't so much bring Joy Division's journey to the heart of darkness to an abrupt halt as freeze it for all eternity at the brink of discovery.'[10] Dave McCullough, who had struggled with the band's truculent attitude on his first attempts to interview them, yet remained deeply moved by their music, wrote a despairing obituary in *Sounds*: 'That man cared for you, that man died for you, that man saw the madness in your area.'

Closer was released on 18 July 1980. The record has an entirely different feeling from *Unknown Pleasures*, no longer scored to a backdrop of industrial decay but a more sumptuous, luminous mood, redolent not just of the Doors but also those lusciously arranged Scott Walker Jacques Brel interpretations Bowie had hitherto latched onto, with shimmering keyboards and glittering drums acting like orchestral layers above the fluid depths of Peter Hook's anchoring bass. Ian's voice takes on the more sensitive tone of a Sinatra-style crooner, infused with a sense of wonderment that implies he really has seen things beyond the realm of the commonplace.

'Love Will Tear Us Apart', released as a 7-inch in June 1980, still cannot be heard without all the hairs down the back of the neck standing to attention. While Ian's vocals exude tenderness and regret in equal measure on such self-lacerating lines as 'Why is the bedroom so cold turned away on your side?/Is my timing that flawed, our respect run so dry?' conversely, Bernard Sumner's guitar sounds close to ecstatic. The song became the band's only chart hit – reaching number thirteen – and was *NME*'s Single of the Year.

Most Joy Division fans bridle at the dread word 'Goth', but it's hard to imagine Oscar Wilde himself fashioning a story of beautiful doomed youth more tragic than that of Ian Curtis and the people who knew and loved him.

'It was a breakdown of his relationship, accentuated by the amount of barbiturates he was taking to subdue his epilepsy,' Sumner would tell Jon Savage on the subject of Ian's death.

'Barbiturates make you so you're laughing one minute, crying the next. He'd had a physical breakdown, a relationship breakdown, which caused an emotional breakdown . . . Now I accept these things: if it's going to happen, it's going to happen. Also, I don't really believe it ends there.'

You Only Live Twice

'Where there is error . . .' What of that dynamic duo who started all of this, by opening the Manchester Pistols portal at the Lesser Free Trade Hall back in 1976? Howard Devoto and Pete Shelley debuted their band Buzzcocks in the place where Joy Division first convened, but despite the runaway success of their self-financed debut *Spiral Scratch* EP, Devoto wouldn't be long for the world of acerbic punk pop that Shelley was perfecting. The erstwhile Howard Trafford – whose adopted surname is a Latin-derived term for 'bewitchment' – was not of a mind to share bodily fluids with the more thuggish, gob-hawking elements of his audience, nor to pledge any tribal allegiance to punk. Not now that it was a game anyone thought they could play.

He did take one parting gift from Shelley, however. A riff that became the first Magazine song, an ode to nonconformity called 'Shot by Both Sides', which he put together with a new combination of wild talents after finishing his psychology studies at Bolton Institute of Technology.

The best interpreter of that riff came via Devoto's sometime girlfriend, punk Pop Artist and singer with avant-noiseniks Ludus, Linder Sterling, who had designed the arresting cover of Buzzcocks' 1977 single 'Orgasm Addict' with a cut-up of pornography and domestic appliances that neatly satirised how women were perceived in the dream homes of the late '70s. Linder shared a student house with Greenock-born guitarist John McGeoch, who was similarly inspired by pioneer painter and graphic artist Robert Rauschenberg to apply Pop Art principles to his playing. 'Rauschenberg's ethos was that if he made a mark he'd seen before, he painted it out,' he told Toby Manning in 2004.[11] 'I applied the same rule to my playing.' McGeoch's starkly elegant, angular guitar riffs left a distinctive, spider-legged trail across some of the greatest music of the '80s; Magazine are only the first band in this book to benefit from his talents.

They were also the first musical flowering of the hugely influential and singularly gifted Barry Adamson, for whom 'Shot by Both Sides' could equally be an expression of the racially volatile world he grew up in. This Hulme son of a white mother and black, *Windrush*-generation Jamaican father never felt at home in any social pack until the first time he saw the Buzzcocks play. Born with a debilitating condition called dyschondroplasia, with both his arms and hips dislocated, he was forced to endure multiple operations and terrible discomfort as a child in the '60s. He found his great escape in the era's most glamorous depictions of espionage, all the sharp-suited playboys and beehived femme fatales depicted in Sean Connery's Bond movies and TV series like *The Avengers*, *Man in a Suitcase* and *The Man from U.N.C.L.E.* The urbane accompanying jazz- and bossa nova-inflected soundtracks by John Barry, Laurie Johnson, Ron Grainer and Jerry Goldsmith lodged deep in his brain for future reference.

'Walking down the street with a suitcase of toy guns and spy cameras, that was very much me,' he told Simon Henwood of *Purr* in 1993. 'I was very much in my own head then. I don't think I felt very safe. The messages I was getting already were: "Well you're a little different, and because you're a little different, we're gonna push you outside." So I think a natural thing for me to do was: "Right, before you do that to me I'm going to leave first, I'll save you the bother."' It's a sentiment many in his audience would be able to concur with.

Barry was studying graphics at Stockport College at the time of his Buzzcocks' awakening: 'I don't think music and graphics are correlated, but it's still about training the senses. At the time I didn't really know what use that was going to have in the rest of my life, but it has done, in terms of how I approach something, the perspective.'

Fate also lent a hand: the nineteen-year-old Adamson had acquired a bass guitar and while out buying strings for his new instrument, spotted Devoto's Magazine recruitment ad in Manchester's Virgin Records store. He stayed up all night teaching himself how to play his new instrument and got the job conjuring up a bassline for 'The Light Pours Out of Me' the very next day.

Drummer Martin Jackson completed the original quartet, who recorded 'Shot by Both Sides' and were duly snapped up by Richard Branson's Virgin. The definitive Magazine line-up would be complete when original keyboardist Bob Dickinson was replaced by Dave Formula, a slightly older veteran of the Northern Soul scene so vital to the musical DNA of the left-hand path of the Pennines – see also how Joy Division turned a cover of N. F. Porter's Wigan Casino floor-filler 'Keep on Keeping On' into the haunted dancehall of their own 'Interzone'.

Formula came of age in the mid-'60s, where 'the last gasps of the Manchester beatnik, modern jazz met the would-be existentialists' in the Cona and Left Wing coffee bars. The latter would evolve into the legendary Twisted Wheel, where under the canny eye of promoter Roger Eagle's Saturday All Nighters, the greatest American R&B artists and upcoming UK acts like Steampacket and component members Rod Stewart, Long John Baldry, Julie Driscoll, Brian Auger and the Trinity would perform.

'Roger had a fantastic record collection that completely opened the whole blues and R&B scene for us,' Formula recalled. 'He had stuff that you would never hear, as he was so absolutely in love with that whole, wide American black music genre and spent God knows how much money importing stuff.'

Formula's first band was irresistibly named the Satanists – sharp-dressed mod rockers who would convert into St Louis Union under Eagle's enthusiastic patronage. The Hammond Inferno that Formula created in those heady days would enrich Magazine's musical references and widescreen out their sound. But to begin with, it was Devoto who was the band's motivating force and wellspring of ideas and cultural connections. 'The most important man alive,' as one *NME* headline writer mischievously put it, delighted in playing mind games with his devotees, the besotted men in the music press.[12] 'Devoto is a hidden gem,' wrote Paul Morley in his *NME* introduction to Magazine (8 October 1977). 'He is not a minor writer! His approach is consciously different, his intentions not obvious.'

'He has the air of a man who's been *somewhere else*,' concurred Morley's colleague Charles Shaar Murray, 'on stage he gives the impression that he's just been somewhere other than a sleazy dressing room, that he's arrived at the gig by time/space warp and that the fact doesn't bother him unduly.'

Indeed, Devoto's stage presence was a strong part of the band's otherworldly allure, somewhere between Roxy-era Brian Eno, the idiosynractically shaven-headed Peter Gabriel of 'Supper's Ready' Genesis and Bowie's *The Man Who Fell to Earth* Thomas Jerome Newton in full knicker-wetting alien reveal. Though there was something about this same presence and that of Dave Formula's banks of keyboards – a veritable bridge of the *Starship Enterprise* on stage – that suggested Magazine could secretly be guilty of that most verboten of all Punk Year Zero Thoughtcrimes: *Prog*.

In fact, Magazine's music was so visionary that, when they reformed in 2009, the freshness and possibility sealed into those songs initially recorded between 1978 and 1981 was such that it seemed they had foreseen the next three decades and were wondering what had taken Johnny-come-latelies like Radiohead and Franz Ferdinand so long.

Perhaps it's because there is more ambiguity to Magazine – Devoto is knowingly camp and sexually evasive, whereas, despite Ian Curtis' forays across the border, Joy Divison exude a firmly heterosexual northernness. Peter Hook especially looks like he can hold his own in a pub fight, and that, according to Deborah Curtis, is the main reason Pete Shelley used to like standing next to him at gigs. Inspired by the Pistols, Joy Division created a music from their immediate surroundings, while Magazine incorporated unexpected elements from beyond punk's remit. The B-side of their second single 'Touch and Go' was a cover of 'Goldfinger', the Bond theme written by Anthony Newley, Leslie Bricusse and John Barry, originally belted out by Shirley Bassey, who legendarily whipped off her bra while recording to give those vocals her diva all.[13] They would go on to create a skeletally groovesome cover of Sly and the Family Stone's 'Thank You (Falettinme Be Mice Elf Agin)' and gave Captain Beefheart's 'I Love You, You Big Dummy' a Linder-style graphic art makeover, with Adamson's ice funk bass and Devoto's arch-android vocals colluding to sound as if they were the song's authors.

In the same feature that he nailed the singer's space alien presence, Charles Shaar Murray also noted: 'John Barry would seem to be a hilariously unlikely "influence" for a Modern-World band like Magazine, but those menacing tempos, eerie Duane Eddy guitar licks and red-alert horn parts (expertly evoked by Formula's synthesiser) are oddly echoed in much of the rest of Magazine's work.'

This perfect summation of Magazine's sound just goes to show how ahead of the game they were. Following the '90s wave of cinematic dance imaginings from Portishead, Massive Attack, Andrew Weatherall, David Holmes and Tricky – and largely thanks to the body of work created by Barry Adamson – John Barry's music is hilarious no more, but a serious, aspirational influence.

Because You're Frightened

Magazine caught the sense of great geopolitical shifts in their songwriting, refracted through the lens of all those Cold War spy themes. On their 1978, John Leckie-produced debut *Real Life*, this was evident on 'Definitive Gaze', 'Shot by Both Sides' and 'The Light Pours Out of Me' but especially in the portentous 'Motorcade'. On this epic of crime scene reportage, McGeoch's guitars are the assassin's bullets, cutting across the procession of vehicles choreographed by Formula's keyboards, so that it simultaneously recalls the Zapruder footage of the JFK hit – news of which Dave can recall first hearing at the Cona coffee bar – and predicts further scenes of outrage soon to beam into our sitting rooms.

Following Magazine's first tour, Martin Jackson packed up his drumsticks to be replaced by John Doyle, whose more forceful style of playing added a further layer of drama. Sadly, John Barry was not available to be their producer of choice on their second LP, but Colin Thurston, veteran of Bowie's *Low* and Iggy's *Lust for Life*, took the controls as the band spent the freezing January of 1979 making a musical dead drop into the evocatively titled *Secondhand Daylight.*

In this magisterial recording, they reached the apex of their Gothic glamour. They'd been touring in Berlin with Patti Smith before the recording, soaking in the ominous sights of Checkpoint Charlie, the razor wire along the top of the Wall, those dead-eyed men with machine guns making sure this strangely small and unimposing-looking structure effectively kept east and west a chasm apart. Added to Thurston's presence on those two previous pivotal recordings made in Hansa Studios, this Germanic influence infused the LP with a perfect *The Spy Who Came in from the Cold* ambience.

'It's always raining over the border,' begins opener 'Feed the Enemy', which goes on to describe the 'border guards' as 'actors' in a play everyone is colluding in – both the heads of state who issue their orders and the audience safe at home watching 'the replay'. 'How many friends have we over there?' Devoto speculates on the lives of unseen others passing only metres away. Ghosts of Berlin's more distant and decadent Weimar Republic past are awoken from under the 'Permafrost' by Barry's pickaxe bass and Devoto's immortal lines, rendered with the utmost in detached distain: 'I will drug you and fuck you/On the permafrost'. What Belladonna-eyed Gothic princess could resist?

The album was released on 30 March 1979, two days after James Callaghan's Labour government lost a motion of confidence by one vote, triggering the general election, and the day after the Irish National Liberation Army's attack on Airey Neave. Magazine's oblique snapshots of momentous times convey the atmosphere of the spring of 1979 with unerring accuracy. To listen again is to see the *Nationwide* wheel spinning once more on the pixelated TV screen of memory. But – and this is also part of why their songs have endured while more earnest diatribes date – Devoto's teasing, impressionist lyrics refrain from ever making direct commentary. 'Scepticism was really important to me,' he told journalist Toby Manning. 'I've always been quite apolitical because of my weakness for seeing both sides of things. Or thinking I do.'

But across Britain, sides were being taken, battlegrounds prepared. Seventeen days into office, on 21 May 1979, Margaret Thatcher announced her government's plans to sell off all nationalised industries, starting with British Petroleum (BP). In September came news of plans to regenerate London's Docklands and Thatcher presided over the opening of Central Milton Keynes, validating Johnny Rotten's 'Anarchy in the UK' prophecy that: 'Your future dream is [now Britain's largest] shopping scheme'. Stormclouds gathered over this rapidly shifting landscape, demarking where the biggest fissures of the '80s would come – as staff on *The Times* came back to work after a year-long dispute on 13 November, the National Union of Mineworkers rejected a pay deal and threatened to strike.

Two days into the new decade, it was British Steel workers who were downing tools. In a warning shot that such action would no longer be accommodated, Thatcher dealt them a Bloody Valentine, announcing state benefit to strikers was to be halved. With news of 11,000 job cuts to come just three days later, those who still held positions limped back to work on 2 April. An irreversible force had been set into motion that would end up impacting on the communities that had supported her in the heavily industrialised parts of Britain – especially the north of England – hardest of all.

Magazine channelled all of that fear into their next album.

Crib Notes from Underground

Both Joy Division and Magazine drew much inspiration from their combined voracious reading, another pastime common to the auto-didact working-class youth of the '70s, who were always making good use of their library cards and passing well-thumbed existentialist tracts, pulp paperbacks and doorstopper-sized nineteenth-century novels between them. Ian Curtis mined Joseph Conrad's 1899 novella *Heart of Darkness* for *Closer*'s 'Colony' and took the title of 'Atrocity Exhibition' from J. G. Ballard's experimental 1970 novel of interlinked short stories – another massive influence on the generation who picked it up alongside copies of *Roxy Music* and *Ziggy Stardust*.

Not to be outdone – and in keeping with Curtis' penchant for East European literature – Devoto turned Fyodor Dostoevsky's premier existentialist novel *Notes from Underground* into Magazine's 'A Song from Under the Floorboards' on their third long player, May 1980's *The Correct Use of Soap*. The song begins as the novel, with the arresting line: 'I am angry, I am ill and I'm as ugly as sin'. In quoting the Russian author's nameless retired civil servant narrator, Devoto could just as well have been talking about a British equivalent. Lines like 'I know beauty and I know a good thing when I see it' bring to mind the caustic world view of Nigel Hawthorne's civil servant supreme Sir Humphrey Appleby in the new satirical BBC comedy *Yes, Minister*, which first aired on 25 February 1980 and would provide expert insider commentary throughout the Thatcher years.

Barry Adamson, meanwhile, had discovered Hubert Selby Jr's 1964 *Last Exit to Brooklyn*, a novel that vividly inhabits the territory the Velvet Underground[14] would later claim and unfolds, just like *The Atrocity Exhibition*, as a series of linked short stories, mapping the geography of the author's home terrain through Benzedrine-driven tales of transgender hookers, closeted gay macho men and vicious young switchblade-packing hoodlums. It was a book the UK courts tried to ban, but its right to be published was successfully defended in 1968 by the same QC who would quash a similar obscenity charge against *Never Mind the Bollocks* nine years later – John 'Rumpole of the Bailey' Mortimer.

It's from *Last Exit to Brooklyn* that those Duane Eddy references bleed in, the cavernous sound of his 'Peter Gunn' guitar the perfect soundtrack for a knife fight. Eddy's sound was created by producer

Lee Hazlewood recording him inside a grain silo and this was a formative influence on the young John Barry, who went to Los Angeles to learn techniques from Lee while recording *Watch Your Step* with the John Barry Seven in 1961.[15] The osmosis would continue with Adamson.

'I understood [*Last Exit to Brooklyn*] completely,' Barry recalled of his first immersion in Selby's work, 'and I read everything else I could get hold of by him. I knew that somewhere in me, I wanted to explore those same areas.'

By the time they came to record their third album, the band had started to pull in different directions. Devoto's father died suddenly while Magazine were touring America in 1979 and as a result, the singer put away his make-up box and stepped aside from his dominant role in writing music as well as the lyrics, letting the rest of his increasingly confident band members take over.

Keeping things closer to home this time, Martin Hannett was employed to bring his talents to *The Correct Use of Soap* – perhaps perversely, considering Devoto thought he had 'dominated' *Unknown Pleasures* to a detrimental degree. The more forthright singer managed to restrain his producer from employing any of his drummer torture techniques on John Doyle, but Hannett still managed to introduce this 'fairly straight bunch of fellows', as Adamson described them, to 'all these illegal substances in the back of cassette boxes' – bringing on his Hubert Selby Jr studies in earnest.

The Cold War frosting still lingers over *The Correct Use of Soap*, released on 30 May 1980, twelve days after Ian Curtis' passing. Opening track 'Because You're Frightened' perfectly captures the psychic weather of the nation with lyrics that could be a paean to the allure of our stern PM, Devoto declaring he is falling in love: 'Because I'm getting frightened/Of the things you somehow make me do.' By then, Thatcher was in need of some loving – as unemployment approached 2 million, an *Evening Standard* poll reported six out of ten Britons were dissatisfied with her first year's performance.

Further strife sizzles through 'I Want to Burn Again' with its references to customs men and suitcases with holes blown out of them. Explosions and politically motivated murders continued to splatter the headlines, the most spectacular being the August 1979 Bank Holiday assassination of Lord Louis Mountbatten, claimed by the Provisional Irish Republican Army (IRA). While sailing off the coast of his holiday home in County Sligo, Queen Elizabeth II's second cousin and last Viceroy of India's 29-foot fishing boat was reduced to what one eyewitness described as 'a lot of matchsticks floating on the water' by 50 pounds of gelignite – a portent of more Troubles to come from across the Irish Sea.

The Correct Use of Soap sadly also marks the fork in the road where the first, splendidly isolated and far-sighted Magazine went their separate ways. While Devoto, Adamson, Formula and Doyle would make one last album together, July 1981's *Magic, Murder and the Weather* – perhaps their best album title of all – they had lost one vital ingredient. By then John McGeoch was over the hills and far away, lured by a siren's call.

The Cry of the Banshee

'Where there is discord . . .' 'I first saw John on *The Old Grey Whistle Test* playing "The Light Pours Out of Me" with Magazine and thought: He's the one,' Siouxsie and the Banshees' bassist Steven Severin recalled in 1988. Four years and two albums into their existence by then, his band had already got through four guitarists and three drummers, one of each in a recent and very public mid-tour spat – so McGeoch appeared as the answer to their prayers. And although this new relationship was also doomed to end in tears, with an increasingly alcohol-addled McGeoch being given his cards a scant two years later, the partnership would see the Banshees produce arguably their finest three LPs. Which was no mean feat, considering how far and fast they'd progressed from the first incarnation that stepped out onto the 100 Club stage on 20 October 1976, the first night of the two-day Punk Festival masterminded by Malcolm McLaren. Siouxsie and Steven Severin – or 'Suzi and Two-Tone Steve of the Bromley Contingent' as

Melody Maker's on-the-spot reporter Caroline Coon had them in her review – were part an outré group of misfit friends from the same outer south London suburbs David Bowie had come of age in the decade before them. Like him, they were aliens in Metroland and quickly began to make their own entertainment – in Siouxsie's case, from an early age.

Her first interviews reference an isolated childhood existence in Chislehurst, south-east London, rife with parental neglect. The youngest of three children, while her older brother and sister were faces in the Swinging London Mod milieu, latchkey kid Susan Janet Ballion was letting herself in and making her own food by the age of seven. In further shades of Bowie's childhood, she had a strained relationship with her mother Betty, a bilingual secretary whom she described to *Sounds*' Vivien Goldman in December 1977 as 'acutely schizophrenic, paranoid'. Relations with her dad were also clearly problematic, with Siouxsie adding in the same interview that when her father, a lab technician with an alcohol problem, suddenly died when she was fourteen: 'I just laughed.' In a January 1978 interview with Paul Morley, she described pretending to commit suicide to try to gain her parents' attention: 'I used to do things like fall on the floor upstairs so that they'd think I'd fallen downstairs, and I'd have bottles of pills in my hands. I've always felt on the outside, really.'

Like a true pre-teenage witch, Sioux surrounded herself with cats ('I'm more affectionate with them than I am with people. They're so useful for talking to') and her siblings' record collections, which mirrored the sounds Dave Formula had been drinking in at his Manchester coffee houses. In particular, the mysterious, androgynous Julie Driscoll caught her attention: 'I was besotted by her, by the way she looked, by her voice. It was very different from watching Lulu on *Top of the Pops*, this woman with a shaven head and huge black eyes. I thought she was incredibly beautiful, very spiky and strong and tough – not at all cute and cuddly and feminine. And I loved the song "This Wheel's on Fire". It conjured up all sorts of fantastic stories to me.'

Although they lived only streets away from each other, Siouxsie didn't meet the teenage Steven Bailey – whose family had moved him to the neighbouring suburb of Bromley from Archway in north London when he was eleven – until fate took a hand at a 1975 Roxy Music gig at Wembley Arena. She hired an outfit from theatrical costumiers Bermans & Nathans for the occasion and looked like 'a cross between a mermaid and a chorus girl'.[16] A large part of Sioux's appeal stems from how she seems to have stepped out of a fairytale – the earthly incarnation of the sinisterly beautiful fairy Queen Maleficent, created by Marc David for Disney's 1959 *Sleeping Beauty*. Indeed, as if anticipating Maleficent's punk reincarnation to come, David instructed the actress who spoke her lines, Eleanor Audley, that 'the voice is the most necessary thing in the world'. Maleficent, it may be noted, curses the titular princess to die when she pricks her finger on a spinning wheel . . .

Sioux certainly cast her glamour over Bailey that night and they soon became a couple, pooling their resources of record collections and likeminded friends. Catching an early Sex Pistols' gig at Ravensbourne College of Art in 1976, the dynamic duo finally found their tribe, rapidly becoming part of the band's inner sanctum. In the unprecedented heat of that summer, they seemed to change their monikers as rapidly as they altered their hair colours – Steven Bailey was also known as Steve Spunker, Steven Havoc and Steven Deville before finally settling on a surname taken from the Leopold von Sacher-Masoch character mentioned in the Velvet Underground's 'Venus in Furs': 'Severin, down on your bended knee/Taste the whip, in love not given lightly'.[17]

With Bromley pals Simon Barker and Simone, Sioux and Severin were part of the Pistols' entourage who shot to tabloid infamy after appearing on the Thames Television *Today* programme, verbally jousting a soused Bill Grundy on 1 December 1976. 'Siouxsie's a Punk Shocker' was the *Daily Mirror*'s headline the next day, accompanied by an arresting photo: bleached Julie Driscoll crop, Aladdin Sane-meets-Alex Droog eyeflash, mannish white shirt and black trousers with braces and polka-dot bow tie. The image provided a clue of a still more clandestine world wherein the adventuress Siouxsie had been taking style notes: Madame Louise's, a lesbian club on Poland Street, in the heart of sinful Soho.

Just as it was in Manchester, London's gay clubs – some of which had been established decades before and were preserved in all the damask, red velvet and candles of a bygone age – were crucial to the gestation of punk and its further mutations. These were places straight society was not supposed to find, yet thanks to a tip-off from her go-go-dancing older sister it was Siouxsie who not only discovered Louise's but was the first of the punks to pass muster with its gatekeeper. Madame Louise presided at the door, judging who might become a member of her exclusive supper club, as often as not with '50s Soho's greatest roué Francis Bacon, just visible through a cloud of cigarette smoke beside her. Of course she would have been impressed by this vision of Sally Bowles' beaming back from Weimar Berlin. Siouxsie knew how to present a confident demeanour – she'd once walked her girlish gay best friend Bertie Marshall down the streets of Chislehurst on a collar and lead as if he were her dog.

The nineteen-year-old, who subsequently made her stage debut at the 100 Club, was wonderfully evoked by Caroline Coon as 'nothing if not magnificent. Her short hair, which she sweeps in great waves over her head, is streaked with red, like flames. She'll wear black plastic non-existent bras, one mesh and one rubber stocking, and suspender belts (various), all covered by a polka-dotted, transparent plastic mac.'

The first Banshees' guitarist was a seventeen-year-old Marco Pirroni, who would go on to great fortune as Adam Ant's chief collaborator; and their drummer his mate John Beverley, aka Sid Vicious, who would go on to eternal infamy. They performed a twenty-minute version of 'The Lord's Prayer' laced with chunks of 'Twist and Shout', '(I Can't Get No) Satisfaction' and 'Deutschland Über Alles' in a performance stage-directed by Pirroni – the only one of them with any prior musical experience – that achieved the prerequisite madness.

'I thought we were doing "Sister Ray" or something,' he recalled. The Velvets' influence is a common thread with their Manchester peers and, uncannily, one of the other songs they discussed playing was the theme from *Goldfinger*. With their first statement of intent, it seemed the Banshees were throwing the past thirty years – all the horrors of the Second World War, the '60s and the false dawn of the Summer of Love, not to mention the rapidly waning influence of the Christian Church – into their musical grinder. Unlike the rest of the bands on the bill, they really were making it up as they went along, but, said Marco: 'We didn't think it would get us a good profile or make us famous, or anything. It was just the urge. The subconscious urge that you had to do something.'

Re/make Re/model

The Banshees would go on to fashion new forms of beauty from the resultant shards on their stunning debut album *The Scream* (1978), having dispensed with their second guitarist Pete Fenton, in a line-up that temporarily solidified with John McKay on the six strings that drew blood and Kenny Morris on drums. This pairing provided a distinct framework for the Banshees' sound, the self-taught McKay's guitar traversing similar oblique angles to McGeoch's in Magazine and Morris's echoing drums working a potent Krautrock-meets-Glitter Band beat to Severin's dominant, rhythmic bass. *The Scream* was starkly different from its spiritual parent, *Never Mind the Bollocks*. Eschewing rock 'n' roll archetypes it instead absorbed the Germanic influence of Neu!, Can and Kraftwerk so dear to Steven Severin and the film scores of Bernard Herrmann – in particular, the screaming strings of the shower scene he created for Alfred Hitchcock's 1960 masterpiece *Psycho* – that Siouxsie would later acknowledge as another vital 'obsession'.

Co-producer Steve Lillywhite's work on the recording of these instruments – especially the drum sound, in which the bass and snare were recorded first and the cymbals and tom-toms later – would be a major influence on Joy Division. Stephen Morris acknowledged in his 2019 memoir, *Record Play Pause*: 'It would be Siouxsie & the Banshees to whom I most felt some kind of affinity . . . the bass-led rhythm, the way first drummer Kenny Morris played mostly toms . . . The Banshees had that foreboding sound, sketching out the future from the dark of the past.'[18]

The lyrics were just as arresting. The two original Banshees turned the scenes of their troubled adolescence into a Surrealist portrait of a madness-inducing prison of conformity with such outstanding tracks as 'Overground' ('This limbo is no place/ To be a digit in another space') and 'Suburban Relapse' ('I was washing up the dishes . . . When my string snapped'). They even transformed the menu of their local Chinese takeaway into their first hit single, the irresistible skewed pop of 'Hong Kong Garden'.

Sioux gave Vivien Goldman a fascinating insight into her lyrical process, describing how she kept clippings of news stories for inspiration: 'You always find people doing the weirdest things, like this bloke who put his leg on the railway line because he wanted to claim more money as a war hero. And the woman who wheeled a chopped-up body around in a pram. It's all there, in *The Sun* every day.'

This was a habit she would keep, finding subject matter in the outer reaches of bizarre human behaviour – tribal and sub-cultural rituals, or myriad forms of male-on-female oppression – and researching them to create a database of absorbing lyrics for decades to come.

The only non-original track on *The Scream* was a vertiginous cover of 'Helter Skelter', the Beatles' *White Album* track that inspired Charles Manson to pull the curtain down on the '60s in a homicidal rampage.[19]

It's interesting how some of the points Siouxsie makes to Vivien Goldman echo Margaret Thatcher's philosophy: 'I think everyone should help themselves,' for example – and, perhaps as a result of her upbringing – 'I've just got a low tolerance of people who can't help themselves.' However, while there was only ever room for one woman in Thatcher's cabinet, Siouxsie wanted to be a conduit:

'I don't see myself as a Joan of Arc or anything, but it would be great if other women would follow in my footsteps.' As we shall see, she did more than offer words of encouragement to her fellow female travellers.

They Used Dark Forces

Before the arrival of *The Scream*, the Banshees had spent two years vying with their friends and regular live bill sharers Adam and the Ants for the title of Biggest Unsigned Band in Britain, making their first recordings for John Peel's Radio 1 *Sessions*. Eventually it was New Zealander Chris Parry – who was narrowly beaten to signing the Pistols and the Clash, but had already taken the Cure under his wing – who nabbed them for Polydor, providing a deal that gave the band the artistic control they sought.

The reluctance of major label A&R men to go near them largely came down to the Banshees' desire *not* to please. Or, as one early supporter, *Sounds*' Jane Suck, put it in June 1977: 'It's the Nazi vibe that is holding back the potential horde.'

This apparent flirtation with fascism is an issue that still rears its head, much to the band's chagrin. But the swastika was a dangerous image to play with while the right-wing National Front (NF) Party was gaining political power, picking up 120,000 votes in the May 1977 Greater London Council (GLC) elections – more than it had acquired from the entire British electorate at the previous general election of 1974. It was recruiting in cash-strapped, inner-city areas and punk gigs quickly become targets. The organisations Rock Against Racism (RAR) and the Anti-Nazi League (ANL) were formed as confrontational responses, building a network of activists and putting on gigs in venues across the country, the latter with the support of the hard left Socialist Workers Party (SWP) and sponsorship from some trades unions.

The NF countered with provocative marches through areas largely inhabited by black and Asian communities, where they spouted their tirades with an inordinate amount of police protection.

The murder of Blair Peach occurred at one such demo, where 2,876 police, ninety-four of them mounted,[20] lined a route through the largely Sikh and Hindu area of Southall, west London, on 23 April – St George's Day – 1979. The 33-year-old schoolteacher, an active SWP member, was on an ANL counter-protest when he was struck on the head by a member of the notorious Metropolitan Police unit the Special Patrol Group (SPG) and died of his injuries in Ealing Hospital the next day.

For anyone who did not experience the '70s first-hand – and if you didn't, any episode of ITV's *The Sweeney* picked at random will put you in the picture – perhaps the most shocking aspect of this event is just how much of the press reports at the time put their sympathies with the racists and the police.

The Banshees refused to play any RAR benefits, Siouxsie explaining to Tom Vague of fanzine *Vague* that: 'We found that patronising. It was like saying blacks couldn't do anything for themselves.' However, they would find other ways to deal head-to-head with racists who invaded their gigs in the future.

Joy Division also had critics within the music papers who were understandably uncomfortable with the fact the band's name was taken from a chilling expression for a concentration camp brothel that Ian Curtis had gleaned from *House of Dolls*, the second volume of memoir-as-fiction by Holocaust survivor Ka-Tzctnik 135633, first published in Britain in 1973.

The end of the Second World War was thirty-one years distant from the beginning of punk and many of the Pistols' generation grew up playing on the bombsites still left over from the conflict, with family members who had served in it. Deborah Curtis makes no bones about how horrified she was by her husband's choice of band name and hoped the public would not realise where he had got it. The fact that Bernard Sumner was at the time calling himself Bernard Albrecht[21] and the band's fans' taste for grey clothes and utility haircuts – 'depressives dressing for the Depression' as Mrs Curtis wryly put it – enhanced the impression they also had found something glamorous in the strife of the '30s.

In the Banshees' case, similar accusations could be traced all the way back to the 'Baby Belsen' homemade T-shirt sported by 'Belsen Was a Gas' author Sid Vicious at the 100 Club; Sioux's teaming of a swastika armband with an open-cup bra to attend the Pistols' Screen on the Green gig in 1976 and an early version of 'Love in a Void', which contained the line 'Too many Jews for my liking' – subsequently amended to 'Too many bigots for my liking' to make it clear they were laughing at and not with *Till Death Us Do Part*'s Alf Garnett.[22]

Could the fact that Siouxsie still draws more flak for this than the surviving members of Joy Division – who went on to trade under the name New Order, an expression used by Adolf Hitler in his autobiographical manifesto *Mein Kampf* – be attributed to the fact that female transgressors of any stripe are always held up to greater scrutiny than their male counterparts? I think so. The '70s were every bit as misogynist as they were racist (cf. again *The Sweeney*) and Sioux experienced police brutality first-hand, having by then spent a night in the cells for wearing shoes deemed 'offensive weapons' to a Heartbreakers' gig at the Rainbow. As Vivien Goldman, herself the Jewish daughter of German refugees, pointed out: 'Siouxsie is very obviously intelligent. Too intelligent and articulate . . . One look into her level, inquiring brown eyes is all it takes to know she's as likely to take shit as I am to flog my typewriter for a new frock.'

Both the Bromley contingent and Ian Curtis were massive fans of Bob Fosse's *Cabaret* (1972), from where the taste for Weimar, Dada, suspenders and fishnet stockings, green fingernails and throwing glasses of Champagne into the face of impending doom can all be traced. Recent history compelled the enquiring minds of a generation growing up under the shadow of potential nuclear Armageddon to wonder how little men like Hitler, Mao and Stalin could bend the fate of entire continents to their will. Vivienne Westwood and Malcolm McLaren's designs drew heavily on the imagery of totalitarianism – Siouxsie's swastika armband was part of their Anarchy shirt, which was also adorned with a removable Karl Marx patch, a Maoist red armband stamped with the word CHAOS and the Situationist slogan 'Be reasonable – demand the impossible' emblazoned across the front. Simon Barker was wearing one on the Bill Grundy show and, as he said: 'I don't remember a lot of fuss about that going out at six in the evening. But at the same time, [Second World War veteran] Spike Milligan used to do his joke with a traffic warden who was Adolf Hitler, Freddie Starr used to do it and [Inspector Cyril] Blakey from [ITV's] *On the Buses* had a Hitler moustache.' The looking glass of '70s popular culture offers a reflection of sensibilities that seem warped compared to ours, and when it comes down to it, the early punks were all possessed with the primal teenage urge to shock. 'In Europe you're not allowed to show a swastika, they're hypersensitive about it,' said Simon Barker. 'But I think we had a better way, because we ridiculed it, we laughed at it. We had no respect for anything.'

Aesthetically, as Jane Suck observed, the Banshees were much 'more akin to Visconti's *The Damned* than the Third Reich' anyway. Though it was Gordon Hessler's 1970 film *Cry of the Banshee* that the band got their name from.[23] Along with Sioux's love of Bernard Herrmann's *Psycho* score, the Banshees shared Magazine's fondness for John Barry, *The Avengers* and spy themes in general, with their appreciation of Gerry and Sylvia Anderson's Supermarionation secret agents expressed in their live cover of the theme from *Captain Scarlet*.

However, the band that had gelled so perfectly around *The Scream* did not last much longer than it took to make their second album, *Join Hands*, before McKay and Morris made a shock departure on 7 September 1979, at the start of a tour with the Cure. What happened next was crucial to the evolution both of the Banshees and their fellow suburban subversives, who hailed from even further down the railway line out of London Victoria, to a place we may fondly refer to as 'Creepy Crawley'.

Boys Don't Cry

'Where there is doubt . . .' Despite his image as the voice of the lost and the lonely, Robert Smith was born into a large and happy family on 21 April 1959, the third of four siblings, two boys and two girls, all of them blessed with prodigious musical abilities. His first home was in Blackpool and his first, rather prophetic, memory was the taste of sand on the beach. But Robert was only three when his father Alex found better employment prospects at Upjohn Pharmaceuticals in Crawley and moved his brood down south to what was then a booming New Town in the commuter belt of Surrey/West Sussex. Robert would spend his adolescence experiencing first-hand the results of the post-war town planners' dreamscape, in a location equidistant from the capital and the dramatic chalk cliffs and South Downs of the Sussex coast.

Though the original village dates back to the thirteenth century, Crawley's position between London and Brighton meant it grew exponentially with travel technology, first as a coaching post, then, with the coming of the railway in 1841, and finally, the expansion of nearby Gatwick from small aerodrome to major hub by 1958. It was given New Town status by the Attlee Labour government in 1947 and thereafter the village and its surrounding settlements of Ifield and Three Bridges began their transformation into a sprawling civic, commercial and residential conurbation, which went from housing a mere 9,500 people to 60,000-and-growing by the time the Smiths arrived in the early '60s. It was designed to offer hope and prosperity to just their kind of young family, and its location must have made it seem ideal. But, just like the music Robert Smith would go on to make, Crawley has a sinister and macabre side.

It was here that the infamous post-war serial killer and con man John George Haigh set up the workshop where he would dissolve the bodies of his rich benefactors in oil drums full of sulphuric acid. While ostensibly working as a salesman and bookkeeper for a cosmetics company – and wooing the owner's young daughter with trips to the seaside and classical concerts in London – Haigh defrauded and killed a succession of at least six friends and acquaintances drawn in by his particular brand of pencil-moustachioed charm. The Acid Bath Murderer only finally came unstuck when he got the ratio of the chemicals needed to dispose of his final victim, Mrs Olive Durand-Deacon, wrong. Police, alerted by her concerned friends, raided his workshop to find her gallstones and one denture remaining. Although Haigh's crimes turned the stomachs of the detectives who heard his confessions – which included vampiric claims to have drunk his victims' blood – he fascinated the journalists who covered his trial as much as he had his prey. 'My spirit shall remain earthbound for some time: my mission is not yet fulfilled,' Haigh wrote to his mother on the eve of his execution on 10 August 1949.[24]

Perhaps his shade was waiting for the arrival of Robert Smith, who shares a few things in common with Crawley's creepiest proto-Goth. Haigh was also born in the north of England to parents of strong religious faith, in his case the extreme Protestant sect the Plymouth Brethren, whose methods of strict Bible study alongside sadistic child discipline also gave the world the English occultist Aleister Crowley, the 'wickedest man in the world'. Young Robert adhered to his parents' Catholic faith, diligently attending the Friary in Crawley into his twenties and continuing to wear his rosary to this day. Despite appearing captivating to the opposite sex, both Smith and Haigh had but one true love. Robert has been with his wife and muse Mary (née Poole) since the age of fifteen. Their relationship has inspired several of his most poignant songs – 'Siamese Twins', which he recorded with her looking on, and 'Charlotte Sometimes', the 7-inch of which featured a blurred photo of Mary on the cover, an image that would recur on the sleeve of 1990's 'Pictures of You' – and he has always been at pains to keep his life with her as private as possible. Haigh maintained a six-year-long chaste relationship with Barbara Stephens, which began when she was fifteen. Despite everything she heard at his trial, Stephens remained in love with him to the last.

Finally, both singer and serial killer evinced strong musical gifts in childhood – Haigh won a choral scholarship to Wakefield Grammar School at the age of ten and sang High Anglican Mass every week at the Cathedral, entranced by the figure of the crucified Christ. By the age of six, as Smith encountered his first founder member of the Cure, Laurence 'Lol' Tolhurst, on the bus to St Francis Primary School each day, he had already fallen under a still more powerful divine force: his older brother Richard's record collection. Robert's earliest musical revelations would continue to inform his songwriting – as an adult, he would fluctuate between beguiling whimsy and outright nihilism – and his questioning of his own faith would provoke some of his greatest and most extreme music.

His musical ear was drawn both to the Poptimism of *Help!*-era Beatles and the mysteries of Jimi Hendrix, whose abilities with chord structures and tonal effects he would make a study of when he first began to grapple with the guitar at the age of thirteen. Rather than admiring Lizard King Jim Morrison, Smith found inspiration in the autumnal oeuvre of tragic English Lost Boy Nick Drake (1948–74), whose guitar playing was as erudite as his lyrical rendering of woods and waters, pain and loss.

The first album Robert bought for himself was *Ziggy Stardust* in 1972. But though Smith was as entranced by the strangeness of the Starman as any of his peers, he grew more closely enamoured of the powers of a pirate-striped, black-eyed Scotsman. Never mind Bowie's 'My Death', Alex Harvey's stunning 1973 cover of Jacques Brel's 'Next', performed with guitarist Zal Cleminson in full tragic Pierrot make-up on the BBC's *The Old Grey Whistle Test*, chanelled all the trauma of the song's subject matter – a young First World War soldier forced inside 'a mobile army whorehouse' for a grim coupling that stains the rest of his life – as if Harvey had gone through the ordeal himself. Perhaps a life of thwarted fame on the rock 'n' roll circuit is comparable – battered in both physique and vocal cords, Harvey would drop dead from heart failure the day before his forty-seventh birthday, on a ferry home from a gig in Belgium, on 4 February 1982. But he conferred his potent Celtic magic on the fourteen-year-old Smith, who followed the Sensational Alex Harvey Band to as many gigs as he could.

'Alex Harvey was the physical manifestation of what I thought I could be,' Robert told *The Guardian*'s Will Hodgkinson three decades later. 'He never really got anywhere, even though he had something so magical when he performed – he had the persona of a victim, and you just sided with him against all that was going wrong.' It was precisely these qualities that Smith would embody when it came to be him standing under the spotlight.

Already experimenting with his sisters' make-up palettes and his mother's black velvet dresses – and getting beaten up and suspended from school for his efforts – Robert's initiation into the art of stage magic began in 1972. Together with brother Richard and younger sister Janet – already a virtuoso pianist – he formed the magnificently Wheatleyan-sounding Crawley Goat Band, playing cover versions on whatever instruments they could lay their hands on at home or from the music room of Notre Dame Middle School, where Robert, Lol Tolhurst and Michael Dempsey were now pupils. The first incarnation of the Cure would evolve out of a band formed by the latter trio in 1976.

With Robert on guitar, Dempsey on bass and Tolhurst on drums, the suspiciously proggishly named the Obelisk evolved over the course of that long hot summer – and all that was stirring down the tracks from Bromley to the King's Road – into the more punk-sounding Malice. Dad Alex built them a studio to rehearse in and they acquired an additional guitarist, Janet Smith's boyfriend Porl Thompson, along the way. From then on, their covers of Bowie's 'Suffragette City', Hendrix's 'Foxy Lady' and the Troggs' 'Wild Thing' began to evolve into original material. It didn't take Robert long to tune in – by January 1977, high on the smart punk-pop of Buzzcocks and Elvis Costello, he'd cut his shoulder-length hair, renamed his band the Easy Cure and resolved to seize the day.

Strangely, Smith was not initially the band's lead singer – a bewilderingly fast succession of vocalists with such unlikely names as Gary X and Peter O'Toole (no relation to the erstwhile *Lawrence of Arabia*) preceded him. But it was on Smith's initiative that they got their first record deal, when he spotted an ad in *Melody Maker* placed by Germany's largest independent record label Hansa – home of perennial '70s chart-toppers Boney M. – scouting for new acts aged between fifteen and thirty.

The Easy Cure recorded a demo tape of two Smith compositions, 'Killing an Arab' and '10.15 Saturday Night' in the Smiths' home studio and sent it off, as requested, with a band photograph. By 18 May 1977, they had their first record deal, pocketing £1,000 – the equivalent of nearly £8,000 today – which they duly ploughed back into buying new equipment. Between then and the autumn recording of their first recording sessions for their new label, Porl Thompson took temporary leave, while Peter O'Toole became the figurative Pete Best of this ensemble – his departure leaving Robert to take over on vocals. Though initially 'paralysed with fear' at the prospect, the already myopic Smith found that taking to the stage wearing beer goggles helped: 'I drank about six pints . . . Of the first three songs, I started on the second. No one even noticed. So I thought, "If I can get away with that, I can be the singer."'

Making a Killing

It wasn't so easy to impress their new record company with the material they recorded at SAV Studios in Wembley, however. Label bosses were particularly offended by 'Killing an Arab', which had been inspired by Albert Camus' novel *L'Étranger* and begins, as on the shores of Smith's memory, 'Standing on a beach . . .' Robert was exploring the existentialist notion of nihilism in his lyrics, that whether he should 'turn and walk away' or 'fire the gun' at the titular Arab – as the book's central character, Meursault, does – the result 'amounts to the same/Absolutely nothing'. Much as John McKay's oriental guitar line that jolted 'Hong Kong Garden' high up the charts, he added an attractive, Moorish-patterned riff to enhance the effect of those words. Again, this was a very teenage urge, prompted by reading such exponents of the absurd as Camus, Jean Genet and Samuel Beckett, as was the wont of many a '70s adolescent. 'The Camus volume in question was simply the most interesting piece of literature that passed by during "O" level time,' as a more sympathetic Nick Kent would point out in *NME*, 'amid the turgid likes of Molière and the usual list of sixteenth-century dullard scribes'. But it made the German label nervous. Neither 'Killing an Arab' nor other Smith compositions 'Meathook' and 'See the Children' impressed Hansa, who, the band told some of their earliest interviewers, were more taken by their photo than their music. Lol Tolhurst recounted the label's reaction to their demo to an enquiring Ian Birch in *Melody Maker*, March 1979. 'This is horrible,' they said. 'Not even people in prison would like this!' The band parted company with Hansa less than a year after signing, cannily retaining all the rights to the material they'd recorded.

Which is where Chris Parry enters the frame. Dropping the 'Easy' part of their name, Smith, Dempsey and Tolhurst recorded a new demo tape of 'Boys Don't Cry', 'It's Not You' and 'Fire in Cairo', which ended up on his desk at the exact time he was setting up his own label. Parry had absolutely no doubts about the worth of what he was hearing. The Cure became Fiction's first signing – although their debut single 'Killing an Arab'/'10.15 Saturday Night' came out on Small Wonder, the indie label operated by Pete and Mari Stennett out of their Walthamstow record shop, as a special one-off deal set up by Parry in late December 1978.[25]

The second coming of this pairing of tracks delighted *Sounds*' resident man-in-a-long-mac as much as it had aggrieved Hansa. Making it Single of the Week in his first pick of 1979, Dave McCullough enthused at the contrast between the 'fresh and crisp' A-side and the muted kitchen-sink drama of its flip, which traversed similar lyrical lines to the Banshees' evocations of suburban ennui, but with a more skiffling refrain to its constantly dripping tap. 'The effect that the single had upon my weary and battle-scarred brain was astonishing,' McCullough wrote. 'I felt alive again.' He hastened to meet the by-now-nineteen-year-olds, marvelling at Robert's 'skinny and alarmingly handsome' looks over drinks in a South Kensington hostelry, close to the Natural History Museum – and the Onslow Court Hotel, from where Mrs Duran Deacon made her fateful last exit to Crawley, thirty years previously.

McCullough followed the band to a gig at West Hampstead's Moonlight Club – the scene, three months later, of Ian Curtis' onstage trauma and also the venue where the Banshees and Ants had established residencies throughout their unsigned years. The skills McCullough witnessed there were testament to the hours the trio had spent playing to their friends at the Rocket pub in Crawley.

'The Cure brought back the spark of rock and roll to me,' the journalist enthused. 'Youth. Energy. Character. Endless potential and hope.' To his question on describing their sound, Parry made the sage-like reply: 'Almost rootless, which makes them very contemporary.'

For a band whose love of polka dots, lashings of eyeliner, smudged lipstick and tarantula hair has become so fixed in the popular imagination, it's disconcerting to discover them being described in Ian Birch's *Melody Maker* article as a 'no-image band'. But the cover of their debut album *Three Imaginary Boys* – released on 8 May 1979, four days after Thatcher's election victory – with a standard lamp, a fridge and a Hoover taking the place of each band member – is a reminder of how reluctant they were to be pigeonholed back then.

The vinyl inside this enigmatic sleeve contained both sides of their debut single and more tracks that demonstrated Smith had plenty to say about coming of age in the commuter belt – much like his Surrey peer and fellow Chris Parry signing, the Jam's Paul Weller of Woking, Surrey. The most enduring, 'Boys Don't Cry' – which would have a decades-long afterlife and become the title of a 1999 film – put into words the thought processes of so many adolescent boys in the flush of their first amorous encounters, with a tune that matched their wrenching stomachs and stinging tears. The most obviously punk track, 'Grinding Halt' envisioned, in staccato couplets, the kind of nuclear Armageddon that all '80s children feared would become their fate: 'No me/No people'. The most atmospheric, 'Fire in Cairo' followed 'Killing an Arab''s muse into the desert, where Smith enacts a Scheherazadian fever dream using his guitar as magic carpet.

'They are trying to tell us something,' wrote Joy Division and Magazine's great champion, Paul Morley. 'They are trying to tell us they do not exist. They are trying to say that everything is empty.

They are making fools of themselves . . .' Morley went on in this offended-intellectual vein for some paragraphs, before concluding, with feeling: 'What they've done here is the equivalent of an album of Enid Blyton . . . packaged as . . . Angela Carter.'[26] It would not be the first time a male journalist took such extreme umbrage with Robert Smith – though it would soon become evident that he could give as good as he got. At the time, though, Smith seemed keen to convey just how down-to-earth his band really were. Although he inevitably took the lead, all early Cure interviews were undertaken with the three-piece and despite being the sole author of most of their songs, the entire band was always afforded songwriting credits. Alone among the lead singers of this chapter, Smith seemed content with his family and his place in the world, unwilling to leave home or indeed look beyond Crawley for anything more exotic – 'I couldn't stand living in London myself.'

Perhaps it was because he knew he wasn't ordinary that he felt he should try harder to be so. Maybe the fact Smith went to a faith school, rather than a state one, kept him sheltered for longer. Whatever: 'I wouldn't want to think people doted on us, hung on every word, or wanted to look like us,' he told Jim Green of the *Trouser Press*, going on to explain how the aftermath of punk's iconoclasm had created its own new clichés, such as everyone wanting to look and sound like the Clash. Amusing as these words may now seem, when the Cure bestrode the world as a stadium-filling Goth Colossus and every small town from Crawley to Chernobyl has its own spiky-haired Smith lookalike: 'We don't want to look like rock 'n' rollers,' was his reasoning for that. But that would change following the events of September 1979, when the Cure set off on tour in support of Siouxsie and the Banshees.

Jumping Someone Else's Train

John McKay and Kenny Morris had begun to feel disgruntled during the recording of *Join Hands*, which began in London's Air Studios in the fateful May of 1979. Prophetically, the album took warfare as its general theme, opening with the tolling of bells on 'Poppy Day', which was based on John McCrae's poem 'In Flanders Fields' and echoed on the album's cover, which depicts four soldiers from the Guard's Memorial to the First World War dead and a Remembrance Day bloom. 'Regal Zone' was written about the seismic Iranian Revolution that raged from 7 January 1978 to 11 February 1979 and saw the end of the last Persian royal dynasty under Shah Mohammad Reza Pahlavi unceremoniously ousted and replaced by supporters of the hardline cleric Ayatollah Ruhollah Khomeini; while 'Icon', about the toppling of regimes and the destruction of sacred imagery, anticipated what would happen next.

Yet the Banshees had not completely broken from the Bromley–Chislehurst borders yet. 'Playground Twist' set chants of childhood cruelty and nursery rhyme to the sound of more church bells and McKay's epically flanged guitars. Edgar Allan Poe once more rose back from the dead on 'Premature Burial', in which Sioux compares the experience of being born into suburbia to that of being entombed alive and, like the medium at a séance, commands her listeners to: '*Join hands*'. In the harrowing 'Mother/Oh Mein Papa', a reworking of a German folk song with double-vocals contrasting her experience to that of a stereotypically normal one, Sioux casts the maternal influence in her life as malignly vampiric: 'So she clutches at her brood (So she gathers up her brood)/ . . . And smothers their last breath (She gave us our first breath)'.

The band worked quickly on the album, recording and mixing the instruments in just one month – but Siouxsie's vocals were added afterwards, at the mixing stage, signalling the band's imminent fragmentation. Just as on *The Scream*, McKay's distinctive guitar – and saxophone on 'Regal Zone' – and Morris's ominous drums played no small part in the drama of sound the Banshees created for *Join Hands*, while Morris's friend, the future film director John Maybury, provided art direction and the illustrations on the inner gatefold sleeve.

But the schism within the ranks began with Sioux and Severin's choice of Mike Stavrou for producer and widened when that selection was reinforced by the band's hands-on manager, Nils Stevenson, with the effect that McKay and Morris's input was marginalised. Perhaps understandably, they began to respond in a somewhat sulky manner – Morris did not attend any of the mixing sessions and both were annoyed by how the album sounded. The pair stare stony-faced from the last band photo session, to which they had been summoned with no prior consultation. Just before they set off on tour, a warm-up show in Belfast was beset with equipment problems for McKay, who had to play without his effects pedals. Then, on the day of the album's release and the start of their tour, things overheated in a record shop in Aberdeen.

The omens were ill. Sioux and Severin were midway through the signing before McKay and Morris knew anything about it and when they came into the shop, McKay removed *Join Hands* from the record player, replacing it with the Slits' new album *Cut* – not quite the helping hand for her punk sisters that Sioux had envisaged. If that wasn't insult enough, Polydor had set up the signing, but not provided enough stock. They took further umbrage with manager Nils for selling promo copies to the kids at £3.80 a shot and started handing them out for free instead. Which was when Siouxsie made a physical intervention and the guitarist and drummer swiftly took their leave.

Severin expected they would cool down – unusually, the tour was being financed out of their own pockets, to stop their record company from 'asking favours' as he ominously put it to *Sounds*' Phil Sutcliffe, who had turned up to review the gig that evening and got himself a scoop. But McKay and Morris absconded from their hotel, leaving their tour passes on their pillows in a last gesture of defiance. After their non-appearance at the soundcheck, suspicious Nils Stevenson caught up with them as they boarded a getaway taxi. Attempting to strangle Morris as the vehicle sped away, he was disgorged onto the pavement screaming: 'You will never work again!'

Cannily, the ex-drummer diverted his driver from taking them to the station, as he would later recall: 'Because that was the first place Siouxsie would look and I knew her. I knew she would be going there, looking through every carriage on the rampage, and she would search under every seat – and she did!'[27]

That night, the Cure played an extended set before Sioux and Severin took to the stage to explain the situation to their audience: 'Two original members of the band are here tonight. Two art college students fucked off out of it . . . If you've got 1 per cent of the aggression we feel towards them, if you ever see them you have my blessings to beat the shit out of them.'

But salvation was only a support act away. Returning to the stage, the Cure plucked some more songs from their repertoire to feed the fans, including one called 'S', which they dedicated to Siouxsie. Then Sioux and Severin, as if rebaptising themselves and their novitiates, came back for a version of 'The Lord's Prayer' that eyewitness Sutcliffe described as: 'A naked event, a moment of truth, a spit in the eye of disaster . . . My scalp prickled at the nameless feelings of it.'

Robert Smith and Lol Tolhurst would stand in for McKay and Morris for the rest of the Join Hands tour. In the process of saving the Banshees from financial ruin, Smith had joined a vastly more worldly and sophisticated outfit – and he would find it hard to ever leave. Although he would be replaced at the end of this tour by John McGeoch – and Morris's role taken by erstwhile Slits' drummer Peter 'Budgie' Clarke, revenge indeed for the Aberdeen Record Store Incident – Smith's association with the band would not end there. Severin, in particular, would take on a role that no one else in the Cure ever seemed to fulfil for Smith – that of an older brother. But: 'Our friendship was based entirely on altered states,' he would tell *Q*'s Robert Sandall a decade later. 'Whenever we went out together, I would never get home until the next day. Mary hated it.'

'He was very clever,' Severin would counter to his band's official biographer Mark Paytress. 'It wasn't just the lipstick he took from the Banshees.'

But that's another story for a later page.

Gothfather: Jim Morrison

'There are things that are known and things that are unknown. In between are the doors.' So goes the William Blake quote, repurposed by Aldous Huxley for his 1954 experiment in psychedelics The Doors of Perception, *which, in 1965, inspired a 22-year-old Jim Morrison to form a band while studying film at UCLA. The son of a US Navy rear admiral, James Douglas Morrison (1943–71) had been kicking against his ultra-conservative background since childhood. At the age of four, he witnessed the aftermath of a road accident in the desert outside Alburquerque – where his father was then working for the American atomic weapons programme – in which a group of Pueblo Native Americans lay dying in the road. He claimed that the soul of one of the departing entered his body and would continue to channel the incident on stage, in song ('Peace Frog') and poems ('Dawn's Highway', 'Ghost Song') ever after.*

At school he was rebellious and precocious, developing a taste for the philosophy of Friedrich Nietzsche and the poems of Arthur Rimbaud, as well as the all-important Beat writers Jack Kerouac, Allen Ginsberg and William S. Burroughs – he even consulted the Library of Congress to peruse liturgies on sixteenth-century demonology, much to the disbelief of his English teacher. Like his admirer, Ian Curtis, Jim could display many different personalities to the people he was close to – especially his girlfriends – being controlling and frightening one minute, vulnerable and romantic the next.

At the beach one day in the summer of 1965, he met fellow UCLA student and pianist Ray Manzarek, who thought his poetic musings were 'rock group material'. Oddly, until then, the smoky-baritoned Morrison had no intention of forming a band, but following the swift addition of guitarist Robby Krieger and drummer John Densmore, that was what they became. Indeed, arguably, the band that best defined the turning-on of the mind-altering end of the '60s – fixed in that time in no small way by fellow UCLA alumnus Francis Ford Coppola's use of their oedipal epic 'The End' over images of burning Vietnamese palms on the opening sequence of Apocalypse Now *(1979).*

From their stunning, eponymous debut album to Morrison's mysterious demise in a Paris bathtub – or not – the Doors' existence was a vertiginous voyage to 'break on through to the other side' of those portals Blake envisioned. The subsequent legends of arrest for alleged indecent exposure, drug and alcohol excess and wild, witchy women have made a heady mythology out of Jim's short life, but tend to overshadow just how brilliant the Doors' music really was. In swift succession, they made six almost flawless albums – The Doors *(1967),* Strange Days *(1967),* Waiting for the Sun *(1968),* The Soft Parade *(1969),* Morrison Hotel *(1970) and* L.A. Woman *(1971) – that combine Jim's leather-trousered, shaman-seer-philosopher-poet persona with the epic, keyboard-led groove cooked up by the jazzwise and downright funky Manzarek, Krieger and Densmore. Shortly after penning his epic ode to the City of Angels, Morrison and partner Pamela Courson moved to Paris in an attempt to escape the pressures of heroin addiction and infamy, but after only four months in the French capital, he somehow found the exit he'd been seeking all along.*

In the official version, Pamela found Jim dead in the bath of their apartment, where he had fallen asleep and drowned. Other witnesses maintain he died at the Paris nightclub Rock 'n' Roll Circus, from a dose of heroin supplied by Marianne Faithfull's dealer boyfriend Jean de Breteuil, who then drove him home and staged his more legal repose. No autopsy was performed so no official cause of death was ever given. Courson died three years later from an overdose, taking her secrets with her.

Jim was interred in Père Lachaise Cemetery in Paris, also the last resting place of Oscar Wilde, where his headstone and a marble bust were repeatedly vandalised and then stolen by fans, just as Wilde's Jacob Epstein-designed tomb would be defaced by lipstick-wearing Morrissey fans. When the music's over . . .

Gothmother: Julie Driscoll

'I had the hots for Julie Driscoll!' Siouxsie Sioux recalled her first exposure to the singer who made Bob Dylan's 'This Wheel's on Fire' and Donovan's 'Season of the Witch' her own with the spellbinding recordings she made with Brian Auger and the Trinity in 1967–68. For a brief moment in time, 'Jools' became 'The

Face' of Swinging London. And what a face – huge eyes with dark shadow and long, long lashes dominated the heart-shaped, pale-lipped visage of this arresting beauty. Needing no unnecessary adornment, she wore her hair close-cropped and moved with a spider's shadowy grace under layers of chiffon and feather boa. Her deep voice was just as captivating and the detached way she deployed her vocals added to the mystique. But perhaps the biggest enigma is how she managed to slip through the cracks of pop history, eluding the success her originality merited, until she re-recorded the song that so captivated the eleven-year-old Sioux with added vocals from Adrian (Ade) Edmondson to become the theme tune for the satirical BBC sitcom Absolutely Fabulous *in 1992.*

Born in London on 8 June 1947, Julie was a teenage mod who got a job as secretary for Yardbirds' manager Giorgio Gomelsky when she was seventeen. The impresario was not slow to recognise her potential – she rapidly went from opening fanmail to performing alongside Long John Baldry, Brian Auger and Rod Stewart in the touring revue show Steampacket in 1965 – a combo that, as many a soul- and jazz-loving modernist will tell you, should have been enormous, but imploded following a short-lived affair between Julie and Rod.

Keyboard wizard Brian Auger put the Trinity together in early 1967, wanting to build a bridge between the rock and jazz worlds he had each pointed toe in. With Clive Thacker on drums, Dave Ambrose on bass and Vic Briggs on guitar, they recruited Driscoll to bring her spectacular vocals to play. So tight were the outfit from playing live that their debut album, Open, *took only six hours to record. A spooksome succession of singles – 'Black Cat', 'Season of the Witch' and a first Dylan cover, 'I Am a Lonesome Hobo' – followed, before the Trinity recorded their definitive 'This Wheel's on Fire' in April 1968. The record flamed its way to number five in the charts and Julie was suddenly the nation's pin-up.*

But trouble was brewing in psychedelic paradise and its name was Giorgio Gomelsky. Under his controlling influence, the band's label Polydor – which would sign the Banshees a decade later – put out all these records as Julie Driscoll releases without crediting Brian Auger and the Trinity. The meddling manager was also filling their schedule with too many extra-promotional activities, so exhaustion set in and tempers frayed. After a series of moody TV interviews, the Trinity recorded their Definitely What! *album without Julie in early 1969, but she rejoined them later that year for another burst of frenetic creativity. The sixteen-track double album* Streetnoise *contained two further classics, Auger's 'Tropic of Capricorn' and Julie's take on Miles Davis' 'All Blues' – which Gomelsky was prevented from wiping only after Auger threatened to break his bones if he tried it, as the musician recalled to* Goldmine's *Dave Thompson, on its re-release in 2008.*

A US tour with Led Zeppelin followed, but that too was sabotaged by the ambitions of Driscoll's manager and ended with her quitting the band. Auger made one more Trinity album, Befour, *then moved on to his current ensemble, Oblivion Express. Julie disappeared from view, resurfacing as Julie Tippetts, wife of modern composer Keith Tippett, whom she married in 1970. Her work with him has seen her incredible voice travel further and further to the outer limits of experimental musical practice. Though she did briefly reunite with Auger to make the* Encore *album of 1978, lack of record company support saw yet another quality recording disappear largely without trace.*

When the Banshees came to record their version of 'This Wheel's on Fire' for their 1987 Through the Looking Glass *LP, Steven Severin recalled: 'It wasn't until I dug it out of my record collection that I realised it was written by Bob Dylan.'*

'And I nearly said: "Let's not do it,"' admitted Sioux. 'I hate him!'

CHAPTER 3

Magic, Murder and the Weather

Casting the runes for the '80s: Killing Joke and Bauhaus

> 'There is no such thing as good and evil – only order and chaos'
> – Sir Humphrey Appleby, *Yes, Minister*:
> 'The Whisky Priest', first aired 16 December 1982

In the First Foundation Myth of Rock 'n' Roll, one dark midnight in the '20s, Mississippi bluesman Robert Johnson met the Devil at the crossroads and made a pact: in return for the ability to play guitar better than anyone else, he would trade his soul. Johnson's subsequent recordings demonstrated awesome powers – his twenty-nine songs about life in the segregated south sent shivers down the spine of popular music, influencing its course and informing its best and most successful practitioners throughout the rest of the century.

In the First Foundation Myth of Goth, one dark midnight in May 1979, Jaz Coleman and 'Big' Paul Ferguson performed a magical ritual at their squat in London's Holland Park. The disgruntled former keyboard player and drummer of obscure post-punk outfit Matt Stagger wanted to start a new band, one that could harness the occult forces Coleman was studying. One into which he could channel all the upheaval he'd seen in his crystal ball to conjur a new sound. Music that would be every bit as extreme and intoxicating as the decade to come.

The pair already had a name for their nascent creation, suggested by a psychiatrist friend who worked at the Tavistock Institute[1] and predicted Thatcher's enthusiasm for free market economics would nurture a new corporate elite, one that would get the last laugh at everyone else's expense. And they didn't want to waste any time auditioning losers.

The next day, they put this ad in *Melody Maker*:

WANT TO BE PART OF THE KILLING JOKE?
We mean it man.
Total exploitation, total publicity, total anonymity.
Bass and lead wanted.

Of all the musicians in the land, only two men were able to decipher this message. Guitarist Kevin 'Geordie' Walker (b. 1958) was the first to arrive. A native of County Durham, transplanted to Milton Keynes by his father's work and desperate to escape from it, he described the scene that greeted him to *Sounds*' Phil Sutcliffe: 'There was this shithole of a flat with this oily rag of a human [Jaz] rummaging in a dustbin outside. I had an argument with him immediately and he seemed to like my sarcasm.'[2]

Geordie in turn recruited eighteen-year-old Martin 'Youth' Glover, sometime bassist with Jimmy (brother of John) Lydon's band the 4 Be 2s[3] after a similar personality reading. This noted Sid Vicious lookalike, then calling himself Pig Youth – as opposed to the Jamaican DJ and toaster, Big Youth – had a fondness for dub reggae and its accompanying mood enhancers that would transmute into his style of playing, though, at his first rehearsal, this was at such an embryonic stage that Coleman and Ferguson were ready to ditch him. Geordie, however, picked up signals from Youth's approach to an instrument he was only just learning to play. Sensing 'he was the man', the guitarist set about constructing a Camberwell Carrot of a riff with him. It became the band's first composition, 'Are You Receiving?'

Dark Entries

Thus, Killing Joke came into existence at 11 Portland Road, W11, a remarkable London leyline. Noted on Charles Booth's Poverty Map of 1886 as the most deprived slum in the Notting Dale area, this street would, by 2016, become the most expensive and sought-after address in a capital living high on the hog of deregulated financial services. But – just like Margaret Thatcher getting selected as party leader – back in the '70s, you wouldn't have bet on it. At the start of her government, the west London district of Notting Hill – notorious for race riots, Rachmanism and radical politics – still had a heady scent of reefer, patchouli oil and Molotov cocktail thrumming in the air.

There were two major encampments in Punk London: the King's Road enclave of the Pistols and McLaren-Westwood and the Notting Hill streets around Ladbroke Grove and Portobello Road claimed by the Clash. Managed by McLaren's former business partner and close rival Bernie Rhodes, this sharp-dressed ensemble of local lads – Mick Jones (guitar), Paul Simenon (bass), drummers Terry Chimes and then Topper Headon, along with Ankara-born singer-guitarist Joe Strummer (née John Mellor, 1952–2002) – were a walking advert for the area's multiculturalism. Their strain of politicised punk fused perfectly with the music the *Windrush* generation had brought when they fetched up in the area's crumbling Victorian piles owned by landlord Peter Rachman[4] in the '40s.

From the turbulent '50s, when Colin MacInnes surveyed the landscape of Ladbroke Grove in his youth culture classic *Absolute Beginners* (1959), a hip outsider scene was fermenting in the streets of W11. Rent parties, held by West Indian migrants in 'mushroom clubs', 'blues' or 'shebeens', rapidly spread throughout the area, sharing the newcomers' love of calypso, ska and roots reggae with the indigenous Modernist youth. In spite of the race riots of 1958, this scene would evolve into the Notting Hill Carnival and infuse music made in the capital ever after.

A decade later, the counter-culture magazines *International Times* (IT) and *Oz* both had offices there. Turner's house in the 1971 Nicolas Roeg/Donald Cammell classic *Performance* is located in Powis Square – the heart of Rachmanland – and the Syd Barrett-era Pink Floyd played gigs at the All Saints Church on its corner. Rough Trade records began life on Kensington Park Road in 1976 and continues to trade just across the Portobello Road at its Talbot Street shop; Virgin records had offices in Vernon's Yard and Mute just over the Grand Union Canal on the Harrow Road; while Chris Blackwell's Basing Street Studios hosted everyone from Roxy Music to Bob Marley and the Wailers while it was Island's in-house recording facility.[5]

Despite punk's outward antipathy towards hippies, plenty of the key faces of the late '60s were still around a decade later – Floyd's manager Peter Jenner now looking after Ian Dury and the Blockheads; Release[6] founder Caroline Coon covering the punk frontline for *Melody Maker*; and *IT* editor Barry Miles and contributing White Panther Mick Farren doing the same for *NME*.

Other forms of alternative lifestyle also flourished in Notting Hill's bohemian terraces – the sort that Dennis Wheatley warned about. Doomed producer Joe Meek conducted fateful séances from his flat in Arundel Gardens in 1958. Occult-obsessed bluesman Graham Bond – who thought he was the son of occultist Aleister Crowley and ended his life under the wheels of a Piccadilly line tube in 1974 – opened the Good Vibrations Club on Westbourne Park Road in 1966. More flamboyantly still, self-styled 'King of the Witches' Alex Sanders and his wife Maxine gathered their coven in a basement flat in Clanricarde Gardens in 1969. Which is why it shouldn't come as much of a surprise that Killing Joke shared their accommodation with a heavily tattooed, fire-breathing magus known as Dave the Wizard, who became a talisman for the band.

It was Dave who inaugurated the first Killing Joke gig by chalking a heptagram – a seven-pointed star representing the seven alchemical substances – on the stage. The band continued this practice, while also retaining his services to dance around them as they played, shooting flames into their audience. The stories the Wizard told them about his rituals – including a claim to have once eaten an aborted human foetus – would make their way into their eponymous debut album, on the song 'SO 36': 'Crime of flesh, control is joyless . . . The smoke on the city with miracles spent'. In his lyrics, Jaz Coleman cast London as a magical place, where any diligent psychonaut might rise above the slums and the squats with the right application of hidden knowledge and illicit substances. And so it would prove.

Killing Joke rehearsed in the same studios as the Clash and Motörhead, whose older frontmen Joe Strummer and Ian 'Lemmy' Kilmister were both former inhabitants of the Wild West squat kingdom of Frestonia that bordered Notting Hill.[7] Each band had an influence on the young pranksters, as Youth later recalled to *Revolver*'s Kory Grow: 'The Clash were starting to use dub influences at the same time we were, but in a different way – and we always wanted to sound louder than Motörhead.'[8]

Indeed, Killing Joke always had a heavy element to their sound, which some early reviewers found difficult both to categorise and to take – that lingering aroma of reefer and patchouli had some of punk's leading intellectuals instinctively wrinkling their noses. But this wasn't the denim-and-leather variety of the nascent New Wave of British Heavy Metal (NWOBHM) currently bursting out of the nation's pubs and bike sheds. The headbanging guitar histrionics and cartoon horror imagery of Iron Maiden, Judas Priest and Saxon were the antithesis of the Geordie's precision heaviosity and Big Paul's brutal backbeat, which harked back further in time to Hawkwind, whose 'Silver Machine' Lemmy briefly steered; the portentous rumble of Black Sabbath's Tony Iommi – who once used *The Devil Rides Out* 'as a handbook on how to be a Satanist'[9] – and Led Zeppelin's grand riffmeister Jimmy Page, who took his occult leanings considerably further. Yet this was also music you could dance to, and – whether a 'Wardance' or a 'Firedance' – Youth's bass and Coleman's keyboards always brought the funk, an echo of many nights spent in the land of mushroom clubs.

Killing Joke had no shortage of subject matter to match the extremity of their sound. The coming of Thatcher provided Jaz with the doom-drenched lyrical inspiration to go with that 'Are You Receiving?' riff: 'Our destination is nowhere . . . This is life in the fall'.

The Cold War and the bleak prospect of a Nuclear Winter informed 'Turn to Red' and 'Nervous System', the remaining two tracks of their debut EP, *Turn to Red*, released on their own Malicious Damage label in October 1979 and an instant John Peel favourite – boosted by the approval of John Lydon, whose post-Pistols' outfit Public Image Ltd were headed in similar musical directions. As were another bunch of sorcerer's apprentices from Northampton, who, two months ahead of Killing Joke's debut had already released the First Foundation Single of Goth on 6 August 1979 – a hair-raising, nine-minute-and-thirty-six-seconds-long, dub-inflected, dread-infected eulogy to a fallen vampire king.

Hex Education

David and Kevin Haskins were the sons of shopkeepers from the county town in the middle of England where, on 14 June 1645, Oliver Cromwell's New Model Army laid waste to the forces of Charles I at the Battle of Naseby. Northampton later became synonymous with the shoe industry, and, of particular importance to the style of the '80s, Doctor Martens boots. Speaking in 1982, older brother David (b. 1957) would describe his hometown as 'a void' and Kevin (b. 1960) 'a negative influence'. But, as all punk's children knew, better to make something out of nothing than decline the challenge of change.

Musically inclined from an early age, the brotherly rhythm section had played bass and drums respectively in several covers bands as they journeyed their way through public school and then, when their parents could no longer afford to stump up the fees, their local grammar. Both ended their formal education at Nene College of Art, where David met his spiky-haired contemporary,

Daniel Ash, a former pupil at the 'madhouse' comprehensive adjacent to, but a social world away from, the grammar school the Haskins boys attended.

Getting into the art college had been a salvation for Ash, who told *The Face*'s Mike Stand he found his secondary schooldays both frightening and frustratingly limiting. With guitar skills to offer, he joined the brothers in punk upstarts the Craze, who played a few local gigs in 1978 before Ash seized his moment of opportunity to throw out a lifeline to a former schoolmate. When the strikingly handsome Peter Murphy became their singer, the band took an entirely more original direction. It came with a carefully thought-out and choreographed look, one that would set the template for the decade ahead. Suitably for an ensemble formed through art college connections, they took their name from a movement begun in Weimar Berlin in 1919 that had turned all previous conceptions of architecture and morality on their head: Bauhaus.[10]

Until given the outlet of sympathetic company in his own band, Murphy was, in his own words, 'very inhibited, lacking in confidence', confining his talents to singing to an audience of letterheads and beer mats in the print shop where he was apprenticed.[11] The youngest of eight in an Anglo-Irish Catholic family from neighbouring Wellingborough, Peter had been offered a place at Nene at the same time as Daniel Ash, but, doubtful of his own abilities, turned it down in favour of learning a trade. While Murphy at first felt protected within his family's faith, by the time he was at school it was a different matter, as he explained to *The Face*'s Mike Stand: 'They would ask who hadn't gone to church on Sunday and if you put your hand up they were down on you with hellfire . . . So if I was told off I'd sit and cry and shout "I hate you, Jesus Christ!"'

This internal schism would be channelled into Murphy's stage persona. As with the Cure's Robert Smith, it was when Peter started using his lyrics to probe the strength of his religious convictions that he came up with the dark stuff – as if double-daring God to prove his existence by incinerating him for blasphemy. Despite never having written any music before, he penned the words to what would become the title track of Bauhaus's first album, 'In the Flat Field', at the band's very first rehearsal. In his 2014 memoir, *Who Killed Mister Moonlight?: Bauhaus, Black Magick, and Benediction*, David Haskins describes the song as a protest against 'the quotidian mundaneness of life in Northampton, and the desire to escape that "flat" existence'.

The same session also summoned up the magic that would introduce this new incarnation of Bauhaus to the nascent Thatcher generation with immediate impact. 'Bela Lugosi's Dead' was inspired by a late-night BBC Two screening of the Hungarian actor's 1931 outing as the Count, the first sound movie adaptation of Bram Stoker's 1897 novel. Recorded live in Beck Studios, Wellingborough, on 26 January 1979, the song's skeletal percussion, scratchy guitar and dub-heavy beats created a funeral shebeen inside Castle Dracula. 'Red velvet lines the black box/Bela Lugosi's dead' intoned Murphy, with all due portentousness.

Released in an original limited-edition white vinyl 12-inch by Small Wonder and relayed across the land through an unseen network of Peel towers, creatures of the night heeded its call to begin throwing shapes in candle-lit bedrooms in earnest. Those curious enough to flutter out and seek the originators of this bone-rattling beat would be treated to an act that was almost certain to be confrontational. Like their German antecedents,[12] Bauhaus put on a spectacular show, Murphy casting forked-tailed shadows against flashing strobe lights, while Ash's towering, spiked quiff and fishnet-stockinged torso marked him out as a new kind of guitar hero – the one the boys in the crowd most wanted to emulate.

'On stage Bauhaus are completely different people,' a gob-smacked Tom Vague, who had just interviewed a seemingly affable fourpiece at the Bournemouth Village Bowl just before Halloween 1980, reported. 'Pete Murphy is Iggy Pop reincarnate and the rest don't look too friendly. Nobody knows what to make of them. The audience don't know whether to stand around posing or dance . . .'

Even *Sounds*' Phil Sutcliffe, who had survived his trip to KJHQ in Portland Road intact, was taken aback: 'The band, who I'd never seen before, have an aggressively weird stage act using lots of make-up, freak hairstyles and darkness cut by strobes, back-lighting and a floodlight occasionally fired at the audience.' On this occasion, at the University of Surrey in Guildford, the gig was infiltrated by NF skins, who gleefully filled up their water pistols at the urinals and then fired the contents all over the band. Murphy responded by laying one of them out cold with his mic stand – his days as a shrinking violet now officially over.

'I get carried away,' he would explain to Mike Stand. 'I see a heavy kid at the front and I go out of my way to make him hate me. Maybe that comes from the blockheads at school. My chance to get back [at them].'

The two halves of the Bauhaus boys' schooldays perfectly illustrate one of the platforms that got Margaret Thatcher elected: the vexed subject of secondary education. Since 1944, children in England and Wales had been divided up at the age of eleven by an intelligence test. Those that passed gained access to the grammar schools and the bright futures gleaned from academic achievement. Those who failed the dreaded 11-plus were condemned to secondary moderns or technical (tech) schools, where they were taught more practical skills, the boys then packed off down the mines, docks and factories, the girls to be secretaries, hairdressers or set up homes.

Worried that entire generations were being unfairly judged by this system, in 1965, Labour undertook to create a new kind of secondary education: comprehensive (comp) schools, where children of all abilities could learn a wide range of subjects together from the ages of eleven to sixteen. But because the task was left to local authorities to implement, the progress of change was slow. Parents who had benefitted from grammar schools wanted to keep them for their children, while critics of comprehensives argued that plummeting standards and loss of discipline would be the results of an idealistic system unable to cope with pupil numbers and needs – which seems to have been Ash and Murphy's experience.

As secretary of state for education and science, Thatcher straddled the fence, appearing to back parents who were resistant to comprehensives[13] while overseeing the opening of thousands of them. By 1979, she had come up with a free market solution for this dilemma, not dissimilar to the idea of Right-to-Buy for council tenants that would be published in the December of that year. It was one that appeared to put the consumer in the driving seat: 'Parents would vote with their children's feet,' as she put it in her memoirs.[14]

Over the course of the '80s, a formula was developed that transferred budgets from local authority control directly to schools, awarding funding in proportion to pupil numbers. Parents effectively became consumers in the education market; while educators were forced into the position of shopkeepers, trying to keep their businesses afloat.

Burning from the Inside

Just as Peter Murphy found he could take revenge against his schoolyard tormentors 'by becoming this superhuman, mad, powerful personality' on stage, so too did Jaz Coleman. Once he stepped out from behind his Matt Stagger keyboards to take the role of Killing Joke's lead singer, Coleman became a formidable frontman. Following the release of *Turn to Red*, Killing Joke spent the winter of 1979–80 touring with Joy Division, on what Jaz would later recall to *Mojo*'s Andrew Perry as 'the Northern Gloom and Southern Stomp' tour,[15] each band giving the other marks for who had played the most eviscerating set. A single, 'Nervous System' – a short-lived liaison between Malicious Damage and Island that didn't end well – followed in December 1979, by which time the band had attracted a sizeable following.

With the influx of trouble-seeking NF skins turning gigs increasingly violent, the need to alchemise all that energy into something empowering was a mission that Coleman would feel perhaps more keenly than the rest of his band. For as, in words even less delicate than Geordie's 'oily rag' comment, Paul Ferguson would explain to Phil Sutcliffe in the unreconstructed language of the '70s: 'The thing is, he's a wog.'[16]

Though he came from more genteel surroundings than Barry Adamson, the young Jeremy Coleman would nonetheless grow up feeling a similar kind of social isolation as a mixed-race child of his time. 'Being in a fight was very much part of my childhood,' he would tell Belinda Nash of *Ragamuffin* in 2016. 'I used to go to school with a knot in my stomach.'

He was born in Cheltenham, Gloucestershire, on 26 February 1960 to two schoolteachers: white English father Ronald and Anglo-Indian mother Gloria (née Pandy), a high-caste Brahmin[17] of Burmese descent. Like Jimmy Page, whom he would come to know via their mutual interest in the Thelemic teachings of Aleister Crowley, young Jaz's first musical forays were as a singer in the cathedral choir, a talent for which he won awards. At the same time, he was studying piano and violin under Eric Coleridge, head of music at Cheltenham College, practising, by his own account, for four hours each day. While being groomed as a classical star at home, school was a place of intimidation and mockery – but as he later said to Nash: 'Being bullied at school is good, you have to deal with it.'

Jaz's way of taking matters into his own hands was to drop out and leave home. Though not, perhaps, without some assistance – he had family in Ladbroke Grove, his uncle, Bob Pandy, a lifelong Labour councillor for the Royal Borough of Kensington and Chelsea.[18] As with Barry Adamson, punk provided the opportunity to channel both Jaz's talents and hurts – not to mention those potent inner feelings about not belonging in any place or to any race. As Coleman would later admit: 'I did have a lot of resentment for a long time about this.'

His band's manners, as curious and critical journalists would soon find out, could also be heavy. Following the acrimonious end to their dealings with Island, who wished to impose the usual record company control over the band, Killing Joke signed a new deal with EG Records – the glam/prog management home of Roxy Music, King Crimson, T. Rex and Emerson, Lake & Palmer – that came with distribution from top Goth-enablers Polydor.

The first fruit of this new endeavour was the instant classic 'Wardance' single of February 1980, its sleeve brilliantly illustrated by the band's graphic design partner, Mike Coles, as a collage of Fred Astaire dancing across the battlefields of the Somme. Initial pressings came complete with mock military 'call-up' papers and, like all KJ's releases to date, colour-coded in the International Anarchist hues of red, white and black.

Happy with the freedom their new contract afforded them, the band began work on their first album, telling *NME*'s Paul Rambali they intended to produce it themselves, learning all they could in the studio during the process. To the journalist's surprise, Youth cited Disco doyens Chic as an influence: 'All that sugar shit on top, you can forget that – but the rhythm's there.'[19]

In an early example of Jaz's Nostradamus-like powers, Killing Joke released their eponymous debut on 5 October 1980 – twenty-two days before convicted IRA paramilitaries began hunger strikes inside Belfast's Maze Prison in protest at the removal of their Special Category Status[20] – adorned with Don McCullin's photograph of rioters in the Derry of July 1971. This stark, black-and-white image of the state bearing down on dissenters with batons and tear gas – a prelude of worse to come on Bloody Sunday on 30 January 1972 – now served as an ominous overture to the decade ahead; and a signal that Killing Joke's antennae were finely attuned to current events.

Within six months of its release, there would be riots in Brixton, clashes between the police and the black community that would fan out countrywide over the summer of 1981 into suburbs such as Handsworth in Birmingham, Toxteth in Liverpool and Moss Side in Manchester, where the descendants of the *Windrush* generation were in no mind to tolerate their lot any more. Meanwhile, over in Belfast and on the day before the Brixton riots, Bobby Sands, the most high-profile of the Irish hunger strike protesters, was elected as MP for Fermanagh and South Tyrone – only to die of starvation on 5 May. That his attempted showdown with Margaret Thatcher over the treatment of Irish Republican political prisoners should go ignored had already been signalled by her infamous remarks at the Tory Party Conference in Brighton on 10 October 1980, when in rhetorical reply to her critics, the PM made it clear: 'The lady's not for turning.' Words the IRA would keep close.

Killing Joke could smell the scent of Molotov cocktail on the breeze because they were immersed in a culture most of their white peers outside W11 would never have experienced. When *Jamming!* journalists Tony Fletcher and Anthony Blampied interviewed Jaz and Youth on the day of the Brixton riots, Coleman would presciently note: 'What's happened over there and what they're putting through the TV are two different things. They haven't given the facts *why* it fucking all happens – it's all "*Black Youths*", you know what I mean? . . . It's just increasing the fucking racial tension.'

In truth, *Killing Joke* didn't sound an awful lot like 'Le Freak' – but it did achieve a potent symbiosis between the sounds of London's marginalised black communities and the sort of minor key riffing first forged in the mechanised Midlands on Tony Iommi's lathe-lacerated fingers. The blueprint, then, for what would in the future be known as 'industrial' music was made on such influential tracks as 'The Wait', 'Requiem' and – perennial live favourite for any edge-of-Apocalypse situation – 'Complications'.

Reviewing the album for *NME*, Paul Morley had the temerity to compare it to the light, Adult-Oriented Rock (AOR) of Foreigner[21] – and for this deliberate provocation was duly summoned to Portland Road to explain himself. Like Sutcliffe and Rambali before him, Morley expressed discomfort with what he thought Killing Joke were projecting: 'Their commitment, their music, even their artwork has this undercurrent of violence, which confuses and alarms.'[22]

Jaz defended the band's position and use of symbolism thus: 'The feeling of a guy in the First World War who's just about to run out from the trenches, right, and he knows his life is going to be gone in ten minutes and he thinks of that fucker back in Westminster who put him in that position. *That's* the feeling that we're trying to project.'

Even if the mainstream music press didn't get it, the fans did. *Killing Joke* rose to number thirty-nine in the UK charts.

The Fifth Element

For both Killing Joke and Bauhaus, playing live was a way of working up a very intentional ritual, a way of altering their audiences' consciousness as powerfully as hashish inhalation.[23] 'There's a fifth member of Bauhaus, which is a sort of spirit entity,' David Haskins told Mike Stand. 'When he isn't there, he's sorely missed. When he is, the performance is invested with real magic.' Jaz Coleman would also refer to Killing Joke having a fifth member, telling *Sounds*' Neil Perry: 'Right from the beginning there's been a guiding force thas we have complete faith in. Something keeps giving us all the facilities to express ourselves with.'[24]

Haskins Sr – or David Jay/J, as he cast himself in his Bauhaus role – was his band's serious student of the occult. He was the author of the Romantic lyrical incantation 'Bela Lugosi's Dead' and, like Coleman, would use the music he began making in 1979 as a pathway to further esoteric enlightenment. The Bauhaus bassist also had a local wizard to apprentice to, one who was just beginning his own parallel career as a graphic novelist.

Alan Moore (b. 1953) began making music with Haskins as occasional offshoot project the Sinister Ducks in 1979, an adjunct to their adventures in ritual magic.[25] He would go on to enliven the DC Comics franchise with *Batman: The Killing Joke* (1988) and write such powerful secret histories as the Jack the Ripperology *From Hell* (1988–98). But back then, he had just commenced producing the *Maxwell the Magic Cat* strip for the *Northants Post* as Jill de Ray – after Gilles de Rais, the sorcerer companion-in-arms of Joan of Arc who was condemned to death for the murders of hundreds of children in 1440s France. The source material for the legend of Bluebeard was a pretty provocative pun.

For shocking unsolved serial murder was very much part of the psychic weather when *In the Flat Field* was released, on 3 November

1980. Two weeks later, on 17 November, the fiend dubbed the Yorkshire Ripper by the tabloid press would claim his thirteenth and final murder victim, twenty-year-old Leeds University student Jacqueline Hill. However, it would be a further two months before the perpetrator of this terrifying six-year reign of violent sexual assault and murder against women in the Leeds-Bradford area was finally apprehended. The climate of fear engendered by this real-life bogeyman and the seemingly hopeless attempts of the West Yorkshire Police to catch him would find potent expression in the work of the artists discussed in this book, as we shall go on to examine, and permeated the atmosphere of records made in these times.

For many of those who bought it, *In the Flat Field* was the record that heralded the Dawn of Goth – and not just because of the way its Pan-like nude cover star is seen trumpeting on his pipe. It was recorded for Ivo Watts-Russell's fledgling 4AD label, a new offshoot of hip independent Beggar's Banquet, which had picked up 'Bela Lugosi's Dead' from Small Wonder and would subsequently become one of the defining labels for artists of the Genre That Dare Not Speak Its Name. The album itself did speak in a highly original way to the time and place it was conceived in and the personalities of Bauhaus's two distinct factions.

The focal point of the band's live act, the glamour duo of Murphy and Ash, exorcised their Catholic upbringings on 'Double Dare', 'A God in an Alcove', 'St Vitus Dance' and, most explicitly, 'Stigmata Martyr': 'Look into your crimson orifice/In holy remembrance'. Meanwhile, further back in the shadows, the urbane Haskins brothers painted a cinematic palette where horror and noir merged, evocative sound settings for tales of teenage transgression.

As the title track attests, *In the Flat Field* is an album that captures all the chiaroscuro shades of adolescent longing and non-belonging. Its Northampton setting, halfway between the reality of this 'solemn place of fill wetting dreams/Of black matted lace of pregnant cows' and a longed-for, sophisticated company of 'Piccadilly whores', frames the lament of the rural outsider for some big-city kicks.

Bauhaus also put their green fingernails on a pivotal Goth quality, one that their own appearances embodied: androgyny. In 'Small Talk Stinks' – another perfectly aimed dig at the provincial mindset – the Murphy who previously dreamt of meeting Soho Meat Rack sinners is treated instead to a small-town vision of gender-fluid youth: 'See the young man in his new gown/Talking up to his bouffant drag'.

With lyrics that implied their authors already had libraries fully furnished with the works of Wilde, Aubrey Beardsley, Joris-Karl Huysmans, Charles Baudelaire, Algernon Swinburne and Gustave Moreau, Bauhaus expressed their desires and longings in language that was either – depending on your taste – supremely intelligent and decadent or blindingly pretentious. If Howard Devoto would have been proud – and Bauhaus's Cold War excursion 'Spy in the Cab' suggests they had been paying attention to him – so might the Banshees also have nodded approval at the band's glam inclinations. Having topped the indie charts with their debut album, Bauhaus swiftly followed it up with a December 1980 single cover of T. Rex's 'Telegram Sam' that was every bit as good as Siouxsie's stomp through 'Twentieth-Century Boy' that had graced the B-side of 'The Staircase (Mystery)' in 1979.

However, few critics were prepared for Bauhaus either. Perhaps all the negative implications of the word 'Goth' can be traced back to Andy Gill's review in *NME*.[26] Under the prog-punning headline 'Gothick as a Brick',[27] he condemned the album as 'nine meaningless moans and flails bereft of even the most cursory contour of interest' and the band as 'a hip Black Sabbath' – as if this was a bad thing. Or perhaps the stigma(ta) stuck when the usually reliable Dave McCullough also turned his back on Bauhaus, asserting that *In the Flat Field* contained: 'No songs. Just tracks (ugh)' and lyrics that were: 'Too priggish and conceited', leading to an overall feel of 'Sluggish indulgence instead of hoped for Goth-ness'.

The clear inference from both reviews is that Bauhaus, like Killing Joke, had been indulging in too many of the unclean pursuits of the pre-punk era. Yet, far from being the turgid grind such reviews suggest, these bands' experiments in alchemising the core elements of rhythm and bruise would energise such diverse adherents as Seattle's grunge propagator Steve Albini, Bristol's trip-hoppers Massive Attack and Brazilian thrash metallers Sepultura. When, at the start of the '90s, former NWOBHM pioneers like Def Leppard began to choke on their own hairspray, an upstart bunch of Seattle scruffs called Nirvana would provide the antidote with a riff on Killing Joke's era-defining 1984 single 'Eighties'.[28]

But be warned: invite an unseen Fifth Member over the threshold at your peril. Bauhaus's magical formula has proved unstable, exploding in spectacular fashion down the years since their inception and pitting their strong-willed lead singer against the rest of the band. Though their bat-signal burned high and bright in the night sky of the early '80s, Bauhaus would – with some assistance from David Bowie – soon impale themselves upon the fickle stake of fashion. Yet – and despite no shortage of dramas to come – latter-day pie peddlers Killing Joke have always managed to rumble on. This, I would like to put down to the psychogeography of their inception.

For there is a crossroads on Portland Road W11, where it bisects Clarendon Cross. To the north crouch the council tenements of villainous Notting Dale past. To the south stand the tall, white-painted Victorian mansions of the upwardly mobile future. At this very interzone in October 1979 – just as *Turn to Red* was released and the Veil was at its thinnest – a man who would embody the philosophical thrust of the decade to come first stepped through a portal named the Winchester Club and into a nation's front rooms.

Like the punchline to the Killing Joke, Arthur Daley could only have appeared at this specific crossroads at this specific time. The star of ITV's *Minder* merged the last of the Second World War spivs with the first of the '80s wheeler-dealers through the toothy, trilby-hatted channel of actor George Cole, a man who had specialised in playing wide boys in the Ealing comedies of his youth. Second-hand car dealer, wholesaler in back-of-a-lorry goods, importer-exporter of novelty items and manager of titular muscle-for-hire

Terry McCann (Dennis Waterman), Arthur was a free market economist supreme. Initially pitched as a starring vehicle for Waterman – fresh from his pivotal role in *The Sweeney* – and made by the same production company, Euston Films, *Minder*'s first seven series ran parallel to the reign of 'Her Indoors at Number 10'.[29] Arthur and Terry's adventures in what would now be called 'the gig economy' – nightclubs, restaurants, fashion, mini-cabbing, the nascent home video industry – and both local and international politics also reflected the struggles of London's working-class/migrant communities, with ex-con boxer Terry suffering the brunt of the 'ag' when his employer's 'nice little earners' inevitably 'went pear-shaped'.

Throughout the decade, and while driving a succession of flash motors, including his trademark Jaguar XJ6, a silver Mercedes 280E or even a Portland beige Daimler, Arthur's VAT (vodka-and-tonic) would remain permanently 'on the slate' at his dubious drinking den. The Winchester Club was situated next-door to the real-life Julie's, an upmarket bistro favoured by exactly the sort of Notting Hill creatives who had the powers to summon this avatar of the new age into existence over a particularly good lunch. In doing so, they managed to capture one of the capital's greatest societal changes in full flux, the transition of a land of used car lots and dodgy spielers into a bankster's paradise.

If Dave was the Wizard foretold of in legend, then Arthur was the King.[30]

But I have stared into the crystal ball too long and speak of things that have yet to pass. For now, let us leave our two most truly magic(k)al bands back in the December of 1980, when the last idealistic dreams of the Love Generation were terminated outside the Dakota building in New York City as Mark David Chapman took aim at John Lennon; and strange lights were seen flickering through a forest in deepest Suffolk, apparently emanating from an Unidentified Flying Object . . .

Gothfather: Aleister Crowley

When Dennis Wheatley wanted to understand the philosophy of a modern magician to inform his 1934 novel The Devil Rides Out*; when MI6 were recruiting for spies to infiltrate pro-German occult organisations during both World Wars;* when, at the height of their power and influence, the Beatles visually represented their heroes on the psychedelic sleeve of* Sgt Pepper's Lonely Hearts Club Band*; and when Aiwass, disembodied spirit messenger of the Ancient Egyptian God Horus, needed someone to take down his commandments – they all turned to one man.*

Aleister Crowley, aka the Great Beast, aka Lord Boleskine of Foyers, aka the 'wickedest man in the world', was born Edward Alexander Crowley in Royal Leamington Spa on 12 October 1875. His father Edward, despite making a fortune from the family brewing business, was a proselytising member of the teetotal puritanical sect, the Plymouth Brethren. Crowley Sr read the Bible aloud for an hour every morning to his unruly infant son – nicknamed the Great Beast by his exasperated mother Emily – and at the earliest opportunity packed him off to the strict Ebor prep school, run by the sadistic Reverend Henry d'Arcy Champney. Crowley's lifelong rebellion against Christianity began in earnest at the age of eleven when Edward Sr died, and by the time he went up to Trinity College Cambridge at twenty, he had rebranded himself as Aleister, the Gaelic form of his middle name after Percy Shelley's poem, 'Alastor, or the Spirit of Solitude'. Now in possession of his inheritance, Crowley spent his student years indulging his lifelong passions: playing chess, publishing deluxe volumes of his own poetry, mountaineering and maintaining a vigorous sex life. Many of his biographers believe that his homosexual awakening at Trinity also opened his third eye to matters mystical and his lifelong search for occult knowledge that would forge his notoriety.

Aleister left Cambridge without a degree in 1898, the same year he was initiated into the Hermetic Order of the Golden Dawn by its founder, Samuel Liddell MacGregor Mathers. Under the personal tutelage of adept Allan Bennett (sadly, no relation), he learned how to perform ritual magic with the help of drugs. For the necessary ambience, he bought Boleskine House on the banks of Loch Ness – later to be owned by Jimmy Page – where he attempted to evoke his guardian angel and lairded it up in a kilt. Crowley's presence in the Golden Dawn – whose HQ was in the same Hammersmith thoroughfare, Blythe Road, as Arthur Daley's car lot – came much to the horror of fellow initiate W. B. Yeats – who thought Crowley insane and, worse still, a bad poet – and eventually caused a schism in its ranks.

By then, Crowley had had enough of them anyway. He went to Mexico, to scale mountains with experienced climber Oscar Eckenstein, who taught him how to harness his powers of will, imagination, visualisation and concentration to serve his magical practice. Thus refreshed, Crowley travelled on to Asia to practise hatha yoga and unsuccessfully attempt to conquer K2.

In 1903 he married Rose Skerrett, sister of the painter Sir Gerald Kelly, with whom he would make contact with Aiwass in Cairo, taking down the words of The Book of the Law *over the course of three days. This document announced that humanity was entering a new Aeon with Crowley as its prophet, proclaiming: 'Do what thou wilt shall be the whole of the Law' – and laying the cornerstone of Aleister's own religion, Thelema.*** *Both Rose, and their daughter Lilith, would soon fall by the wayside of Crowley's ambition, the latter dying of typhoid in infancy on a ill-fated trip to India, the former being committed to an asylum for alcoholism by her husband in 1911.*

Undaunted, Crowley began recruiting for his own order, the Argenteum Astrum (Silver Star), attracting the visionary artist Austin Osman Spare, military strategist Captain John Frederick Charles Fuller and the young poet Victor Neuburg. Neuburg became Aleister's new muse, with whom he would practise sex magic and create a theatrical production, The Rites of Eleusis, *in which Victor took a starring role. This brought them to the attention of Theodor Reuss, Frater Superior of the Ordo Templi Orientis (OTO), an older German society, who appointed Crowley head of his British Branch at a 1912 ceremony in Berlin. Here, Lord Boleskine acquired yet another nom de plume, that of Baphomet – a name all too familiar to Wheatley readers. When the First World War intervened to break the spell between the two nations, Aleister relocated to New York, where he loudly espoused support for Germany – perhaps an elaborate cover for counter espionage – which did his reputation in Britain lasting harm.*

In 1920, he relocated to Cefalù, in Sicily, where he rented the farmhouse he called the Abbey of Thelema, and took in disciples, including his lover Leah Hirsig and their newborn daughter, Anne 'Poupée' Leah. With their leader now addicted to heroin and cocaine, the commune rapidly turned unsanitary – in October 1920 Poupée became Crowley's second daughter to die prematurely. When young Englishman Raoul Loveday contracted a liver infection from which he also died, his widow Betty told a lurid story of life at Thelema to the British periodical John Bull, *who labelled Crowley the 'wickedest man in the world'. The new fascist leader, Benito Mussolini, expelled him from Italy in 1923.*

*After sojourns in Tunisia, Paris and Berlin, Crowley returned to London, where, his fortune long spent, he was declared bankrupt in 1935. Surviving on income from his books, lectures on yoga and contributions from the American Lodge of the OTO supplied by rocket scientist Jack Parsons, he became intrigued by Adolf Hitler, believing he was ripe for Thelemaic conversion. But when the new Führer abolished the OTO in Germany, Crowley offered his services to British intelligence during the Second World War instead. Whether or not he really did mastermind the operation that lured Nazi leader Rudolf Hess to crash land his plane in Scotland in 1941, it was definitely through the soirées of spy-master Maxwell Knight that he met covert operatives Wheatley, Roald Dahl and Ian Fleming. By then, the robust health that had enabled him to climb mountains, father a trail of illegitimate children*** and converse with the gods was failing the Great Beast. He retired to a boarding house in Hastings in 1945 and died of chronic bronchitis on 1 December 1947. Only a dozen people attended the funeral of a man whose reputation was now that of a traitor and degenerate black magician.*

Which was a good enough plateau for his magical revival to begin its ascent . . .

* *Allegedly.*

** *Though the same injunction had been issued before, by the French Renaissance writer François Rabelais (d. 1553), whose fictional giant Gargantua founded the Abbey of Thélème a few centuries before Crowley.*

*** *Despite his convictions, there is no evidence to support former Barnardo's boy Graham Bond's claim that he was one of them.*

Gothmother: Vampira

The time was Halloween 1953, the place Hollywood. Invited to a showbiz party, aspiring actress Maila Nurmi determined to make an impression. It had been twelve long years since she fled the small fishing town in Oregon where her Finnish parents had settled to pursue her dream of stardom. Though her beauty had brought her to the attention of director Howard Hawks and the bed of actor/director/enfant terrible Orson Welles, she had nothing to show for it – she had blown her chance with the former by giving him a piece of her mind when he asked her to see a dentist; and been dumped by the latter when he got her pregnant, the resultant baby boy given up for adoption. All she could rely on were the two qualities she had in abundance – wit and visual flair. At the age of thirty-one, the time had come for Maila to turn Hollyweird.

Taking inspiration from Charles Addams' stylish New Yorker *cartoons, she donned a skintight black dress, turned back-to-front so the neckline plunged from her padded bust to her cinched-in waist. A black wig and 3-inch-long false nails completed the transformation: the blonde beneath was no longer recognisable. That night she cast her glamour on Hunt Stromberg Jr, the new program director at KABC-TV, and within months she was hosting her own late-night TV show, named after the voluptuous character she created:* Vampira.

Through a swirling mist of dry ice, Vampira introduced films of terror and outrage while reclining barefoot on a skull-encrusted chaise lounge: a vision of insouciant beauty roughly halfway between Morticia Addams and premier bondage pin-up, Bettie Page. Because the film industry deeply distrusted and feared its emergent rival, television, Stromberg didn't have anything of real quality to bring to his viewers – but this was of no matter for his rapier-witted hostess. With lines as dry as the Mortician's Martinis she was sipping – 'one part formaldehyde, one part rattlesnake venom, a dash of culture blood, garnished with an eyeball' – Vampira openly mocked the schlocky horrors she was screening.

She was an instant hit. The toast of LA's afterhours nightclubs, Vampira was chauffeured around town in a funereal black 1932 Packard, stood for Night Mayor of Hollywood – on 'dead issues', naturally – and became the consort of a young actor nurturing a deathwish, James Dean: 'We had the same neuroses,' she would later say. Marlon Brando proposed to her; she turned him down: 'He was a sex addict and a hypocrite.' Elvis, too, fell by the wayside: 'The way he moved those hips on stage, I was expecting a symphony, but I got Johnny One-Note.' To maintain her hourglass figure, she strapped a poultice of meat tenderiser around her waist in a corset made of inner tube. Perhaps her greatest uncredited role was in the development of Queen Maleficent herself – Maila filmed 'live action references' for the Disney creation in 1956.

Sadly, Vampira's reign over Hollywood didn't last much further than sunrise. Having a frontwoman who could get cinematic turkeys to lay televisual golden eggs was not enough for KABC, who wanted Maila to sign the rights to Vampira over to them after eight months on the air. She refused and the show was pulled. More personal tragedy followed, as her soulmate James Dean met his untimely demise in 1955. 'He was the first person she ever met that was from the same planet,' explained her niece Sandra Niemi, who managed to construct Vampira's biography from a cache of diaries found after Maila's death in 2008. 'She never got over his death.'

Though Nurmi reprised her creation for Ed Wood's visionary sci-fi–horror mash-up Plan 9 from Outer Space *(1957), it would take the passage of thirty-eight years and the magic of Tim Burton before this film could be truly appreciated by a global audience. By then, Maila had had another bust-up with a television station, having unsuccessfully tried to sue comedy actress Cassandra Peterson and associated parties for stealing her character in the KHJ-TV series* Elvira's Movie Macabre *in 1981. She made a couple of singles with the band Satan's Cheerleaders (featuring future Cramps bassist Candy Del Mar) and appeared in the 1986 movie* Population: 1 *with Tomata du Plenty of LA electropunks the Screamers. Eking out her existence from a tiny rented flat in a converted garage in Hollywood, she supported herself with paintings sold on eBay.*

Only when she died did Vampira finally get to move to her dream home – the Hollywood Forever Cemetery, a place she often used to visit for a picnic – where neighbours include Judy Garland, Rudolph Valentino and Yma Sumac. But the look she created for that fateful night in 1953 is one that has never been bettered – or ever really gone away. As she once remarked: 'My whole life has been a Halloween party!'

CHAPTER 4

Rocket from the Crypt

The envoys of a special relationship: the Cramps, the Gun Club, Lydia Lunch, the Birthday Party

> 'When America found itself having a hard time facing the future, they looked for people like John Wayne. But, since John Wayne was no longer available, they settled for Ronald Reagan. And it has placed us in a situation that we can only look at like a B-movie'
>
> – Gil Scott-Heron, 'B-Movie', 1981

Rendlesham Forest, Suffolk, is in an area of Britain that has long concealed the military secrets of two nations with a special relationship. RAF Woodbridge and RAF Bentwaters were first created on either side of the 4000-acre woodland in 1943 to service aircraft returning from bombing raids on Germany. When post-war relations between east and west frosted into the Cold War, the United States Air Force (USAF) took over the 'Twin Bases', stationing a number of fighter squadrons there from 1951 onwards. Following the US-led boycott of the 1980 Moscow Olympic Games, relations between Washington and Moscow were on a periodic sheet of thin ice when, in the early hours of Boxing Day, American airmen reported a Close Encounter of the First Kind.

A USAF security patrol close to the east gate of RAF Woodbridge first saw lights descending into the forest at around 3 a.m. As the patrolmen approached them, they observed a glowing metallic object, unlike any conventional aircraft, emanating multiple-coloured rays. It moved rapidly through the trees, sending 'the animals on a nearby farm into a frenzy'.[1] But when local police were summoned at 4 a.m., the only light they could see was the beam of nearby Orford Ness lighthouse.[2]

At daybreak, USAF servicemen returned to the clearing and found three small impressions on the ground in a triangular pattern, as well as burn marks on the branches of trees. Again, the local police were unimpressed, dismissing the damage as animal activity. Deputy base commander Lieutenant Colonel Charles Halt visited with more personnel on 28 December to test for radiation and witnessed further star-like lights in the sky. He filed a UFO report to the UK Ministry of Defence, which they declined to investigate on the grounds that it wasn't a national security issue. The disgruntled Halt would later accuse both the US and UK governments of colluding in a cover-up.

'The British Roswell' came one month and twenty-two days after former Hollywood actor and Republican governor of California Ronald Reagan defeated incumbent Democrat Jimmy Carter in the US elections. On 20 January 1981, the swashbuckling 69-year-old was inaugurated as the country's then oldest-ever president, ushering in a new era of American politics during which reality increasingly blurred into a science-fiction film script. Fortunately, some American ambassadors had already arrived at our shores, who were able to make sense of it.

'We are all made from aliens from outer space,' according to UFO expert and founding member of the Cramps, Lux Interior. 'One extra-terrestrial woman was the mother. We all came from her. I firmly believe this.'

'Life,' as his guitar-wielding partner Poison Ivy Rorschach further contextualised from behind her trademark impenetrable black sunglasses, 'is a B-movie.'

The Way I Walk

The Cramps first touched down in Britain in June 1979 and their evocation of the hellfire spirits of '50s rockabilly went down like liquid dynamite. Newly signed to Miles Copeland's Illegal Records, they came as a support act to the Police and could not have provided a more reprobate contrast to Copeland's brother Stewart's Sting-fronted trio of punky-poppy-reggae enforcement officers. Though the '50s revival of the earlier '70s was still loitering around the British charts in day-glo socks and drape suits, unlike revivalists Showaddywaddy, Darts and Racey, the Cramps were unlikely to be appearing at Butlin's any time soon.

Their live act was a jaw-dropping voodoo, described by every reviewer as 'frightening', thanks equally to the dense, primal grind of their twin-guitar attack – 'Link Wray playing at a Black Mass' as *Sounds*' Sandy Robertson put it – and to the way they looked. Lux Interior was a towering six-foot-two in another six inches of black stilettos and about the same height again in raven-black pompadour. His vocal style a unique gibber and howl, like a snake-handling Southern Baptist preacher lost in the trance of the moment, he could find himself chewing glass without getting cut and rarely finished a set without removing his gold lamé or black rubber strides and rolling about in bikini-style panties. He was flanked by his flame-haired paramour, Ivy, a six-string goddess in spectacular combinations of sequins, leopardskin, chiffon and rubber; and the menacing Bryan Gregory. Ghoulishly thin, with a shock of bleached white hair like a cowl around his skull-like visage and sporting a necklace made from chicken bones, Gregory, thought Nick Kent, was 'the handsomest man in rock 'n' roll' – a view not shared by *Melody Maker*'s editor Allan Jones, who opined that the guitarist 'looked like he had driven nails through his face' to achieve his complexion. Meanwhile, surly Elvine drummer Nick Knox – a dead ringer for Martin Sheen in Terrence Malick's 1973 serial killer road movie, *Badlands* – kept their backs and the rhythm like a man possessed.

The Cramps' UK debut EP, *Gravest Hits*, followed in July 1979, culled from their previous two US Vengeance-released singles that were recorded in Ardent Studios, Memphis, with former Box Tops and Big Star singer-guitarist Alex Chilton, who dubbed his protégés 'the greatest rock 'n' roll band in the world'. It stood as testament not just to their comprehensive collection of rockabilly, surf, doo-wop and hillbilly 45s but also their dedication to incredibly strange movies of the likes made by Ed Wood and 'Godfather of Gore' Herschell Gordon Lewis; along with, as Ivy explained to *Melody Maker*'s Penny Kiley, 'Everything I ever saw on TV, everything I ever ate, everything I heard on the radio,' during her itinerant Californian upbringing.

Their covers – a swaggering take on Jack Scott's 'The Way I Walk', a rattlin' bones throw of Roy Orbison's 'Domino' and a conjuration of Ricky Nelson's 'Lonesome Town' as a teenage werewolf's lament – reached a psychotic peak as they cranked the Trashmen's 'Surfin' Bird'. The apex of their live set, it was rivalled only by the spine-tingling 'Human Fly', a sci-fi experiment gone wrong of their own devising that nonetheless tipped its lyrical 'ninety-six tears and ninety-six eyes' to garage forebears ? and the Mysterians. The Cramps made these long-neglected songs sound so much their own it was – and would remain – hard to tell the difference between original composition and cover. When the Ramones found it impossible not to record their own version of 'Surfin' Bird' after seeing the Cramps play it live, they made sure to ask Ivy's permission first.

'This music found us,' as Ivy put it. 'We didn't seek it out, it found us and grabbed us. In that sense it's quite spiritual, it's like religion grabbing people.'

Within the first week of their arrival, the Cramps had knocked the Police off the *NME*'s front cover and had a fanclub, the Legion of the Cramped, set up in their honour by smitten youngsters Stephen Patrick Morrissey and Lindsay Hutton. 'The Cramps should be bigger than the Police, they should be bigger than Blondie,' an equally impressed Siouxsie told Tom Vague of *Vague* fanzine. 'They are really important. I'm impressed by the way they go completely over the top.'

Their mission to spread the rockabilly gospel received such an enthusiastic welcome that it gave birth to an entire genre (see next chapter). One that would also despise the handle the music press gave it, despite the fact that 'Psychobilly' was a word that had first dropped from the lips of original Man in Black Johnny Cash on his 1976 car construction hit, 'One Piece at a Time'.

I Was a Teenage Werewolf

Strangely, that mission hadn't been so easy in New York City, where the Cramps first set up base. Ivy and Lux arrived in punk's transatlantic rival capital in 1975, after reading about wild goings-on at its Bowery epicentre, CBGBs, in *Rock Scene* magazine. By then, the couple had been together three years.

Their paths first crossed in the summer of 1972, when, mesmerised by a vision at the roadside, 25-year-old Alice Cooper fan Erick Purkhiser stopped to pick up nineteen-year-old hitchhiker Kristy Wallace in Sacramento, California. In some of their reminisces, she was wearing cut-off jeans and a vintage '30s top, in others a see-through plastic rain mac and nothing else but high heels, artfully teased red hair and make-up 'like a cross between Julie Driscoll and Marc Bolan'.[3] On the dashboard between them lay a prospectus from Sacramento City College – and it was here that they met for the second time, having both enrolled in a course entitled Art & Shamanism. According to Ivy, this was based on English archaeologist and Dead Sea Scrolls scholar John M. Allegro's controversial 1970 tome *The Sacred Mushroom and the Cross*, in which the author posits first that the roots of Christianity lie in ancient fertility cults whose followers routinely ingested hallucinogens to receive divine messages, and second that Jesus Himself was a product of psychoactive mushroom ingestion – a practice the couple had already engaged in with encouraging results.

The erstwhile Kristy Marlana Wallace was born on 20 February 1953 in San Bernadino, California, the youngest of three children with a mysterious father who worked in the nuclear industry and moved his family around multiple times before finally settling in Sacramento.[4] The child who enjoyed blowing up her Barbie dolls with firecrackers and flying around the room to the Ran-Dells' 'Martian Hop' grew into a rebellious teen, twice thrown out of high school for smoking and dress infractions. She picked up the basics of surf guitar from her older brother and worked out the rest herself – listening to Link Wray and watching Bo Diddley perform with his rhythm guitar sidekick Norma-Jean Wofford, aka the Duchess, resplendent in skintight gold lamé catsuits. Kristy's experiments with hallucinogens began at the age of fourteen when she first got her hands on some Orange Sunshine, made in 1967 by infamous hippy chemist and Grateful Dead soundman, Owsley Stanley. She said she took it for one hundred days without ever having a bad trip.

The former Erick Lee Purkhiser was born on 21 October 1946 in the suburban town of Stow, Ohio, eight miles from the 'Rubber Capital of the World', Akron, where his father, a strict Catholic, was a foreman at the Goodyear tyre factory. Erick was the middle of three brothers and it was elder sibling Ron who introduced him to the joys of Hank Williams and Elvis as a child. A nearby live rock 'n' roll club called the Doghouse and an addiction to EC comics and cult WJW Channel 8 Horror TV host Ernie Earle Anderson, aka Ghoulardi,[5] shaped his destiny. Determined to swerve a life of industrial grind, he was thrown out of the Navy for failing a drugs test and followed an Alice Cooper tour across the States to Sacramento, where, while tripping on mescaline, he received his own personal portent: a plastic 'Dead Babies' torso landed straight on his lap.

Two months later, the couple met, began living together and rebaptised themselves. Erick took his new name from a car ad, Kristy fasted for six days before taking magic mushrooms and receiving the name Poison Ivy Rorschach in a vision. Pooling their considerable record collections, they began to conceptualise a band and took a series of dead-end jobs – from selling clothes in flea markets to working in a circuit board factory – to fund their relocation to New York. All the while, they learned how to sing and play the songs that set their souls on fire.

At first, the Gotham City omens looked good. Lux got a job at the Musical Maze record store at 83rd & Lexington, where he met Bryan Gregory (neé Beckerleg, 1951–2001), a recent arrival from Detroit, who shared Ivy's birthday – the date on which they met in 1976. Having found herself a rare solid-body Lewis guitar in a shop on 48th Street, Ivy bestowed on Bryan her Flying V. Despite his lack of musical training – Gregory had come to New York to study graphic design – he was a kindred spirit. 'We were almost the same size and could fit into each other's pants and shoes,' Ivy said. 'We understood each other because we weren't the boy/girl next door.'[6]

Bryan recruited his sister Pam, aka Pam Balam, to play drums, but never having picked up sticks before, she lasted only a few rehearsals. Her replacement, Miriam Linna, who had equally limited experience, managed to last a year as the Cramps took their first steps in the NY live arena, encouraged by fellow Ohio transplants the Dead Boys and Linna's roommates, Teenage Jesus and the Jerks. After her departure, it was the latter's drummer, Bradley Field, who recommended another Ohio refugee to audition – Nick Knox (aka Nick Stephanoff, 1953–2018), who'd previously drummed for Cleveland's Electric Eels.

This proved more of a trial for Lux and Gregory than it was for Knox. 'The truth is we thought the guy was just too weird,' Lux told *Mojo*'s Bill Holdship, 'he seemed so unfriendly and angry and couldn't talk on top of it – but I told him his hair was too long. That night we ran into him at Max's [Kansas City, another pivotal NYC punk incubator] and he'd cut his hair. "Now will you give me an audition?" – and I was impressed enough to say yes. "Good," he answered, "because if you said no, I was gonna punch your face in."' This attitude went down well with Ivy, then supplementing the band's income working as a dominatrix. Knox was in for the next thirteen years.

Though they also forged a kinship with the Ramones, inspired by their similar stance as a gang of degenerate brothers – a male punk version of the Ronettes or the Shangri-Las in black leather jackets – the Cramps were routinely written out of New York's musical history. As an incredulous Lux told *Sounds*' Edwin Pouncey: '*Spin* magazine wrote an entire issue on CBGBs and that whole scene from '76. We weren't mentioned in it anywhere. We played 50 times at Max's Kansas City and once a month for three years at CBGBs . . . I asked one of the people on that magazine why . . . and they said, "Well, we had a meeting on that and we decided that you're not really a punk band, you guys are just weird."'

Yet the Cramps' weird is very much America's weird – the music they channelled and created is the authentic voice of the real punk, from lipsticked hillbilly hepcat to dragged-up blues howler. Lux and Ivy instinctively understood all that was great about what Ivy memorably called 'the sound of southern culture falling apart in a blaze of pick-ups'. In the same Sandy Robertson interview,[7] Lux divined the difference between his way of thinking and that of one of NYC's more revered punk icons when discussing 'Surfin' Bird': 'I think it stands for the unimportance of words in rock 'n' roll, except for sound. Y'know: *"Thebirdisthewordthebirdisthewordthebirdistheword."* It says something more than Patti Smith might say in a whole side of an album.'

Sunglasses After Dark

At the end of 1979, the Cramps returned to Memphis and their Godfather Alex Chilton to record their debut album, *Songs the Lord Taught Us*, at Sun Studios. However, Sam Phillips' legendary launch pad for Elvis, Jerry Lee, the Big O, Johnny Cash and Carl Perkins didn't welcome them with open arms either.

'We didn't get any respect by the studio. They'd look at us like we weren't a serious recording act,' Ivy recalled. 'The mixing was a problem too 'cos we couldn't get any engineers that could stand to listen to this music. They'd sit there and say: "How can you listen to this distortion all day?" And any time Alex wanted to put his hands on the board to move the faders, it was: "How dare you?"'[8]

Bryan Gregory was also getting twitchy. He had a *Spinal Tap*-style girlfriend who wanted him to leave the band and form another one with her and a still less healthy relationship with heroin. He barely showed up for the recording and when he did, he complained about the material – Ivy had to fill in most of his guitar parts. After the album's March 1980 release, and two days into their US tour, he absconded with the band's truck and all their gear. Reviewing the album for *New York Rocker*, Richard Grabel passed on some gossip: 'One even hears that guitarist Bryan Gregory has left the group for a Satanist cult . . .'

It seems to be the fate of those bands whose music is more akin to a divine mission than a grab for fame to travel a hard and difficult road but the Cramps had learned from Chilton how to produce an album, and not only that, how to 'make it a party'. As the title implies, *Songs the Lord Taught Us* was once more a celebration of those who had inspired them to pick up guitars and holler – Jimmy Stewart's 'Rock on the Moon', the Sonics' 'Strychnine', Johnny Burnette's 'Tear It Up' and Little Willie John's 'Fever'. In their most inspired revival tent moment, they segued Dwight 'Whitey' Pullen's 'Sunglasses After Dark' – I'm'a tell ya how to be cool in one easy lesson/Sunglasses after dark!' – with Ivy's reanimation of Link Wray's killer 'Ace of Spades' riff. A fitting tribute to the man whose first single, 1958's 'Rumble' – recorded after Link kicked a hole in his amplifier to get the right 'live' sound – was the first instrumental to get banned on US radio. The Cramps helped to reanimate his career, too.

Yet again, the material penned by Ivy and Lux was just as great, if not superior. 'Teenage Werewolf' opens with a mournful Lux ruing the 'braces on my fangs'. 'Zombie Dance' takes aim at the living undead who walk among us: 'The kind of life they choose/ Ain't no life at all'. But it's on 'Garbageman', in which Ivy laid down her most infectious riff to date, that Lux proved he could, in fact, write words that stood for something. Weaving lines from 'Louie Louie' and 'Surfin' Bird' into its spell, he laid down the Cramps' gospel: 'Well if you can't dig me you can't dig nothin'/Do you want the real thing or are you just talkin'?'

Somebody out there did. The Cramps needed a new guitarist – and he would soon be making his presence felt.

Papa Oom-Mow-Mow

Disenchanted with New York, Lux and Ivy relocated to Los Angeles in the spring of 1980. This, of course, was the city that had nurtured Ronald Reagan's career: from whence he had become a star of the silver screen and moved into politics, taking office as the Republican governor of California in November 1966. His story illustrates the social upheaval of post-war America and just how much changed between the days Vampira rode around Hollywood in her black Packard in 1953 and Jim Morrison took his leave of the City of Angels in 1971. It also provides plenty of clues as to why, when he came to ultimate power, Margaret Thatcher would become his number-one admirer and ally.

America emerged from the Second World War as a superpower, with no swathes of smoking ruins to rebuild or crippling national debt to repay. To outside eyes, it seemed the Hanna-Barbera animation series *The Jetsons* (1962–63) had correctly divined a jet-propelled, leisure-filled future. One in which all those advances in science, technology and communications learned during the conflict could be put to the common good and not simply be diverted into a four-decades-long face-off with rival superpower the Soviet Union (USSR).

But as any Ufologist will tell you, the very notion of flying saucers – even the cute little one George Jetson propelled his family around in – is inextricably linked to the dark arts of the Cold War. America had been pursuing the spectre of Communism since the '30s, when the House Un-American Activities Committee (HUAC) was set up to investigate alleged disloyalty in anyone from private citizens to public bodies. When, in 1947, they came calling on Hollywood, Ronald Reagan rode swiftly to their aid. During nine days of hearings into alleged propaganda and influence at the movies, Reagan – then president of the Screen Actors Guild – testified alongside Walt Disney in portraying the industry's problems with unionisation as an ideological battle against Communism.

When Reagan launched his political career, Disney, along with fellow Republican big-hitters Bob Hope and John Wayne, saddled up behind him. One of his key gubernatorial campaign promises was to 'clean up the mess at Berkeley'. This, politically febrile campus of the University of California (UCLA), was where political radicals fired up by the Civil Rights movement and Vietnam War met the Beat Generation. During 1964–65 there had been non-stop strikes and protests – the first mass act of civil disobedience at an American college. As Reagan saw it, the university had become 'a haven for communist sympathisers, protesters, and sex deviants' – and he was going to put a stop to it.[9]

Once in office, Governor Reagan appointed himself and allies to the UC Board to oust Berkeley President, Clark Kerr. But his troubles with the uppity students were far from over. In 1967, the Board compulsory purchased a 2.8-acre plot in Berkeley for development into student housing, but ran out of funds to complete the project. The partially bulldozed land became a dumping site until, in the spring of 1969, fed-up locals – residents, businesses and UC students – hatched a plan to turn it into a public leisure space.

As the People's Park Committee began landscaping the waste ground, the Berkeley Board announced plans for a sports field to be constructed there instead. A series of negotiations between the two sides began, but on Thursday, 15 May 1969, Reagan's patience ran out. At the request of Berkeley's Republican Mayor, Wallace J. S. Johnson, the Governor sent Berkeley Police and California Highway Patrol officers into the People's Park at 4.30 a.m. They cleared an eight-block-wide area and put an 8-metre-high chainlink fence around it.

By early afternoon, enraged UC students marched to the People's Park, to be met by 159 police officers assigned to guard the site. The protesters tried to pull down the fence, throwing bottles and bricks at the cops, who responded with tear gas. Police reinforcements were called in as the crowd swelled to 4,000 and a group of sheriff's deputies were chased out of the area. At this point, Reagan's Chief of Staff Edwin Meese called in Alameda County sheriff's deputies, bringing police numbers up to 791, and directed them to use whatever methods they wished to disperse the by now approximately 6,000-strong melee.

Officers in riot gear waded in with nightsticks swinging. Alameda County sheriff's deputies – many of whom were Vietnam War veterans – fired '00' buckshot at the retreating protesters. They also aimed shotguns at those watching from the rooftops, including James Rector, who was hit while on top of Granma Books and died from his injuries on 19 May. At least 128 Berkeley residents were admitted to local hospitals for head trauma, shotgun wounds and other serious injuries. Carpenter Alan Blanchard was blinded by taking a direct hit of buckshot to his face.

That night, Governor Reagan declared a State of Emergency in Berkeley and sent in 27,000 National Guards to patrol the streets, where they remained for the next two weeks, breaking up the most minor of demonstrations with tear gas.[10] It appeared this enemy of Communism was not above learning a trick or two from Eastern Bloc despots when it came to stifling opposition.

'Once the dogs of war have been unleashed, you must expect things will happen, and that people, being human, will make mistakes on both sides,' he declared.[11] Words that would echo down the '80s as similar tactics came to be used in Britain on dissenters Thatcher called 'the enemy within' – striking miners and print workers, the Peace Convoy and the group of women who began protesting the storage of US cruise missiles in Berkshire by chaining themselves to the perimeter fence of RAF Greenham Common in September 1981.

One of America's most astute commentators, the singer-poet Gil Scott-Heron came back to those events on 'B-Movie', his blistering response to the election of 'Ronnie the Ray-Gun': 'Civil Rights. Gay Rights. Women's Rights. They're all wrong. Call in the cavalry and disrupt this perception of freedom gone wild.'

With Ronnie now hanging his Stetson at the White House, Los Angeles was ripe for another wave of deviant insurrection.

For the Love of Ivy

The roots of punk, California style, can be traced to the time of Reagan's governorship and the days of the Electric Prunes, the Standells, the Seeds and the Count Five – garage/psych bands whose oeuvre was collected by future Patti Smith Group guitarist Lenny Kaye on the influential *Nuggets* double-album of 1972; and to McLarenesque hustler-mogul Kim Fowley, who produced a string of novelty hits, including such Cramps-friendly fare as the Hollywood Argyles' 'Alley Oop', and masterminded the career of glam girl rockers, the Runaways.

At the time Ivy and Lux took the lease on an apartment in Hollywood, a host of bands from LA's suburban sprawl – Phast Phreddie and Thee Precisions, X, Weirdos, the Blasters, the Bags, the Go-Gos – were getting their acts together in true garage style; while Circle Jerks, Bad Religion and Black Flag led the emergent hardcore scene. The Cramps had always gone down well in La-La-Land, where, as Ivy told *Sounds*' Sandy Robertson with admirable understatement, 'there's a lotta really nuts people'. The scene converged in several key venues – Cathay de Grande and the Masque in Hollywood; and Madame Wong's West and the Hong Kong Café in Chinatown – where their next guitarist was currently playing in a band that nursed a sizeable crush on the Cramps.

What happened next depends on who's telling the story. Either Bryan Gregory's replacement announced himself to Lux and Ivy by hurling a brick through the window of their new pad,[12] or they hunted him down, offered him a job and – just as they had with themselves – gave him a new identity.

Three years earlier, Brian Tristan (b. 27 March 1959) was a handsomely cheekboned Mexican-American teenager from La Puente, who had fallen in love with the Ramones, travelled back and forth to New York to see them and was now running their fan club. One hot night, outside a Pere Ubu gig at the Whisky a Go-Go, he ran into a kid from the San Fernando Valley who stood out from the crowd even more than he did.

The then nineteen-year-old Jeffrey Lee Pierce was a hulk of a man with a shock of bleached blond hair styled after his idols, Marilyn Monroe and Debbie Harry, all wrapped up in a 'white vinyl trench coat and white cowboy boots', as the erstwhile Tristan would recall to *Mojo*'s Sylvie Simmons.[13] Behind this formidable front was an all-consuming hunger for roots and blues music akin to Ivy and Lux's ravening thirst for rockabilly. Pierce formed his first band, the Red Lights, in which he sang, played guitar and keyboards, with bassist Anna Statman in 1978. In a supplementary career as a writer for LA-based *Slash* fanzine, he'd been exploring Jamaican reggae, hillbilly country, western swing and the Delta laments that Robert Johnson wailed into legend. He looked back at Tristan, a cocky punk throwback to LA's zoot suit rioters of the '40s: 'We should be in a band together,' he said.

However, Jeffrey Lee's quest would lead him quite some distance down the Lost Highway before they finally did: to New York, where he met his punk idols and landed a job handling Blondie's fanclub, briefly joining local ensemble the Individuals; to Miami, where he claimed to have learned Haitian voodoo; over to Jamaica, where he tried but failed to get to grips with Rastafarianism; and then back to LA via New Orleans and San Antonio. Each pitstop took him further into worlds of poverty and resilience, transcendent ritual and the bottom of the bottle. He got beaten up a lot, looking the way he did, but all of it fed into his vision. And he learned how to tell a good story along the way.

Back in his hometown, Jeffrey Lee played drums for a while in the Precisions and formed another band with fellow *Slash* writer and reggae enthusiast, bassist Don Snowden, and novice drummer Brad Dunning. On guitar was Brian Tristan, whom Pierce had taught, via Bo Diddley's 'Gunslinger', the art of one-fingered, open-E-string strum, a style he would perfect with a singular grace. They were called Creeping Ritual, and even then, Don noted, unlike most of their peers, Jeffrey Lee 'was a real musician' who knew how to 'down-tune his low E-string to get that Robbie Krieger sitar-drone effect . . .'[14] But, just like Robert Johnson, nobody seemed to know quite where on his travels Pierce had learned to do the things he could – either on the guitar or with his lonesome whippoorwill wail.

The band needed a better name, though, which was provided by Pierce's flatmate, Circle Jerks' singer Keith Morris, who struck just the right note of southern discomfort with his suggestion: the Gun Club. Their initial foray into gigdom was a residency at the Hong Kong Café, supporting the Blasters. Here, Jeffrey Lee's first Gun Club songs were debuted and they hollered all the way back to rock 'n' roll's primal roots. The juke joint bump 'n' grind of 'Sex Beat' – 'We can fuck forever but you'll never get my soul' – the twangtastic rolling ride of 'Black Train'; 'She's Like Heroin to Me' with its sinister dual-slide guitars and 'For the Love of Ivy', Jeffrey Lee's torch song to the Cramps' leading lady, in whose honour, he decreed, he was going to: 'buy me a gun just as long as my arm/ Kill everyone who ever done me harm'.

Pierce also liked to play the songs the Lord taught him, including Robert Johnson's 'Preachin' Blues' and Tommy Johnson's 'Cool Drink of Water', versions of which found their way onto the Gun Club's debut album. He liked a drink as much as those old bluesmen and had a taste for narcotics, too. 'Our drugs of choice were speed and heroin – great combination – and alcohol,' their first guitarist told Sylvie Simmons. 'We made a career out of being the craziest, drunkest band going.'

Not long after those gigs – at which Lux and Ivy were easily identifiable among the ten or so other attendees – Brian Tristan decamped to Crampsville and would be known as Kid Congo Powers forever after. Undaunted, Jeffrey Lee went into the studio with a bag of speed and came out two days later with the album that made his name as a new kind of Old Testament kind of guy: *Fire of Love*.

Powers' departure was not such an ill wind. For one thing, it was amicable, the reassembled two bands frequently playing together afterwards. For another, it blew a blistering new guitarist through the Gun Club's saloon doors. Cramps' fan Ward Dotson – formerly of hardcore band Der Stab – had offered Ivy and Lux his services the moment he knew they had relocated to LA.[15] When he heard the job had gone to Kid, he approached Jeffrey with the same proposition. Without a note of audition, he was in. Pierce meant business, recruiting drummer Terry Graham and bassist Rob Ritter, both until recently of the Bags, to complete the new line-up. And when *Slash* owner Bob Biggs heard Jeffrey's tape of *Fire of Love* and released it on his Ruby Red label on 31 August 1981, business was good.

Up Jumped the Devil

The record was picked up in Britain by Beggars Banquet and released in June 1982, whereupon journalists who had championed the Cramps fell upon it. 'On days when I would return home in a head-pounding, foul state of erupting rage,' wrote Edwin Pouncey, 'where if a kitchen knife had been handed to me as I walked through the door I might have done something I would later regret, the Gun Club's mighty *Fire of Love* album acted as a release valve for all that seething anger crawling inside.'[16]

The fortunate UK audience would have two albums to revel in when the Gun Club played their first London gig. Because by this time, Ramblin' Jeffrey Lee had retraced his steps to New York, where the band had recorded a second album, produced and released by his old mucker, Blondie's Chris Stein, for his Animal label. Beggars Banquet took that one too, releasing it on 20 September 1982.

With Debbie Harry on backing vocals, *Miami* marked another beauty spot on Pierce's personal map of the blues. The fire had burned itself down to smoke now and a ghostly vision of the Gun Club rose from the embers, drifting through the landscape of America's unquiet dead. All the voodoo skills Jeffrey Lee mastered in the Floridian locale of the album's title are summoned on the shimmering 'Brother and Sister' and its scenario of backwoods murder – 'The sins of me/They buzz and hiss in the trees'. He lured his listeners further into the trees with 'A Devil in the Woods' and 'Like Calling Up Thunder': 'Ghosts, they crawl on the floor/ Wondering at it all'. And he continued to commune with ancestral spirits, summoning hair-raising covers of the old ballad 'John Hardy' and Creedence Clearwater Revival's 1970 'Run Through the Jungle', a song widely perceived to have been written about the Vietnam War.[17]

Jeffrey Lee certainly infused his version with the smell of napalm in the morning, telling Edwin Pouncey: 'My father flew planes in Korea during the war and my cousin was in the Green Berets in Vietnam, stone killer . . . He had to be one of those special forces people that used to have to go on those slay missions, search and destroy missions where they just go through those Vietnamese villages and wipe out everything.'[18] He went on to muse about the possibility that he might one day act on the impulses he expressed in his songs and commit brutal murder – it was something he saw as being part of the American national psyche.

The Gun Club's early adopters, like Pouncey, *NME*'s Richard Cook and *Melody Maker*'s Jim Irwin, were all serious record collectors and aficionados of the music Pierce was exhuming from his country's cultural crypt.

'The Gun Club take and shake the misty lore of the southern bible belt, demolish its respectable trappings,' wrote Cook. 'They renew the terror and violence in a form boiled dry by stupidity and endless reiteration.' The band 'sure ain't pretty,' considered Irwin, 'but their stark, demonic intensity grabs you by the throat and *demands* your fullblooded attention.'

Although some of Jeffrey Lee's bandmates were having trouble coping with such a sensitive interpreter of Robert Johnson's lines: 'The blues, is a low-down achin' heart disease/Like consumption, killing me by degrees'. By the time they got to London, the Gun Club didn't just have a new LP but a new line-up. When Rob Ritter quit to rejoin his old band 45 Grave in June 1982, Terry Graham recommended another of his old Bags' bandmates, Patricia

Morrison (b. 1962), who instantly rectified Jim Irwin's observation about the way the band looked. The fact that native Los Angeleno Patricia bore more than a passing resemblance to Vampira's vexed successor Elvira was no coincidence – actress Cassandra Peterson would later admit she 'borrowed' the punked-up Morticia look from the bass-slinging Bag.[19] Morrison herself was apprehensive at joining forces with Pierce: 'He was just one of those odd people that have an odd personality,' she told *Stomp and Stammer*'s Jeff Clark. 'But I heard the tape for *Miami* and I thought the songs were amazing. So I said, "I'll give it a try."' Jeffrey Lee's songwriting skills were always the key for Patricia. Although he could be difficult to cope with, 'When we got on stage, it just simply worked,' she said.[20]

Pierce came to baptise his UK audience on the night of 5 October 1982 like Robert Mitchum's Preacher Powell in *Night of the Hunter* (1955) – promising redemption from posturing New Romantics and dour agit-punk while all the time nursing a massive switchblade in his pocket. Richard Cook testified: 'Although he looks a little like a cold, uncaring Meat Loaf, Pierce more closely resembles a Presley come back from an awful purgatory, tearing away at his oldest roots. When he swings his great silver crucifix and majestically crosses himself as he stares out at us, the absolution hangs in the balance.'[21]

Smoke in the Shadows

'I was eight years old when all the riots in the United States were going on in 1967,' Lydia Lunch recalled. 'Right outside my front door in Rochester, New York State. I don't remember the riots of '64 because I was five, but the riots of '67 are formative. From whatever information I could glean as a child, I discovered there were a lot of women involved in the Black Panther movement – and that was my biggest inspiration.'

While the rigorous search for Reds had been going on, America's most debilitating problem – the gulf of inequality between its black and white citizens – ignited. The first inner-city race riot, in

Birmingham, Alabama, in May 1963, was triggered by the Ku Klux Klan firebombing of African-American Civil Rights campaigners, including the parsonage of the Reverend Alfred King, brother of Dr Martin Luther King Jr. President John F. Kennedy – who had saved his country from the threat of nuclear war with the USSR in the 1962 Cuban Missile Crisis and was in the process of drawing up equality legislation – was shot dead by would-be Soviet defector Lee Harvey Oswald at Dealey Plaza on 22 November 1963 and worse was to come.

Although JFK's successor, Lyndon B. Johnson, signed the Civil Rights Act into law in July 1964, America's cities continued to convulse with racially polarised violence – and it was the poor black neighbourhoods, like the one Lydia grew up in, that burned. In Watts, California, in August 1965, Chicago in June and August 1966 and then right throughout the country in the summer of 1967, from Newark to New York and Rochester – where Lydia watched the flames of a crashed helicopter from her attic bedroom window, listening to 'Light My Fire' by the Doors – over to Detroit and Milwaukee and down to Houston and Tucson. Following the assassination of Dr King in Memphis on 4 April 1968, there were riots in 125 cities, including Baltimore, Washington DC, New York City, Chicago and Detroit, while in Boston, Godfather of Soul James Brown quelled an uprising by the sheer force of his charisma.[22] The city was fortunate to have had him – for decades after, the damage done during those conflagrations went unreconstructed, creating the equivalent of Europe's bombsites in the most deprived areas of American cities.

The Pop Art future that Hanna-Barbera's *The Jetsons* envisaged was dealt its final blow on 6 June 1968, when JFK's crusading brother, Senator Robert F. Kennedy's pledge to take on organised crime was met by Palestinian Sirhan Sirhan's bullets in the kitchen hallway of LA's Ambassador Hotel. Pile on the overseas disaster of Vietnam, dragging on since 1955, and the inauguration of Richard 'Tricky Dick' Nixon in 1969, and you complete the journey to *Apocalypse Now*.

After her political awakening in the crossfire hurricane of these events, Lydia Lunch (b. Lydia Anne Koch, 2 June 1959) began to process her personal struggles in the flickering afterglow: 'I certainly felt I had more in common with the Black Panthers than any other organised group that's come down the pipe since. Of course, we know what happened to them; they were incarcerated or eliminated because they were too threatening. But when women have a cause they can believe in, they're willing to fight their lives out for it. Makes sense to me.'

She has since gone on to produce the most multifarious body of work of any artist in this book, along the way becoming as articulate a political commentator as Gil Scott-Heron; a torch singer whose music has crossed all genres and a force of creativity whose endeavours link just about everybody else mentioned within these pages. When I first met her, Lydia told me: 'My job is merely to shit in the face of history. I can't compromise my vision, my truth, in order to make more popular opinion. I'm not in the entertainment field, I'm too confrontational.' Yet the record she has left of her life and times will probably be of the highest value to historians.

At the age of sixteen, she left Rochester, and the trauma of the sexual awakening suffered at the hands of her Bible salesman father, and escaped to New York. Which, by the mid-1970s, recalled 'Berlin at the end of the Second World War' according to resident film-maker Vivienne Dick, thanks to the widespread practice of landlords burning out buildings to claim insurance and oust rent-controlled tenants.[23] Lydia affectionately referred to it as 'Beirut on the Hudson'.

Visitors arriving in the city's airports in June 1975 were handed a leaflet announcing: *Welcome to Fear City: A Survival Guide for Visitors to New York* by members of its own police force. If British Chancellor of the Exchequer Denis Healey was having trouble balancing his books at the time, New York's Mayor Abe Beame was facing the disintegration of his city, with President Gerald Ford appearing to wash his hands of it – 'Ford to City: Drop Dead' ran the infamous *New York Daily News* front cover. Murders, car thefts and assaults had doubled in the past decade, rapes and burglaries tripled and robberies increased tenfold, while thousands of NYPD officers were laid off.[24]

Entire blocks along Avenues B, C and D were demolished, while major infrastructure like the East River bridges were left to rust and Grand Central Station was in danger of being bulldozed. During two-day-long power cuts in the summer of 1977, a serial killer calling himself Son of Sam stalked the blacked-out streets, leaving messages for the police that uncannily recalled the inner monologues of Martin Scorsese's Vietnam vet Travis Bickle (Robert De Niro) who prays that 'some day a real rain will come to wash all the scum off the streets' in his monumental 1976 evocation of the fallen city, *Taxi Driver*.[25]

Yet among the ruins of the Lower East Side thrived a vibrant artistic community. Like the Cramps before her, Lydia was welcomed into it by the Dead Boys, who would honour her with a song called 'I Need Lunch'. But it was Mink DeVille's Willy DeVille who gave her the nickname that stuck, thanks to her Robin Hood-like ability to provide free food for the dirt-poor bands that clustered in CBGBs, Max's Kansas City and the surrounding derelict buildings where they made their homes. This milieu of runaways and squatters – a vertiginous equivalent of London's Frestonia – also included the saxophonist James Chance, avant jazzers the Lounge Lizards, Sonic Youth's Thurston Moore and the film-makers Beth B, Vivienne Dick, Richard Kern and Nick Zedd – all of whom Lydia would work with, igniting and documenting the transgressive New York guerrilla art/music/film scene.

She formed her first band, Teenage Jesus and the Jerks, in 1976 after encountering Bradley Field 'setting a homeless person on fire outside CBGBs, which I proceeded to stamp out'. She had just turned down the chance to be the Cramps' replacement for Pam Balam – her friend Miriam Linna got the job instead. But it was through the medium of percussion that Lunch helped channel Field's murderous proclivities into art. With one drum and one cymbal.

Even more so than Lux and Ivy, Lydia was stripping music back to its core. While living with James Chance – who would have a brief dalliance as a Jerk before forming his own outfit, the Contortions – she had got hold of a guitar and taught herself to make some noises with it that matched the rhythmic intensity of the words that spewed forth in her first public exorcism: 'From the original inception of Teenage Jesus, the music imitated the words, which were percussive and brutal. But the words were always the most important element.'

Her musical vision had been nurtured in Rochester on Johnny Cash, Billie Holiday – whose 'Gloomy Sunday' she covered – and Lou Reed's post-Velvets' output, notably *Berlin* (1973): 'I've aspired to make records that brutally real,' and *Metal Machine Music* (1975): 'I couldn't stop playing it for the first three weeks after I bought it, throwing myself into some kind of psychic psychotic trance which barely prevented me from killing my entire family.' The Stooges and Alice Cooper also played a role: 'There's yet to be any one as sexy and death-obsessed as Alice. Snakes, guillotines, black make-up, a big nose – what more could you ask for from a rock star?'

Suicide, the vastly underrated duo of sculptor-turned-singer Alan Vega and keyboard wizard Martin Rev, whose astounding electronic-vocal music sounded like Elvis lost in space, were mentors to the youthful Lunch.[26] But it was Mars, the freeform experimental boy/girl outfit of singer Sumner Crane, guitarist China Burg, bassist Mark Cunningham and drummer Nancy Arlen, whose first gigs electrified her into starting her own band.

Lunch is as refreshingly unafraid of the G-word as she is of anything else. Her Catholic-school education had already provided her with the props of rosary beads and sacred hearts, symbols of gruesome saintly sacrifice and the deification of suffering, to go with the hilarious moniker of her first band and her raven-haired, baby doll killer looks: 'I was basically a Goth by the age of thirteen, in 1973, when everyone else was dressing glam.' She is much more disdainful of the word 'punk', considering just about every band to be filed under its name as dead-end rock 'n' roll revivalists. She called what she was doing not New Wave but No Wave.

Not Waving but Lounging

Lydia served up the first strange fruits of her wrath in the short, sharp shock of the 'Orphans'/'Less of Me' single, released on Migraine Records in 1978. To a stark, militaristic beat, she painted a bloody picture of the end of innocence on the A-side – 'No more ankles and no more clothes/Little orphans running through the snow' – and got to grips with the job of processing her own psyche on the flip: 'Sensitivity turns to hardcore/The further you go the deeper entwined'.

By this time, the Jerks had mutated: Gordon Stevenson had come and gone as a bassist, to be replaced by Greek-Italian New Yorker Jim Sclavunos, a striking figure who, at 6 foot 7, towered over even Lux. Kid Congo Powers, who had previously befriended Bradley Field's partner Kristian Hoffman in LA, watched the band rehearse while staying with them on trips to New York. Talking to author Nick Soulsby, he compared the experience to being 'invited to learn a different language. The songs were so minimal, shorter than anyone's, but anyone could understand the expression. How could such basic music be so difficult?'

Watching one of their minimalist sets ('the longest was thirteen minutes. You did not need more') at the Artist's Space on 6 May 1978, in a bill that also included James Chance fighting with his audience, was a visiting Brian Eno. Inspired by what he saw, he would go on to produce the *No New York* album that showcased Teenage Jesus, Mars, the Contortions and DNA for Antilles, a US subsidiary of Roxy Music's parent label, Island. Each band was given half a side of the album and delivered their goods, in the words of *Melody Maker*'s shell-shocked reviewer Ian Birch, 'like a psychic battering ram'. He found Teenage Jesus 'so over the top I hardly know what to say. Lydia's banshee wail and the band's fat-fuzz minimalism are unremittingly nightmarish.' The back sleeve of the LP presented the performers in a series of police-style mugshots and, as a masochistic design quirk, the album came with its lyric sheet embedded in its sleeve, so you had to rip it apart to read it.

Yet, if this was the aural evocation of Son of Sam's New York, then a little over a year later, Lydia would be dancing with the ghosts of an earlier age, working with Tommy Dorsey big band veteran, trombonist and arranger Billy VerPlanck on 1980's *The Queen of Siam*. Made for Michael Zilkha and Michel Esteban's influential ZE label and recorded in 1979,[27] this jazz noir masterpiece was largely written by Lydia and future *SpongeBob SquarePants* composer Pat Irwin, with Richard Hell's guitarist Robert Quine, Contortions bassist George Scott and Lounge Lizard Dougie Bowne on drums. There are two cover versions, each casting their singer in a different light. Lydia pays tribute to Billie Holliday on 'Gloomy Sunday' – written by composer Rezso Seress in 1933 and supposedly responsible for a spate of suicides, including his own, in his native Hungary. It was given English lyrics by Tin Pan Alley tunesmith Sam Lewis in 1936 and recorded by Lady Day in 1941, whereupon the BBC banned it for being 'too upsetting'. Lunch then demonstrates the yin and yang of Goth by turning unexpectedly upbeat. Her version of Mike Shapiro and Buddy Buie's 1967 Halloween classic 'Spooky' even outdoes Dusty Springfield's cool take of 1968.

Listening across the Atlantic Ocean, Barry Adamson pricked up his ears. 'That record joined another set of dots for me because a large part of it was done with a jazz ensemble, but it was still as punk as fuck,' he told Nick Soulsby. Equally impressed was the Australian guitarist in a band that had not made New York yet, but had just crossed half the world to arrive in London at the time of *Queen of Siam*'s release, in February 1980.

The Neighbours of the Beast

Rowland S. Howard, together with singer Nick Cave, bassist Tracy Pew, multi-instrumentalist Mick Harvey and drummer Phill Calvert, had made the time-honoured passage of their countrymen to a damp basement flat in Earl's Court at the dreg-end of a perishing British winter. Their band, newly baptised the Birthday Party, were relocating from the sun-drenched beaches of Melbourne at the behest of manager Keith Glass, who thought they could go further in London than was possible back home. Previously and misleadingly known as the Boys Next Door, they were also leaving behind a reputation for trouble.

Cave was Lux's serious rival for the scariest frontman of the early '80s and though they had followed a different path, something in the Birthday Party's music tapped back into their country's roots the way that the Cramps' and the Gun Club's did. Describing their style as 'sophisticated primitivism' in one of their first interviews with the British press in June 1981, *NME*'s Andy Gill asked them if they had been affected by aboriginal culture. 'Aboriginal culture's just been razed to the ground,' Nick replied. 'The only "walkabout" is from one aboriginal bar to another aboriginal bar.'[28]

Although he and Jeffrey Lee Pierce had yet to meet, Cave shared the Gun Club frontman's lyrical preoccupations and the manner of conveying them. Before very much longer, Cave would also be sharing a guitarist, when Kid Congo Powers jumped ship from the Cramps. Meanwhile, departing guitarist Rowland S. Howard, whose sound made up a big part of the Birthday Party's power, would find his finest musical foil in Lydia Lunch.

Rowland was born in the city that styles itself Australia's cultural capital on 24 October 1959. He had joined the others as lead guitarist and songwriter in 1979, after his former band, the Young Charlatans, disintegrated. As the name suggests, he was cutting a swathe from an early age. According to his younger brother Harry, by the age of ten, the long-haired, black-clad Rowland would walk the streets of their Swinburne neighbourhood twirling a walking stick, followed at a nervous distance by a trail of awestruck girls.[29]

Bearing an uncanny resemblance to original anarchist Percy Bysshe Shelley, this pre-teen Pied Piper was as gifted as he was alluring. Encouraged by his parents, who played in a folk band, he first learned piano, then took up guitar, an instrument he approached in as original a manner as John McGeoch, creating a style that many would emulate but never better. While the Magazine man's Pop Art approach yielded the ultimate manifestation of urban anxiety, Rowland summoned the elements through his six strings and used them in just as painterly – in his case, Expressionistic – a way.

Painting was something else he excelled at, leaving home at sixteen to attend Prahran Art College, where he joined his first band, the Obsessions. The Young Charlatans were formed in 1977, when Rowland met singer Ian 'Ollie' Olsen. 'Ollie had the ability to make you think he was a complete genius,' he told Nick Cave's first biographer, Ian Johnston, 'and he gave me the ability to take myself seriously as a guitarist.'[30] It was at this time that he wrote the song for which the Boys Next Door would become most famous, 'Shivers'. He also introduced Cave to fellow Prahran art student, the beautiful, red-haired Anita Lane, who would become his partner and muse. Howard was just the suburban alchemist the Boys Next Door needed to catalyse their evolution.

The band had been knocking around in different formations since Nick Cave (b. 22 September 1957) was sent to Caulfield Grammar at the age of twelve. An aficionado of local hero, the outlaw Ned Kelly, he had just been expelled from Wangaratta High for attempting to pull an older girl's knickers down. His father Colin, an English teacher, hoped the private all-boys' school would instil some discipline in his wayward youngest son. In this, the institution failed. As with other sons of authority figures we have met previously, Cave Minor was already a very naughty boy, adept at fighting, drinking, smoking and inspiring rebel tendencies in others. But the new school did facilitate his meeting a soul brother in Tracy Pew (1957–86, threatened with expulsion for repeated hair offences) and the less visually flamboyant but crucially more practical vicar's son Mick Harvey (b. 29 August 1958), their original guitarist. Phill Calvert (b. 11 January 1958) was destined for the Pete Best role in Cave's career.

Like Jaz Coleman, both Cave and Harvey began their musical careers as Anglican choirboys – Cave's first recorded appearance being on a Christmas single of 'Silent Night' – but by the time they met, Nick's soul was in hock to the Sensational Alex Harvey Band. He spent his last years at Caulfield Grammar in the art room with Pew, Harvey, Calvert and friends, learning the repertoire of the Glaswegian Mephistopheles and becoming the Boys Next Door. Once school was out, the pragmatic Harvey got work in his local tax office in order to avoid university, Cave started a fine art course at Caulfield Technical College and Pew began taking bass lessons from neighbour Chris Walsh, exploring his extensive record collection in the process. He was particularly drawn to Hank Williams and Johnny Cash – a black Stetson nicked from Walsh would form an indelible part of his image – as well as the debut album of da brudders Ramone. As the Sex Pistols' call to arms resounded through Melbourne, the Boys regrouped, playing their first gig as a punk band at Harvey's father's parish hall in 1977.

Nick and Tracy already looked the part – the former now boasting a Sid Vicious hairstyle, so that his rangy frame was augmented by spikes from head to winklepickered boot; the latter a moustachioed cross between Johnny Cash and Muscle Mary. The ferocious presence of these two, who had gained some experience in seeing off skinheads as part of their drinking, fighting and car-thieving leisure activities, would come in handy when the gig was invaded by them; the ensuing brawl only curtailed by the arrival of the police. From this auspicious beginning, the Boys rapidly gained a reputation as the best live act in Melbourne, bringing them to the attention of Barry Earl, label boss of Suicide records, a New Wave subsidiary of Australian major label, Mushroom. He had them record three tracks – a cover of Nancy Sinatra's 'These Boots Are Made for Walkin'', their own 'Masturbation Generation' and Harvey's song 'Boy Hero' – for the *Lethal Weapons* compilation, released in 1978.

By then, at the age of twenty-one, Cave had acquired a heroin habit and lost his father. Colin Cave was killed in a car accident on 11 October 1978, while his son was being questioned by police at St Kilda Station on charges of vandalism and being drunk and disorderly. Nick was sitting in a cell with his mother, Dawn, when his younger sister Julie and Anita Lane arrived to break the news.

'Nick's got this incredible drive that's got him through everything,' Anita told Ian Johnston. 'When his father died, I wondered what was going to happen to Nick's drive, but it just got stronger.'

It was shortly after this bombshell that Howard – by then, also nurturing his own opiate addiction – joined the band. Though the Suicide label collapsed, the Boys were still under contract to Mushroom, which wanted an album for its investment. Further material was recorded at Melbourne's Richmond Recorders in January 1979 with young engineer Tony Cohen, who would forge a lasting working relationship with Cave. This resulted in the *Door, Door* album, from which 'Shivers' was extracted as a single – something Rowland would come to bitterly regret: 'It's the only song people ever come up to me and talk about, like it's the only song I've ever written, particularly in Australia.'[31]

With both the band and Cohen learning the ropes, nobody who had seen them live considered the record much of a representation of what they were capable of. But, though it marked the end of the line with Mushroom and Barry Earl, it attracted the attention of Keith Glass, an old hand on the Melbourne music scene. He signed them to his Missing Link label and put them and Cohen back in Richmond Recorders, where they taped an album's worth of material. Howard's presence pushed the band in a distinctly different direction, opening them up to experimentation and giving Cave, initially at least, a flint to strike his fire off. The first fruit was 'Hee Haw', a five-track EP of paradigm shift.

The new formation seemed perfectly attuned: Rowland's guitar and Phill's drums rollicked like a bucking beast, Tracy's bass and Mick's guitar rumbled, while Nick's inner werewolf began to bristle, baring his fangs on 'The Hair Shirt'. Adding notes of jazz discord, Harvey skittered drunken piano across Cave composition 'Faint Heart', while Howard blew distress noises from an outraged clarinet on his own 'Death by Drowning'. Nick's lyrics initiate the triumvirate of obsessions that would last his career: murder, hauntings and religious iconography, all served up – like the gin and tonic of stigmatic blood in 'A Catholic Skin' – with lashings of blasphemous glee. 'If you turned it up,' noted Tony Cohen, 'it bloody blew your bloody head off.'[32]

The band took their new name from a scene in Fyodor Dostoevsky's *Crime and Punishment*, where bereaved consumptive Katerina Ivanovna throws a grotesque wake for her husband that Cave misremembered as a birthday party. Like Ten Pound Poms in reverse,[33] their passage to Blighty was paid for by the AUS$5 per night they had amassed from a year's worth of gigs, plus assistance from Glass.

But the dirty streets of London came as a shock to their system.

Nick the Squatter

Mick Harvey lasted two weeks in Earl's Court before getting himself a temping job and a better place to live. The others, soon joined by their girlfriends, moved around en masse, first to a shared house in Fulham, then to a squat in Walterton Road, Maida Vale, where they rummaged in skips and bins for sustenance, home furnishings and anything they could possibly sell – 'a miserable Dickensian situation' as Nick would later describe it to *NME*'s Biba Kopf. Not realising they could sign on the dole, they took menial work – Tracy cleaning Heathrow Airport, Nick picking up litter at London Zoo. With only two communal records as a distraction – *Metal Box* by Public Image Ltd and *Buy* by James Chance & the Contortions – Cave fashioned two songs of self-loathing, 'Nick the Stripper' ('hideous to the eye') and 'King Ink' ('feels like a bug/And he hates his rotten shell'), which summarised his grimy predicament. 'He was reading Samuel Beckett,' Rowland recalled in the same interview. '*Watt*, things like that, depressed, sort of dirty; and that, I think, influenced him into writing about this whole sort of squalor thing . . .'[34]

Meanwhile, with little help coming from Keith Glass, the job of trying to get a UK record deal fell to Harvey and Calvert, who, after pounding the pavements and knocking on doors, managed to get a couple of singles culled from their last Richmond session – 'Happy Birthday/Riddlehouse' and 'Mr Clarinet' – stocked in independent record shops. Crucially, this brought them to the attention of the legendary DJ John Peel.

Their luck took another upwards swing when they got a gig supporting German electro-punks Deutsche Amerikanische Freundschaft at the Moonlight Club on 10 July 1980. This came only three months after Ian Curtis' last hellish appearance at the venue and two since his death, a raw wound still to Peel, his listeners and Joy Division's admirers in the music press. In the audience that night were two men who would change the Birthday Party's destiny – Ivo Watts-Russell of 4AD and his friend, Daniel Miller of Mute, who was working with the headliners.

Though their set was shambolic – it was the first time the band had ever been given a rider – both men were impressed with the raucous Australians. Miller would have signed them to his fledgling label, but at the time he was putting DAF up as guests in his home as well as putting their records out, so lacked the means. Watts-Russell, with some money from parent company Beggars Banquet behind him, was able to make an agreement with Missing Link and, by October 1980, released the single 'The Friend Catcher'.

This was another track from Richmond Recorders, with Cave this time playing the Big Bad Wolf to a feedback inferno created by Rowland and an array of effects pedals and tape echo machines, all cranked up to eleven. Peel loved it so much he played it twice in one night and gave the band their first *Session*. The Birthday Party took the opportunity to record four new songs, including 'Figure of Fun' and 'King Ink' in the BBC Maida Vale studios, close to their squat HQ. With enough money advanced from 4AD to go back to Melbourne and record an album, the band took temporary leave of their crumbling pile and flew home, playing a kiss-off gig at the Moonlight Club on 3 November.

This small corner of West Hampstead has acted like a portal in our story so far, pointing Ian Curtis towards the exit, while summoning Nick Cave forwards. When the Birthday Party came back to London in March 1981 with an album called *Prayers on Fire*, it was to Cave that those left bereft by Curtis' passing would look, both as shamanic frontman willing to risk all for their enlightenment and a projection of their own deepest fears and desires.

Blood on the Rise

'There's no way you can possibly go on stage and have a pleasant relationship with your audience,' Nick told Ralph Traitor in an interview of April 1982. The *Sounds*' writer was asking him and Rowland about an incident at a recent gig when he had attacked a punter with his microphone. 'He seemed to be staring at me, absolutely pleading for it,' the singer replied. Traitor – who doubled as Jeremy Gluck, frontman of Canadian surf punks the Barracudas – said that he detected 'a desire to treat people badly'. Rowland indignantly replied that the audience 'treat us badly when we're onstage. They take Nick's clothes off and punch him and pull him to the floor and spray him with stuff.'

'But surely Nick asks for that, wandering around taking slugs off a whiskey bottle and doing his Jim Morrison rave-ups?' Traitor enquired.

'I can't answer that question,' Cave snapped back.[35]

The Birthday Party recorded *Prayers on Fire* with Tony Cohen at Armstrong's Audio Visual Studios in Melbourne between December 1980 and January 1981. The sessions were described by those present as being more akin to a party, with friends wandering in and out, and, in the case of Philip Jackson, Mick Hauser and Stephen Ewart from Melbourne group Equal Local, contributing horns to 'Nick the Stripper', earmarked as the first single. Anita Lane wrote the lyrics to future Peel favourite 'A Dead Song' and Howard's girlfriend Genevieve McGuckin penned the lyrics for 'Capers', while film students Evan English and Paul Goldman, who had shot the promo for 'Shivers', brought in their friend John Hillcoat to work as an editor on a video for 'Nick the Stripper' – the beginning of another significant creative relationship for Cave.

The promo was envisioned as a Felliniesque carnival of the damned, to be filmed in a tip in the suburb of Camberwell on the eve of the band's return to London. Over 1,000 extras, exhorted to dress in the most outrageous way, joined a legion of Melbourne's down-and-outs, headed by a veteran hippy, wearing Jesus robes and blitzed on acid, and a recent inmate of an asylum, dressed as an Egyptian eunuch, who spent the night howling at the moon. The band wandered through this motley crew, headed by Cave dressed in a loincloth. Shooting went on until dawn, by which time some of those present had made away with the generator English had borrowed from his film school.

'It was appalling,' he said, describing the night's activities to Ian Johnston.[36]

Between recording sessions, the Birthday Party had played a New Year's Eve gig at the Crystal Ballroom, where Tracy Pew had kicked off a stage invader, breaking his ribs. When the injured party came backstage to remonstrate afterwards, he was sent packing with the words 'tough shit' ringing in his ears.

The band had decided that their time in London had been ill-spent – they hadn't done enough to distinguish themselves from their peers. From now on, they would take a confrontational attitude towards their fans that went with the increasing violence of their music. It was to attract followers like moths to a flame.

They returned to London, Nick and Anita to the Walterton Road squat. Mick Harvey, meanwhile, had found nearby accommodation with fellow Melbourne ex-pat and music-head supreme Jim Thirlwell (b. 29 January 1960), who, as well as playing live with the The, had begun to mastermind a series of extraordinary records under the name of Foetus, starting with the 7-inch 'Spite Your Face'/'OKFM' on his own Self-Immolation label. Also in attendance at the Birthday Party's gig on 19 March 1981 at the Venue in Victoria Street, supporting Wire's Colin Newman, was guest DJ Barry Adamson. The circle of talented individuals drawn to the sound of this Party was increasing as exponentially as their audience.

Prayers on Fire was released on 6 April, five days before the Brixton riots kicked off a summer of violent uprisings across the UK. Cave did his best to incite a similar reaction from the audiences on the band's first nationwide tour that June, supporting Bauhaus, but to little avail. The Birthday Party did not enjoy the experience of sharing a bill with Bela Lugosi's disciples, whom they held in similar esteem to their critics in the music press. Which is perhaps why, for their next single, they chose a song debuted on their second Peel *Session* that April, the pulverising comedy vampire classic 'Release the Bats'.

Barry Adamson was present at the recording. 'They seemed to be expressing stuff that was inside me that I didn't have a clue how to get out,' he recalled. 'I wanted to be a part of it.'[37] Conversely, Phill Calvert's days looked numbered. His suggestion of recording a Beatles' song to go with the A-side had not gone down well with his bandmates and Mick Harvey had to work out the drum parts for 'Release the Bats' for him. It was a sore that would continue to fester as the band made their first trip to America that September.

Their initial two shows in New York proved even more exasperating than those supporting Bauhaus. The first, a jetlag-fuelled drunken farrago at the Underground in Union Square – a disco full of uncomprehending hipsters – was curtailed by management after four songs; the second, at the Ritz, was patrolled by a phalanx of burly security guards who had got wind of their crowd-provoking tactics. After this, a number of promoters decided to cancel the gigs they'd booked with the Birthday Party further across America. But they still had one New York date left, on 3 October at Chase Park, off Broadway – and it was attended by one unquiet American who really did appreciate their attitude.

Lydia Lunch had been living in Los Angeles since August 1980, fetching up in the Venice Beach surrounds of the Doors' inception. She had led three more bands since we last saw her – and that's not counting Beirut Slump, her horrorcore collaboration with Jim Sclavunos, Vivienne Dick and Liz and Bobby Swope, who existed concurrent to Teenage Jesus and dissolved at around about the same time as the '70s. As 1979 became 1980, she formed 8 Eyed Spy with Sclavunos, *Queen of Siam* collaborators Pat Irwin and

George Scott and Michael Paumgardhen – a No Wave supergroup who shocked and delighted their audience by playing, as guitarist Thurston Moore put it, a 'semblance of boogie chords'.

In their year's existence, 8 Eyed Spy gigged across the States and Europe and released two albums of live and recorded material before Lydia put a halt to their burgeoning success: 'One night we had a show and it was sold out – and the look in people's eyes sickened me so much, I said I can't go on with this. Don't look at me with that false look in your eye because it doesn't mean anything to me.' Their extreme coda came on 5 August 1980, when George Scott died from a heroin overdose at the age of twenty-six.

Lydia's next move was the down and dirty blues band Devil Dogs, who lasted three months and had two different line-ups, including future Fuzztones singer-guitarist Rudi Protrudi, who played bass for them. They also did a cover of 'Run Through the Jungle' – perhaps it was something in the California air. Lydia's music altered as it attuned to her new environment.

Under the hot sun, she began dreaming of the Manson Family out in Spahn Ranch and more recent night stalkers terrorising dreamland – the Hillside Stranglers, Kenneth Bianchi and Angelo Buono Jr, who abducted, tortured and killed ten women between 1977 and 1978. Thus, her next band, 13.13 – with ex-Weirdos Greg Williams, Dix Denney and Cliff Martinez – awoke the spectre of psychedelia and the Summer of Hate, 'taking what had been ugly and condemned and elevating it up to a new altar'. Chilling songs like 'Afraid of Your Company' and 'Suicide Ocean' mapped the psycho geography of the Big Nowhere by night: 'The clock died at a quarter to midnight/Frozen angels on my bedpost/Tripping over some senseless beggar/A simple case of mistaken face/My how nothing changes/Different men in the same positions/Just this side of motel's end/At suicide ocean'.

By October 1981, 13.13 were in New York to support Siouxsie and the Banshees, who had clocked Lydia playing with Devil Dogs at the Mudd Clubb the autumn previously and bonded over their mutual love of Alice Cooper. Lunch had got hold of a copy of *Prayers on Fire* two weeks before the Birthday Party's show at Chase Park: 'And I just had to go and pledge my undying devotion to the very vampiric Rowland S. Howard. Who could resist?'

That was the end of 13.13. 'We just knew,' said Lydia. 'Rowland had heard *Queen of Siam* and proposed we did a cover of "Some Velvet Morning". I fell in love with a ghost and moved to London.'

Gothfather: Lee Hazlewood

The song that Rowland and Lydia would record, 'Some Velvet Morning', is the masterwork of a man who cut a singular path through the American music industry, pursuing a dream of making music that was 'not normal'. Sometimes called 'cowboy psychedelia', it's a strange brew of country and fairytale, mariachi and Greek tragedy, all served up in its author's suggestive, smouldering baritone. Hazlewood's songs were chart-toppers on both sides of the Atlantic but his novelistic albums, hauntingly orchestrated by Wrecking Crew regular Billy Strange and beautifully produced by himself, lay forgotten for decades – but for successive generations of musicians who kept rediscovering his elusive genius.

Barton Lee Hazlewood was born in Mannford, Oklahoma, in 1929, the son of an itinerant oilman, whose wanderings across the south imbued his son with a taste for the cowboy lifestyle and its music. Having served for his country in the Korean War, Lee began working as a songwriter and producer for rockabillies Sandford Clarke and Duane Eddy in 1956, hitting upon the novel idea of recording the latter's guitar inside a grain silo to really make it twang.

In 1965, after producing Dean Martin's take of his wandering man song 'Houston' – and bonding over a mutual love of whisky – Lee was asked by Frank Sinatra to come to the rescue of his daughter's career. Nancy Sinatra had been marketed as a sweet young pop thing and her career was floundering. Hazlewood had a song he'd written for Duane Eddy that might sound better coming from a girl. Issuing her with the instructions: 'You can't sing like Nancy Nice Lady any more. You have to sing for the truckers,' Lee recast 'These Boots Are Made for Walkin'' and Nancy staked her claim to immortality.

After performing 'Some Velvet Morning' together on a 1967 TV special Movin' with Nancy, *it was released as a single and then cast in its most majestic setting, 1968's* Nancy & Lee. *Its enigmatic riddle of a lyric and otherworldy layering of fey folk with rugged country, cloaked in Strange's psychedelic strings, crystallises a moment between the optimism of the Summer of Love and the darkness on the desert horizon that was manifested in rogue hippy Charles Manson.*

Nancy's singing on 'Some Velvet Morning' is more the voice of an elemental, heightened by the name Phaedra – in mythology, the treacherous wife of Theseus. Many of Hazlewood's songs, including Nancy & Lee's *'Summer Wine', involve sprite-like beings casting spells on cowboys that result in the loss of senses and spurs; and he based the logo of his record company LHI (Lee Hazlewood Industries) on a classical Greek profile.*

Sinatra would record another memorable album with the man she described as 'part Henry Higgins and part Sigmund Freud', Nancy & Lee Again *(1971), before he made a mysterious exit to Sweden at the height of his popularity. They reunited on her fiftieth birthday and played a series of gigs together in 1995, by which time Lee had become a cult figure, his songs recently covered by Gallon Drunk, the Earls of Suave and Tindersticks, not to mention Barry Adamson and Anita Lane's epic 1991 version of 'These Boots . . .'. Sonic Youth's Steve Shelley reissued a batch of Lee's albums on his Smells Like label and in 1999, Hazlewood was moved enough to release his first album for twenty years,* Farmisht, Flatulence, Origami, ARF!!! and Me *and appeared live at the Nick Cave-curated Meltdown festival at London's Royal Festival Hall. After enjoying his renaissance, Lee was diagnosed with cancer in 2006 and set about recording a farewell album,* Cake or Death, *which included Duane Eddy reinterpreting that song originally intended for him; and a new recording of 'Some Velvet Morning', which Lee duetted with his granddaughter – Phaedra is her name.*

He died peacefully at his home in Henderson, Nevada, in 2007, a few days after his seventy-eighth birthday party.

Gothmother: Bobbie Gentry

Another song recorded in the Los Angeles of the Summer of Love that sounded like it beamed in from another time, another place. Another singer-songwriter-producer who hailed from the south and did not walk the line. Bobbie Gentry's 'Ode to Billie Joe' held a nation spellbound on its 1967 release and has still never given up its secret. Its author, a smoky-eyed swamp witch with a towering cascade of raven tresses, remains one of the greatest mysteries of popular music history.

Bobbie Gentry was born Roberta Lee Streeter on 27 July 1942 on a farm owned by her grandparents, just outside the small town of Woodland, Mississippi, in the heart of the blues-haunted Delta. She remained there when her parents split, singing in church from the age of three and learning the piano her grandmother traded for one of her cows: 'I used to sit and listen to jazz music and blues music from New Orleans on an old battery-powered radio, then I'd go over to the piano and try to pick up the tunes. I always used to try to play on the black keys, because I remembered the lady who played in church always played on the black keys! I had no real playmates as a child, and so the piano became my best friend.'

At the age of thirteen she moved to Palm Springs to live with her singer-guitarist mother, Ruby Meyers. By then she had also mastered the guitar and banjo, as well as the art of the seamstress, standing out from her classmates by making her own eye-catching clothes. She was performing as a duo with her mother at the local country club when the 1952 King Vidor melodrama Ruby Gentry *gave her the idea for a stage name that was both homage to her roots and a reflection of Jennifer Jones' character in the film, who risks it all to rise above her poor background.*

Bobbie studied philosophy at UCLA before transferring to the Los Angeles Conservatory of Music, where she took composition, music theory and arranging, paying her way sewing and teaching guitar by day and singing and dancing by night. She began her recording career with rockabilly legend Jody Reynolds, cutting the single 'Stranger in the Mirror' with him in 1966. In the same year, she met Bobby Paris, blue-eyed soul singer of 'Night Owl' and Northern Soul hero. In return for her playing rhythm guitar for him, he engineered a demo of her songs, including 'Ode to Billie Joe'. This ended up on the desk of music publisher Larry Shayne and once she had a deal with him, Gentry was able to sell it to Capitol. With arranger Jimmie Haskell adding cinematic strings, Bobbie wove a dark tale of forbidden love and dark secrets in a rural outpost very much like the one where she grew up.

The central mystery of 'Ode to Billie Joe' – just what the song's narrator and her accomplice Billie Joe MacAllister were seen throwing off the Tallahatchie Bridge shortly before he launched himself off after it – Gentry never revealed.

There was even a 1976 film made with the same title, in which Bobbie gave screenwriter Herman Raucher free rein to interpret in any way he liked. His conclusion made the film a cult gay hit.

'Ode to Billie Joe' went to number one in America a month after its release, the album of the same name painting an intimate portrait of life in an America of cottonwoods and muddy waters, where stealing small pleasures in flowers, food and fooling around bring some longed-for colour to a dusty, hardscrabble world. Bobbie drew on her lonely childhood for lyrical insights and though the music paints the beauty of the landscape vividly, she does not romanticise it: the footstomping 'Mississippi Delta' contains an old Delta slave hex, while one of her few comments on 'Ode to Billie Joe' was her insight that: 'If [its characters] weren't indifferent to tragedy, they wouldn't be able to stand life as it really is.'

Like the siren of Tennessee, Dolly Parton, Bobbie took control over all aspects of her output from the start, writing and producing her six solo albums, designing her stage costumes and, in an unprecedented move, masterminding her own 1968 series for the BBC – the first time a female songwriter had been asked to host such a format. She had a golden touch with other people's material too – her cover of Bacharach and David's 'I'll Never Fall in Love Again' was a UK number one in 1969 and she made Betty LaVette's 'He Made a Woman Out of Me' and Mose Allison's 'Parchman Farm' sound like she'd written them herself. Her one album of duets with Glenn Campbell in 1968 is her most disappointing work –he was no Nancy to her Lee. But so complete was her talent that she even provided the cover art for her albums Patchwork *(1971) and* Fancy *(1970).*

From the latter came the hit single that drew a sly comparison with her own journey to fame and that of the song's courtesan, turned out by her mother one desperate night. 'It's difficult when a woman is attractive,' she would later understate, 'beauty is supposed to negate intelligence – which is ridiculous.' Nonetheless, she understood that implication, and the misogyny behind it, all too well: 'Just be nice to the gentlemen, Fancy/And they'll be nice to you.'

After the release of Patchwork *in 1971, Bobbie followed the route of Tupelo's most famous son and took up a residency in Las Vegas. Not only did she design her own bejewelled jumpsuit to wear and choreograph a Mardi Gras procession with six carnival floats as centrepiece of the show, but she also performed 'Lucy in the Sky with Diamonds' while swinging from a star-spangled trapeze.*

Then, in 1981, it all came to an end. Gentry called time on Vegas and the music industry, walked away from the spotlight and never looked back. Quite possibly, it was the smartest move any woman in the music industry has ever made: 'I might have been born just plain white trash/But Fancy was my name.'

CHAPTER 5

London After Dark

To the Batcave with the Banshees, Marc Almond, Annie Hogan, Foetus, the Immaculate Consumptive and f(r)iends, then on to Klub Foot for a Psychobilly freakout

Vyvyan: 'I must be hallucinating. What's a good thing for a hangover?'
Mike: 'Drinking heavily the night before.'

– *The Young Ones*: 'Nasty', first broadcast on BBC Two, 29 May 1984

One month after Prince Charles and Princess Diana announced the birth of their firstborn son, William Arthur Philip Louis, on 21 June 1982, a new club opened on a corner of London's Soho with a long history of infamy – number 69 Dean Street. Not unknown to royalty, this townhouse at the junction of Meard Street was once the love nest of King Charles II's mistress, the celebrated actress Nell Gwyn. It went on to further notoriety as the Gargoyle Club when David Tennant – brother of Bright Young Thing and Bowie/New Romantic role model, Stephen – took a fifty-year lease on it in 1925. He invited Henri Matisse, Edwin Lutyens and Augustus John to design the interiors and Somerset Maugham, Noël Coward, Virginia Woolf, Duncan

Grant, Nancy Cunard and Dame Edith Sitwell to dance the night away at its opening.

Singer Olli Wisdom and guitarist Jon Klein could not have found a more ideal location when they needed a regular gig for their band, Specimen, and were offered a free Wednesday night slot in the top-floor room there, above what had since become the Nell Gwyn strip club.[1] Though still shy of a label, the idea of starting a club where they were the house band proved to be a smart one, as Specimen took the lead in the new scene fermenting in the capital. With a nod to Adam West and a wink to the *Rocky Horror Show* costume department, they called it the Batcave – and its signal was soon attracting a guest list of Dark Young Things every bit as impressive as Tennant's.

You entered the club via the same small, rickety lift that was bringing down the strippers from the end of their shift. Then a doorway framed by a real coffin was the portal to this underworld, theatrically transformed into themed areas, some showing 8mm movies and promo videos, others offering cage dancers, drag acts, fire-eaters and mud wrestling – this being Soho, after all. Specimen's keyboard player and pin-up, sweet transvestite Jonny 'Slut' Melton, described the scene beautifully in Mick Mercer's *Gothic Rock*: 'It was a light bulb for all the freaks and people like myself who were from the sticks and wanted a bit more from life. Freaks, weirdos, sexual deviants . . . There's people around who'll always be attracted by something shiny, glittering, exciting . . . The Batcave was more Gotham City than Aleister Crowley.'[2]

Marc and the Mambas' Annie Hogan and Hamish MacDonald of Sexbeat were regular DJs, spinning sets that included rockabilly, old school R&B, soundtracks and exotica as well as glam staples and the latest releases from the Banshees, the Cramps, Killing Joke, Bauhaus and the Birthday Party. Nearly all of whom were to be found cavorting, plotting and propping up the bar of a Wednesday evening, catching a rampant dose of what older residents of the 'Dirty Dozen' streets in this area of London would diagnose as 'Sohoitis'. From one band arriving at midnight, three offshoots might well have emerged before the first light of dawn.

Daughters of Darkness

Top of the guest list would be Siouxsie and the Banshees, who had just begun work on their fifth album, *A Kiss in the Dreamhouse*, at producer Mike Hedges' Playground studio in Camden Town. This would turn out to be their third and final LP with John McGeoch and followed another tumultuous period in the band's history.

Since we last saw them, at the end of the Join Hands tour in 1979, Sioux and Severin had reassembled what they hoped was – and many still regard as – an unbeatable line-up. Following the break-up of Magazine, and after a brief dalliance in Visage with Barry Adamson and Dave Formula, John McGeoch had been persuaded to throw in his lot with the Banshees. For Budgie (b. 21 August 1957 in St Helen's, Lancashire), this was more of a fateful progression – he had played his first ever gig as a drummer for the Spitfire Boys,[3] while supporting Siouxsie at Liverpool's Eric's in 1977. The experience led him astray from the career in fine art he had been studying for.

Budgie would go on to play in Liverpool's punk supergroup Big in Japan, whose revolving line-up also contained, at various times, Jayne Casey, Holly Johnson, Ian Broudie, Clive Langer, Bill Drummond and Dave Balfe. But it was his work on the Slits' Dennis Bovell-produced *Cut* album of 1979 that marked him out as the era's most innovative drummer. Founded on a love of ska – the Upsetters' 'Return of Django' was the first record he ever bought – and strange Mancunian beat beasts like Hotlegs' 'Neanderthal Man' and John Kongos' 'He's Gonna Step On You Again', Budgie's polyrhythmic beats hit the space between reggae, jazz, funk and punk. 'Buddy Rich is the guy I want to be,' he told writer Tom Vague, 'but Animal is the guy I really am.'

Those innate abilities were given immediate rein on the drumless demos he received from Sioux and Severin. 'I remember my introduction to the first song I played with them,' he told *Peek-a-Boo*'s Danil Volohov, '"Red Light" starts like mechanized beats, like the shutter of a camera and so it wasn't punk! I felt like I was straight away allowed to be an inventor.'[4]

The new Banshees' sound was debuted on the 'Happy House' single of March 1980. Its proto-Tim Burton video – actually directed by Clive Richardson – had Budgie and Severin performing in an *Alice in Wonderland*-style multi-dimensional house while Sioux, wearing a Harlequin costume, strums a ukulele and peers through the window as the rooms grow bigger and smaller.[5]

'Christine', the subject of their next single, did indeed turn out to be the same person(s) as Molly Fountain's neighbour in *To the Devil a Daughter* – or at least, she sprang from the same source. The original 'banana-split lady' was Christine Beauchamp, the patient in Morton Prince's 1906 *The Dissociation of a Personality*, who had a 'bad' self she believed was controlled by the Devil. In 1957, psychiatrists Corbett H. Thigpen and Hervey M. Cleckley published *The Three Faces of Eve* about another Christine suffering from disassociated personality disorder. Dramatised as an Oscar-winning film the same year, this was the story of Chris Costner Sizemore, who had a good self, 'Eve White', and a bad self, 'Eve Black' – by no coincidence, the name of the track on 'Christine''s flip.

Kaleidoscope, the album that followed on 1 August 1980, was as multi-faceted as its name implies. The band had gelled immediately as they got into the studio, exploring the use of synthesisers and drum machines for the first time on tracks like 'Red Light' and 'Lunar Camel', and with McGeoch's crystalline guitar refracting all the colours through their midst. Hitting their stride as a unit, they released the single 'Israel' in November 1980 and stylishly got the last word on any lingering NF elements in their audience by performing it wearing Star of David T-shirts. Tom Vague records skinheads chanting '*Sieg Heil!*' (Hail Victory!) to the band at Derby Assembly Rooms in February 1981, at which point they left the stage, returned wearing said shirts and proceeded to play 'Drop Dead': 'Siouxsie's vocals are even more venomous than when they were applied to Morris and McKay,' he noted. 'The skins drift off into obscurity, probably not realising the significance of the Star of David.'[6] 'Israel' was recorded with a Welsh choir to add to its festive feeling. By contrast, the band's next album was a venture into the heart of darkness very much influenced by current events.

On 2 January 1981, a man loitering in a car with a young woman in Sheffield's red-light district was arrested by a couple of suspicious beat bobbies. Sgt Bob Ring and probation officer PC Robert Hydes had finally managed to do what the rest of the West Yorkshire force had been unable to achieve for the past half-decade and apprehend the Yorkshire Ripper. Thirty-four-year-old lorry driver Peter Sutcliffe – who had been questioned by detectives and released nine times previously – was charged with thirteen counts of murder, tried at the Old Bailey and found guilty on 22 May 1981. Less than three weeks later, on 6 June, the Banshees released the album they had forged while he was still at large, a terrifying séance of black magic and murder called *Ju Ju*.

Honed in the live arena, it was, remembered Severin, 'the first time we'd made, for want of a better word, a "concept" album that drew on darker elements'.[7] These included the subjects of witchcraft and voodoo, a nod to the maestro Alfred Hitchcock on 'Spellbound' and a Scheherazade-cloaked tale of female oppression on 'Arabian Knights', both of which made intoxicating singles. But the real horror played out on its centrepiece, 'Night Shift', a song that hit much closer to home.

Long before the police caught up with Sutcliffe, it seemed that Siouxsie – who had spent her precarious teenage years in private clubs with runaways and sex workers – had divined exactly what kind of predator this phantom Ripper was, perceptively fashioning a Photofit of a man 'always silent and kind, unlike the others' with his vocational 'love with a knife'. As survivors of his attacks testified, Sutcliffe disarmed his prey with his dapper appearance and remarks about the weather before hitting them over the head with a ball-peen hammer. Attempting to plead insanity in court, he claimed to have heard the voice of God commanding him to kill while working as a gravedigger. The violence of 'Night Shift''s lyrical exoration to annihilate all of femalekind inhabited his blank heart. Bringing the bleak Pennines' weather with them, McGeoch's guitar fills in the lightning flashes of the hate-charged atmosphere, while hard rain beats its tattoo from Budgie's clattering drumsticks.

Preceding 'Night Shift' – and ending side one on a suitable note of foreboding – the relentlessly mechanistic 'Monitor' imagines snuff movies made for mass entertainment and an Orwellian crime prevention technique. In the age of the video nasty – when, before the intervention of conservative activist Mary Whitehouse, my eleven-year-old brother could have checked out uncertificated copies of *I Spit on Your Grave*, *Driller Killer* and *Cannibal Holocaust* from our local petrol station – this scenario did not seem too implausible. Nor did the audience's collusion when the victim seems to stare accusingly out of the screen: 'As if her pain was our fault/But that's entertainment'.

Listening from the flat field, *Ju Ju* came to me as a warning. That the spookiest 'it happened to me' ghost story spun in the Belton bus shelter, the goriest horror film the garage had to offer, all those Dennis Wheatley and James Herbert paperbacks – even the perceived padding of Old Shuck's feet behind me on the long, unlit walk home – were as nothing to the terrors one apparently normal man was capable of. A bitter truth I would recognise decades later, in the black novels of Derek Raymond and David Peace, but one that was never quite so viscerally conveyed as in the time of the Ripper by the combination of Siouxsie's voice and John McGeoch's guitar.

Creatures of the Night

Though it was Siouxsie and Budgie who were creating the off-stage fireworks. The track 'But Not Them', recorded during the *Ju Ju* sessions while Severin and McGeoch were taking a break, rapidly evolved into *The Wild Thing* EP by the Creatures, released on 25 September 1981 as a twin-pack of 7-inch singles. The cover shot featured the couple doing a good approximation of the wild thing in a hotel room shower. Romantically, Severin and Sioux had since gone their separate ways without acrimony – it was Severin who came up with the name for the Creatures' debut, thinking it sounded like the music the monsters were dancing to in Maurice Sendak's 1963 children's classic, *Where the Wild Things Are*. But manager Nils Stevenson was also a former beau of Siouxsie's and he didn't find this new situation half so much fun.

His relationship with her and the rest of the band unravelled, both personally and professionally, on the Banshees' five-month tour of Europe and the States, coming to a head at a Peppermint Lounge show in New York on 13 November 1981. 'One particular situation got out of control and John pinned him up against a wall and said, "Just fucking go home,"' Sioux told *Uncut*'s Garry Mullholland. 'He was too obsessive towards me and I felt suffocated by it.'[8]

Stevenson was fired shortly afterwards.

Returning home, Severin continued a conversation begun with Lydia Lunch and Banshees' guitar tech Murray Mitchell, back in New York. Together with Kristian Hoffman, they began performing what Lydia called 'the first spontaneous rock improv' as the Agony Is the Ecstasy, in support to the Birthday Party. Their act was underpinned with a prerecorded backing track of atmospheric guitar, drums and sound effects made by Mitchell and Hoffman, which the ensemble embellished live, in performances described by Murray as 'totally freeform feedback with Lydia ranting over the top. To say it wasn't well received is an understatement. By the time we got to Hammersmith Palais there were three thousand people chanting: "Fuck off!"'[9]

One of these dates, at the Venue on 26 November 1981, was captured on *The Agony Is the Ecstasy*, a split live EP with the Birthday Party's *Drunk on the Pope's Blood* on its flip, released by 4AD in February 1982 – the perfect Bloody Valentine's gift. Rowland and Lydia's cover of Nancy and Lee's 'Some Velvet Morning', backed with their own 'I Fell in Love with a Ghost' followed on as a 4AD 12-inch with Barry Adamson playing double bass, Mick Harvey on drums and Genevieve McGuckin's piano.[10] By this time, Barry was also standing in on bass for the Birthday Party.

Shortly after the band had returned to Melbourne to record their second album, *Junkyard* with Tony Cohen in December 1981,

Tracy Pew was arrested for drunk driving. When he gave his name as Peter Sutcliffe – actually, one of his Melbourne friends but an unfortunate coincidence – suspicious police uncovered two more outstanding warrants for minor theft in his real name and Pew was sent to a labour farm for eight months. Phill Calvert's shortcomings were further revealed during recording, with Mick Harvey able to do what producer Cohen called 'animal drumming' much more convincingly than he could.[11] Calvert would not last much longer, playing his final gig with the band at *Zig Zag* magazine's club night in Westbourne Grove on 10 July 1982.

As well as the Banshees, the Batcave became a regular place to hang for Nick Cave, Barry Adamson, Lydia Lunch and Jim 'Foetus' Thirlwell – all of whom were now living in west London, between Ladbroke Grove, Earl's Court and Chelsea. Joining them at the bar were two other pivotal figures in our story. Blixa Bargeld, of Berlin's premier experimental noise terrorists Einstürzende Neubauten, who had met the Birthday Party at a gig in Amsterdam in June 1982 and would shortly be helping them to relocate in his home city; and chart-topping Northern Soul transformer, Marc Almond of Soft Cell.

Non-Stop Erotic Cabaret

Marc Almond and Dave Ball met at Leeds Polytechnic (now Leeds Beckett University) in the year that the two sevens clashed. Almond (b. 9 July 1957) was studying performance art, a slight, kohl-eyed boy who looked like Judy Garland, slept under pin-ups of Diana Dors and Jayne Mansfield and, for his degree, wrote theatre shows called *Glamour in Squalor*, *Twilight and Lowlives* and *Zazou*, the latter of which was described by the *Yorkshire Post*'s critic as 'one of the most nihilistic depressing pieces that I have ever had the misfortune to see'.

Ball (b. 3 May 1959) was a burly Northern Soul boy with a huge record collection, a talent for computer technology and a knack for putting the two things together. Annie Hogan vividly recalled her first encounter with him at their student house in Leeds' Leicester Grove: 'I went into Dave's room and he was at his synth. Petula Clark's "Downtown" was playing through his synths and he was doing this amazing remix on the spot.' Both Ball and Almond grew up by the seaside – Dave in Blackpool, Marc in Southport – nurtured on the tacky glamour and transient cheap thrills of summer Saturday nights, the ever-present threat of violence and nausea that went with all the underage drinking and hormonal raging; and the consolations of Northern Soul all-nighters that come with being on the neo-Mod scooter run circuit. Marc had a formative Thursday night memory that tallies with my own experience of seeing 'Tainted Love' performed for the first time in August 1981, sandwiched between Anneka's 'Japanese Boy' and Shakin' Stevens' 'Marie Marie': 'When I was at home, watching T. Rex doing "Ride a White Swan" and David Bowie doing "Starman", everyone was so uncomfortable in the room. It was suggesting things that you never talked about with your family. Men wearing make-up and glitter and a sexuality that hinted at something else.'

Though a wave of synth bands labelled 'Futurists' were on the ascendant and would dominate the charts of the early Thatcher years, Soft Cell seemed more at home in the past. In the video for their next single, 'Bedsitter', Marc's reading matter was the same 1961 Penguin paperback edition of John Braine's *Room at the Top* that my parents had bought as students. Three years before Morrissey arrived dropping lines from Shelagh Delaney's *A Taste of Honey* (also 1961) on the Smiths' eponymous debut, Marc was already styling himself in winceyette pyjamas and an overflowing kitchen sink. In many ways, punk and its immediate aftermath recalled the era of Skiffle, Beat Boom and British New Wave Cinema, being a sudden window of opportunity from which smart working-class kids could steal their fortune. A northern dreamer with a penchant for brassy blondes and tall stories, Marc could have been a Billy Liar for the '80s – except for the fact that he and Dave *did* get on the train from Leeds to London. In the end destination of Soho, they fashioned their own version of an Angry Young Man novel, the *Non-Stop Erotic*

Cabaret album.[12] Along the way, they recorded demos with Daniel Miller and Pete Maben, which found their way to an exceptional young manager called Stevo Pearce.

Like Malcolm McLaren, Stevo also started his career on the King's Road, in his case as a sixteen-year-old DJ at the Chelsea Drugstore, playing music by the likes of Cabaret Voltaire, DAF and fellow Mute signings Fad Gadget and Non. As a key location in Kubrick's *A Clockwork Orange*, it was an appropriate venue for a young man whom the industry feared was a reincarnation of head Droog Alex. Stevo's Electro Tunes night moved to the Hammersmith Clarendon and earned the interest of *Record Mirror*, who got him to compile an electro chart for them, and then *Sounds*, who called his weekly listing the Futurist charts.[13] These comprised demo tapes by unsigned new bands, which, logically enough, he turned into a sampler called *Some Bizzare Album*.

As well as Soft Cell's 'The Girl with the Patent Leather Face', this also featured Depeche Mode's 'Photographic', Blancmange's 'Sad Day' and The The's 'Untitled'. But, strange as it is to relate now, the band that caught the ear of major label Phonogram, and led to them signing Soft Cell via Stevo's Some Bizzare label, were B-Movie. This poppy boy band from Mansfield reached number sixty-one in the charts with 'Remembrance Day' on Phonogram subsidiary Deram in 1981. At the same time, Soft Cell went to number one and subsequently sold 1.35 million copies of their cover of 'Tainted Love', a Northern Soul standard first performed by Marc Bolan's wife, Gloria Jones. Which came as a surprise even to the band, who had been cultivating an intimate, arty stage show with film and slide shows performed on a purpose-built set in the shape of a white padded cell with pink and blue neon bars, made with student friend Huw Feather. A band who told one of their earliest champions, *Record Mirror*'s Betty Page, 'We're more like a cabaret band than a rock band, really.'

It was this aesthetic that separated them from even their closest Futurist neighbours, Sheffield's Cabaret Voltaire and the Human League, whose Philip Oakey was no stranger to black eyeliner and lipstick and also cultivated a bit of a croon. Soft Cell were not about Brutalist architecture, motorways and J. G. Ballard. The electronic duo they had the most in common with was Suicide and they also adored *The Queen of Siam*. It wouldn't be long before Marc was performing an extraordinary version of Suicide's 'Ghost Rider' with Jim Thirlwell – who would sign his Foetus identity to Some Bizarre in 1983 – and covering 'Gloomy Sunday' himself. He liked to sing songs from a woman's perspective.

Which made Almond a bit of a dangerous figure, someone who parents recoiled from the way his own had from Bowie and Bolan – Phonogram had predicted as much when they asked him not to go on *Top of the Pops* looking the way he did. He was more likely to be a danger to himself than any corrupter of naive youth, though. The early '80s charts might have been populated by 'gender benders', as the popular press of the day put it, but this was still not a safe time to come out and admit you were gay. Punk had broken down barriers for bold women like Siouxsie and provided a haven for gay men and women within an established – and still clandestine – subculture in London and Manchester, but none of this had reached very far out into the provinces yet.

Even in big cities like Leeds to walk around looking suspiciously effeminate on a Saturday night was to take your life into your own hands, let alone smaller outposts like Great Yarmouth, where there was no such thing as a gay bar or club. Marc's performance sent out the signals to those who were able to decipher them, but in interviews he was deliberately ambiguous, always deflecting attention from his sexuality and using Diana Dors and Jayne Mansfield like metaphorical blonde bombshell bodyguards.

Once they were famous, Soft Cell used other deflective tactics to have fun with the scandal-hungry tabloids, who had been quick to discern that Marc was not like the other New Romantic/Futurist boys. Video maestro Tim Pope directed a mock-porn promo for *Non-Stop Erotic Cabaret*'s most deliberately provocative track, 'Sex Dwarf', featuring the titular person of restricted growth in fetish gear, chainsaw-wielding ladies of the night, raw meat, maggots and

Almond in a codpiece. It was banned immediately and remains so to this day though it didn't take my brother long to find a dodgy VHS of it – and not, I think, from the petrol station.

Twilights and Lowlives

As entranced by the gilded gutter life as those who had hobnobbed in the Gargoyle Club's golden age, Marc was a natural f(l)it for the Batcave. Both he and Ball became voracious collaborators outside of Soft Cell and in the corner of sinful Soho where Stevo's other protégés mixed, the side-projects flowed like Mortician's Martinis. Marc and the Mambas began life as a collaboration with fellow Some Bizarre artist, The The's Matt Johnson and Almond's former housemate, the inspired pianist and now resident Batcave DJ, Annie Hogan (b. 1961), whom he had first met when she was mixing up Glam, New Romantic and post-punk on the decks of Leeds' Amnesia Club.

Hogan relocated from Leeds to London at the same time as Almond, first staying in Lydia Lunch's flat on Westbourne Grove while Lunch was in the States: 'She had left her records, so I quickly discovered Yma Sumac's magnificent *Mambo!* (1954) and, although I already loved John Barry from a kid, Lydia had *Beat Girl* (1960), which just blew me away. *The Queen of Siam* was one of my all-time favorite LPs and I played them all down the Batcave. Marc and I did play there too, with backing tapes, a Farfisa organ and the Venomettes. We played a wild rendition of the Velvet Underground's "What Goes On" that night and I felt entrancingly inspired, the Velvets' spirit lingering. Then I'd go back to Lydia's flat and take Pervert the poodle for a walk and feel genuinely stimulated by everything going on around me.'

Their *Untitled* double album, recorded in the summer of 1982 and released that September on Some Bizzare, was both an introduction to friends Marc had made through Bowie – Scott Walker's 'Big Louise', Lou Reed's 'Caroline Says', Jacques Brel's 'If You Go Away' and Syd Barrett's 'Terrapin' – and a soundtrack to the night world around them. The title track and 'Angels' bear the signature of co-writer Matt Johnson, while the rest of the music was largely improvised by Hogan. One atmospheric interlude took its très Sohemian name from Marc's old stage production, 'Twilight and Lowlives'. Almond, Hogan and Johnson were joined by Cindy Ecstasy, the New Yorker who had provided sultry backing vocals on *Non-Stop Erotic Cabaret*'s 'Torch' and 'Memorabilia'; and photographer/sometime the The drummer Peter Ashworth on percussion.

'"Empty Eyes" was very much an on-the-spot track I came up with on electric piano and developed from there,' recalled Hogan. 'Marc and Cindy's backing vocals added a loose, 1960s girl group feel. It was that Velvet Underground influence which underpinned many of the tracks and gave the album an overall psychedelic feel.' Unconventionally released with one disc that played at 33 rpm and the other at 45, *Untitled* was a brave move, considered Annie: 'Soft Cell basically had a teenybopper audience, so to choose those covers – and even encourage my solo pseudo classical piano piece – must have split his fanbase.' But Almond was astute enough to realise that his most devout fans were the ones for whom this material would have the strongest resonance. The front cover painting depicted him with a halo. The back was a photomontage of Marc and collaborators hanging out with the likes of Divine and Andy Warhol – Soft Cell did very well in New York – and came with the line, 'It's my happening and I'm freaking out!', an exclamation like the one first uttered by transsexual svengali Z-Man Barzell in Russ Meyer and Roger Ebert's superb '60s satire, *Beyond the Valley of the Dolls* (1970). Yet more signals for those in the know.

The Batcave's supergroup, though, was an idea hatched there by Lydia, who had been asked by Danceteria in New York if she would put on a show for them at the most magical time of the year. She asked Marc Almond, Nick Cave and Jim Thirlwell – with whom she had just begun a long creative and romantic relationship – if they would like to go to New York for Halloween and join her in a Weimar-style cabaret she called the Immaculate Consumptive.

A setlist of covers and original new work was decided on and, like 'The Agony Is the Ecstacy', the ensemble first created backing tracks at Alvic Studios in West Kensington, where the Birthday Party had been working on additional material for *Junkyard*. They utilised the talents of Barry Adamson, Mick Harvey and Blixa Bargeld; and also Annie Hogan, who played piano on Cave's cover of Elvis's 'In the Ghetto' and would record a further track with him, 'Vixo', which appeared on her *Kickabye* EP of 1983.[14] It was Anita Lane who came up with the title *Kickabye*: 'Nick and Anita were the sweetest people to be with,' Hogan recalled, 'entirely kind, intelligent and funny.'

The Immaculate Consumptive played three shows, opening at the 9:30 Club without Thirlwell on 27 October, then going on to Danceteria on 30 and 31.[15] In the audience, Lydia's future manager Tom Garretson watched open-mouthed: 'It was the closest thing I've seen to the hysteria and friviolity of what Berlin cabaret was in Weimar . . . At one point Nick came out and was going to do a solo song on the piano and he told the audience: "We borrowed this piano from Brian Eno." He started playing and the piano broke so he started telling jokes . . .'[16] Eno's piano had been trashed the night before by Jim walking on it while performing 'Halo Flamin' Lead'. But, as Marc remembered, 'Nick came on and stole the whole show singing "In the Ghetto". It ended up being his show, really.'

In Fear of Fear

The Batcave's position on such a powerful Soho leyline was no doubt a reason Youth was also a regular in the year that 'Empire Song', the first single from Killing Joke's third album, *Revelations*, elevated them to their first appearance on *Top of the Pops*. But on that historic occasion, in March 1982, Paul Ferguson had to take over on lead vocals, while a heavily disguised figure in an outfit that could have been made for a deep-sea diving beekeeper masquer-aded behind Jaz Coleman's keyboards. Their singer had done a bunk on them, his whereabouts unknown to the rest of the band, until, on 3 April, *NME* reported that he was in Iceland, 'staying with local band Theyr (or Peyr, depending on your translation), a group who share Jaz's interest in the occult'.[17] Their manager, Gudni Agnarsson, explained they were 'building our own community beyond the system', including constructing a studio that could be operated underwater. 'We just know there will be disasters,' he went on to bespeak, 'so we want it to withstand the Last Wave. Jaz had his reasons for coming.'

This message was retranslated throughout the music press. Jaz had discovered that Margaret Thatcher was the antichrist. What's more, numerically her new suitor's name, Ronald Wilson Reagan, added up to 666. Coleman had foreseen the apocalypse and gone to perform a ritual on an Icelandic leyline to avert the end of the world. As usual, his predictions could be found encoded in the lyrics of his own sonic book of *Revelations*, released by EG in July 1982.

Killing Joke had enlisted the talents of distinguished Kosmische producer Conny Plank – famed for his work with Can, Neu!, Kraftwerk and DAF – after self-producing their second album, *What's THIS For . . .!* the year earlier. They wanted to learn more and Plank didn't dissappoint Ferguson and Geordie – especially when he compared the sounds they made on drums and guitar to his childhood memories of the noises of circling bombers and crackling radios during the Second World War.[18] Youth, however, was not happy at losing his autonomy in the studio. Fired up on a volatile mix of dope, speed and acid, the first incarnation of Killing Joke had become a ticking time bomb.

Witnessing them at work in Plank's HQ, just outside Cologne, *NME*'s Barney Hoskyns walked into the full black cloud of their budding paranoia. Jaz spoke about bringing his classical training to bear on the new material: 'We were experimenting with fourths, because in conventional music you're never allowed to use intervals of fourths, it produces an undesirable effect, just like in the litanies in church music.' Meanwhile, Plank, Hoskyns observed, had 'sluiced out the system, extracting the spleen from the guts of the sound and ridding the apocalyptic stomp of its unnecessary military bombast'.[19] This sonic clarity resulted in their most compelling – and foreboding – album to date. From the opening 'The Hum', through 'Empire Song', 'The Pandys Are Coming' and 'Land of Milk and Honey' to the closing 'Dregs', Killing Joke wove nightmarish nursery rhymes about the cost of colonialism and an inevitable, impending war.

Another parallel between the early '80s and the era of the Angry Young Men was the return of the Campaign for Nuclear Disarmament (CND). Founded in 1957 by philosopher Bertrand Russell, the organisation was supported by many musicians during the years 1958–62, when annual protest marches to and from the Atomic Weapons Research Establishment at Aldermaston, Berkshire, were organised. So it was at the coming of Trident, with CND membership between 1980 and 1983 increasing to 90,000 with 250,000 local branches. Marches and mass demos were back on, with Glastonbury Festival putting its weight behind the cause, raising £1 million in donations between 1981 and 1990[20] and Labour adopting a policy of unilateral nuclear disarmament at its 1982 conference. Killing Joke played the 1981 CND Rally in Trafalgar Square, which was attended by 250,000 people.[21]

Of all their *Revelations*, 'Empire Song' seemed most clairvoyant: 'Back to square one, and the old school backfire/It's just begun, let's watch the blind eyes turning,' Jaz intoned.

The day before the *NME* revealed Jaz's whereabouts, on 2 April 1982, Argentina invaded the British dependent territories in the South Atlantic: the Falkland Islands, South Georgia and the South Sandwich Islands. Thatcher's December 1981 rating as the most unpopular leader in post-war history – fanned by the summer of riots and unemployment reaching a record 3 million – was spectacularly reversed when she led the nation into battle. From 5 April, when the Royal Navy task force first set sail, until the Argentinian surrender on 14 June 1982, the Tories shot back to the top of the opinion polls for the first time since the 1979 election.[22] As if to give a divine blessing to Britain's retaking of the islands, Pope John Paul II began a visit to the UK as the Battle of Goose Green commenced on 28 May and was at Canterbury Cathedral the next day when the Argentines were defeated.[23]

Ronald Reagan, however, was not in a position to give Mrs Thatcher his full public support for the mission, since Argentina was a Cold War ally against the Soviet Union. Instead, he sent Secretary of State Alexander Haig to try to broker a peace deal between the two nations – much to Thatcher's fury. Still, this was no grounds for Ronnie and Maggie to break up. Within weeks the US were providing British troops with covert assistance,[24] and Reagan was given a state visit on which he became the first US President to address a joint session of Parliament. That same day, 8 June, forty-eight British servicemen en route to recapture the city of Stanley were killed when supply ships were bombed near Bluff Cove. But despite this catastrophe – along with the controversial torpedoing of the Argentine warship *General Belgrano* on Thatcher's order, and a further loss of 207 British servicemen plus three female civilians – this sudden test of the Iron Lady's mettle served to re-enchant the nation.[25]

Was this what Jaz had seen in his crystal ball? Over the years since, he has given several reasons for his flit to Iceland, the most Crowleyan being that he wanted to invoke his Holy Guardian Angel – as the Great Beast did when he spoke with Aiwass – and had the realisation that he needed to go back to his classical work. All was resolved once Coleman had written a symphony in the land of the Norse gods and thereby reconciled the two musical halves of his persona. Although, after Geordie had gone over to join him and took to the idea of living 'off grid' for a few months, it would take a bit longer for the rest of Killing Joke to see the funny side.

Back in London, a disgruntled Youth took a trip too far, had a psychotic episode and was hospitalised and given electric shock therapy after being caught trying to break and enter the Freemasons' Hall in Covent Garden.[26] Afterwards, he went his own way, rediscovering his Chic muse and creating dance music with future Justified Ancient of Mu Mu Jimmy Cauty in Brilliant; and making his name as a producer. Meanwhile Big Paul nursed a grudge for the way he had been left in the lurch that would continue to fester, despite the further sucesses that were coming the band's way.

Interview with the Vampire

And Northampton's children of the night, what music did they make? Parking the customised hearse they were using as a tour bus at the mouth of the Batcave,[27] Bauhaus used the venue to tackle their critics in the music press head-on. 'I've certainly never been as scared as when a rapier-thin Murphy darted into the crowd, grabbed me by the lapels and forced me backwards,' Mick Mercer recalled in *Gothic Rock*. 'There he was, with the lights of the strobes shooting up from the floor, suddenly smashing mirrors with the microphone stand . . . In the grip of the sodding vampire, mate!'[28]

By the time of their second album, *Mask* in October 1981, Bauhaus had been assigned back to 4AD mother-label Beggars Banquet due to the size of their audience, boosted by such chart forays as 'Telegram Sam', 'Kick in the Eye' and the fact that when Adam and the Ants released their shock pop crossover masterpiece *Kings of the Wild Frontier* in November 1981, their hardcore base deserted them to follow the hearse instead. With Banshees/Creatures/Cure producer Mike Hedges at the helm, *Mask* was an album of expansive evolution, with room for both the punchy, skeletal funk of 'Kick in the Eye' and 'In Fear of Fear' – the latter featuring a sax solo from Daniel Ash – and the epic fairytales 'The Passion of Lovers' and 'Hollow Hills', songs that invited the epic interpretive dancing with hand signals that became known as 'lightbulb changing' in the dark places of Great Yarmouth where such secretive rites were practised. The band even created their own Hammer Horror by sneaking into an abandoned shoe factory in their hometown that was due for demolition and filming the video for 'Mask', powering the impromptu set with their car batteries. 'It was really dangerous,' David Haskins told Loring Kent of website *Cover Our Tracks*. 'It was also situated directly across from the police station.'[29] Naturally, Murphy took the Christopher Lee role as an ancient, desiccated vampire who is reanimated with the help of the others' bodily fluids.

However, for Bauhaus's loudest and most determined critics, there was only one cracked actor Murphy was continually measured up against and found wanting. Never ones to shirk from confrontation, when their next single, 'Spirit' failed to crack the top thirty, they turned instead to a song originally recorded for a Radio 1 David 'Kid' Jensen *Session* – an audacious cover of 'Ziggy Stardust', released in plenty of time for Halloween 1982. The accompanying video, directed by Mick Calvert, was shot in another crumbling building – the basement of Camden's Roundhouse, the converted railway shed at the epicentre of the counter-culture during the '60s but, due to lack of funding for most of the ensuing decade, now in some state of disrepair. Bauhaus played to an ecstatic audience of fans on the stage where the Doors, Jimi Hendrix, Led Zeppelin, Pink Floyd and Bowie himself once trod. Then they wrapped the single in a David Haskins-designed sleeve that transposed the Ziggy flash over their own logo. Peaking at fifteen, it scored their highest-ever chart rating.

Less successful, however, was their attempt to put the frighteners up their most deadly critic, *Melody Maker*'s Steve Sutherland, when they dared him to an onstage verbal duel at the Lyceum on 14 October 1982. Standing his ground like Peter Cushing with a pair of candlesticks, the supremely self-confident Sutherland was able to talk his inquisitors into a corner – Murphy even ended up defending the journalist against the crowd's cat-calls.[30]

But this indignity did nothing to prevent their trajectory. It was upwards into Daniel Ash's stunning representation of a negative image of the sun that adorned the sleeve of 1982's self-produced *The Sky's Gone Out*. Confidently remaining in Berlin-Bowie territory with 'Swing the Heartache' and a cover of Brian Eno's 'Third Uncle', Bauhaus also reached for the moon with the ballad 'All We Ever Wanted Was Everything' and the triptych 'The Three Shadows', a return to the haunted landscape of 'Hollow Hills'. The atmosphere of these tracks converged with my reading of

Rosemary Sutcliff's renderings of ancient Britain and what might have gone on inside the ancient tumuli, barrows, standing stones and chalk carvings that chart the country's leylines. It seemed that every time Bauhaus got to the centre of the city where all roads meet – 69 Dean Street or the basement of the Roundhouse could both vie for the terminus of all Goth leys – they had to return to the fields. Though, perhaps indicative of the internal fault lines already starting to splinter the band into two factions, Murphy's most pertinent lyric was delivered on 'Silent Hedges': 'What happens when the intoxication of success has evaporated?'

His desire 'to be massive' would be achieved in 1983. First, when he appeared as the face of Maxell videotapes, staring down a wind machine from a black leather armchair in one of the most memorable TV ads of the decade. Then came the ultimate accolade – and a defiant two-talon salute to Steve Sutherland – their vindication by the Über Nosferatu. At the behest of film director Tony Scott, Bauhaus were invited to appear in the opening scenes of his 1983 adaptation of Whitley Strieber's *The Hunger*, performing 'Bela Lugosi's Dead' in the nightclub stalked by the film's vampire lovers – Catherine Deneuve and David Bowie himself. Their scene was shot, poetically enough, at another subterranean venue run from a former wine cellar beneath London's Charing Cross Station, the gay nightclub Heaven – but at the decidedly Dracula-unfriendly hour of 7.30 a.m. on 22 March 1982. The appearance of Bowie – 'sporting a very resplendent black silk suit and jet black pompadour wig' – as Kevin Haskins recounts in *Bauhaus Undead*, spurred Murphy on to 'an electrifying performance'. After they had wrapped their scene, much to Bauhaus's delight, Bowie drew the band around an old Wurlitzer jukebox in an adjacent room, making selections and sharing stories from his earliest Mod days, of watching the Kinks, the Yardbirds and the Pretty Things at Eel Pie Island and the original Marquee Club on Wardour Street.

Yet, just as Bauhaus sealed their most perfect moment in cinematic amber, everything started to disintegrate. Before they could begin recording their fourth album, *Burning from the Inside*, at Rockfield Studios in Monmouthshire, Murphy was hospitalised with pneumonia. Ash and David Haskins took over the production, raising one last top-thirty single with the baroque 'She's in Parties' and laying the ground for their future, Murphy-less work in Tones on Tail and Love and Rockets. The concluding song 'Hope' had Bauhaus fans weeping into their snakebite-and-blacks after the band played a final gig, at Hammersmith Palais, on 5 July 1983 and left *Burning from the Inside* to serve as their epitaph. 'I didn't want the band to end,' Murphy told *Uncut*'s Stephen Dalton in April 2008. 'But we were so up our arses, so repressed, we never really communicated. Being in that band was like being in a concentration camp. It was cold as ice, very British, very stuck-up. Not human.'

'Rest in peace,' were David Haskins' final words on the night, before the daylight flooded in and Bauhaus were out for the Count.

Some New Kind of Kick

The Batcave left its Dean Street belfry for a new destination at 28 Leicester Square in February 1983, then flittered over to Fooberts in Foubert Place before returning to roost at number 69 – which, having been through its New Romantic incarnation as Billy's was now renamed Gossips – in 1984. Despite – or maybe because of – the reverence in which the club's founders held them, the Cramps were not so impressed when they finally got to meet them.

'We had nothing to do with the Specimen supporting us,' Lux told *The Face*'s Fiona Russell Powell after they had shared the bill at a July 1984 gig at Hammersmith Palais. 'I saw them on TV one time and all they did was talk about their make-up for 15 minutes. It was *so* boring.'

But what had kept the Cramps so long? Falling foul of the IRS – in the shape of Miles Copeland's record company – and their perennial bad luck with finding second guitarists who could stick around, that's what.

Kid Congo Powers had seemed like the perfect match when he eloped with Lux and Ivy in 1980. The band recorded their second

LP, *Psychedelic Jungle*, at A&M Studios in Hollywood, a further history lesson for scholars of incredibly strange music, which this time took a detour around the acid-fried end of the '60s. Once more, Crampsified cover versions occupied half of the fourteen grooves, perfectly complementing new material and the Anton Corbijn cover-shot of the band seen through a fish-eye lens, lettered in shades of purple and green – a nod to *Pebbles 3*, in the series of compilation albums that had picked up the baton from *Nuggets* and were steadily cataloguing freakbeat releases from 1965–68. Once more, without studying the credits, it was difficult to discern which tracks were homage and which were Lux and Ivy originals – 'Goo Goo Muck', for instance, sounds like the natural descendent of 'Garbageman' but was actually first performed by Ronnie Cook & the Gaylads;[31] while 'Caveman' sounds like something Link Wray cooked up in his 3-Track Shack, but is really Kid Congo channelling those converted chickenhouse vibes through a Rorschach/Interior composition. 'One of the few overdubs was us screaming and throwing chairs and metal ashtrays around,' he recalled. 'That became a blueprint for my approach to making music.'[32]

The shows for *Psychedelic Jungle* saw the band reach peak levels of insanity – at Hammersmith Palais in the summer of 1981 Lux jumped into the audience; the next night at Brighton Top Rank he stripped off completely and ended the gig lying on the stage, rubbing his mic up and down a speaker to create a deafening wall of feedback – a spectacle he would go on to repeat throughout the European leg of the tour, coming close to getting the band arrested. 'I'd have to pull that whole scam every time he wrecked the joint,' Ivy told *Vive Le Rock!*'s Dick Porter. 'I'd have to say, "I don't know what got into him – I'm scared to be near him!" And they'd feel so sorry for me they'd say, "Okay now, just go."'[33]

But, despite the success of these gigs, the band were getting little financial support from their record company. Unhappy with both their lack of forthcoming royalties and the way the 12-inch of 'The Crusher' single had been rushed out with a demo version of 'Some New Kind of Kick' on its flip, the band issued a lawsuit against IRS in January 1982. While pending, they could release no further new material, so they took to playing covers-only gigs. It didn't take long for enterprising elements of their audience to start taping these and rush-releasing poor-quality bootlegs masquerading as official merchandise. Affronted on both sides, the Cramps stopped playing at all – and Kid's activities led him back to his original guitar teacher and fellow recreational substance enthusiast, Jeffrey Lee Pierce. 'I was going on with my life – and my life included doing a lot of drugs,' Powers told Dick Porter. 'I really reconnected with Jeffrey at this point. I was kind of itching to record with [him].'

Meanwhile, Ivy boned up on her law studies, learning enough to eventually take over all management duties, and she and Lux also poured their energies into recording a demo, which they used to sketch out powerful new material including 'The Most Exalted Potentate of Love' and Lux's homage to childhood inspiration Ghoulardi, 'Call of the Wighat'. In February 1983, the band played two shows at the Peppermint Lounge that were recorded and eventually released as *Smell of Female* in November, after IRS finally made an out-of-court settlement in September. Cramps' fans had been dealt another IRS re-release of old material, *Off the Bone*, back in June – a compilation that even cover artist and ardent Cramps' fan Graham Humphries didn't know had come out without the band's blessing. Copeland's crew would release a similar, cynical reiteration, *Bad Music for Bad People*, in June 1984.

At least the Cramps were able to work out an amicable parting deal with Kid. 'It was quite undramatic,' Congo Powers told Dick Porter. 'And I was on so much heroin it wouldn't have mattered to me anyway.' Nick Knox's brother Ike replaced him in the band that arrived back in Britain in 1984. And the man who had helped Ivy release *Smell of Female* was a true rockabilly rebel. He'd been promoting the cause since the days of punk and was now overseeing the birth of the two scenes' outrageous mutant offspring: Psychobilly.

Rockabilly Psychosis and the Garage Disease

Belfast natives Roger Armstrong and Ted Carroll had both dabbled in band management, with Horslips and Thin Lizzy respectively, before joining forces in London in 1975. Their fledgling Chiswick label was funded by a stall they ran, selling rare rockabilly records to punks on London's Golborne Road and catering to the connoisseurs at legendary Teddy Boy pub the White Hart in Tottenham, 'where you could get a retro band, a pint and a good kickin' if you didn't look the part,' as Roger recalled. Fortunately, the ever-stylish Ted and Roger were 'given the nod' by legendary King of the Teds, Sunglasses Ron, and so were able to thrive on both sides of what, by 1977, would become a yawning tribal chasm between the punks and their bequiffed forefathers. Joined by former EMI/Tamla Motown employee Trevor Churchill, they began putting out records by new bands such as Whirlwind, who despite being 'a very straight-ahead rockin' outfit, were not part of the old Teds scene'; as well as reissuing pivotal back catalogue by Link Wray.

By 1979, the Teds vs Punks King's Road showdowns had passed into legend and new bands eschewed the trad Ted watering holes in favour of punk clubs. Bands like the Polecats, featuring future Morrissey collaborator Boz Boorer, the influential Levi Dexter & the Ripchords and wandering Americans, Stray Cats, whose smash-hit eponymous debut of 1981 was produced by Rockpile singer-guitarist, Chiswick associate, roots music enthusiast and all-round genius Dave Edmunds.[34] At the same time, the *Pebbles* albums had begun to spawn more exciting, stripped-down sounds from the likes of Billy Childish's the Milkshakes (originally Mickie and the Milkshakes) from Chatham, Kent.

'The two scenes collided and found common cause in wild rock 'n' roll hybrids,' Armstrong considered. 'I don't think that punk rock and Psychobilly were ever bed-fellows, they just shared an attitude. By then, punk rock was sort of over, and so Psychobilly, as it had been named, became the place to be young and go berserk. Of course looming over all of the bands were the Godfathers/

Mothers of the whole scene – the Cramps.' Roger, Ted and Trevor responded with two labels that catered for their concurrent obsessions. Big Beat for the new bands, including the Cramps, who they licensed direct from Ivy, and Ace – named after, and with the blessing of, the original Mississippi label – for re-releases of the kind of lost classics they had been selling on their original stall.

One of the architects of Psychobilly was Nick Garrard, who began managing a rockabilly three-piece called Raw Deal, whom he renamed the Meteors in 1979. Inspired by the Cramps and his love of both punk and straight 'billy, he saw the way forward as 'a fusion between the two styles'. With the talents of bassist Nigel Lewis, drummer Mark Robertson and singer-guitarist P. Paul Fenech, it didn't take long for his theory to be proved right. The release of the 'Meteor Madness' and 'Radiocative Kid' EPs (both 1981) on Big Beat proved that the world was ready for psychotic tales of mutant teenagers set to a stomping, horrorbilly beat.

Along with *Smell of Female*, these two EPs inspired an eruption of rockabilly psychosis. Bands began picking up guitars and double basses, teasing their hair into gravity-defying pompadours and generally psyching out. Leading lights were the Guana Batz, Frenzy and Batmobile, along with the more garage-inspired Sting-rays, the Vibes and so-called 'Cowpunk' bands like the Shillelagh Sisters – who more closely resembled the Pogues – and the magnificently named Blubbery Hellbellies. For Sting-rays' singer Bal Croce, this was a golden era: 'People would actually pay to see me jump up and down! The rest of the band were very talented, but as I had absolutely no musical ability at all, it was the perfect vehicle. Oh, and our proudest achievement – apparently we were the most graffitied-about band in the toilets at Hampstead Girls School, circa 1984.'

Perhaps the most spectacular – and certainly the most commercially successful – band to emerge from this wave was also the one with the biggest barnets and most comical attitude. King Kurt had names like Smeg, Thwack and Maggott. Their mascot was a rat and their gigs resembled the set of Saturday morning anarchic kids' show *Tiswas*, with flour, eggs and shaving foam splattered about with gay abandon. Sometimes they only allowed men in if they were wearing dresses. On one infamous occasion, a schoolboy boasted he'd lost his virginity *onstage* at a Kurt koncert.

'Yes, our audiences liked being humiliated,' recalled guitarist Paul Laventhol, aka Thwack, noting that – as 'Monitor' predicted – nowadays, 'we find this is the basis for all popular entertainment.' Kurt snagged themselves a deal with Stiff and Dave Edmunds stepped up once more to produce their debut LP, *Ooh Wallah Wallah.* The single 'Destination Zululand' hit the charts in 1983. They might have seemed like the least serious of the Psychobillies, but Paul considers the band were a necessary reaction to the Thatcher years: 'Art always thrives under oppressive regimes. We did a march when Ken [Livingstone] was head of the GLC [Greater London Council] and he made all the fares really cheap – then Thatcher overruled him and disbanded the GLC and we played "The Way I Walk" on the back of a truck.'

Pyschobilly's dancehall was the same Victorian boozer in Hammersmith that had given the world Stevo: the Clarendon. Klub Foot was run by punk promoter John Curd from its packed first floor. 'The night the first *Stompin' at the Klub Foot* LP was recorded, I think they rammed 1,200 people into the venue – flouting all known fire regs,' recalled Sting-rays' guitarist Mark Hosking. 'We couldn't get off the stage – never mind anywhere near the bar . . .' Bal Croce still marvels at the memory: 'Packed, sweaty, usually pretty violent – but great atmosphere. I remember a lot of punch-ups at our gigs – and slightly ashamed to say, it didn't half add to the night.' Nick Garrard's memories were similarly golden: 'The groupies, the riders, the free beer! The joy of John Curd ringing up and asking if you wanted to support the Cramps or Killing Joke, bands who you loved.' The *Stompin' at the Klub Foot* LPs, on Curd's ABC label, and Ace's *Rockabilly Psychosis and the Garage Disease* caught the scene at its sweaty height.

'It was a broad church, and even the Pogues sort of came out of it,' Roger Armstrong considered. 'It was all about taking music from the past and being irreverent about it at the same time as having an obvious love of it.' Indeed, Bal Croce remembers the first Pogues' gig – supporting the Sting-rays, the Milkshakes and the Cannibals at the 100 Club – Shane MacGowan's crew then billed as the Black Velvet Underground.

But in 1984, Lux raised an eyebrow at the thought of being the scene's Godfather, summarily dismissing these bands: 'I don't think they're *psycho* at all!' That's probably because, as Armstrong said: 'The Cramps are not part of a scene. It's their life's work. They can't grow out the green quiff and get a day job.'

Gothfather: Link Wray

'I was in the death house, dying from my army wounds, and God says: "Hey! We gotta help this guy!" And he gives me "Rumble". Zap!' This was how Link Wray described how he conceived his most notorious 45, the banned 1958 instrumental, when I met him in 1993. With a new LP called Indian Child *out on Epic, a new grunge audience who had come to him through namechecks by Nirvana and his '50s back catalogue all dusted down and rereleased by Ace, he was playing UK shows with devotees the Fall as his backing band. It was one of the periodic highs in his whirlwind of a life.*

Frederick Lincoln Wray Jr was born on 2 May 1929 in Dunn, North Carolina. His parents were Shawnee, but living in a town that was basically run by the Ku Klux Klan, they lived a precarious existence, passing as white. 'I was brought up on the blues, the painful music,' he recalled. 'When I was eight years old, this old black blues guy named Hambone showed me the way. He tuned my guitar for me and played his music at me and that was that. And I got into it, 'cos I was never going to be educated.' Utilising this raw talent, he formed his first band with brothers Vernon (1924–79) on bass and Doug (1933–84) on drums. Link Wray & the Wraymen sounded like they'd just stepped out of a flying saucer movie.

Drafted in 1951, like Harry Crews and Lee Hazlewood, Link fought in the Korean War (1950–53), where he contracted tuberculosis and had to have a lung removed. Surgeons predicted he would never sing again, but instead his year-long hospitalisation gave him the idea that would make his name – bringing the machine-gun sounds of mechanised warfare into rock 'n' roll. While Lee used a grain silo to create Duane Eddy's twangtastic sound, Link's approach was to kick a hole in his speaker until he achieved the desired effect: 'When "Rumble" came out it was like: "Hey! That's not Elvis! That's not Chuck Berry! Who is this insane person?" I had to create my own fuzzbox, right? I couldn't buy it, 'cos it wasn't there!'

With his two brothers, he moved to Washington DC, where the fearsome sounds of 'Rumble', 'Run Chicken Run', 'Ace of Spades', 'Comanche' and 'Jack the Ripper' went down a treat in the 'knifer club' where the Wraymen took up residency.

'The first night I came in, the bouncer took out a .45 and stuck it in my guts and said: "Are you scared, Link?" I said, "Shoot, no, I been dead already, shoot the motherfucker!"' Eventually tiring of the hazardous biker nightlife, he and his siblings settled on a farm in Accokeek, Maryland, where they created their 3-Track Shack out of a chickenhouse, recording with the sounds of the indigenous wildlife around them as back-up. In 1977, rockabilly revivalist Robert Gordon ('Bryan Ferry carried to the logical conclusion,' according to Trouser Press's *Jon Young) made a record with him, which, together with the Cramps' incessant championing, brought him to the attention of the punk generation. But, despite peaks of recognition – an inclusion on the* Pulp Fiction *soundtrack was the commercial crown of the grunge years – Wray was beset by hard times. He fell out with his brothers in the late '70s and, in a strange parallel to Lee's Swedish sojourn, ended his days in Copenhagen with his fourth wife, Danish national Olive Povlsen Wray, passing from heart failure in 2005 at the age of seventy-six. Four years later, the Library of Congress selected 'Rumble' to go into their National Recording Registry for 2008, an honour for recordings that are 'culturally, historically or aesthetically significant'. It was further selected for the Rock and Roll Hall of Fame in 2019. Whatever would he have made of his newfound respectability?*

It wasn't just that Link's guitar sounded scarier than anyone else's. In his black leathers and with his monumental raven pompadour, he walked the walk more convincingly than any of his peers – just ask any bouncer. It was Wray's verboten 'Rumble' that would turn the ear of the choirboy Jimmy Page, electrify the young Pete Townshend and call Poison Ivy to do what she did, remaining her formative influence: 'He had the most apocalyptic, monumental sound I ever heard.' He was, after all, a kindred spirit. 'I only live for rock 'n' roll,' he told me. 'I don't believe in politics, I don't believe in tradition, I just believe in my music.'

Gothmother: Nico

'And what costume shall the poor girl wear to all tommorow's parties? . . . A hand-me-down dress from who-knows-where?'

Nico sang Lou Reed's words to 'All Tomorrow's Parties' on 1967's The Velvet Underground and Nico, *her double-tracked vocals betraying no emotion. They described what Reed had seen going on, night after night, in Andy Warhol's Factory: the parades of Times Square transvestites, Uptown socialites, wannabe actors, singers, dancers, models and hustlers from across the United States and beyond, who passed through its silver-lined walls for the Pop Artist's delectation. Yet what makes her vocal so powerful is the story the nineteen-year-old German was concealing behind the flawless façade of Andy's 'Pop Girl of '66'.*

Christa Päffgen was born in a perilous place at a dangerous moment in time: Cologne in 1938. Her Catholic father Wilhelm was the scion of a wealthy brewing dynasty, her mother Grete a working-class Protestant. At the outbreak of the Second World War, Wilhelm was conscripted in the Wehrmacht, his spouse and daughter cut off by his disapproving family. Following a nightmarish few months when she was forced to leave Christa in an orphanage while taking up work in an armaments factory, Grete moved them both to live with her parents in the Spreewald Forest, just outside Berlin. Here, they were relatively safe from bombardment – though Nico would later recall seeing the trains bound for Auschwitz pass by, describing the rail lines as 'a ribbon of death'. She would never see her father again – accounts of his demise vary, all equally grim – and his shade would haunt her ever after. Her biographer Jennifer Otter Bickerdike suggests that when, as an aspiring model in her early teens, the fashion photographer Herbert Tobias renamed her 'Nico', this new identity created a 'protective shield' around her.

It certainly worked. She rapidly moved through the epicentres of the fashion world: Paris, New York, Milan and London, becoming fluent in seven languages. Federico Fellini gave her a role in La Dolce Vita *(1960), Jean Paul Belmondo in* A Man Named Rocca *(1961) and her first single 'I'm Not Saying' was written by ill-fated Rolling Stone Brian Jones and produced by Jimmy Page. It was Jones who introduced Nico to Warhol and she was soon starring in his and Paul Morrissey's experimental films, most famously* Chelsea Girls, *in her golden year of 1966. After singing with the Velvet Underground, she recorded her own 1967 album* Chelsea Girl, *with songs by Greenwich Village folksinger friends Tim Hardin and Bob Dylan. It was Jim Morrison – 'my soul brother', as she described him – who suggested she should write her own. The resulting* The Marble Index *(1968), recorded with John Cale, returned to the forests of her past. There, she discovered the harmonium and patterned her vocals around rhythms created on the instrument, recording those two things separately first. Cale then fashioned sounds around her mesmeric drone that suggest the tumultuous journeys of her past: electric viola, glockenspiel, bells and a bosun's pipe. When she first heard the finished product, he recalled, she burst into tears.*

Two more albums followed, Desertshore *(1970, produced by Cale and Joe Boyd) and* The End . . . *(1974, produced by Cale). By this time, she had grown back her natural dark hair and dressed in black, the weird sister of her Warhol incarnation, whose music anticipated Joy Division's glacial urban tundra and the Banshees' enchanted netherworld. Sharing a taste for courting controversy, with Brian Eno on synth and Cale on piano, she triggered a riot in Berlin performing the German National Anthem (also performed on* The End . . .*) live, complete with verses that had been banned after 1945 because of their association with Hitler.*

In October 1978, just as Sid Vicious was arrested for the murder of his girlfriend Nancy Spungen, she briefly toured with the Banshees. Far from finding an understanding audience, she was bottled onstage by angry punks and left the tour after only three dates. Her typically uncompromising response: 'If I had a machine gun, I would shoot you all.' Though she did share one thing in common with Vicious, himself nicknamed after a Lou Reed song – a heroin addiction that would last the rest of her days. She would find another (platonic) soulmate – and drug buddy – in John Cooper Clarke. Relocating first to Manchester, then to Brixton with him, she made music with Blue Orchids and the Invisible Girls, appeared at the pivotal 1982 Futurama Festival and, despite the drugs and almost constant poverty, remained productive both in the studio and live. Many who were close to her describe how she wilfully deconstructed her once-perfect appearance when that protective shield turned into a gilded cage of idealised femininity, glimpsing flashes of creative freedom only through her music.

Nico made her last recording with Cale, Camera Obscura, *in 1985. Developing an interest in Egyptian music, she was getting a new band together in 1988 when she recorded what was fated to be her last vocal performance, 'Your Kisses Burn', a duet with Marc Almond for his* The Stars We Are *album. The experience did not go quite as Almond and his musical arranger Annie Hogan had hoped.*

'When we came to do the song, it became very evident that it was very difficult for her,' he said. 'She was taking methadone and getting more stoned and out of it as the day was going on. So we were pushing her and coaxing her and eventually we got something like a vocal, but not without a lot of tears and frustration. We had to piece her vocal together by studio trickery, really. I think, on the whole, it's always bad to meet the people who have been your heroes and heroines and work with them. Although it's thrilling, you're walking on dangerous ground.'

A month later, Nico was dead, an ending suitably Dadaist in its strangeness. She was on holiday in Ibiza with her 23-year-old son, Ari, when she cycled off into town on the morning of 7 July 1988, in search of marijuana – or 'hish-hash', as one witness on the Banshees' tour remembers her calling it. Ari later described how she carefully wound a black headscarf around her head, before departing into the blistering heat. A taxi driver found her lying unconscious by the road and, when he eventually found a hospital that would admit her, she was pronounced dead at 8 p.m. – the cause, a massive cerebral haemorrhage.

Ari took her back to the forest, burying her in the Grunewald Cemetery, close to Berlin. 'Everything was turbulent about her, starting with the bombs during her childhood,' considered her friend, Danny Fields, who signed both the Doors and Nico to Elektra. 'You can hear it in the words of her songs. It's a mythical thing that I think we are going to be trying to explain for a long time.'

CHAPTER 6

Goth's Own County

The Harrying of Leeds: Soft Cell, the Mekons, the Sisters of Mercy, the Three Johns

'For a few weeks after the election, we would draw a stick figure on the palm of one hand and a scribble of pen on the other. Showing the hand with the stick man to our audience and miming the actions, we chanted: 'Here's Margaret Thatcher/ Throw 'er in the air and catch 'er/Squishy squashy squishy squashy/There's Margaret Thatcher.' The chant finished with the grand reveal of the scribbles on our alternate palm: Margaret Thatcher has been squashed into nothingness.'

– Children's playground game of 1979,
described by author Jennie Godfrey

'Only two words on the wall: LEEDS and HATE.'

– David Peace, *Nineteen Seventy-Seven*, first published 2000

Soft Cell met in a city of fear. Leeds was where the Yorkshire Ripper had taken the life of his first victim, Wilma McCann, in 1975 and remained central to his nocturnal activities until his capture in 1981. Six of the thirteen murders he was convicted of took place in the suburbs of Scott Hall, Roundhay Park, Chapeltown and, as his frenzy increased, the environs of Leeds University. Four more local women survived his brutal attacks, made between 1976 and 1980, at great personal cost.

Leeds is a city of night. Its coat of arms was designed around three silver owls, taken from the heraldry of Sir John Savile, the city's first Alderman, elected in 1626. Savile was a descendent of Ibert de Lacy, a favourite of William the Conqueror, who granted him a vast northern estate that stretched from Lincolnshire to Lancashire. Owls, called Night Hags and Corpse Birds by the Celts, are linked to the underworld and considered malevolent in many folkloric traditions – wherein they are nearly always represented as female. But those that de Lacy wore into battle with William kept Leeds safe when, having disposed of King Harold, the monarch alternatively known as the Bastard, laid waste to the northern shires and any rebels they may have been shielding in the Harrying of 1069–70. While William's army put an estimated 150,000 to the sword, Leeds' population of at least 200 went about their business unharmed.[1]

In 1147, the foundation stone of Leeds' first and most epic piece of Gothic architecture was laid by the Cistercian monks of Kirkstall Abbey and the town remained a prosperous cloth-trading centre through to Tudor times. During the Wars of the Roses (1455–87), it was Sandal Magna in neighbouring Wakefield that saw the bloodiest of battles between the rival Houses of Lancaster and York, when up to 2,500 Yorkists were slaughtered and the head of Richard, Duke of York, and his son, Edmund, Earl of Rutland, were taken for display on Micklegate Bar in York. Trouble revisited in the Civil War (1642–51) when Leeds was garrisoned for the Royalist cause by Sir William Savile and routed by Sir Thomas Fairfax one cold January morning in 1643. The Black Plague followed on the Parliamentarians' heels in 1644, laying waste to 1,300. But at the Restoration, Charles II gave Leeds a new Municipal charter – and the Savile family, along with their owls, were back in business.

Medieval Leeds was rebuilt during the Industrial Revolution (1760–1840), when the cottage industry of weaving was rapidly transformed into the mills that dominated the skyline of a conurbation granted city status in 1893. The Victorian iteration was captured in all its glowering glory by Leeds' foremost painter of nocturnes, John Atkinson Grimshaw (1836–93) – still the best name of any artist born in Yorkshire.

After the Second World War, Leeds entered its Brutalist phase, when architect and freemason John Poulson (1910–93) began covering his home city and most of the Northeast in dubiously constructed tower blocks and municipal buildings – a clandestine collusion with powerful public figures for which he would end up being jailed in 1974.[2] It was the birthplace of gifted wordsmiths: youthful *Beyond the Fringe*-r Alan Bennett (b. 9 May 1934) and Billy Liar's creator Keith Waterhouse (1929–2009), whose work captured the post-war public imagination; and the pithiest poet of them all, purple-shirted Jake Thackray (1938–2002), whose genius songs of Yorkshire life included the tales of the bewitching 'The Hair of the Widow of Bridlington' and a coven of Satanic housewives operating in Castleford.[3]

While they were all getting on the train to 'That London' to become National Treasures, another Leeds man named Savile was introducing the first-ever *Top of the Pops* in 1964, the fruition of a career as a disc jockey that had begun at the city's Mecca Ballroom in 1949. The story of Sir James Wilson Vincent Savile, OBE, KCSG, that began to unfurl after his death in 2011 was one of corruption, depravation and horror to rival that of his friend, Peter Sutcliffe's. While Jim fixed it for the nation, Leeds United Football Club dominated Division One from 1961–74 under the winning spell of magus-like manager Don Revie. Their emblem was another bird with mythic status, the peacock: symbol of birth and renewal, royalty and power, chariot for Hindu war gods and harbingers of rain. There would be more of the latter in United's forecast after Revie's departure to become England manager. But the man who would seize the city's Heart of Darkness and secure its crown as the Capital City of Goth did not arrive at Leeds Station until the autumn of 1978.

Some Kind of Stranger

He did have a name: for the present, it was the rather unassuming one of Andy Taylor. Until recently, he had been studying French and German at St John's College, Oxford, but left under a cloud at the end of the previous academic year, when his tutors refused to let him switch to learning Chinese. In the furtherance of that aim, the nineteen-year-old had enrolled to pick up his studies at Leeds University. He stepped off the train after packing not much more than 'one pair of shoes' and 'this old pair of trainers I'd been wearing since I was fifteen'. Surveying the landscape through a pair of dark glasses that seldom left the peaks of his cheekbones, he shrugged his shoulder-length red hair and made his way to his new, much less salubrious student digs in 'a housing estate of utter grimness' under the shadow of Elland Road.[4]

United had gone through three post-Revie managers in rapid succession by then. The latest, Jock Stein, had been appointed on 21 August and would be on his way again by 4 October, lasting little longer than Brian Clough's tumultuous two months of 1974, before Jimmy Adamson ushered in a period of relative stability that lasted until October 1980. Andy Taylor had better fortune to bring the city's way.

This was the first time he had ever ventured to the north of England. Taylor was born on 15 May 1959 in the watery East Anglian realm of Ely, whose previous most famous son, Anglo-Saxon chieftain Hereward the Wake, had led a rebellion against William the Bastard in 1071. Though defeated, Hereward managed to evade capture, disappearing with his men through the secret causeways of the Fens and into the mists of legend. Emerging from a similarly mystifying labyrinth of railway architecture beneath Leeds Station known, appropriately enough, as the Dark Arches, Taylor would transform himself into Andrew Eldritch, frontman of the Sisters of Mercy and Goth Lord of the North, via a portal called the F Club.

This was the brainchild of Leeds' promoter John Keenan, who had started putting on punk gigs at Marc Almond's alma mater – Leeds

Poly – in 1977, but was voted out of the venue by Common Room Committee. The F Club – the name an expression of his opinion of said students – began life in a faded cabaret theatre called the Ace of Clubs. After a 'suspicious fire' of the sort not uncommon to ailing provincial nightclubs, Keenan moved to Roots Club in Chapeltown, a former synagogue that catered to Leeds' West Indian community, playing reggae most nights of the week in a parallel universe to the Ladbroke Grove of Killing Joke. The F Club opened at Roots with a Magazine gig on 1 February 1978 and went on to host Wire, Wayne County, the Banshees, Joy Division, Big in Japan and Suicide.

'Chapeltown was also a red-light district, where the Ripper was at large at the time,' recalled Paul Hollins, now professor of Cybernetics at Bolton University, then a young Banshees/Suicide fan who could smell the dry ice of change in the air. 'When I think about it now, it was downright dangerous.' Though Leeds had a reputation for clannish violence quite apart from nurturing a serial killer, few of the city's resident punks nor student intakes seemed cowed by the risks of clubbing or gig-going. Jon Langford (b. 11 October 1957) arrived in the city from his native Newport in 1976, to take up an art degree at Leeds University: 'As soon as I got there, punk rock happened. The Pistols came and played a couple of months later and everybody wanted to form bands. I had a drumkit – I was a youth club basher, I knew a bit of Black Sabbath – so I was in demand!'

On his first day, Jon met Kevin Lycett, Andy Corrigan, Tom Greenhalgh and Mark White, with whom he would form the Mekons – named after *Eagle* comic superhero Dan Dare's Venusian arch-enemy. He was the only person who could competently play an instrument and their novel approach to making music was best described by *Melody Maker*'s ever-perceptive Mary Harron: 'If the Mekons owe something to the early Velvet Underground, they belong just as much to the traditions of British music hall. There is the same camaraderie with the audience, the same informality, the same mixture of songs and patter.'[5]

Their same year-group also produced Gang of Four and Delta 5, angular, post-punk/scratchy funk combos with strong Marxist leanings – perhaps unsurprisingly, as they had all been tutored by T. J. Clark, the only British member of the Situationist International who 'came in like Che Guevara in blue denim,' as Langford remembered. 'There was a sort of Marxist revolution in the art department. It was just turmoil and it was just brilliant.'

Annie Hogan, who arrived at Leeds University in 1979 to study International History and Politics, had her career transformed by the city's nightlife: 'I would say I defied the Ripper and consciously walked everywhere at night,' she remembered. 'Young and inebriated, I even slept in the park a couple of nights. Now I think what an idiot I was, but then I thought, "Fuck you" – if I even thought at all – and just did as I felt.'

There were other oppressive factors abroad in those Yorkshire nights. The NF had a nest in Leeds, whose members tried to disrupt events. Jon Langford recalled: 'From the early days of punk there was some hostility between the students and the townie kids, there was quite a lot of edge and there was some really weird politics.' When Marxist newspaper *The Leveller* suggested the F in F Club stood for Fascist, Keenan renamed his operation the Fan Club when he moved operations to Brannigan's pub in the October of that year. Here, he began running regular slots for new local acts, billed as the Sheepdog Trials. Those who passed muster would get the prestigious support slots that could make a band's fortune.

It didn't take long for Andy Taylor to find it. In his first term at uni, he was able to see Wire, the Damned, Cabaret Voltaire, Joy Division, Pere Ubu and the Human League at the F(an) Club. More importantly, it was where he met resident DJ Claire Shearsby, who, opined Paul Hollins, was 'the coolest thing in Leeds. Every girl wanted to be her and every guy wanted to be with her. Including me. And I never even got a passing glance but she went out with Andrew.'

Elvis was actually Claire's first love. She recalled falling for him at the age of ten, before being abducted by David Bowie: 'My first two singles were "Suspicious Minds", followed by "Life on Mars" and then Alice Cooper *School's Out* was my first LP.' She began collecting records at Scene and Heard on Kirkgate and then on to the Virgin store: 'You had to be really brave to go upstairs – they had joss sticks and everything. Listening booths and the guy behind the counter would happily put on anything you asked him for. Then it moved down the road and you had the Singles Bar with chairs and ashtrays, and woman called Sharon who'd make you a cup of coffee while you listened. I had a Saturday job and singles were 50p when I started seriously buying. Initially, I just got a collection of punk stuff – it was charming. Even the bad stuff had its charm.'

As a teenage punk, Claire went out in her dad's suit, brothel creepers and cropped, hennaed hair. 'I'm about five foot eight, and I was really good at sport at school. Quite often, if I was in a shop and I had my back turned, people would go: "Yes, sir, can I help you?"' Like Langford and Hollins, she was part of the select audience who saw the Sex Pistols play the Fforde Grene pub in Harehills in 1976, and began her DJing career in the Leeds Poly common room the year after.

'I used to hang out where students went, rather than my local. I directed myself towards the creative people. So I was hanging out with the Mekons and one of the guys was DJing at the common room. I'd go with him and help – and then about three weeks later, he went off to London to seek his fortune and I just took over.'

Claire's DJ booth became the focal point of the F Club: 'My record collection was not very big, it would all fit into one bag. I had things like *Funhouse* and *Raw Power*, New York Dolls, *Nuggets*, then all the new 7-inches that had just come out. At Brannigans, where the club was at the longest, it was more of a venue than a disco, so people didn't dance very much. If I played "Electricity" by OMD [Orchestral Manoeuvres in the Dark], everybody would get up and "Spanish Stroll" by Mink DeVille – but most of it was just too energetic. They'd bounce up and down when the shows were on, but that was it.'

Claire had her own way of dealing with troublemakers: 'There were always three or four lads that everyone said were NF. I was playing a track one time and the dancefloor was empty and one of them came on and started goose-stepping and saluting, so I just pulled the faders back and stared at him until he walked off. He didn't do it again, that's for sure.'

By this time, she had grown her hair longer, experimented with Crazy Color and then bleached it out: 'It was quite big and blonde for a while – I'd had a few lumps fall off, when it got exhausted from all the bleach. I was known as "Haystack".' Her nightclubbing attire was chic yet functional: black Lycra, black leather jacket and biker boots, 'so you could walk home afterwards.' A dab hand with a sewing needle, she could also run up her own creations, one favourite being a velvet cloak bought from a jumble sale and tailored into a jacket: 'Based on *The Masque of the Red Death* – there were loads of good ideas in that film.'

What did Andy Taylor have that all her other hopefuls didn't? 'He used to come down to Brannigans and he used to come on his own. Smoking his cigarettes and hanging out by the DJ booth and asking for the Stooges. He did that a few times and I started talking to him. He had dark jeans, a Ramones T-shirt, a leather jacket, shoulder-length hair, sunglasses. In the darkest nightclub ever. And he did look quite a lot like David Bowie so that made him quite attractive.'

Claire and Andy became Leeds' glamour couple, her flat above a chemist's shop off Belle Vue Road his merciful release from those Atkinson Grimshaw-like student digs and the afterhours hangout for the F Club crowd. Visiting *Melody Maker* journalist Adam Sweeting described how 'This room in which we sat bore many of Andy's hallmarks. There are long rows of cassettes, each one carefully indexed by typewriter or in Andy's thin, careful lettering. Shelves of books are arranged with utmost aesthetic appeal — orange Penguins, grey Penguins . . .'[6]

Jon Langford was a frequent visitor: 'Andy was the first person I knew with a video machine. We used to watch *Doctor Who* on a little tiny black-and-white TV he had hooked up to it. In the afternoon, with the curtains drawn. He was incredibly insect-like. A guy who always wore shades and never went out in the daytime.'

By then, after a spate of indie Singles of the Week with 'Never Been in a Riot' and 'Where Were You?', the Mekons had managed to defy their own manifesto and sign to Virgin records: 'Everything we ever said was negative,' Langford recalled. 'Our manifesto was all things that we would never do – like anybody cared. Then, as soon as any reality came along, we would just do those things anyway. We ended up in the Manor, having breakfast with Richard Branson. Even asking him for the bacon he hadn't yet eaten.' Having spent his advance on a 'ridiculous silver Pearl drumkit', Jon sold his previous rig, lovingly customised with tropical fish vinyl from Woolworth's, to Andy: 'And he painted it black! With emulsion paint – he did a terrible job of it, I couldn't believe it.'

The second most important ingredient in Taylor's transformation blew in just a little later. Just as David Bowie could not have become Ziggy without a guitarist from Hull, nor did Andy become Spiggy without his Mick Ronson, Mark Pearman (b. 1959). Via the F Club, this young man would also be rebaptised, his new identity possibly inspired by the Mekons/Gang of Four's brand of Commie-DIY: Gary Marx.

Dark Habits

Despite its track history with the Spiders from Mars, Hull in the late '70s was a dead end compared to Leeds – stuck out at the edge of the Humber Estuary on the North Sea coast, its once-prosperous port and fishing industry now in steep decline. Mark Pearman took the M62 out of there to visit a friend at Leeds Uni in 1979, saw the Mekons and Gang of Four a few times and never looked back. Taking a job in a carpet shop, he discovered the existence of the F Club via Leeds' premier punk outfitters Xclothes, who were selling membership cards for a quid.

Pearman was soon a regular fixture at Brannigans, regaling John Keenan with his plans to get a band together and marvelling at Claire's choice of records: 'She just seemed to have everything you could possibly ask for . . . It was really wide ranging, not just punk.'[7] Andy and Mark got talking at the DJ booth and soon enough, Mark was asked to audition for Andy and Claire's band.

This short-lived ensemble had been instigated by bassist Jonny Plumb and they were also rehearsing a singer called Keith Fuller, the F Club's top Dave Vanian lookalike. Plumb assumed leadership – but, from his original position behind the black drumkit, Andy managed to argue both Jonny and Keith out of the door. 'He was so swashbuckling in his ability to get stuck into an argument,' Pearman recalled. 'He just seemed to absolutely buzz about falling out with people. It was astonishing.'[8]

Claire never made it onto the stage either: 'It started really amorphously. If you had a keyboard and an amp you could join in, so we all gave it a bit of a go. Then my amp caught fire and I thought, I don't really want to be onstage. I want to be at the back, in the dark. DJing, or I thought doing sound engineering might suit me. I don't need that much adulation, really.'

Like novitiates in Holy Orders, Taylor and Pearman took on new names when they became the Sisters of Mercy, named after the Leonard Cohen song: 'A nice 50:50 balance between nuns and prostitution, which seemed like a very suitable metaphor for a rock band,' as Andrew Eldritch told Adam Sweeting. 'All this pseudo-faith business and high ritual, and yet . . . prostitution.'

He and Marx produced the first single under this name in 1980, recording at RicRac Studios – a shed in a run-down industrial estate in Wortley, south Leeds. 'Damage Done' took Neil Young's 1972 'The Needle and the Damage Done' and turned his lament for his many junky contemporaries into Andy's amused commentary on the speed-crazed kids at Brannigan's ('See the rebel and the damage done'); tossing in a bit of T. S. Eliot along the way: 'Somebody tell me about the rhythm of the dance floor (This is the way the world will end)'.

The experience was a learning curve, as Eldritch writes on the Sisters' official website: 'The guitar parts were played upon the guitar, but that three-watt practice amp sounded like a three-watt practice amp. The bass parts were also played upon the guitar. The drums were played so badly that you can hear Andrew dropping the sticks at one point. The production was terrible and the songs themselves were never much good.'[9] Nonetheless, they got it all the way from the shed to independent record distributor Red Rhino in York and then on to John Peel's turntable. But they still needed to increase the numbers of their flock.

Craig Adams (b. 4 April 1962 in Otley, west Yorkshire) was a veteran of John Keenan's Sheepdog Trials, as the keyboard player and rhythm guitarist of the Expelaires. This collection of talent had become the F Club's house band and would provide the nucleus for a new wave of Leeds' bands – bassist Mark Copson became singer of Music for Pleasure, guitarist Dave Wolfenden joined Red Lorry Yellow Lorry, Darren Carl Harper became drummer for Girls at Our Best! and singer Paul 'Grape' Gregory founded 3000 Revs with Adam Pearson, later a Sister himself.

Adams also had a sideline, an electronic duo called the Exchange with Jim, the legendary dancing bar manager of the Faversham, another much-favoured watering hole. According to Jon Langford, this pub was: 'Goth Central. There was a scene on a Friday night, you'd go in the men's bathroom and there was a lot of big hair and "Hey, can I borrow your hairspray, please?" Big lads – plasterers, builders – in the bogs of the Faversham, all doing their nails.' In this alternative version of Soft Cell, the flamboyant Jim was Marc while the taciturn Craig was Dave. Langford produced a session for them; Jim rewarded him with a pewter stein engraved with the words: *To Welsh Jon from the FIC* [Faversham In-Crowd].

But Adams' destiny lay in another band and on another instrument. Taking over on bass, he joined the first Sisters line-up to actually step on a stage, at the University of York, on 16 February 1981. By then, Eldritch had dispensed with the black drumkit and acquired his first Boss DR55 drum machine, which he named Doktor Avalanche.[10] This allowed him to take centre stage, though sartorially, the Sisters had yet to get their habits together: 'Craig [looked] like he had put on someone else's school uniform,' Marx recalled. 'I was a spotty kid with a Trutex shirt. Andy [looked] like Lenny Kaye or Joey Ramone.'[11]

Adams had a secret weapon. 'The first few gigs people thought there was something wrong with Craig's bass,' recalled Shearsby. 'It was because he'd put a fuzz pedal on it and no one had done that before. So I would stand next to the sound guy and say: "The bass is supposed to sound like that." Then they wanted echo on stuff. I watched that for a bit until I knew I could do it and became the band's sound engineer.'

While their music was still finding its form, Marx considered the embryonic Sisters more akin to Killing Joke, in that 'our roots were in aggression'. They were drawn to the same sources of heaviness: the Stooges, Motörhead and Hawkwind, especially *Space Ritual*, the 1973 live album that captured the Ladbroke Grove psychonauts in full cosmic effect. Adams took on Lemmy's role as fearsome bassist, underpinning the Sisters' sonic attack while Eldritch's vocals ranged from a Jim Morrison whisper to screams worthy of Alan Vega. Marx was the showman/shaman of the group, the violent sound electrified through his flailing, lanky frame, his workmanlike white shirt soon to be replaced by a succession of flouncy girls' blouses. And Doktor Avalanche kept the beat stomping on, a machine incarnation of Eldritch's beloved Glitter Band. Other lodestars were bands witnessed at the F Club – the Cramps and Cleveland, Ohio's other greatest contribution to uneasy listening, Pere Ubu. London visitors the Psychedelic Furs would play a vital future role in the Sisters' success, as would Bauhaus's tricks with mirrors and lights.

Like that other Pop Artist named Andy, Eldritch was a fan of rock 'n' roll as sheer, rebel outsider spectacle. While they had yet to make a great record, he had designed his band a great logo with which to brand their Merciful Release label; first seen on the back cover of 'Damage Done'. This he achieved by taking a plate of a dissection of the head, face and neck from *Gray's Anatomy* and superimposing it over a Pentagram: Motörhead meets Mocata.

In the succession of Sisters releases to come, Eldritch would put his scalpel-like skill with language to similar effect, anatomising the teenage rituals that powerfully connect pop music with superstitions, rites and sacred ritual – what he would refer to as 'false spiritualism'. Unlike Jaz Coleman, he would do it with a knowing wink concealed behind those mirror shades. Spiggy Topes was *Private Eye*'s spoof Mick Jagger/Lennon/McCartney hybrid before he morphed into Eldritch, via the shared name of Claire and Andy's cat.[12] 'I don't see why you shouldn't be able to frighten people and amuse them at the same time,' he told writer Adam Sweeting, 'and excite them and inspire them. Because that's what it does to us, it does *all* those things to us.'

Event Horizon

John Keenan's other gift to the era's youth culture was the Futurama Festival, which he first staged at Leeds Queen's Hall, between 8–9 September 1979. Billed as: 'The World's First Science Fiction Music Festival', its stellar line-up included Joy Division, the Fall, Echo and the Bunnymen, Cabaret Voltaire, Orchestral Manoeuvres in the Dark (OMD), the Teardrop Explodes and an eagerly anticipated appearance from Public Image Ltd. Keenan also intended it as a launching pad for his F Club protégés, but visiting *NME* correspondent Andy Gill was hardly impressed: 'The Expelaires, prole-rockers with a masturbation fixation, ground on for far too long,' he sneered, 'and the Void would be well advised to change their name, it being embarrassingly appropriate.'[13]

Local bands fared a lot better at the second event, held in the same, cavernous former tram depot, between 13 and 14 September 1980. Though only two bands away from opening the first day's bill, Soft Cell seized their opportunity. Noticing DJ John Peel in the audience, Dave Ball gave him a copy of their debut EP 'Mutant Moments', made in their Leicester Grove student flat and financed with money borrowed from his mother. Stevo was listening when Peel gave the duo their first national airplay and the deal with Some Bizzare soon followed. More immediately, they attracted the attention of Annie Hogan, who by then had been spending more time getting lost in music than actually at her studies.

'I had been wasting time, spending afternoons in the Faversham playing pool, jacking up all the new alternative music on the jukebox and watching the Bowie fanatic barman going through his moves,' she recalled. By night, she had become a DJ at Amnesia: 'At first, I got a job behind the bar and struck up a friendship with the in-house DJ, Ian Dewhirst. I was coming into contact with the wilder and weirder characters on the Leeds scene. There were a pair of girls who wore tweed suits and twinsets who played me *Reproduction* by the Human League for the first time, which blew my mind. Ian reacted to my perpetual requests for alternative music by getting me to DJ while he went for a drink – but as I quickly got more experienced, he encouraged me to play for longer and longer, while he chatted up women, paying me with cocktails and cigarettes. This situation suited everyone.'

But not even the Faversham barstaff had prepared Annie for what she witnessed at Futurama 2[14]: 'Soft Cell encapsulated everything I wanted out of music – and, by the magic in the Leeds air, it was music that brought us together. They found their way to Amnesia, dug my set and, when I started to book gigs, played an amazing show there. A room came available in the flat they shared and I was asked if I wanted it. Of course I did! I moved into a small bedroom and shared kitchen and bathroom with Dave, Marc and whoever else was moving through at the time.'

The lower end of the Futurama 2 bill also contained early incarnations of future pop stars – Sheffield's Vice Versa, who would become ABC, and Manchester's Frantic Elevators, fronted by future Simply Red blue-eyed soulboy Mick Hucknall, then a Magazine devotee. The Bunnymen returned – one place higher up the running order than U2 – and Siouxsie and the Banshees headlined Saturday, while Gary Glitter's appearance on Sunday suggests the influence of a certain individual on Keenan's booking choice.

Perhaps the most arresting performance came from Dublin's the Virgin Prunes, who came on stage wearing loincloths with pigs' heads attached to their crotches and stood, confronting the audience in silence, for a large part of their set. Equal parts art instillation and pagan offensive, the Prunes, fronted by the charismatic Gavin Friday, a friend of U2's Bono, and guitarist Dik Evans, brother of the Edge, were highly influential on those who managed to catch one of their rare UK shows. Gleeful provocateurs, who delighted in challenging the easily outraged with heavy cross-dressing, wore more make-up than even Pete Murphy and had an ancient Irish way of singing, the *Sean nós*, that brought to mind the legendary cry of the Banshee, they would release their first single, 'Twenty Tens', on Baby Records, via Rough Trade in January 1981. Rightfully described by *Sounds*' Dave McCullough, on his first sighting in September 1979, as 'closer to the genius of the (true) Sex Pistols than any band in Britain today', we shall return to them on a later page.

By the time of the third Futurama festival, on 5–6 September 1981 at Stafford's New Bingley Hall, the Sisters of Mercy were occupying Soft Cell's former position, third from the bottom of Saturday's bill, and still struggling to find a permanent second guitarist. But by the time February 1982 had come around, so had eighteen-year-old Ben Matthews (b. 1964 in Clapham, London), via a recommendation from the Expelaires. 'The [Sisters] rang me up . . . and asked me if I wanted to join,' Ben told Mark Carritt and Steve Trattles of *Whippings and Apologies* fanzine in August 1983, 'I said no at first because I was in the middle of my A-levels. So they spent ages convincing me that they were going to be the biggest thing Britian had seen since the Stones or the Beatles. I didn't really believe it and asked them the name of the band. They said we're the Sisters of Mercy and I said okay.'

Their shy, bespectacled recruit was given his own convent name – Ben Gunn, after the cheese-obsessed castaway in Robert Louis Stephenson's *Treasure Island* (1883). With him onboard, the Sisters had finally got their bearings.

The Quality of Mercy

The Mekons' tenure on a major label was a short one, lasting no longer than their first album, 1979's *The Quality of Mercy Is Not*

Strnen – an allusion to the infinite monkey theroem reflected in their chimp-as-journalist cover star, not quite reproducing Portia's quote from *The Merchant of Venice* that 'the quality of mercy is strained'. 'We got dumped by Virgin,' Jon Langford recalled, 'then we had an independent album out on Red Rhino,[15] then we went to Europe for a bit. But there was no money for anything, so me and Tom went back to finish our courses, and did our final years. I was really painting then – I'd got rid of all this rock 'n' roll and I was going to be a painter – but then I fell in with a different crowd, which became the Three Johns, with John Hyatt and [Philip] John Brennan.'

The Three Johns were a furious aural response to the state of the nation. Langford gave up the drums in favour of guitar, letting whichever model of drum machine Eldritch was currently employing fill in that role for him, too: 'He became my drum machine guru. Every time he got a new one, he'd show me how to work it, then I'd get the same one for the Three Johns.'

The results of this arrangement were electifying: with Brennon on bass and Hyatt vocalising with Rotten-esque aplomb, the Three Johns whipped up a mighty storm, using both Jon's Francis Bacon-esque satirical paitings and lashings of dry ice as onstage enchancers.

'We set up our own label CNT with Adrian Collins,[16] who asked me to be the in-house producer,' Langford explained. 'Again, people thinking I could do things like that, because I'd been to the Manor and eaten Richard Branson's bacon.' However, the role of older brother was one that came easily to the then 24-year-old: 'By 1980–81, we were really big mates with Red Lorry Yellow Lorry, the Sisters, the Expelaires – and it was like that barrier had disappeared, the kids had grown up and the bands that had been that nasty, politically, disappeared. It was our Summer of Love – in the mortuary!'

Collins asked Langford to produce the Sisters' second single, 'Body Electric'/'Adrenochrome', for which he found a much better outhouse studio: 'It was a garage in Bridlington, KG Sounds, run by Ken Giles, who had a gear shop empire in Wakefield, and I was his little apprentice. He would set up a massive PA that they'd use for rock gigs in his garage. Then they'd pump [Doktor Avalanche] through the PA. We'd put all these mics in there, trying to capture something. We'd spend days just on the bass drum sound, adding all these things to make it sound epic . . . Yet it was just a cheap little drum machine, going through all this gear. So we'd play it back and it would still sound pretty much like a cheap little drum machine.'

Nonetheless, tangible black magic was captured on this release, which was recognised as a *Melody Maker* Single of the Week. Eldritch continued to work the theme of 'Damage Done' into his own Atkinson Grimshaw word painting, a vision of Leeds nightlife cut with speed and strobe lights, illuminated on the A-side by: 'The body electric flashes on the bathroom wall/Crawling to the corners where the idiot children call'. On the flip, the city's factions perform their manic danse macabre under the Gothic spires and the railway arches: 'Wide eyed/Sped on adrenochrome'.[17]

Before the single was released, on 7 May 1981, Langford found himself stepping into Craig Adams' shoes for a gig at York University when the bassist disappeared to the Canary Islands for a month's assignment as a photographer's assistant. Here, Jon learned some valuable techniques that would be applied to the Three Johns. 'The biggest piece of equipment on the stage was the smoke machine. Andy had a music stand he'd customised that had the drum machine on it and the drum machine didn't have any pre-sets in it: it was just a number of rhythms and then a dial for the speed, so we had a piece of masking tape with little pencil lines coming out of it – I had to do the same thing myself for the Three Johns. In between songs, you'd have to minutely adjust it so it was the right speed. We were standing next to this massive PA with the smoke machine, all playing into fuzzboxes. We didn't have guitar amps or anything, everything was coming back through the monitors.'

The dry ice was an integral part of the Sisters' stage artistry, literally cloaking them in mystery, so Eldritch could throw shapes through the gloom like a medium moving through an ectoplasmic séance room.

'He once did an interview when he said that even when he went shopping, he took a smoke machine with him,' Langford chuckled. 'He couldn't imagine walking around Morrisons without it.'

By the time of Adams' return to cloisters, Andy and Claire had moved from their flat above the chemist's to one above a rehearsal studio in Village Place, Burley, where the band honed their material: not just an impressive set of originals, but some cover versions that proved as essential to their legend as those chosen by the Cramps. Quite the reverse of Lux and Ivy's obscure rockabilly resurrections, though, these were all songs by master-crafters of the tearjerker at their sublime best: Hot Chocolate's 'Emma', ABBA's 'Gimme Gimme Gimme (A Man After Midnight)' and Dolly Parton's 'Jolene' – with Eldritch just as unafraid as Marc Almond to sing a woman's part.

'There was a really passionate group of fans from Wakefield called the God Squad,' recalled author David Peace, then a black-clad teen from neighbouring Ossett. 'They would follow the Sisters everywhere and bootleg everything and then, upstairs in Wakefield indoor market, there was a guy called Reg selling the tapes. So, if you wanted to have the versions of "Emma" or "Jolene" or "Gimme Gimme Gimme", you had to go and get the bootlegs.'

These songs became highlights of the Sisters' live experience, along with more likely choices: the Stooges' '1969', Suicide's 'Ghost Rider', the Rolling Stones' 'Gimme Shelter' and that favourite cover of Joy Division's, the Velvet Underground's 'Sister Ray'. Perhaps Dave McCullough had seen something coming in his crystal ball when he began his 1979 review of *Unknown Pleasures* with the words: 'Andrew looked out through the misty, musky curtains and saw that morning was on its way like a messenger of doom.'

Though in fact, now was the dawn of this Andrew's finest hour.

From Her to Eternity

A year previously, a performance by the Psychedelic Furs at the F Club made an impression on Andrew Eldritch: 'I saw all twenty-five of them lined up across the stage, all of them in black, all of them wearing shades and just bringing the house down,' he told Sisters biographer Mark Andrews. So he accompanied Claire, who was DJing, to the Furs' soundcheck at Huddersfield Polytechnic on 29 May 1981. They got a Sisters demo to saxophonist Duncan Kilburn, who played it on the tourbus to the rest of the band on the way back to their hotel. Guitarist John Ashton was taken by the intense amphetamine logic compressed onto the tape and offered the Sisters full support on the Furs' next tour. Not only that, but when they visited Bridlington again, in the autumn of 1982, he took over production on their third single, recording four songs that they had previously tried out on their debut John Peel *Session* that August. This time, the two tracks that winged their way out of the garage and onto their initial 45 vinyl setting had the sound to match their authors' ambition.

A-side 'Alice' told of a tragic figure, recognisable from any impromptu house party in grotty student digs at pub-kicking-out-time throughout the '80s, bringing with her the scent of joss sticks, the tinkling of charm bracelets and pin-eyed stare of the damned. We first find her 'pressed against the wall/So she can see the door', wearing her best party dress but not looking for that kind of score. 'I wrote it in ten minutes about pills and tranq[ulliser]s when I used to care about watching people I know get dragged down by that,' reflected Eldritch to *NME*'s David Quantick in 1990. His anguished scream of: 'Alice! Don't give it away!' caused an eruption of outwardly thrust arms and splayed palms among those performing what was known as 'chicken-dancing' to this drama at gigs and across the nation's dancefloors.

But Alice's tragedy was very nearly upstaged by her flipside, 'Floorshow', an apocalyptic Death Disco inferno of Adams' ultimate fuzzoid bass, Gunn's undulating six-string funk and the Doktor's beat discipline versus Marx wreaking havoc on Jon Langford's Shergold guitar. On it, Eldritch fashioned the masterpiece of his Leeds noctournes, a rock 'n' roll preacher pitching to his unwitting flock: 'The old religion redefined/For the facile futile totally blind'.

Were the Sisters somehow mocking their audience? Adam Sweeting was obliged to ask. 'It's not really that,' Eldritch replied, 'it's just that they don't have a lot to compare it with. And what they *do* have to compare it with, they're being continually given at face value.'

'And ours stands up on face value,' added Gary Marx.

The Sisters dropped their G-Bomb on 21 November 1982 and its aftershocks are still being felt.

'The Sisters had this really immediate impact,' considered David Peace. 'What's amazing, looking back, is that how all these little towns – Batley, Dewsbury, Wakefield – they all had their little Gothic club.[18] I started going to the Hellfire Club in Wakefield. It was in Heppy's, this kind of dinner and supper club, up an alleyway behind the Strafford, which is in *Red Riding*. But Leeds was always the place I really wanted to go. If you wanted to buy records or books it was the best place, but it was also a scary place to go on your own, especially if you were fourteen, fifteen.'

Luckily, David and his schoolfriends found a dad willing to drive them between Ossett and Leeds to catch the Sisters in their prime. It was April 1983 and the Sisters played two gigs in two weeks at the Warehouse, headlining on the 7th and supporting the Gun Club – now with Patricia Morrison on bass – on the 19th. The band had their pedal to the metal. A new 7-inch, pairing Eldritch's 'Anaconda' – which, following in 'Alice''s wake, likened the taking of drugs to the embrace of said serpent – with the Ennio Morricone-chanelling Adams/Marx instrumental 'Phantom', was out in March. Closely followed by the 12-inch of 'Alice', with an added '1969' that, according to David, regularly turned the Hellfire Club into a Battle of Wakefield re-enactment.[19]

'I know it's a Sisters cliché but the Ben Gunn line-up was the best,' he considered. 'And it was at the Warehouse, where Marc Almond used to work on the door and Claire Shearsby used to DJ. For me, as with Joy Division, it was all about the bass. The way Craig used to look – before he started wearing velvet and hanging out with [future Sisters guitarist] Wayne [Hussey] – in a leather jacket with studs in it; he looked like he was in the Ramones and he would thrash the bass. They were so powerful live. The perfect marriage of Motörhead, Stooges, Suicide and Ramones.'

'The Reptile House' EP came slithering after 'Anaconda' in May, as Eldritch chilled to a new theme, scoring six songs that conflated conflict with twisted desire: 'Kiss the Carpet', 'Lights', 'Valentine', 'Fix', 'Burn' and an uncredited reprise of 'Kiss . . .' 'It was the most serious record we ever made,' he told New York's WNYU-FM Radio in September 1983, 'but it was also the most perverse. Everything about that record is perverse. It's really slow, it's really long, and I just love the way all the lead lines are hidden in the mix, involved in all the effects, completely submerged, you really have to fight with that record.' Indeed, some of his best lyrics since 'Floorshow' were buried in this smouldering self-production. Analogies between love and war abounded in 'Valentine', 'Burn' and 'Fix', the latter in particular seeming most clairvoyant: 'Love for the fix for the fabrication/Love for the corpse for the corporation'. Perhaps, also, it was Margaret Thatcher he had cast as the red-eyed femme fatale of 'Kiss the Carpet'.

It was these songs David Peace would come back to when opening the time tunnel to write his occult histories of Yorkshire, the *Red Riding Quartet, GB84* and *The Damned Utd*: 'The Sisters *were* the Gothic, industrial, Ripper Leeds. The Three Johns capture the political tension in a very direct way, but the Sisters capture the decay. Like Pere Ubu in Cleveland, you can hear the Dark Arches and the dripping water. They *were* the pivotal Leeds band and I still think "Reptile House" is the most Leeds record you can ever listen to.'

Waiting for Another War

As this chapter's opening schoolyard ditty demonstrates, for the children of miners, steelworkers and dockers, the coming of Margaret Thatcher was not something to celebrate. But, even as 1983 dawned with record unemployment up to 3,224,715 and those in the homes of heavy industry hit proportionately worse than their counterparts in the south-east, these plucky little northern tykes were not going to hex her away so easily. It wasn't just the Falklands 'bounce' that saw to Maggie's second landslide general election victory on 9 June 1983. The PM had already put strategies in place to maintain control over the electorate's thinking long before that.

Back in 4 January 1981, she had invited a special guest to dinner at Chequers.[20] Australian mogul Rupert Murdoch (b. 11 March 1931) had bought his way into the British newspaper industry when he acquired ailing *Daily Mirror* sister title *The Sun* from Cecil King in 1969. Until that point, the left-wing King had been the most powerful press baron in the land with an empire, International Publishing Company (IPC), that included *The Times* and over 200 other titles. During the '60s, under the editorship of charismatic Welshman Hugh Cudlipp, the *Mirror* was its best-selling daily paper, whose strapline, *Forward with the People*, gave readers the assurance it did kowtow to power. But King came unstuck towards the end of that decade, when, while starting to take leave of his senses, he attempted to engineer a coup against former PM Harold Wilson in 1968.

As part of the ensuing clean-up operation, Cudlipp was forced to sell *The Sun* to Murdoch, knowing he was inviting a vampire over the threshold. As he reflected: 'It was the dawn of the Dark Ages of tabloid journalism when the proprietors and editors decided that playing a continuing role in public enlightenment was no longer any business of the popular press . . . when journalism . . . shed its integrity and became intrusive journalism for the prurient . . . and the basic human right to privacy was banished in the interest of publishing profit.'[21] A similar fate awaited the *Mirror* after his retirement, at the hands of Robert Maxwell, who purchased the newspaper on 12 July 1984.

Murdoch had expected to join Britain's coterie of ennobled newspaper proprietors but was swiftly disabused of that dream by the reality of the class system. The barons of Fleet Street had no intention of inviting the 'Dirty Digger' from the colonies into their elite club – giving him an aggrieved outsider status he shared with the Cromwellian Thatcher. Murdoch evinced his revenge by casting spells over the proletariat instead, capturing both the *Daily Mirror*'s readership, then their Sunday reading when he acquired his most pernicious scandal rag the *News of the World* in 1969, and eventually even turning that most cloth-cap of all British pursuits, football, into the corporate fiefdom of the world's richest capitalists via his Sky TV domination of the Premier League.

At the time of their meeting at Chequers, Murdoch had ownership of *The Times* and the *Sunday Times* in his sights, which would, were his bid to be successful, give him control of over 40 per cent of the British press. As such, he was liable for referral to the Monopolies and Mergers Commission. However, a mere month and eight days after the clandestine conflab, on 12 February 1981, by sinister sleight of hand – a tiny cabinet reshuffle that replaced the current trade secretary, tough negotiator John Nott, with the inexperienced John Biffen – he took control of both titles, his bid having passed through the entire political system unopposed.

Like Ronald Reagan setting about a bunch of unarmed hippies with the National Guard, Margaret Thatcher enabling what amounts to state control via Rupert Murdoch's newsgroup does not read like the actions of an avowed enemy of Communism. The former *Sunday Times* and *Times* editor Harold Evans, forced out of his post by Murdoch in 1982, likened the subterfuge surrounding the Chequers' meeting to a 'KGB dead drop'. John Biffen reflected that the process he had been manipulated into seeing through revealed Thatcher to be a 'Stalinist . . . a tigress surrounded by hamsters'. Except, perhaps, for her original mentor, Alf 'Red' Sherman.

With Murdoch as Thatcher's policy mouthpiece, a remarkable chain of events was set in motion, starting with his 12 February announcement that he had struck a new deal with unions about manning levels and new technology. The very next day, the National Coal Board announced plans for widespread pit closures.

The fix was in, the battle lines being drawn.

The Sisters' final single of 1983, and their last both with Ben Gunn and as a truly independent release, came out on 8 October.

'Temple of Love' was classical Gothic worthy of those other famous Yorkshire sisters, the Brontës: all high winds, black rains, 'and the devil in black dress watches over/My guardian angel walks away'. Still more portentous were the two songs on the flip side. In the yearning 'Heartland', Eldritch sings: 'Leave the sirens far behind me . . . My heartland fade across the line'. Then, on their closing cover of the Rolling Stones' 'Gimme Shelter', he completes his warning: 'War, children/It's just a kiss away . . .'

Gothfathers: Suicide

In the influential record boxes of Leeds' premiere DJs Annie Hogan and Claire Shearsby, Suicide's eponymous debut album stood out like a bloody cleaver. Singer Alan Vega (1938–2016, born Alan Bermowitz in Brooklyn, New York) and his onstage partner, electronic keyboard player Marty Rev (born Martin Reverby, 18 December 1947 in Brooklyn), resembled the cycle sluts of Kenneth Anger's Scorpio Rising *with leather caps and Elvine quiffs, billing themselves as 'punks' as early as 1971. Hallmarks of their early appearances, framed by neon artist Vega's violet tubes that so inspired Soft Cell's set dressing, included self-laceration by safety pin and bike chain and hazardous stage-diving à la Iggy. Their audience responded in kind: 'Everything was thrown at me,' Vega told* New York Rocker's *Lisa Jane Persky in May 1976. 'Punches, chairs, bottles, cigarettes, instruments – you name it.' And that was only the beginning.*

Vega and Rev first met in 1970 at a studio on Broadway and Waverly, where Alan constructed his light sculptures. Marty studied piano under avant jazzer Lenny Tristano and hankered to apply minimalist principles to rock 'n' roll; Vega had been gifted with the perfect voice to express his love of Elvis. Their unique formula took all the guitars and drums out of rockabilly and compressed it into Marty's keyboards, while Alan screamed, crooned and hollered up its lovelorn shades. Between the Velvet Underground and No Wave, theirs was the blasted '70s, where Warhol's Factory met the New York Dolls in Max's Kansas City and CBGBs.

'It was the best of times, it was the worst of times,' Vega told Uncut's *David Stubbs in 1998. 'We were freezing our asses off, we were starving our asses off, but we all had the feeling that we were creating something that was affecting the world . . . Ironically, we were the only ones who weren't doing drugs, with a name like Suicide. [Suicide] was a social expression: "America is killing its youth".' But the way their audiences treated them, it would come to seem as if they did have a death wish.*

It was the Dolls' first manager, Marty Thau, who funded Suicide *(Red Star, 1977), a Rosetta Stone of Goth. It contains Marc Almond and the Sisters' beloved 'Ghost Rider' (inspired by the hero of Vega's favourite Marvel comics); 'Girl' – given the Barry Adamson treatment on his* As Above, So Below *album of 1998 – and the epic, ten-minute-26-second terror inferno of 'Frankie Teardrop', covered by Lydia Lunch on a series of Vega seventieth-birthday tribute EPs put out in 2013 by Blast First. Produced by Craig Leon, using studio effects learned from Bob Marley and Lee 'Scratch' Perry, to this day,* Suicide *sounds light years ahead – and yet somehow still drenched in the same magic Tupelo moonlight as the night of Elvis Presley's birth.*

Suicide came to Britain for the first time in 1978, to be met with extreme violence by appalled Clash fans – Vega later recalled an axe being thrown at his head at the Glasgow Apollo. They accompanied Elvis Costello to Belgium and caused more riots, the ensuing chaos recorded for posterity as 23 Minutes Over Brussels. *Their next studio album,* Suicide: Alan Vega and Martin Rev, *was produced by Ric Ocasek of the Cars, with whom they had recently been touring, who worked without pay at the Power Station studios used by Chic. With a disco groove and a glossy S&M sleeve, it was released by ZE in January 1980 – the track 'Diamonds, Fur Coat, Champagne' reflecting the upper echelons of New York nightlife observed from the gutter. Despite being an obvious antecedent of the entire New Romantic/Futurist movement, it too disappeared from history in the blink of a mascaraed eye.*

After which, they drifted apart. Vega rode his space rockabilly persona high into the French charts with his 'Jukebox Babe' single made with guitarist Jim Hawke, a side gig that the singer had envisioned as a one-off but 'in fact, lasted all the way to 1986'. In July of that same year, he became a ghostly presence on the Andrew Eldritch-masterminded The Gift *album by the Sisterhood. Though he is credited on the sleeve, it remains unknown to all but insiders whether Vega actually appears on it. 'He was possibly part of the Chorus of Vengeance on the track "Rain from Heaven",' suggests its Wikipedia entry. When further questioned by* The Quietus's *Ben Graham on the subject in 2011, Eldritch responded: 'Andrew went back to Vega's apartment with a DAT recorder, played him the tracks and explained the scenario. Andrew has a permanent visa to Planet Vega, because the two of them get on very well. Nobody else talks to Vega like Eldritch talks to Vega.'*

Suicide were subsequently reunited and went on to make a second Ric Ocasek-produced album, 1988's A Way of Life *(Wax Trax), which contained Vega's vitriolic response to the Reagan years in 'Rain of Ruin' and foreshadowed Detroit techno with 'Heat Beat'. The duo was now cited as a key influence on industrial bands like Nitzer Ebb, Nine Inch Nails, Front 242 and Chicago's Al Jourgensen-fronted Ministry and Revolting Cocks, who shared their new record label. In the UK, Blast First's Paul Smith re-released their first two albums and they played triumphant shows at the Barbican and John Peel's Meltdown, notable for the absence of brickbats, bottles and boos. However, that had taken almost their entire lifetimes. They recorded two more albums, one in each ensuing decade:* Why Be Blue *(1992) and* American Supreme *(2001), after which live shows became rarer. After suffering a heart attack and stroke in 2012, Alan Vega died on 15 July 2016.*

'Every ten years we're rediscovered,' he told David Stubbs in 1998. 'Now, there's kids getting into us who weren't born when we started. Every ten years they pull us out of the closet, just as we're thinking of retiring. It's vindication, I guess . . .'

Gothmother: Tura Satana

She came burning across the white desert plains, a vision in black. Raven-black hair, matching leather gloves, jeans, biker boots and cleavage like the prow of a battleship. Heavy black liner across her lids, her eyebrows and mouth set in rigid lines, like a Kabuki mask. In the dust behind her, a trail of broken bodies.

There never was a girl like Varla before. In the sunkissed California of 1965, she appeared in stark monochrome, the centrepiece of a film conceived and directed by former Second World War cameraman Russ Meyer. Faster, Pussycat! Kill! Kill! *tells the story of three go-go dancers who get sick of taunting drooling males and set out across the desert in souped-up Porsches, racing, fighting and spitting out acid one-liners. They encounter a wholesome couple and kill the boy, take the girl hostage and drive further into the wilderness. Stopping for gas, they discover a delinquent family sitting on a stack of cash, a sick old man and two sons who could have staggered out of John Steinbeck's Dust Bowl thirty years earlier. Conniving to relieve them of their fortune, the girls' lust for cash and kicks ends up a bloodbath.*

Faster Pussycat *is much more than an exploitation film. Meyer's army training taught him many skills – fast-cut editing, stark angled shots and the ability to make a low-budget production look astonishingly good. Cinematographer Walter Schenk frames the landscape in superb high-contrast black-and-white, rendering every frame iconic. The ball-busting banter and sheer surrealism of the characters are a delight. But integral to the movie's allure are the She-Devils themselves. Bouffanted blonde Billie (Lori Williams) is the all-American babe gone bad. Smouldering Rosie (Haji), a Latina in* Rebel Without a Cause *T-shirt and blue jeans, an aloof mystery. Centre stage is Tura Satana (1938–2011).*

There could never have been a girl like Varla unless there was a girl called Tura first. Born Tura Luna Pascual Yamaguchi, the daughter of a silent screen actor of Japanese/Filipino descent and a Cheyenne/Scots-Irish circus performer mother, Satana's startling beauty brought her trouble from the start. At the age of nine she was gang-raped by five men as she walked home from school. Her assailants were never prosecuted so Satana made a vow to exact her own revenge. With the help of her Karate expert father, she turned herself into a skilled martial artist then she tracked down each and every one of her rapists. 'They never knew who I was,' she later recalled, 'until I told them.'[1]

The genesis of Varla continued throughout Satana's adolescence. At thirteen, she joined a girl gang who carried razor blades around their necks, switchblades down their boots and wore leather gloves for fighting. Thus, Varla arrives on the big screen authentically dressed for combat. When Lori Williams first clapped eyes on her, she thought: 'She looked like a mass-murderer.'[2]

The truly scary thing about Varla is how she appears from out of nowhere to turn a swell couple's day out into a nightmare – and all for sport. Varla is a future apparition of Clint Eastwood's High Plains Drifter *(1973), Rutger Hauer's* The Hitcher *(1986) and Dennis Hopper's* Blue Velvet *psycho Frank Booth (1986) foretold into one malevolent female entity. No, there never was a girl like Varla before.*

1 *From Jimmy McDonough,* Big Bosoms and Square Jaws: The Biography of Russ Meyer *(Crown Publishing, 2006).*

2 *Lori Williams interviewed for* Go, Pussycat, Go! *a documentary that accompanied the 2005 fortieth anniversary re-release DVD of* Faster Pussycat, Kill! Kill!

CHAPTER 7

Cowboys and Indians

The style tribes: Southern Death Cult and Theatre of Hate

'Prepare yourselves to meet the human of the future. Neither man nor woman. Greater than either.'
– Professor Millar (Graham Crowden), *Britannia Hospital* (Dir: Lindsay Anderson), released 22 May 1982

In February 1983, *NME*'s Richard North identified a new movement of loosely affiliated bands. He traced their lineage from 'the erotic politics of the Doors and the tense dusky danger of the Velvet Underground' to the Sex Pistols' punk restart; further distilled through the dark glasses of the Banshees and Ants. He noted a shared taste in the esoteric – though not, he was swift to point out, anything to do with Tolkien-reading hippies, Black Sabbath or 'a Killing Joke stench-of-death gloomier-than-thou slice of fanaticism'. Instead, this bunch of pagan spirits offered what he called 'Positive Punk'.

Though he didn't mention the G-word, the sharp-eyed North was observing a social group he belonged to who were regularly meeting at gigs and clubs and shared a style aesthetic apart from their peers, the neo-Mods, skinheads or cartoon punks posing down the King's Road for the tourists: 'A green-haired spike-topped girl wearing a long black pleated skirt, white parachute top and bootlace tie passes a tasseled, black-haired mohawk in creepers, white socks, red pegs and self-made, neatly designed T-shirt. Something clicks. They smile in acknowledgement.'

At a distance of forty years, it may be slightly easier to separate the mohair strands. Some of the bands Richard covered – Sex Gang Children, Blood and Roses, Specimen and the Virgin Prunes – had taken cues from the early, bondage-trousered Ants and, particularly, the Banshees. By 1982, the look Siouxsie had perfected on *Ju Ju* – tarantula spikes of hair, fishnet stockings on arms, legs and across torso, heavy leather gauntlets adorned with bells – had been adopted not just by other bands but swathes of the teenage population across both sexes. A form of adoration the singer herself would come to despise: 'I'm gonna start wearing purple dresses and yellow polo-neck jumpers,' she told writer Tom Vague back in June 1981, when he asked her what she thought of her copyists. 'I'm vain, it's flattering but it's not why I'm doing it.'

Others – the Mob and UK Decay, who we will come to in the next chapter – were bands born of punk's divergence into the self-sufficient strain of anarcho-punk: much more politically minded and far less androgynous. It was Brigandage, fronted by the supremely stylish Michelle[1] and with North himself on bass, who actually most personified the notion of Positive Punk – and his finely drawn description of the boy and girl smiling at each other in recognition.

There were two other bands on Richard's list and they were the most influential; both formed in 1980, at opposite ends of the country. Each looked to have claimed their visual aspect from the rival factions of the Old West and were soon gathering sizeable followers who styled themselves likewise. Following the birth of Psychobilly and its kissing cousin, Cowpunk,[2] and after Vivienne Westwood launched her influential 1982 Buffalo collection – featuring full pleated *pollera* skirts and bowler hats and inspired by native North and South American cultures – it seemed that everyone was playing Cowboys and Indians.

Do You Believe in the Westworld?

Lying further west and tucked beneath the dramatic foothills of the Pennines, Bradford has always been Leeds' rival. Laid to waste in the Harrying of 1070, the Manor of Bradford was part of Ilbert de Lacy's pillage package from William I and remained in his family's hands until 1311. Established as a small town by the Middle Ages, Bradford sided with the losing Lancastrians during the Wars of the Roses. Despite this, magnanimous Yorkist King Edward IV granted the town the right to hold two annual fairs, enabling it to thrive as a wool-trading centre, which, by the reign of Henry VIII, had exceeded Leeds in prosperity.

During the Civil War, Bradford was garrisoned for the Parliamentarians and unsuccessfully attacked by Royalist Leeds forces in 1642. Legend has it that one unfortunate Cavalier captured in the city begged for 'quarter' – meaning mercy – and was instead 'quartered': hacked to pieces by his laughing Roundhead foes. Hence the saying: 'Getting a Bradford Quarter'. But Leeds got their revenge the next year, when they besieged the town from the hilltop Bolling Hall. Although the Royalists ultimately lost their cause, Bradford had suffered such famine and pestilence it took a hundred years to recover – during which time, Leeds flourished.

Yet Bradford's abundance of coal fuelled its Industrial Revolution comeback when the town became known as 'Woolopolis' for its manufacture of worsted cloth, and non-conformist industrialists Titus Salt, Henry Ripley and Samuel Lister built not just factories but model villages for their workers to live in. It received its charter as a city in 1897. Prosperity attracted overseas attention: three notable German merchants and philanthropists, Charles Semon, Jacob Behrens and Jacob Moser, founded major textile firms and helped to establish the Chamber of Commerce during a Victorian golden age. Charles Semon became the first foreign and Jewish Mayor of Bradford in 1864 and Moser the first Jewish Lord Mayor. Following the Second World War, communities from Poland and

Ukraine settled in the city. From the '50s onwards, there were further arrivals from Bangladesh, India and Pakistan.

Bradford's own national treasures include Pop Art pioneer David Hockney (b. 9 July 1937), composer Frederick Delius (1862–1934), who escaped from his German industrialist family to compose bucolic music in France, and John Boynton 'J. B.' Priestley (1894–1984), the socialist writer who penned the influential state-of-the-nation study *English Journey* in 1933, the evergreen play *An Inspector Calls* in 1945 and helped to found CND in 1958. Little of Bradford's medieval architecture survives apart from Bolling Hall; the city's Gothic treasures, including an abundance of refurbished mills, are largely Victorian and built from the attractive, honey-coloured local sandstone that seems to flood the city with light. It's one of the few places in the UK where you will still find a statue of Oliver Cromwell in the City Hall.

Perhaps this long history of non-conformity and socialist tendencies explains why, as David Peace put it, 'The Bradford scene always seemed more overtly political.' Yet, as was the case with Leeds, the enigmatic frontman who would stake Goth's claim on this city was also an outsider.

A Tribe Called Quest

Ian Astbury was born on 14 May 1962 in Heswall, Cheshire, but moved with his family to the steelmaking city of Hamilton, Ontario in Canada, in 1973, when he was eleven and his father, a former Merchant Navy engineer, was chasing work. Ian has described a tough adolescence, helping to raise his younger brother and sister after his father suffered a near-fatal car crash and his mother became ill with cancer, to which she eventually succumbed on his seventeenth birthday. 'Both my mother and father contracted cancer in that city and subsequently died of their cancers,' he recalled. By his own account, he had attended twelve different schools before the family returned to Britain.[3] In one of them, he made a friend who would have a lasting influence: 'I remember being in a class one day, and this one Indigenous kid didn't like what the teacher was teaching, so he got up and walked out. I was blown away. I thought that was so cool, I started hanging out with him and his brother . . . I really wanted to know more about their background. I quickly became fascinated with their culture and that's when I started to read up on it.'

The Astburys moved back to Britain in 1979, initially settling in his mother's native Glasgow, where she passed away. Here, Astbury had what he described as 'a religious experience' during a trip to the cinema, experiencing the Doors 'The End' on the soundtrack of Francis Ford Coppola's *Apocalypse Now*. After his mother's death, his father returned to Canada with Ian's sister, leaving him and his brother with relatives in the Liverpool area, where he had lived as a younger child. He would continue to find solace in the music of both Jim Morrison and his earlier disciple Ian Curtis – eventually being asked by the surviving members of his idol's band to step into the spotlight as frontman for the Doors in 2002.

In his first *NME* interview, with Paul Morley in October 1982 – a cover story before Southern Death Cult had even released their first single – Astbury talked of having been in the army for a while, before finding an alternative path within the following of anarcho-punk kingpins, Crass. Both a band and anarchist collective, Crass operated – and still do – out of Dial House, a sixteenth-century cottage in Epping, where they recorded, manufactured and distributed their own records and became a beacon for others looking for the opportunity to create and thrive at a time of mass unemployment.

Crass's ideals came both from a previous generation's counter-culture – founder members Penny Rimbaud (b. Jeremy Ratter, 1943) and Gee Vaucher (aka G. Sus, b. 1945) met at art college in Essex in the early '60s – and from the punk scene that spawned younger band frontman Steve Ignorant (b. Steven Williams, 1957) in 1977. They forged links and shared information with CND and the Greenham Common Peace Camp, whose numbers had swelled considerably from the initial thirty-six-strong protest in September 1981 as their actions and ongoing eviction battles with Newbury

District Council became first national and then international news. In December 1982, 30,000 women joined hands around the base in response to NATO's decision to house nuclear missiles on British soil; in April 1983 70,000 made a human chain between the Greenham and Aldermaston bases, and 50,000 encircled the fence again in December 1983.

Crass also played a host of anti-establishment pranks, from hiding feminist flexi-discs inside teenage photo-love-story magazines to manufacturing a telephone conversation between Thatcher and Reagan, which both the US State Department and the Murdoch-owned *Times* believed to be the work of the KGB. The hoax tape, in which the two leaders appear to discuss the 4 May 1982 sinking of HMS *Sheffield* during the Falklands War, was distributed to the press in the run-up to the 1983 election. The band followed this up with their Falklands-related 'How Does It Feel to Be Mother of a Thousand Dead?' single, which led to the PM being questioned about them in Parliament. Conservative MP Timothy Eggar attempted to have Crass prosecuted under the Obscene Publications Act but withdrew proceedings following a radio interview in which Penny Rimbaud claimed the intellectual upper hand.[4] However, there would be repercussions.

Astbury, who recalled being given a copy of John Neihardt's *Black Elk Speaks* (1932) at Dial House, told Paul Morley that it was through following Crass associates the Poison Girls – led by the excellently named Vi Subversa – that he landed up in a house in West Bowling, Bradford. It was future *NME* journalist and self-styled 'seething poet' Susan/Steven Wells who in fact led him from a Poison Girls' gig to West Yorkshire's equivalent of Dial House, a place with a makeshift rehearsal room in the basement where local punk bands congregated. Here, Ian met bassist Barry Jepson, guitarist David 'Buzz' Burrows and, from Bradford's Pakistani community, drummer Haq Nawaz Qureshi, then known as Aki or Aky, of punk band Violation. They needed a singer and, Astbury felt, destiny had finally put him in the right place at the right time.

The renamed Southern Death Cult's debut single 'Fat Man/Moya' was released on Beggar's Banquet offshoot Situation 2 in December 1982. Pulsing with rhythmic energy, heavy drums and bass, and with strafing guitar, it trod a wardance somewhere between Killing Joke and the Burundi beat of Adam and the Ants, with Ian's distinctive vocals giving them a keening, hypnotic edge. Sporting bowler hats, feathered earrings and the sort of Mohawk Richard North was talking about, SDC shared more than just musical ground with the Kings of the Wild Frontier.

The Ceremony is About to Begin

The name Southern Death Cult, Astbury said, represented the place where Britain's authority lay: 'All the main branches of government are in London, all the main branches of the military, the media, the music business, the multinational companies'.[5] Later explanations refer to the fact that 'Southern Death Cult' was a former name for what became known as the Southeastern Ceremonial Complex, an archaeological term referring to the iconography, ceremonies and mythology of the Native American Mississippian culture. Ian did tell Morley about his absorption in America's indigenous peoples and how this had influenced both his look and stagecraft, but in a way that expressed wariness: 'We've looked like this for years, not just because [there's] some kind of new wave we want to lead . . . When we started, people were calling it redskin rock, and I just felt sick. My interest in North American Indians is nothing so superficial.'

This came only a few months after Adam Ant had been taken to task by Native Americans for his use of Apache feathers and the white war line he painted across his face when the *Kings*-era Ants were unveiled, intended as 'a declaration of war with the music business'.[6] On receiving a letter from ten leaders of the Nations expressing their dismay, the singer went to meet with them. 'They showed me their system and their history and I basically said to them: "Come to the show and if you don't like what I'm doing, or if you think that I'm taking the piss I will take the stripe off and not wear it again,"' he told *Louder Than War*'s John Robb in 2014. 'Fortunately they liked the gig. But I had to go to them to speak to them – it's their country. I don't do politics, but this is beyond politics . . . It's about justice . . .'

Southern Death Cult strained to avoid being labelled by the music press: 'Oh God, they might think of some shit name for whatever it's supposed to be!' Astbury predicted. But what's more interesting is how the band *did* reflect the differing tribal make-up of Bradford, and how Aki Nawaz struggled with squaring his involvement in a band of white punks with his Pakistani Muslim background.

'They all thought I was moving away from my community, becoming Westernised, but I don't think that's true at all,' he considered. Though he had lost friends through his involvement and: 'When I'm just called Aki the Pakistani drummer it really pisses me off, as if I'm the token wog in the band or something. I hate it.' However, when Morley asked if he might be inspiring younger kids from his background, Nawaz concurred: 'They go back to their parents and say, "Oh, I really like Aki's style, I want to be like that." And their parents just smack them over the head with a chapati. I'm not saying they should all totally break out of it; I want them to hold onto that something. They have got something that a lot of English kids haven't got . . . I have come from a really solid culture, the kind of background of morality or something that is really fucking lacking in this country.'

Margaret Thatcher was still four years away from making her infamous comment to *Woman's Own*: 'Who is society? There is no such thing.' But Ian Astbury's own rootless background, his family fractured by lack of economic stability, spoke volumes about the Britain that already existed, let alone the further, still more extreme divisions that lay just along the pike.

Given that Killing Joke were the only band in Aki's peer group to be fronted by someone whose origins were also in south Asia, it's not surprising he was a fan: 'I can sit in my bedroom and listen to them over and over again and they really do something for me. They make me feel aggressive . . . not in like smashing something, but a personal power, an inspiration.'[7]

Southern Death Cult's attempts to inspire a more respectful – and positive – understanding between the different strands of British working-class youth put them on a difficult road but, they said, they were prepared to ride it out. 'It revolves around the fact that despite what we are and what we want to do when we get onstage, the emotion that comes through is a very powerful one,' considered the aptly named Buzz.[8]

The Wild Bunch

With his immaculate, bleached white flat-top, Davy Crockett-style buckskin jacket, blue jeans and white Gretsch guitar, the young Kirk Brandon looked like James Dean reborn as a punk rocker. He shared an edgy ambiguity and propensity for danger with the original Rebel Without a Cause, too – and although he managed to stay alive past the age of twenty-four, Brandon has never had an easy relationship with fame or the media either. But he has always had something to believe in, and his ability to get this message across – in a soaring wail reminiscent of Johnny Rotten at his most possessed – would ignite a sizeable passion in his audience.

Born in Westminster on 3 August 1956, Brandon moved with his family to Torbay in Devon when he was ten, to aid his sister's recovery from bronchial pneumonia – but it didn't take him long to find his way back to London again. Kirk formed his first band at the age of sixteen after seeing the Sex Pistols in 1977. The short-lived Stigmata began as a two-piece, grew to four and then folded before they could play their debut gig at Covent Garden's punk hub, the Roxy. He played bass with his second outfit, the Cane, who made a home in a community of squatter anarcho-punks – including the bands the Straps and Crisis – in Clapham. Following the departure of original vocalist-guitarist Chris Skornia, in 1978, the Cane became the Pack, with Brandon taking over those duties, Scotsman

Rab Fae Beith on drums and two ex-pat Canadians, Simon and John Werner, on guitar and bass respectively.

'All band members, myself included, I would describe as a fairly unhinged bunch,' he would recall, 'and what passed for normal among the band and its constant crowd of friends and supporters did not tie in necessarily with the outside world as a whole. Life consisted at the time of trying to survive on the streets and squats of south London – the whole period was funny, violent, grim and all at the same time, the band mirrored its surroundings.'

Managed by future *Arena* documentary-maker Paul Tickell, the Pack played their first gig at the Camden Film Co-Op after a screening of Marlon Brando in *The Wild One* – the audience getting more rebellion than they'd bargained for. 'What actually happened was about 150 people with thousand-yard stares stood stock-still, stunned at the power at the noise of the band – we were fucking angry!' Brandon recalled. Mini-riots followed many of the Pack's performances and venues got trashed. 'One night we played the Crypt [in Deptford, south London], and I recall thinking: "Great, everybody's dancing!" Only, when we'd finished our set, everybody was still dancing – in fact, they were all trying to kill each other. We left the stage as the Crypt was being deconstructed.'[9]

According to Tony Drayton's *Kill Your Pet Puppy* (*KYPP*), a fanzine written from within the same squat scene, the Pack's debut single 'Heathen' was 'simply one of the greatest sides ever produced by a punk group . . . guaranteed to clear the room of anyone over thirty if dropped on the decks in public.' It came out on the unfortunately named SS Records, an informal offshoot of Stiff run by Kirk's next manager, Terry Razor – very much of an Arthur Daley figure, memorably described by *Melody Maker*'s Adam Sweeting as 'a likeable, roll-your-own spiv from Paisley'.

SS, as both Brandon and drummer Rab Fae Beith later told the *KYPP* website, stood for Secret Service Records – after the name of the shop in Covent Garden that Razor ran – but was abbreviated at the pressing plant. 'Terry stole or borrowed Stiff's mobile recording truck,' recalled Rab. 'He turned up at a rehearsal room in Market

Street, Islington with Liam Steinberg, the then in-house producer at Stiff for Rachel Sweet and Kirsty MacColl. He also wrote "Walk Like an Egyptian" [for the Bangles'] a few years later . . . The Pack had nothing to do with the mixing or choosing the record label. The first we knew was when we received a single. SS does stand for Secret Service, Terry's office.'[10] Though this wouldn't be the last time apparently sinister allusions to the Nazis would be perceived in Brandon's oeuvre.

The Pack's next single, 1979's 'King of Kings', was picked up by Geoff Travis' Rough Trade records, which began life in 1978 from the original shop on Kensington Park Road. Having organised its own record distribution network, the Cartel, with similarly minded record shops across the land – thus enabling the likes of Factory and Mute to sell their records across the UK – Rough Trade released its first single, 'Paris Maquis' by French punks Metal Urbain, swiftly followed by Cabaret Voltaire's 'Do the Mussolini (Headkick)' and Stiff Little Fingers' 'Suspect Device'.[11]

By this time, Rab Fae Beith had been replaced by original PiL (Public Image Ltd) drummer Jim Walker, who lifted their game still further with the apocalyptic 'King of Kings', loaded with references from the actual Book of Revelations – as opposed to Killing Joke's – written in blood-red medieval-style script on the single's back cover.

The band's following were so big by then that they were in danger of making a success of things. Not only was this anathema to Kirk's punk principles, but the scene around him was also turning nasty: 'One of the roadies died,' he told journalist Malcolm Wyatt, 'and it all got too much. The whole thing was crazy.'

God's Lonely Man

The Pack split after a sell-out gig at the 101 Club in Clapham and Brandon retreated to a job at Booth's gin factory and a change of scene in Ladbroke Grove, from where he entertained himself watching gangster films, Westerns and all-nighters at the Electric Cinema on Portobello Road: 'I saw *Taxi Driver* twenty-seven times!' This was thirteen times more than Ronald Reagan's would-be assassin John Hinkley Jr, who took a potshot at the President while in the grip of a mania inspired by his obsession with the film on 30 March 1981. The cinema had a much more improving effect on young Brandon. Accompanying soundtracks, by the likes of Bernard Herrmann, Elmer Bernstein and, in particular, Ennio Morricone, would fill his head with ideas about how to create more tension and drama within his own music. He also rekindled his friendship with Terry Razor, who was by then ducking and diving around Blackhill Enterprises – the offices of original Pink Floyd/T. Rex managers Peter Jenner and Andrew King, now representing Ian Dury and the Clash – near to Stiff's Royal Oak HQ.

By 1980, Brandon had put together a new band from the remains of the Clapham squatter groups: from the Straps came bassist Stan Stammers (b. 19 May 1961 in Saffron Walden, Essex), who would prove Kirk's most loyal, longstanding comrade, and from Crisis, drummer Luke Rendle. They were joined by guitarist Steve Guthrie and, inspired by Andy Mackay's work in early Roxy Music, Brandon also brought in Canadian saxophonist John 'Boy' Lennard to lend further texture to their sound. They called themselves Theatre of Hate after French dramatist Antonin Artaud's concept of the Theatre of Cruelty, which – perhaps anticipating Suicide – called for the emotional involvement of the audience in a production. Theatre of Hate would have no trouble inspiring it.

Reflecting their previous band's live reputation, ToH's first release, November 1980's double A-side 'Original Sin'/'Legion' went straight to number five in the Independent Charts. Released on Razor's SS label, the two songs built upon Brandon's best Pack moments (the brooding 'Brave New Soldiers' and the ferocious 'King of Kings' respectively) and took their sound into widescreen, with a twin-guitar ricochet, Lennard's saxophone effectively mirroring Kirk's impassioned vocals and rollicking drums and bass. Brandon's lyrics had always carried resonances of his Catholic upbringing and, like 'King of Kings', the stomping 'Legion' attacked the hypocrisy of organised religion and those politicians, like Ronald

Reagan, whose rise to power was assisted by right-wing Evangelist Christians: 'In gods they trust to hide the sins/Which they commit themselves'. Its flipside lyrically as well as literally, 'Original Sin', hinted at a closer conflict tearing Brandon's soul: 'Since you came in my life/I've had to re-arrange my whole reality . . .'

Between the Pack and Theatre of Hate, Kirk had got in with a different bunch of squatters living in and around Warren Street, W1. Unlike the Clapham anarcho-punks, they were a flamboyant clique of budding celebrities, all of whom had been directly inspired by the example of McLaren-Westwood. They included the milliner Stephen Jones, BodyMap designers Stevie Stewart and David Holah, the ballet dancer Michael Clark, club hosts and future pop stars Steve Strange, Rusty Egan, Philip Sallon, Jeremy Healey and the formidable Australian, Leigh Bowery. Most charismatic of all, from a squat on 21 Carburton Street, came George O'Dowd and his glamorous friend, Marilyn.

Dressing up was this crowd's politics and through them, and the clubs they created and inhabited – Billy's at 69 Dean Street, the Blitz in Covent Garden – the early '80s of the Futurist/New Romantic would be defined and remembered. Sometimes a fashion statement could make an effective protest – as when designer Katharine Hamnett surprised Margaret Thatcher at a Downing Street reception for London Fashion Week wearing a T-shirt proclaiming '58% DON'T WANT PERSHING' in March 1984. In reference to an opinion poll about the proliferation of American cruise and Pershing nuclear missiles across the Continent, the PM's reaction, recalled Hamnett to *The Guardian* in 2019, was to 'squawk like a chicken', and the TV cameras and paparazzi certainly made the most of the moment.

A new sort of youth publication was born from this coterie, too. Having steered *NME* through its initially awkward transition in the punk years, introduced new writers and boosted circulation to 180,000 per week, Nick Logan had become disillusioned with his corporate paymasters at IPC. He jumped ship in 1978, pitching new ideas to East Midlands Allied Press (EMAP), who were developing a new magazine division. His beautifully designed and consumer-astute creations, *Smash Hits* and *The Face*, both launched in 1980. Between them, these magazines navigated the kids of the new decade on a journey from youth – when they could learn the lyrics to their favourite 45s in the glossy, fun-packed former – to the daring leap into clubland and the rebirth of cool with the style-conscious latter, which featured many of Logan's *NME* punk protégés, including Julie Burchill. *The Face*'s rival, *iD* – engineered by former British *Vogue* editor Terry Jones – came hot on its heels. The knock-on effect was felt through *Sounds*' subsequent subdivisions. Having diverted the energies of its chief metal correspondent Geoff Barton into producing the glossy, A4 weekly *Kerrang!* in 1981, the paper also for a brief time (1981–83) produced their older sibling's rejoinder to *Smash Hits*, the similarly formatted, lyrics-inclusive *Noise!*, which was sub-divided into Punk-Herbert news, brought to you by Garry Bushell, Betty Page's Electrobop, Steve Rapport's Psychedelix and the hard-working Barton's Metal round-up.

Despite their origins in the Pistols' orbit, the Warren Street crowd was a far cry from anarcho-punk, so it's hardly surprising that none of them were on Richard North's list. But, through Kirk Brandon, ToH had a pointy boot in both the squat scene of *KYPP* and the Blitz kids. Which would prove to be dangerous ground.

Blazing Saddles

For now, Theatre of Hate were gathering around them one of the biggest live followings in the country and you were just as likely to see them in the pages of *The Face* and *iD* as you were in the fanzines. Which was just as well because, Richard North aside, they didn't have many friends on the weeklies. *NME*'s Andy Gill predicted they 'could well end up as merely minor heroes of the bleak, post-punk Gothic goons along with Killing Joke, Bauhaus and all those other names etched in white paint on black Lewis leathers'.[12] While his colleague Paul Morley, so thoughtful with Southern Death Cult, produced one of his most unappealingly self-indulgent rambles, drawing attention to the singer's sticking-out lugholes – 'Kirk's ears, when sucked, must drive one beyond the reach of reason,' he imagined.[13]

Then there was *ZigZag*. Founded in 1969 by Pete 'Rock's Family Trees' Frame to cover elements of the underground rock, folk and psych scene ignored by the weeklies, it underwent a punk makeover in 1977, when historian Frame handed over to hip young gunslinger Kris Needs. Gothfather Mick Mercer replaced him as editor at the end of 1981, bringing with him writing talents nurtured in fanzine land: Richard North – aka Richard Cabut – Tom Vague, Tony De La Fou (aka Tony (D)rayton), future *Sounds* writers Mr Spencer, Robin Gibson and, from *Leeds Other Paper*, Ann Scanlon. *ZigZag* also operated their own club out of the beautiful art-deco former cinema at 22–24 Great Western Road, W9, close to Portobello Road, putting on gigs by just about everyone mentioned in this book. Attractively designed by Caroline Grimshaw,[14] the magazine perhaps played the biggest part of all those contemporary publications in speaking to the spike-topped girls and mohawked boys out there in the shires.

Theatre of Hate's first album was an 'official bootleg' – i.e. one made and put out by their manager with 'PAY NO MORE THAN £2.49' stamped across the back. *He Who Dares Wins (Live at the Warehouse, Leeds)* was released to counter the tide of live bootlegs flogged less legally on Portobello Market and in the record shops of Soho.

Two more singles followed: 'Rebel Without a Brain'/'My Own Invention' in April 1981 and 'Nero'/'Incinerator' three months later – SS having morphed into Burning Rome records by now. Under the firm guidance of Terry Razor, each release reached a higher position in the indie charts. Talking to *Smash Hits*' Dave Rimmer in 1982, Kirk and his manager outlined how the whole band were living on £40 a week, with Brandon's publishing royalties going towards the recording of their first album.[15] Kirk's lyrical preoccupations returned to politics on 'Rebel . . .' and its B-side, the latter an uneasy example of serial killers becoming media celebrities, 'Yorkshire Jack' and 'Charlie Manson/Diseased and handsome' being two examples. The analogy made by 'Nero' was of the present geopolitical situation mirroring the last days of Rome – hence their label's new identity. 'For the old world, this is a dangerous situation,' Brandon told Rimmer. 'Kids have no option but a lousy job or the dole. All I'm saying is, they've a right to say no. And the more they say no, the better they'll feel. I don't lie to people, I don't confuse them. I just say: "know the score".'

Only 'Incinerator' continued to nag away at more personal concerns: 'The reflection was a dream, a falsehood . . . it was all lies'.

ToH were *ZigZag* cover stars in October 1981, by which time they had recorded two Peel *Sessions*, including one that aired on 24 August and featured the song that owed the most to Kirk's nights spent at the Electric Cinema, 'Do You Believe in the Westworld?' As its spectral Spaghetti Western sound twanged across the nation's night skies, even the most remote Norfolk hamlet incubated its own Kirk clone, making larger gatherings a saloon of bleach, fringed suede, bootlace ties and spotted neckerchiefs. My photo album from this era reveals at least two or three different 'Kirks' in every shot – some of them looking almost as good as the original.

Making full use of his connections, Razor got his protégés into the studio with the Clash's Mick Jones in August 1981,[16] to record the album that would seal their legend: *Westworld*, released in February 1982. To this day, Brandon considers the Clash guitarist 'a genius', whose production work, with its backwards drum loops and echoey, dub-style spaciousness was 'way ahead' of its time. He certainly found a sympathetic Morricone to bring out the Sergio Leone inside him as he drew on the imagery of the cowboy film – and the original 1973 *Westworld* movie – to collage a picture of the current incumbent of the White House riding roughshod across the world. 'Judgement Hymn', 'New Trail of Tears', 'Conquistador' and the closing 'The Klan' – a clear rebuttal to those who saw Brandon in a far-right light – managed to make music that was as stirring, evocative and romantic as it was political. Clearly the perfect support act, they then toured with the Clash – and 'Do You

Believe in the Westworld?' rode its Morricone riff straight into the nation's front rooms, when the band pitched up on *Top of the Pops* in March, fittingly introduced by John Peel in his first appearance on the show for fourteen years.

This landmark performance also marked the debut of a new guitarist and drummer. Steve Guthrie left the band after the release of *He Who Dares Wins* – all the guitar on *Westworld* having been played by Brandon – and Luke Rendle departed shortly after the recording. Guthrie's replacement was Billy Duffy (b. 12 May 1961 in Manchester), a kind of northern twin of Sex Pistol Steve Jones, who had had a brief songwriting stint with a teenage Morrissey in his first band, Ed Banger & the Nosebleeds, and, separately, taught Stephen Patrick's future Smiths' sidekick Johnny Marr the rudiments of guitar. Duffy moved to London in 1979 when he joined Studio Sweethearts, the new band formed by fellow Mancunian punkers Slaughter & the Dogs' Mick Rossi and Zip Bates, with former Eater drummer Phil Rowland. They released one single – 'I Believe' (DJM Records) – and promptly broke up. The other three headed back to Manchester and a reformed Slaughter & the Dogs. But the style-conscious young guitarist remained.

He had got himself a job working for tailor Lloyd Johnson, whose World's End shop – just around the corner from Vivienne Westwood's boutique – featured in the very first edition of *The Face*. One of the original Mods, the then 34-year-old Johnson also had a stall in Kensington Market, where all of Richard North's tribes gathered, and counted the Stray Cats, Madness, the Jam and Ian Dury's Blockheads among his clientele. Johnson's latest range was inspired by what he called 'Vampire Rock 'n' roll' – the sort played by Lux's Cleveland forefather, Screamin' Jay Hawkins, and his London admirer, Screaming Lord Sutch, who, in February 1983, had freshly entered the political fray as leader of the Monster Raving Loony Party. Labelled La Rocka!, these beautiful, western-styled clothes, shoes and boots were, for my friends and I, the stuff of dreams. We saved our pennies from summer jobs in guest houses and seafront tourist traps to fund longed-for day trips to

London, while attempting to emulate the look from the charity shops of Yarmouth; homemade clothes cut from my mother's '60s Butterwick patterns and the bounties of the indoor market at St Benedict's in Norwich, which sold copies of clothes featured in *The Face* and *iD* as well as attire that was yet to be called 'vintage'.

Duffy loved working for Johnson and was spending his evenings playing pub gigs with Lonesome No More before he was pointed out to Kirk Brandon as a likely replacement for Steve Guthrie in September 1981. One conversation about Gretch guitars and a rehearsal later, he was in. Shortly after, the twenty-year-old Birmingham-born Nigel Preston took up his position behind the drumkit. The new boys stepped straight up into the limelight of international festivals and primetime TV.

As the band hit the top forty for the first time, in the eyes of most observers, Theatre of Hate had it in them – the rousing songs, the devoted following and the inspiring frontman who knew just how to talk to his audience – to become every bit as big as the Clash or the Jam.

But it was not to be.

Going Native

Ian Astbury first introduced himself to Kirk Brandon while helping to load gear out of a Theatre of Hate gig in Leeds, handing the singer a Southern Death Cult demo tape as he did so. The move was reminiscent of Andrew Eldritch with the Psychedelic Furs – and paid similar dividends. Kirk was so impressed, he asked Terry Razor to line them up as support on the next tour, even going so far as booking the Bradford lads studio time in London, where they recorded the tracks that would become their first single. His hunch that his fans would take to Southern Death Cult was spot on: 'People described it as "Cowboys and Indians" – silly, I know, but there was a grain of truth to it, looks-wise,' he recalled. Certainly, those old photos of mine reveal that just as many members of my peer group took their cues from Astbury – pierced noses, crimped black-and-white hair, shaved at the sides – as they did from Brandon. Unlike the Kirks, though, at least half of these Ians were female.

As the 'token Northener' in ToH, Billy was happy to be back among his 'lot' and was blown away by Astbury's stage persona: 'Ian came on with his Mohawk and his moccasins, his bells and self-made chaps, doing that weird little dance across the stage he used to do, and when he opened his mouth it was the loudest thing I'd heard in my life.' A genuine feeling of camaraderie grew between the two bands, Duffy and Stammers even acting as sound and light technicians for SDC on occasion.[17]

Billy's first date with ToH had been the 5 September 1981 Futurama 3 gig at Stafford Bingley Hall, with Bauhaus and the Sisters, shortly followed by European dates, which included sharing a bill with Einstürzende Neubauten at the West Berlin Tempodrom. Their set from this gig was recorded for a second, *He Who Dares Wins*, official bootleg, released simultaneously in London and West Germany in February 1982. The guitarist played on one more single, 'The Hop'/'Conquistador', which came out in May – by which time this promising arrangement had come to a premature end as Duffy and Theatre of Hate abruptly parted ways.

What happened?

Like the end of the Pack, it appears to have been a chaotic time for Brandon and a subject he still finds hard to talk about. 'I think we literally were rebels without a brain,' he told *Designer* magazine's Sean Egan in an interview of 2003. 'It started as five guys playing this crazy music, but by the end of the band, which was under two years, it had gone from having a jar of ale straight through to heroin . . .' The drug abuse he was talking about was that of Nigel Preston, who would follow the rock 'n' roll trajectory all the way down to his early death on April Fools' Day, 1992. Going on to allude to problems with management, Brandon also blamed added pressures that *Top of the Pops*' appearance had brought his way: 'There was people outside my door every night, I couldn't walk down the street. From being absolutely nowhere I was on TV shows and the covers of newspapers. That was quite hard to deal with. I was only 25.'

Duffy retreated to the Brixton flat he shared with ToH's merchandising man – or 'swagman', as they were known – 'Little Ian', and a day job at Kensington Market. He was hatching a plan with Steve 'Abbo' Abbott of UK Decay to form a new band when a familiar face stopped by; someone else who had found the weight of expectation heaped upon his band all too much to bear. Ian Astbury had split with the rest of Southern Death Cult and was wondering what Billy might be up to.

In their last ever interview, given to Tom Vague, SDC were tearing themselves apart over how much musicians could achieve politically in the fraught run-up to the 9 June general election. Ian was firmly supportive of the provocations made by his old allies Crass, although: 'I'd be scared to do some of the things they do. I wouldn't want the SPG knocking on my door and taking me away.' Aki and Barry Jepson were more sceptical, the latter unwilling to foist his opinions on an audience: 'Ian wouldn't be writing lyrics if they weren't there to be seen by people. When it gets to the stage where you're the indoctrinator, that's when it's wrong.' Clearly, they were headed for the door marked 'Musical Differences'. Where Astbury would emerge next was signified by his closing comments: 'I went to a Sex Gang Children gig the other night and it was brilliant . . . Great attitude. Everyone just jumping on each other. The concert situation is about the only thing left.'[18]

Death Cult is perhaps the ultimate Goth name and, fittingly, the first incarnation of this band was recruited by Astbury and Duffy directly out of the Batcave. In a 1994 interview with the Alternative Press, Ian would even claim to have invented the term with the nickname he bestowed on Sex Gang Children's singer, Andi: 'I used to call him the Gothic Goblin because he was a little guy, and he's dark. He used to like Edith Piaf and this macabre music, and he lived in a building in Brixton called Visigoth Towers. So he was the little Gothic Goblin, and his followers were Goths. That's where Goth came from.'[19]

Death Cult's first drummer, Ray Mondo (born Raymond Taylor-Smith in Sierra Leone), came from Ritual, a Harrow-based band who had been flittering around 69 Dean Street with Astbury's new favourite band. He in turn brought Ritual's guitarist Jamie Stewart (b. 31 January 1964) in when he agreed to switch to bass – there could be no other Gretsch God in this band. Death Cult released their eponymous debut EP on Situation Two in July 1983. Its striking sleeve depicted the singer and guitarist's twin obsessions: the front cover, a shot taken by Vietnam War photographer Tim Page, the latter a band logo of a skull wearing Mickey Mouse ears designed by Jamie Stewart. Weird scenes from *Apocalypse Now* permeated not just the lyrics of 'Christian', which references the tiger stripe camouflage worn by US forces, but also Duffy's current look, which consisted of those very fatigues along with a green beret. 'Ghost Dance' continued Astbury's quest for knowledge about America's indigenous peoples, using quotes from Paiute spiritual leader Wovoka, who advocated this ritual practice to displace the white settlers; while 'Horse Nation' comes directly from Dee Brown's 1970 history of the nineteenth-century displacement and massacre of the tribes, *Bury My Heart at Wounded Knee*. The opening track 'Brothers Grimm' was one Duffy had actually written with Abbo but seems to aptly describe the relationship with his new frontman: 'Brothers forever blood forever'.

Tom Vague wrote the sleevenotes and followed Death Cult's trail across Europe and back for their first gigs in Britain, where he reported in *ZigZag* that a nation was now firmly divided: 'Basically there's two categories of death cults. On the one hand there's the Goths, spawned by the likes of the Banshees, Bauhaus and Killing Joke, and epitomised by the Batcave . . .' These sensitive souls were constantly under threat from rival, chicken-dancing goon squads: 'Then there's the cult of the billies, fuelled largely by Theatre of Hate . . . It's real easy to join, all you've got to do is pay your £2.50 to get in, spend you dole at the bar and then go mental to King Kurt . . .'

While Vague was writing his piece – and witnessing further tribal skirmishes with Sisters fans, the God Squad, in Leeds – in

September 1983, Ray Mondo was replaced via a straight swap with Nigel Preston, who had been spending post-ToH time in Sex Gang Children. With this line-up, Death Cult would release one more single, 'Gods Zoo' in October 1983, before metaphorically severing Goth ties by reinventing themselves one more time as simply – yet more ambitiously – the Cult.[20]

Of Mice and Men

What of those jettisoned by all these devastating, cross-tribal allegiances? In the aftermath of the second Thatcher landslide election victory of 1983, Astbury's former SDC comrades became, appropriately enough, Getting the Fear. They recruited a striking new singer in Paul 'Bee' Hampshire, who was so androgynous he had the honour of inspiring the first Gothabilly gender confusion anthem. 'I Blood Brother Be' (EL Benelux, 1984) by Shock Headed Peters was written when formerly ruggedly heterosexual singer-guitarist Karl Blake mistook Bee for a girl and, unable to contain his feelings, penned the lines: 'I want to walk through Sodom with a boy on my arm/Who's so damn pretty I don't know where I am . . .'

Just to add to the gender confusion, Barnsley-born Hampshire was previously connected to Danse Society, who also had a singer, Steve Rawlings, that many people, including Mick Mercer (*Gothic Rock*, p. 46), initially mistook for a girl. Bee played keyboards in the pre-Society combos Danse Crazy and Y, before moving to London, where he modelled for fetish magazine *Skin Two* and worked on the door at their club.[21]

Though Getting the Fear signed to RCA, an internal record company shake-up meant they only released one single, the prophetically titled 'Last Salute' – 'If this must end let it pass me by/I'll remain your friend, only flowers die'. In order to escape the ramifications of their contract, they split: Bee and Barry Jepson continuing as the more darkly romantic Into a Circle, while Buzz and Aki formed the funkier Joy with a new vocalist, Danny, and bassist, Eddie.

Neither act lasted very much longer, but Aki did manage to go his own way and by 1988 was running his label, Nation Records, from an office two floors down from the Banshees' management company in All Saints Road, Ladbroke Grove. In the end, the drummer became the most politically overt member of the former Southern Death Cult. Through his own music and his label's output, he has sought to combat racism, examine the causes of Islamic fundamentalism in British youth and create a unity between Britain's Asian and Afro-Caribbean communities – from one of the best addresses to do so in the land.

Kirk Brandon, meanwhile, had signed to Epic records and regrouped with Stan Stammers, drummer Chris Bell and the brilliant saxophonist Lascelles James as Spear of Destiny. They rapidly produced an album, *Grapes of Wrath*, released on 15 April 1983, debuting two of its most outstanding tracks on Channel 4's *Switch*. 'The Preacher' continued *Westworld*'s journey into a mythic landscape, conjuring a philosophical duel between the narrator, the titular Man of the Cloth, and the Devil with effectively stark, minimalist instrumentation and personal favourite 'The Wheel' – a song I would replay in my head as if it were an enchantment to protect me every time I had to walk home from the Belton bus stop after dark.

However, it appeared that yet again, Brandon had shot himself in the foot with this new choice of name. I knew from my Dennis Wheatley (*They Used Dark Forces*, 1964) and James Herbert (*The Spear*, 1978) that it referred to the spear that pierced the side of Christ, which Adolf Hitler was desperate to acquire to ensure his victory by nefarious Black Magical means. But I didn't assume that Kirk had chosen this moniker because he was a Nazi – neither, presumably, did the British-Caribbean James. Brandon's work had so often equated abuses of power within politics and organised religion, I supposed he was drawing another analogy along those lines. But *NME*'s Amrik Rai felt differently and during a heated interview, the singer flailed to defend himself against being charged as a neo-Nazi – and a barrage of other, more personal asides.

The subsequent feature, which ran on 5 May 1984, remains an eye-watering piece of character annihilation. Years later, Brandon told Sean Egan he was advised by his solicitors not to sue the music paper: 'Which in retrospect was incredibly stupid because it caused so much trouble that in reality we just should have sued them . . . In reality, we would have won.'[22]

Instead, before Spear of Destiny's debut appearance on *The Tube*, on Friday, 13 April 1984, Brandon made the anticipatory statement: 'I am not a Nazi.' Swiftly followed by a rebuff to Rai's most insidiously posed question, the one that had him wondering aloud whether his inquisitor wasn't some kind of fascist himself – 'and I'm not gay.'

But those were words that would come back to haunt him.

Gothfathers: The Scream Team

As Poison Ivy previously alluded, there is something in the Cleveland, Ohio, air. Jalacy 'Screamin' Jay' Hawkins was born there on 18 July 1929. Of uncertain parentage, he was put up for adoption at eighteen months and would claim he was taken in and raised by Blackfoot Indians. The truth was more prosaic: he was brought up in a Cleveland boarding house by a woman who may have been a Native American. But clearly Jay had a gift for storytelling, which, when coupled with enormous visual flair and a taste for the macabre, made him an unconventional star. His biggest hit 'I Put a Spell on You' was recorded in 1956 by canny Okeh records producer Arnold Maxim, who made sure Hawkins and his band had a skinful before he rolled the tape. The result sounds just like the denizens of the underworld having a party – the singer recorded his vocal lying flat out on the floor and could later remember nothing about it. But, despite a profound lack of interest from virtually all radio stations, the public loved the raw voodoo trapped within its grooves and bought the single in their droves, inspiring a host of cover versions, none more impressive than the one made by Nina Simone in 1965.

The influential rock 'n' roll DJ and impresario Alan Freed soon got in touch with Hawkins, offering him $300 to emerge from a coffin onstage. Despite his reservations – 'No black dude gets in a coffin alive – they don't expect to get out!' – the audience's wild reaction set him off on his theatrical path of high ghoulishness. He would regularly perform in a Dracula cape with bones up his nose and a cigarette-smoking skull sidekick he called Henry, performing 'spell-casts' which, given his formidable presence, were downright scary to behold. And although the civil rights body NAACP were not impressed with his appearance, ticking him off via ambassador Sammy Davis Jr, he would spawn the entire genre of 'shock rock' that passed on to Alice Cooper, Marilyn Manson, GWAR et al.

Perhaps his greatest admirer was David Edward 'Screaming Lord' Sutch. Born in London in November 1940, Sutch was cutting an outrageous figure on the capital's music scene of the early '60s, sporting 12-inch-long locks before the Rolling Stones had grown theirs past their collars. Recruiting his band, the Savages, from the Cannibal Pot coffee shop on the Harrow Road, he teamed up with record producer Joe Meek, who shared his taste for the supernatural. Together, they created the classic 'Jack the Ripper' single, which they promoted by driving a hearse around the Whitechapel streets of 1962. Armed with a pair of buffalo horns, his auntie's leopardskin coat and some joke shop novelties, Sutch terrified his teenage audience – in his youth, he looked almost identical to the Damned's Dave Vanian.

Both Jay and Sutch managed to get trapped inside their stunt coffins on occasion – a spectacle parodied beautifully in Slade's 1975 film Flame *with Slade frontman Noddy Holder as Stoker, lead singer of the Undertakers. Jay continued his career in music, picking up film roles from admirer Jim Jarmusch in* Mystery Train, *collaborating with New York garage revivalists the Fuzztones and releasing in the Grunge year of 1991 the hilariously named* Black Music for White People *LP, before moving to Paris in 1993. Sutch, however, turned to politics. First in 1963, when he stood as a candidate for his own National Teenage Party in the by-election in Stratford-upon-Avon caused by the resignation of disgraced MP John Profumo. He reactivated his political career two decades later, still in his leopardskin coat and top hat, launching his Official Monster Raving Loony Party at the 1983 Bermondsey by-election. He went on to finish off the SDP – after he scored more votes than their candidate Jack Holmes at the May 1990 Bootle by-election, they promptly dissolved themselves. Though he held the* Guinness Book of Records *title for most parliamentary elections contested and lost – thirty-nine – many of his manifesto pledges have since become law. These include 24-hour drinking, lowering the voting age to eighteen, the abolition of dog licences, the legalisation of commercial radio (Sutch ran his own illegal Sutch Radio from a Napoleonic sea fort in the Thames Estuary, also featured in* Flame*), the pedestrianisation of Carnaby Street, pet passports and – get this, Margaret Thatcher – the abolition of the 11-plus.*

Tragically, Sutch's comedic mask concealed a troubled soul – he took his own life at the age of fifty-eight on 16 June 1999, shortly after the death of his beloved mother, Annie Smith. Jay lived on to the – in rock 'n' roll terms – ripe old age of seventy, before passing on 12 February 2000. He left behind a

31-year-old French widow; five previous wives and at least fifty-seven – perhaps even as many as seventy-five – children, who were reunited by film-maker Maral Nigolian via his jayskids.com for his Cutting Edge Channel 4 documentary 57 Screaming Kids, *which aired in 2001.*

Gothmother: Karen Dalton

In the Greenwich Village folk scene of the early '60s, Bob Dylan was floored by her: 'My favourite singer in the place was Karen Dalton,' he wrote in his memoir, Chronicles Volume One *(Simon & Schuster, 2004). 'She was a tall, white blues singer and guitar player – funky, lanky and sultry. Karen had a voice like Billie Holiday's and played guitar like Jimmy Reed, and went all the way with it.'*

What he was listening to was a true product of the Dust Bowl, the voice of a 21-year-old with two children, who had left two failed marriages behind her in Enid, Oklahoma. Dalton had learned to play the twelve-string guitar by listening to Leadbelly, was adept on the long-neck banjo and could sing Lady Day's 'God Bless the Child' in a way that made all the hairs stand up on the back of your neck – like she knew her own life was to prove to be every bit as nasty, brutish and short.

For a time, on the crossroads of Bleeker and MacDougal, she found a home among the folk singer crowd, playing with Dylan, Tim Hardin, Richard Tucker and the prodigiously gifted Fred Neil, a fellow twelve-string virtuoso who shared her deeply melancholic bent. When Fred – now best known for 'Everybody's Talkin'', as sung by Harry Nilsson on the Midnight Cowboy *(1969) soundtrack – heard Karen performing his material, he said she could have made him believe it was her own.*

She was a regular at the Café Wha?, where she would play traditional songs and blues covers, but she was nervous onstage and unwilling to share with an audience anything she had written herself. Her lack of self-confidence and perilous subsistence, trying to care for her five-year-old daughter, Abbe Baird, in a tenement apartment with no working toilet, triggered wild mood swings. Like Billie Holliday, drugs, booze and men blurred the pain away – but never for long. Talking to The Guardian *in 2021, Baird remembered her mother losing two bottom teeth trying to break up a fight between two of her boyfriends.*

She eventually married Richard Tucker and moved with him and Abbe to Colorado. But by 1969 – after the folk scene had long since decamped to Laurel Canyon – she was back in New York and signed to Capital Records, for whom she recorded the album It's So Hard to Tell Who's Going to Love You the Best. *It was not an easy experience. Producer Nick Venet had to bring Fred Neil into the studio and trick Karen into thinking there were no tapes rolling in order to capture her, recording a set of covers by Neil, Hardin, Jelly Roll Morton and Booker T. Jones, all in one night.* Village Voice's *critic conveyed all the gut-wrenching impact of those hard-wrung takes as 'the antithesis of Joan Baez's boring clarity . . . This record makes me feel like crying.' But, too dark, stark and raw for lovers of Baez, Joni Mitchell or the Mamas and the Papas, it didn't sell and Karen was subsequently dropped.*

She recorded a second album, In My Own Time, *for Woodstock promoter Michael Lang's Just Sunshine label, at the Bearsville Studios in Woodstock set up by Dylan's manager, Albert Goldman, in 1971. With fuller instrumentation and songs especially tailored for her – Dino Valenti, author of 'Get Together' by the Youngbloods, wrote opening track 'Something's on Your Mind' for Dalton and it fitted like a glove – it aimed at a more commercial sound. But Lang scuppered his own charge by putting her on as an opening act for an arena tour with fusion behemoths Santana, an experience she couldn't cope with.*

Dalton's failure to perform like the proverbial chicken on a hotplate triggered the spiral of drug abuse and shared needles that would eventually end with her death from AIDS at the age of fifty-five, in a mobile home in Woodstock in 1993. Her unsettling and uncompromising oeuvre was subsequently rediscovered, with notable interpreters including Nick Cave. Documentary film-makers Robert Yapkowitz and Richard Peete also recently completed a painstaking search to piece together the fragments of her life in their film Karen Dalton: In My Own Time, *released in the US in October 2021.*

Of the rumours that sprang up about Dalton after her death, the most persistent was about her heritage. Her friend, the singer Lacy J. Dalton (no relation), told The Guardian's *Laura Barton on the 2007 re-releases of both Karen's albums: 'Her mother, Evelyn, was Cherokee. She would sleep on a brass bed in her backyard.' Speaking to Jim Farber of the same newspaper in September 2021, Abbe Baird laughed this off, but added: 'She was a lot like her own mother. They were both very volatile people – happy and excited one minute, then very depressed and negative.' Although Karen's parents were both strict Baptists, it was her father who had the Indigenous heritage. Though it's not hard to imagine why this willowy singer, with her long black hair and voice that seemed to channel elemental forces of nature and human pain, could want to find solace in the displaced nations of her land.*

CHAPTER 8

Ranters, Diggers and Levellers

Militant tendencies: UK Decay, the Mob, New Model Army, Joolz

> 'If Margaret Thatcher is re-elected as prime minister on Thursday, I warn you . . . I warn you not to go into the streets alone after dark or into the streets in large crowds of protest in the light. I warn you that you will be quiet – when the curfew of fear and the gibbet of unemployment make you obedient. I warn you that you will have a defence of a sort – with a risk and a price that passes all understanding.'
>
> – Neil Kinnock, speech at Bridgend, 8 June 1983

After Thatcher's 1983 election victory, the formerly most unpopular leader in post-war history now seemed unassailable, her opposition in disarray. Three days later, on 12 June, Michael Foot resigned as leader of the Labour Party, swiftly followed by Roy Jenkins, who stood down as head of the once threatening SPD-Liberal Alliance on 14 June, to be replaced by Dr David Owen. Both of these men had previously deserted Labour, launching the breakaway SDP with fellow moderates Shirley Williams and Bill Rodgers on 26 March 1981. This Gang of Four's formation spoke volumes about the bitter internal rifts that had prevented Labour from becoming an effective opposition.

A bastion of Old Labour values, the CND-supporting, Aldermaston veteran Foot (1913–2010) pledged unilateral nuclear disarmament, the renationalisation of all recently privatised industries and the abolition of the House of Lords in Labour's election manifesto *The New Hope for Britain* – subsequently described by New Labour MP Gerald Kaufman as 'the longest suicide note in history'. Before overseeing Labour's worst election result since 1918, Foot had struggled to contain the warring factions within his party and deflect the scorn and ridicule poured on him by the Murdoch press, led by *The Sun*'s Kelvin MacKenzie, appointed editor two months after the secret meeting at Chequers, in April 1981.

Thatcher's most vociferous cheerleader during the Falklands, MacKenzie described his target reader as 'the bloke you see in the pub, a right old fascist, wants to send the wogs back, buy his poxy council house, he's afraid of the unions, afraid of the Russians, hates the queers and the weirdos and drug dealers'.[1] He boosted his paper's circulation up to 4 million in 1982 by introducing bingo to its pages, celebrated the sinking of the Argentine *General Belgrano* with the headline 'Gotcha' and asked readers: 'Do you really want this old fool to run Britain?' above an unflattering photo of Foot on election eve.

Foot's successor, coal-miner's son Neil Kinnock (b. 28 March 1942 in Tredegar, Blaenau Gwent), elected on 2 October 1983, made strenuous attempts to oust the extreme Militant Tendency from within his party. Initially followers of *The Militant*, a Trotskyist newspaper founded in 1964, its supporters had won favour with Labour's youth in punk Year Zero 1976 and had since been elected to Parliament and key positions within borough councils – most notably the combative Derek Hatton, who became Liverpool council's deputy leader in 1983. A still more prominent figure on the left with whom Kinnock had previously tussled was Arthur Scargill (b. 11 January 1931 in Worsborough, West Yorkshire), since December 1981 the leader of the National Union of Mineworkers (NUM).

Scargill first rose to prominence during the coal strike of 1972 when his 'flying picket' tactics got the better of Edward Heath's government during the Battle of Saltley Gate coke depot in Birmingham. Arthur led several hundred of his fellow Yorkshire miners to assist in preventing supplies of fuel from being delivered to the rest of the UK, overwhelming the police and ultimately getting the dispute resolved on NUM terms. In May 1973, he became president of the Yorkshire NUM and was instrumental in the strike that brought down the Heath government in 1974. Since February 1981, Thatcher's government had stepped back from plans to close down twenty pits on economic grounds after the NUM threatened to ballot for a strike. But, as the PM recorded in her diary, the settling of old scores was 'only really a question of time'.[2]

Kinnock and Scargill – an ally of Kinnock's arch-rival, the hard left Tony Benn – had already traded public insults at the schismatic 1981 Labour Party Conference. That these two red-headed men – both so gifted in the skills of oration yet so far apart on their definition of socialism – made each other see red was yet another gift for the PM.

Her first move was made on 1 September 1983, when Ian MacGregor was appointed chairman of the National Coal Board (NCB). This tough old troubleshooter – seventy at the time of his appointment, the same age as Michael Foot – had come to the government's aid before when Sir Keith Joseph appointed him chairman of British Steel in 1980. He subsequently made 80,000 redundancies in a workforce that had been costing the taxpayer nearly £2 million per day. By now, British Coal was losing around £1.5 million daily[3] and on his first meeting with Scargill, MacGregor laid out plans to improve the balance sheet with a programme of pit closures. The NUM leader had called three ballots on industrial action since 1981 and each time he had been rebuffed by his members. But this changed things. First, MacGregor insisted he would not improve a below-inflation pay offer. Second, he chose a pit in Scargill's heartland – Cortonwood in South Yorkshire – as the first to go. This appeared deliberately provocative. Cortonwood's coal seam was far from exhausted and its workers decided to fight the closure, with neighbouring mines coming out in sympathy. Then MacGregor disclosed the extent of his plans: twenty pits to close with the loss of 20,000 jobs. But Scargill refused to believe it, claiming to have seen a government secret hit-list that condemned more like seventy mines.[4]

The red flag went up. Across the familiar plains of Britain's previous civil wars, on 12 March 1984, fresh battle commenced.

Still Living with the English Fear

As we saw in the previous chapter, the story of Goth's own militant tendency began with Crass and the ideas that radiated out of Dial House, seeding the nation's dole-queue youth with some different designs for life. Two of the most influential bands to come out of this anarchist counter-culture had already gone their separate ways by the time the Miners' Strike began but the ideas they engendered and the connections they forged continued to haunt the musical landscape in ways that make it impossible to tell this story without them.

UK Decay came out of the unglamorous surrounds of Luton in 1979. This Bedfordshire town, heavily bombed during the Second World War when its Vauxhall Motors plant was given over to the manufacture of Churchill tanks, was afterwards rapidly rebuilt as a London overspill. The new suburbs of Farley Hill, Stopsley, Limbury, Marsh Farm and Leagrave that went up in the mid- to late '60s gave Luton the outward appearance of a gigantic Brutalist estate, surrounded by rings of motorway, with planes from its satellite airport soaring overhead.

From these Ballardian vistas, Steven 'Abbo' Abbot (b. January 1960) took every opportunity to get on the train to London and collect records from Soho Market, or follow the Clash, Ants and Banshees around on tour. Inevitably, this led to him joining a punk band, the Rezistors, whose initial songwriting attempts – 'Necrophilia', 'Pervert', 'Mystery Society' and 'Abbo's Acne' –

revealed something of the darkness inside him. Before long, novice guitarist Abbo had taken on vocal duties and renamed the band UK Decay after a *Daily Mirror* headline from the Winter of Discontent. Now comprising himself, Steve Harle on drums and Martin 'Segovia' Smith on bass, they released 'Split Single' in 1979 with fellow Luton punkers Pneumania, from whom Abbo then poached the more seasoned six-stringer Steve Spon, allowing him to concentrate on singing.

Early gigs saw them sharing bills with fellow Banshees' disciples Spizzoil, Killing Joke and a pre-'Bela' Bauhaus, Abbo recalling to Mick Mercer how 'totally blown away' he was when given a tape of their debut single: '["Bela Lugosi's Dead"] just came from nowhere . . . so left of field of what everyone else was doing.' Yet UK Decay's own preoccupations shared much in common with Bauhaus' crypt of curiosities, starting with their debut 'Black Cat' EP, released on their own Plastic Records in early 1980, with the assistance of Rough Trade's Geoff Travis. 'And suddenly we had a record in the indie charts, which was packed with Toyah and all these people we considered really big.'[5]

This prompted Alex Howe, the Soho Market stallholder from whom Abbo had bought so much vinyl, to offer them a deal with his upstart Fresh Records. The first result was September 1980's indie chart smash 'For My Country', in which Abbo appeared to anticipate the Falklands War by two years with some *Jerusalem*-quoting lyrics about the nation's doomed youth. A tour with the Dead Kennedys – led by arch provocateur Jello Biafra, the most Crass-alike of all US punks – followed. Then, with Social Unrest's Creetin (or Jason) K-os taking over from the departed Segovia on bass, UK Decay toured America themselves, in such like-minded company as Circle Jerks and Black Flag. They also found time to produce their own fanzine, *The Suss*, and run the clothes/record shop Matrix in Luton – entrepreneurial activities that would stand their singer in good stead when, at the end of the decade, he started up his own label, Big Cat.

After another new bassist, Eddie 'Dutch' Branch, aka Twiggy, and two more singles, 'Unexpected Guest' and 'Sexual', UK Decay unleashed their debut album, *For Madmen Only*, in October 1981. In keeping with its Halloween release, the record's claustrophobic atmosphere – all clattering drums, pulsating bass and titles like 'Dorian', 'Decadence' and 'Unexpected Guest' – felt like the sonic equivalent of being locked in a haunted house all night. It was sleeved just as unnervingly, in a reproduction of Dutch-Indonesian painter Jan Toorop's 1894 *The Disintegration of Faith*, in which he depicts mankind drowning, with the heads of his contemporaries, writers Willem Kloos and Lodewijk van Deyssel, just visible above the water. Sticking out of the ground are the bayonets of the sovereign power, intent on restoring order through violence. It wasn't too difficult to read that analogy in the political climate of the time and unfolding events would confirm the accuracy of Abbo's scrying mirror.

In an interview with *Sounds*' Steve Keaton, the singer described the album as 'punk Gothique', joking that the band should put out gargoyle-shaped records and only play in churches. Within the next six months, UK Decay would find themselves on bills with Southern Death Cult, Sex Gang Children, Theatre of Hate, Brigandage and Blood & Roses – the slightly older players at the centre of a scene that left the then 21-year-old Abbo 'feeling like Grandpa!'[6]

Fresh records collapsed at the beginning of 1982, but with the help of Crass-associate John Loder's Southern Studios, UK Decay managed to buy the rights to their back catalogue. Through Loder, Penny Rimbaud produced their next EP, the aptly named *Rising from the Dread*, released on Crass's Corpus Christi imprint in August 1982. It is this record that contains the most genuinely unnerving of all their releases, the ten-minute epic 'Werewolf', which in places sounds like the band and Rimbaud actually managed to capture a field recording of a lycanthropic transformation. The effort of which left them exhausted and shortly afterwards an emotional Abbo called time at the Hammersmith Clarendon Klub Foot on 30 December 1982: 'To me it'd become a dinosaur.'

Abbo not only mentioned the G-word some considerable time before Ian Astbury's claimed invention of it, but he was also writing songs with Billy Duffy first. Still, he remained magnanimous: 'Ian came round and said: "We've been offered a £100,000 deal and I don't want it." He was very shrewd because in a very short space of time he'd realised that as soon as he stepped into that big label monster, his future was gone . . . I was actually rehearsing with Billy Duffy and had written four or five songs, but we couldn't get on, that's how him and Ian got together to form Death Cult, who I thought were very exciting and would go on to big things . . .'[7] This was something the UK Decay frontman would also achieve for himself – although, perhaps tellingly, by largely keeping to a background role.

For My Country

Just as UK Decay had conjured poltergeists and werewolves from Britain's troubled national psyche, so the Mob evoked the grim spectre of Matthew Hopkins, self-styled Witchfinder General during the English Civil War, in their brooding *Let the Tribe Increase* album of 1983.[8] Its ominous closing track, 'Witch Hunt', could have provided the template for Neil Kinnock's pre-election prophecy at Bridgend, should he have been an anarcho-punk: 'Changing your course for another way . . . Under pressure from the witch hunt'.

The band formed in the tiny hamlet of Stoke-sub-Hamdon, near Yeovil in Somerset, from whence hailed singer-guitarist Mark Wilson, bassist Curtis Youé and drummer Graham Fallows. Here, they existed on a leyline to the place where hippy and punk converged – Stonehenge and its Free Festival, which began as a retaliation to violent police suppression of the 1974 Windsor Free Festival and would be yet more brutally curtailed in 1985, seeing its last summer solstice sunrise in 1984. The Mob came up, playing support to such veterans as Here & Now, and attended the Free Festival as often as they could.

'The real shining light of Yeovil for me was living near Stonehenge,' recalled Mark.[9] 'From about 1977 to 1978 the whole Yeovil scene would decamp to Stonehenge for weeks on end.'

Which is where they came into contact with Crass and the Poison Girls, who played in 1979, the year the Mob released their first single 'Crying Again' on their own All the Madmen label. This was followed by 'Witch Hunt' in 1980 and their one Crass Records single, the post-apocalypse blues 'No Doves Fly Here', produced by Penny Rimbaud and recorded at Southern Studios in 1981. Played alongside 'For My Country', it made the perfect uneasy listening in those days when it seemed Ronnie the Raygun and Leonid Brezhnev could unleash Armageddon at any moment.

Having learned the ropes of communal living in Wiltshire, the Mob moved to London in 1981, following their second drummer, Joseph Porter, to a squat in Hackney's Brougham Road, acquired for £40 – 'the amount [the previous inhabitant] had spent getting the water turned on and changing the Yale lock'. They soon became involved with the KYPP collective, at events at the Crass-sponsored Autonomy Centre in Wapping and then the Centro Iberico – an abandoned school at 421 Harrow Road, close to the ZigZag venue. They also aided the Black Sheep Housing Co-op, playing benefit gigs and helping to restore buildings for habitation. For a time, it must have felt like it really was possible to sustain a meaningful, self-help lifestyle outside of mainstream society.

Let the Tribe Increase – its title a reflection of that commitment – was another venture between the Mob and KYPP. This one also helped on its way by Rough Trade's Geoff Travis, who paid the pressing costs in return for the band funding their own studio time.[10] To their astonishment, it sold 20,000 copies, but by 1983 the Mob had run their course. Drummer Joseph formed the more folk-inclined Blyth Power, who exist to this day, while Mark took off as a traveller.

Like UK Decay, the Mob's recorded output carries with it the grainy, visceral rawness of music made outside the corporate recording industry, on as low a budget as possible – basically, crowd-funded by a community of gig-goers, fanzine writers and activists, with Geoff Travis and Crass acting as godparents. These were bands who truly excelled live, the vinyl imprints they left behind a ghost image of what it was like to see them in the flesh, what bonded their fans.

The followers of both bands were part of their own travelling societies, a huge segment of early '80s youth culture at a time when large swathes of them had little else to keep them occupied and engaged. As Pete Scott wrote in *Vague* 14: 'If you're on the dole, make the most of it.'

But you can just imagine Kelvin MacKenzie's *Sun* readers' response to that.

Which is why you can also hear an alarm call sounding in the subtext of these records. Those who live on the margins are acutely aware of how vulnerable they are. Those who knew their history would have recalled the fates of their distant antecedents, the Ranters, Diggers and Levellers, who tried such experiments in utopian communal living after the last Civil War and ended up either slaughtered or transported for the democratic dreams.[11]

War and Peace Studies

Then over the hills from Bradford came a three-man New Model Army.

They could hardly have emerged from a more suitable place than this northern bastion of non-conformity, where Cromwell still stood in the City Hall. They could hardly have comprised a more useful, compact and purposeful unit either, drawing all the electricity from the gathering storm into their debut single. 'Bittersweet', released on the misleadingly named Quiet records, was the exact taste of the June 1983 post-election blues. 'Caught in this struggle for power/Where only blood ever tastes sweet,' a singer called Slade the Leveller announced himself, via John Peel's turntable. 'Everything else is so sour/The numbing failures and defeats'. There was nothing muddy about the sound of this band, no doubting the conviction of their vocalist. 'But there's always another morning,' he rallied despondent listeners: 'We're never dead 'til the last breath.'[12]

This New Model Army had arrived just in time for the next civil war. By the November of 1983, they had a deal with Abstract records and a new single – 'Great Expectations' – a neat summary of the politics of greed and a track Peel was again very keen to share. NMA had already attracted a small legion of ardent fans by February 1984, when they were invited to play on Friday night's most essential televisual viewing, Channel 4's *The Tube*. Within ten minutes, they had transmitted to the teenage nation why they were going to succeed in pushing their message further than UK Decay, the Mob or even Crass.

'There's a nightmare coming,' Slade the Leveller warned on opening salvo 'Christian Militia', a song about Ronald Reagan's fanbase. His dark eyes shone, face cracked into a grin that revealed missing front teeth. 'There's a witch hunt coming,' he continued, notes slicing off his red Fender SG and ricocheting against the bass of the astonishing Stuart Morrow. A deceptively slight-looking lad, with black hair pushed up into a sailor's cap, Morrow appeared to have trapped the spirits of both Lemmy and Bootsy Collins inside his instrument and bounced about the stage, legs twitching maniacally with the effort of containing them. Ruthlessly keeping the pace was their Saxon warhammer, big blond Robert Heaton (1961–2004), a man who had once been in Hawkwind and would later be described by veteran Rolling Stones/Led Zeppelin producer Glyn Johns as the most perfect drummer he had ever worked with.[13]

NMA's fans – today fondly referred to as 'The Family' or 'The Following' – were then known as the Militia and were feared by the gig-going public almost as much as Cromwell's pikemen of yore. *Tube* viewers witnessed a dervish of multi-coloured and spiked-up hair, leather jackets adorned with hand-painted band logos – white background, red circle, heavy black stencilled lettering – and shod in traditional working men's clogs, handmade at a mill in Hebden Bridge. They chicken-danced their way through 'Christian Militia' and 'Smalltown England', climbing onto each other's shoulders and spinning, almost as mesmeric to watch as the band. The camera was drawn to a girl with bright red hair at the centre of the skirmish who looked straight back into the lens, laughing.

In their leathers and clogs, New Model Army certainly looked the part of incendiary rebel leaders, throwbacks to tumultuous times past. Introducing them, *Tube* host Muriel Gray reported they were 'the ugliest band in rock 'n' roll' – but their audience begged to differ. Before much longer, NMA's debut LP *Vengeance* would knock gladioli-waving Mancunians the Smiths off the top of the indie charts, catching the climate of 1984 in a witch bottle forever more. Yet both its contents and creators remain a mass of contradictions.

Slade the Leveller was born Justin Sullivan on 8 April 1956. He hailed from the Quaker village of Jordans in Buckinghamshire, founded in the seventeenth century by the followers of George Fox and still administered on cooperative principles to this day.[14] His parents practised a mixture of the Quaker faith and Subud, a religion founded by Indonesian mystic Bapak Muhammad Subuh Sumohadiwidjojo, who travelled to England to spread the word during the '50s. Though Quakers[15] are usually viewed as heirs to the socialist ideas first spread by the Levellers, the Sullivans hedged their bets and sent their offspring to a prestigious prep school, the Dragon School in Oxford. Justin metaphorically wore this dichotomy on his sleeve on *The Tube* – his russet captain's coat not a battledress but an officer's mess dress tunic, though its Royal Corps of Signals badge suggests communications is his area of expertise. And, despite all these connections, the name Slade the Leveller was, the singer told *Sounds'* Jack Barron in June 1984, 'an in-joke. But it does tie in. I'm very keen on that period of history.'

Sullivan first came to Bradford in the late '70s to train as a social worker, taking Peace Studies at the university – the first such course to be offered in Britain.[16] He formed a band with Stuart Morrow (b. 1966, the only member of NMA born in Bradford) while living in the same house to which Ian Astbury was taken from a Poison Girls gig to meet his Southern Death Cult destiny. 'I could play a few chords,' Justin remembered, 'but Stuart was amazingly gifted.'[17]

Like Joe Strummer, Sullivan honed his craft busking. He also got involved in what he described as 'trade' – driving convoys of Transit vans to Pakistan, loaded with engine parts and white goods. 'Plus you sold the van itself when you got there,' he told *Q*'s Phil Sutcliffe. 'We went out in convoys of six, 6,000 miles in two weeks, driving eighteen to twenty-two hours a day.'[18]

The girl with the red hair in the middle of *The Tube*'s moshpit is just as important to this story. Julianne Mumford came into this world on 9 April 1955 at Colchester Barracks, the daughter of a territorial SAS officer. She was born dead and was only resuscitated by a transfusion that was thick, she said, with her father's whisky-laced blood. Growing up in Harrogate, she was a teenage poetry prodigy: 'I'd had my work critiqued by Ted Hughes when I was eleven, via a teacher who must have known him, so I was tipped for the top,' she recalled. 'I'd been in a poetry performance group when I was fifteen, sixteen. We did Bolton Town Hall and I remember there was a man in the front row in a Gannex mac who was eating hard-boiled eggs out of a paper bag for the entire performance. I'd found a musician to go on stage with me, and no one else had thought of doing that. Well – they had in America, but not in Yorkshire. It was all very Beat Generation.'

But despite these highlights, Julianne's teenage years were a tumult – her controlling mother tried to restrict her eating, growth and hormones with a combination of Tetracycline, Valium, sleep deprivation and diets. To escape this misery, she plighted her troth to a member of the Satan's Slaves motorcycle gang at the age of nineteen. Biker Kenneth Denby brought her to the outskirts of Bradford and left her in a 'bloody freezing' £7-a-week flat in Baildon, a village on the edge of the moor, while he went prospecting. Not one to sit at home knitting for long, the biker bride utilised her knowledge of combat techniques, taught to her by her soldier father, and got a job working on the door of Queen's Hall – the city's first female bouncer, a blue-haired punk now known as Joolz.

They were still married by the time she met Sullivan in a Bradford shebeen, optimistically named the Champagne a Go-Go but referred to locally as 'Slaggers', in 1979. 'He had his back to me and when he turned around, I saw this face I had all my life been drawing, in the corners of my rough book,' she recalled. In an eerie premonition of Muriel Gray: 'I called it my Ugly Face! So I was a bit taken aback. We started talking and we haven't stopped talking for forty, fifty years.'

Joolz began managing New Model Army, outlining a plan for longevity on the back of a gas bill and creating the distinctive artwork that has adorned the band's recorded output for four decades since. 'You've basically got to build such a strong relationship with the fans that they understand they're part of the process, not just passive receptors,' she said, explaining her strategy. 'They are a bonded unit and they will follow him – because he will change, he can't remain static and just repeat himself. So my magic spell that I wrote in a café in Bradford Arndale Centre goes: Nobody gets left behind, everybody gets a fair share of the money, everybody gets a fair crack at the credits. And everybody is as honest as is humanely possible.' This is about as far from Malcolm McLaren's Ten Point Plan in *The Great Rock 'n' Roll Swindle* as can be imagined. 'Cultivate hatred' was one of his strategies – 'It's your greatest asset.'

Joolz and Justin bonded over childhood experiences that, while different, characterised them both as outsiders who had a particular gift for words. Intellectual equals, they also looked perfect together, as though they'd met in a previous life while fighting off the Roman invasion. In their ramshackle student house, with its makeshift, eggbox-lined basement rehearsal room, the social worker transformed into a firebrand frontman, while the bouncer – with encouragement from gobby housemate, Ian Astbury enabler and future *NME* journalist Steven Wells – became 'ranting poet' Joolz.[19]

It was a job she would need all her father's SAS steel for: 'The thing you learned from the very beginning was that if you gave an inch, showed any vulnerability whatsoever, they would have you. You'd stand on stage and people would be throwing bottles, glasses, lighted cigarettes to try to set your dress on fire. And with a whole can of Boots Extra Strong hairspray on my head, I would have gone up like a human torch.'

New Model Army went through a couple of local drummers, Phil Tompkins and Rob Waddington, before, in 1982, they found the man who completed their training from raw recruits to the battle-ready combo who stormed *The Tube*. Robert Heaton was born in Knustford, Cheshire, on 4 November 1961 and learned both drums and guitar at a young age, inspired by his father's collection of jazz, classical and Johnny Cash records. His skills as a composer would expand NMA's musical palette and prove a perfect foil for Sullivan's lyrical muse. But for now, with Sullivan and Morrow as the main songwriters, it was full-on attack.

Our Life, Our World

New Model Army's debut album *Vengeance* was released in April 1984. In the same month, the Women's Peace Camp was forcefully evicted from Greenham Common; WPC Yvonne Fletcher was shot dead outside the Libyan Embassy and 100 pickets were arrested following clashes at collieries in Creswell, Derbyshire and Babbington, Nottinghamshire. With only forty-six of the 176 British mines remaining operative, on 12 April, Arthur Scargill took the controversial step of ruling out a national ballot of members to continue the strike.

It was a decision that would put him on a collision course with Neil Kinnock, with recriminations that continue to smolder forty years on. The NUM leader knew from regional canvassing that a chunk of his members was opposed to going all out – particularly in Nottinghamshire, where many miners had taken the opportunity Thatcher had handed them and bought their council houses. A ballot could have exposed the same sort of divisions within his ranks that had riven the Labour–SDP split. Instead, Scargill believed that, as had been the case with the tipping point, Cortonwood, industrial action would be spontaneous and the course of events would sustain the strike's momentum.

His opponents this time, though, were a government that had learned from Edward Heath's failures and enacted the 'Ridley Plan' – a 1977 report, drawn up by Tory Nicholas Ridley, which made explicit recommendations for the privatisation of coal, steel, ports, railways and all other industries nationalised since the Second World War. The National Coal Board (NCB) had stockpiled millions of tons of coal; the government had armed themselves with tough new industrial relations laws and devised a system, the National Reporting Centre (NRC), for coordinating police forces across the land. Forces that, after the summer of riots in 1981, were, if not literally spoiling for a fight, at least much better equipped to deal with one than those who'd faced off the Saltley Gate picket nine years earlier. Daily, the pages of *The Sun* were devoted to demonising the miners and their leader, who was routinely accused of inciting mob rule, his members of being 'the scum of the Earth'.[20]

The centrepiece of the strike was the Orgreave coking works, a massive plant set in fields outside Sheffield, where coal was processed to make fuel for a power station in Scunthorpe, twenty miles away. The NCB had an agreement to only transport the bare minimum of fuel, enough to keep the Scunthorpe furnaces burning, but the NUM believed they were exceeding this quota. Pickets arrived and the response of the South Yorkshire Police escalated. On 30 May, Scargill was arrested and charged with obstruction. He called for a mass picket and, on 18 June, members arrived from across the land.

Where previously police had done their best to obstruct flying pickets from reaching their destinations, on that day witnesses remember officers courteously guiding miners to the site, in particular the 'topside' field to the south of the plant – where a six-deep cordon of coppers awaited. Men who were fully equipped with riot gear, round shields and truncheons – equipment previously only used in Northern Ireland – flanked by dog handlers on each side, plus mounted colleagues carrying staves twice as long as truncheons. Official figures that tally are hard to come by, but the pickets – all of whom were unarmed and wearing only light, summer clothing – did not outnumber the police by very many.[21]

Those present have described what happened on that hot summer's day as not a battle but a rout, in which it was a miracle that no one was killed. Having herded the miners into a position where it was very difficult to escape – the only route out of the topside was to scrabble up a steep railway embankment to a narrow railway bridge over live train tracks – dozens of mounted officers charged into them, lashing out with their truncheons. Fifty-five miners were rounded up and arrested at the topside, then charged with 'riot' – an offence that, at the time, carried a potential life sentence. Forty more were arrested on the 'bottom' side of the plant and charged with the marginally less serious 'unlawful assembly'. None would ever be prosecuted.[22]

On the BBC News that evening, footage was presented in a manner that suggested the police were defending themselves against stone-throwing miners. But there was little that even the sharpest editor could do to disguise the terror on the faces of those being hunted down, nor the severity of the injuries inflicted. Yet Margaret Thatcher did not look askance upon the scenes of police violence at Orgreave. Instead, she was busily drafting a speech that she intended to deliver at the Tory Party Conference in October, in which she described not just the miners, but the entire Labour movement as 'the enemy within' and Neil Kinnock as nothing but a 'puppet' leader of a party that had been 'hijacked' by 'the enemies of democracy'.[23]

New Model Army would be the first band to put into words what happened at Orgreave, in their song '1984': 'The servants of our great nation/Have lied in the name of us all/While the officers of peace and order/Are busy breaking every law/There's hundreds on trumped-up charges/Hundreds on the streets/The future of our villages/Sown with bitter seeds/And hatred starts to rumble where there was no hate before/In our own sweet green and pleasant land in 1984'.[24]

Whether he agreed with the NUM leader's tactics or not, Kinnock's election-night prophecy had swiftly come true.

Gothparents: Percy and Mary Shelley

Rise like Lions after slumber
In unvanquishable number,
Shake your chains to earth like dew
Which in sleep had fallen on you
Ye are many – they are few

So concludes The Mask of Anarchy, *written by Percy Bysshe Shelley (1792–1822) in 1819, after the Peterloo Massacre on 16 August of that year. On St Peter's Field in Manchester, a crowd of over 60,000 had gathered to demand the right to vote and been cut down by the 15th Hussars, who charged on them with sabres drawn, killing fifteen and injuring hundreds more.*

The poetic defender of their cause was exiled in Liverno, Italy, at the time, but responded quickly to the news, completing The Mask of Anarchy *in two weeks flat. But his British publisher, Leigh Hunt, feared prosecution – his client had long been under surveillance for promoting subversive ideas on everything from politics to vegetarianism, free love and atheism. So this great rallying call, which would be taken up by protestors against tyranny the world over in the centuries to come, would not see the light until ten years after Percy's untimely demise.*

Rather, as it remains the case today, to be a successful anarchist in the early nineteenth century required a private income. The trouble for Shelley was that he kept losing his. Though heir to the vast estates of his grandfather, Sir Bysshe, it was his father Sir Timothy, a Whig MP, who held the purse strings and used them as a means to attempt to control his rebellious son.

Beloved of W. B. Yeats, Thomas Hardy, Aleister Crowley, campaigning journalist Paul Foot and Buzzcock Pete McNeish, Percy Shelley was born on 4 August 1792 in Warnham, West Sussex. A sensitive child, plagued by nightmares, somnambulism and hallucinations, he was equally drawn to tales of the supernatural and experiments in science. He enlivened an otherwise miserable time at Eton by administering electric shocks to his masters, blowing up trees with gunpowder and attempting to raise the dead – all the elements of a story, about a scientist who manages to reanimate a living being from mortal remains, that would bring literary immortality to his future wife Mary (neé Godwin, 1797–1851).

But, before he'd ever met the daughter of pioneering feminist Mary Wollstonecraft and political philosopher William Godwin, Percy had already been disinherited because of his first marriage. He'd eloped with sixteen-year-old taverner's daughter Harriet Westbrook shortly after being expelled from Oxford University in 1811 for authoring the anonymous tract, The Necessity of Atheism. *The couple lived an itinerant existence, Shelley always looking over his shoulder for moneylenders and government spies as a result of his activities: in Dublin in 1812, Percy had published and distributed three political tracts calling for Catholic emancipation, the repeal of the Acts of Union and an end to the oppression of the Irish poor – reports of which were sent to the home secretary. Setting a pattern for the rest of his days, Percy preferred to always live à trois, and his life with Harriet was spent either accompanied by her sister, Eliza Westbrook, or 28-year-old teacher Elizabeth Hitchener, whom he called 'the sister of my soul'.*

For a while they settled in Wales, where Percy wrote his first major poem, Queen Mab, *which anticipates Crass in surmising the evils of the society as commerce, war, the eating of meat, the church, monarchy and marriage. With little thought for his own matrimony, he deserted Harriet soon after she'd given birth to their daughter, Eliza Ianthe, in June 1813. While visiting William Godwin in Somers Town, London, he'd fallen in love with Mary.*

The leading anarchist of his day, Godwin lived in a house full of children from his own first marriage, to Wollstonecraft – who had died shortly after Mary's birth – and his second to Mary Jane Clairmont; plus daughters that both wives had previously had. With Clairmont, he established the magnificently subversive Juvenile Library, the Dial House of its day, which nurtured the minds of the young with radical fairytales and histories written under the pseudonym Edward Baldwin and published in-house. Mary cut her writing teeth on stories for this venture.

Repeating the pattern of his careless love, Percy took off with the sixteen-year-old Mary and her step-sister Jane 'Claire' Clairmont for revolution-ravaged

France in July 1814. He would go on to enjoy dalliances with two of his next wife's sisters – both Claire and Mary's other half-sister by Wollstonecraft, Fanny Imlay – with tragic consequences. The threesome was back in London four months later, when the birth of Shelley's son Charles to Harriet and the will of the latterly departed Sir Bysshe forced Sir Timothy into providing Percy with an income.

He would need every penny. In January 1816, Mary gave birth to their son, William – she had already lost a daughter, conceived during their flight to France. Percy published Alastor; or The Spirit of Solitude, *the poem that would inspire Crowley to change his first name some eighty years later. It vividly evoked the wandering poet, searching for divine meaning in ruins and wild places rather than enjoying the 'sweet human love' at his disposal. A cautionary tale both for its author and every future Goth, its climactic depiction of a tumultuous and ultimately fruitless sea journey anticipated Shelley's own fate.*

The Shelleys would undertake a momentous journey of their own in what became known as the Year Without a Summer. It began in London, when Claire Clairmont began an affair with prototype rock star, the 'mad, bad and dangerous to know' George Gordon Lord Byron (1788–1824). Then more famous for his scandalous sex life than his poetry, Byron had publicly humiliated former lover, Lady Caroline Lamb, and been discovered conducting a liaison with his half-sister Augusta while married to heiress Annabella Milbanke – all of which precipitated his move to Italy in May 1816. Accompanied by the Shelleys, Claire hurried to meet him at the Villa Diodati, on the shores of Lake Geneva. Here, in the perpetual twilight caused by volcanic ash from the eruption of Mount Tambora, Byron challenged his guests to each write a ghost story.

The eighteen-year-old Mary conceived the plot of Frankenstein; or The Modern Prometheus *– hailed as the first science-fiction novel by no less an authority than Brian Aldiss; and, along with Bram Stoker's* Dracula, *the fount of the horror motion picture industry – in one, vision-filled evening. 'I saw the pale student of unhallowed arts kneeling beside the thing he had put together,' she wrote in the 1831 preface to her book. 'I saw the hideous phantasm of a man stretched out, and then, on the working of some powerful engine, show signs of life, and stir with an uneasy, half vital motion . . .'*

The party broke up after Claire became pregnant – she would give birth to Byron's ill-fated daughter, Allegra, in January 1817. The Shelleys came home to a reckoning of two suicides triggered by Percy's desertion – Fanny Imlay's, from an overdose of laudanum, in September and Harriet's death by drowning in the Serpentine in December 1816. After a lengthy court case that ultimately decreed him an unfit father, Percy and Harriet's children were given to foster parents.

Moving to Marlow, Buckinghamshire, they were joined by Claire and Allegra, whose presence wore on Mary's nerves. She gave birth to Clara in September 1817 and somehow also managed to finish writing Frankenstein*; while Shelley composed* Laon and Cythna, or The Revolution of the Golden City, *which was suppressed by publisher Hunt for fear that its story of an insurrection, bloodily repressed by Church and Crown, would violate laws of blasphemous libel.*

The household moved back to Italy to meet with Byron again in 1818 – the year Frankenstein *was first anonymously published in London – and tragedy followed apace. Clara died from dysentery in Venice that September, then, travelling between Rome and Naples while Percy drafted* Prometheus Unbound, *the Shelleys lost their older child, William, to malaria in June 1819. Claire's Allegra would follow them into an early grave, dying from typhus at the age of five.*

Percy and Mary had one more child, Percy Florence Shelley, in November 1819. The only one who would survive into adulthood, he became the third Baronet of Castle Goring and lived to seventy, a ripe old age compared to his parents. Mary suffered a further miscarriage, from which she nearly died, on 16 June 1822 – Percy saved her by putting her into a bath of ice, which stanched the bleeding. It was the last dramatic act of love between the doomed Romantics.

Ironically, Percy was writing his final – and most despairing – poem, 'The Triumph of Life', when fate caught up with him. After sailing to Livorno to meet with Lord Byron and Leigh Hunt, on 8 July 1822, Percy's boat – named Don Juan, *after Byron's poem – was lost in a storm. The 29-year-old's body was washed ashore ten days later and cremated on a beach near Viareggio on 16 August, a scene romanticised in Louis Édouard Fournier's 1889 painting,* The Funeral of Shelley, *and around which another legend grew. According to Captain John Trelawny, who built the funeral pyre, Shelley's heart refused to be consumed by the flames and was instead taken away by Hunt and preserved in wine.*

Following her husband's death, Mary lived for a year with Hunt in Genoa, where she often saw Byron and transcribed his poems. She returned to England, first living with her father, and then, when Sir Timothy begrudgingly gave her an allowance, with Percy Florence in Harrow. Frankenstein *was published under her own name in its second French edition of 1821 and would never go out of print.*

Mary faithfully collected all Percy's works, publishing with them her own annotations, which enabled her to swerve around a ban on biography forced on her by her father-in-law. She died in 1851 at the age of fifty-three, from a suspected brain tumour. On the first anniversary of her death, Percy Florence opened up her box-desk and discovered locks of all her dead children's hair, a notebook she had shared with Percy – and a copy of his poem Adonaïs *folded around a silk parcel containing the remains of his heart. It was finally laid to rest with his son's remains, at St Peter's Church in Boscombe, Dorset.*

CHAPTER 9

Through the Looking Glass

Back to the future: Echo and the Bunnymen, Marc Almond and the Willing Sinners

'I myself favour an Irish education. Anyone who has encountered *The Book of Kells* cannot help but be impressed by the labyrinthine coils of the Celtic imagination'

– Pendleton (Charles Kay), *Edge of Darkness*, first broadcast 4 November 1985

To the west of the Pennines, in the domain of Neil Kinnock's other arch-enemy, Liverpool Council deputy leader Derek Hatton, the year of 1984 had begun under a rather more auspicious moon.

'I sat bolt upright in bed,' remembered Ian McCulloch, 'with this phrase in my head: "Fate up against your will/Through the thick and thin/He will wait until/You give yourself to him". The whole lyric just poured out and I had to rush off and write it down.'[1] Echo and the Bunnymen's lead singer had become the conduit of his own miracle, a song 'I always half credit to God' that would light the nocturnal path for his band's fourth and greatest album, a magical parallel universe to the grim realities of 1984. Reflecting on its moment of creation thirty years later, he told *The Guardian*'s Dave Simpson: 'It's about everything, from birth to death to eternity and the eternal battle between fate and the human will. It contains the answer to the meaning of life.'

Nothing of minor significance ever happens in Liverpool – even its name means 'Pool of Life' in Old English. It is, of course, the place where all Pop life began, bursting out of a sweaty cellar club one monochrome post-war lunchtime and turning on all the colours of the '60s. As if the Beatles weren't enough, it also gave us the man born John Robert Parker Ravenscoft (1939–2004) but better known as John Peel, without whom you would not be reading this book.[2] Not to mention the world's greatest football team, steered into their most glorious years in the '70s and '80s by first the sublime management skills of Bill Shankly and then the redoubtable Bob Paisley.[3]

The place began modestly enough though in the time of King John (1199–1216), as a grid of seven streets on the banks of the River Mersey. It maintained a discreet presence until the seventeenth century, when the River Dee in nearby Chester – the main port to the Irish Sea since Roman times – began to silt up. As maritime trade looked sharp for an alternative, Liverpool built its first commercial docks in 1715 and the rapid flow of trade – sugar, coal, cotton, tobacco and slaves – brought the city growth and prosperity, grand architecture, beautiful parks and gardens. By the nineteenth century, there were times when the Second City of Empire had more money than even London.

Liverpool was a haven for Irish migrants fleeing the Great Famine of the 1840s and their descendants would play a substantial role in the city's destiny: John Lennon (1940–80) and Paul McCartney (b. 18 June 1942) cut their musical teeth on R&B records made by black Americans that floated back across the Atlantic some 250 years after the first slave ship set sail in 1699.

Liverpool is the home of Britain's oldest black community, first arriving as Loyalist soldiers from the American War of Independence in 1775. A sizeable Jewish population joined migrants from Greece, Italy and Scandinavia from the 1800s onwards. The city's multicultural make-up is like the sailor's stew from whence its residents take their nickname, contributing to its prowess at sport, music and the arts. Like their dockland Cockney counterparts, Scousers have a distinctive sense of humour – sharp, acerbic and delighting in cunning wordplay that bends into the surreal. The port gives and the port takes away: during the Second World War, the city suffered a Blitz second only in size to London's – though, contrary to myth, John Lennon was not born in the middle of an air raid,[4] a belief perhaps sustained by the fact he was given the middle name of Winston.

The DIY music scene that emerged in the late '70s was in very much in the same spirit as the skiffle boom that Lennon and McCartney seized upon as '50s kids, and Liverpool's landmark punk venue Eric's was the natural heir to the Cavern Club. This was partly down to the influence of Eric's co-owner Roger Eagle, the Northern Soul DJ who steered Manchester's ace faces into the Twisted Wheel a decade earlier.

Like the Cavern, Eric's was a basement club and it first opened its portal below the Fruit Exchange on Victoria Street on 1 October 1976. Its other owners were Ken Testi and Pete Fulwell – who both managed bands and, in Pete's case, ran the Inevitable label – Testi giving the club a down-to-earth name at deliberate odds with the faux-glamour of discos like Tiffany's or Samantha's. It would eventually move to a space opposite the Cavern on Mathew Street and – before it was closed down following a 1980 drugs raid – every significant Liverpool band of the '80s got their first break there. Inevitably, it was where teenage Bowie fan McCulloch met future Bunnymen, guitarist Will Sergeant and bassist Les Pattison, outside the ladies' lavs, some enchanted evening in 1978.

A Promise

Ian Stephen 'Mac' McCulloch (b. 5 May 1959) was the son of a car factory shop steward, a compulsive gambler who his son recalled often forging the rent book to try to cover his losses: 'But for all that, he was the greatest. He was like Eric Morecambe meets Bill

Shankly.' With his brother, sister and 'unconventionally religious' mother, he was brought up in the industrious working-class enclave of Norris Green, on the grandly monikered Parthenon Drive. 'I've turned into him, totally,' the motormouth Mac reflected on his paternal heritage. 'I always think you can get away with anything by being a cheeky little bastard.'[5]

Later diagnosed with a compulsive disorder, McCulloch was an able student at Alsop Comprehensive, getting A-levels in English and art. He decided on his choice of career before he left school – a Starman showed him the way – and spent his teenage years perfecting his own riff on the Ziggy Stardust quiff by applying orange juice and Coca-Cola to his bountiful dark locks. The results would wield a similar power over the next generation – for every Kirk or Ian Astbury of my acquaintance, there were at least two Macs.

McCulloch's roots were Scottish rather than Irish, but he evinced a Lennonesque knack for a one-liner from an early age. When, on their first meeting, Sergeant and Pattison asked him what he was waiting outside the bogs for, he replied: 'The gift of vision.'[6] As well as venerating Bowie, he shared Ian Curtis' fascination with Jim Morrison – and Jim's with Frank Sinatra – and from their earliest recordings, the Bunnymen sounded as though they'd stowed away on the Crystal Ship. Pattison was a genuine seadog who worked at Hesketh Bank boatyard, while Sergeant was a short order cook who was particularly inventive with a guitar. Both adventurous by nature, this pair of old schoolfriends from Deyes Lane Secondary Modern frequently took off exploring – by ferry, plane or pushbike – bringing back musical ideas from distant shores, which, as we shall see, would give the Bunnymen a much broader soundscape than many of their rivals.

McCulloch also shared Andrew Eldritch's predilection for master lyricist Leonard Cohen and had the ability to follow through with highly literary, often drug-tinged observations, delivered in a velvet baritone made for afterhours clubs and moonlit nights: 'As a kid, I'd always loved *The Sky at Night* and *Star Trek*, and I remembered the moon landing,' he told Dave Simpson. 'I was up all night wishing

I had a telescope.' Before his fortuitous run-in with Sergeant and Pattison, he was part of Eric's most mythologised of combos, the Crucial Three, with fellow Scouser Pete Wylie and Tamworth migrant Julian Cope. But the laws of physics could not possibly contain three natural lead singers in one band for more than a handful of rehearsals – Wylie went on to front the various incarnations of his soulful stompers Wah!, while Cope was briefly a pop idol as the Scott Walker look-/soundalike from the Teardrop Explodes.

Initially a trio – Echo was their drum machine – the Bunnymen signed to Liverpool indie Zoo records in March 1979, five months after their first ever gig at Eric's. Their darkly glamorous debut single 'The Pictures on My Wall' opened on a statement of intent, a call to the listener to open their ears to: 'Something changing/On the merry-go-round tonight'.

Stars Are Stars

The Bunnymen put their fate in the hands of an older generation of punk rockers, Bill Drummond and David Balfe, who created Zoo to put out work by their own band, Big in Japan, in 1978. They also released the first three singles by the Teardrop Explodes, for whom Balfe played keyboards. Drummond and Balfe produced the first Bunnymen single, Drummond also taking on the role of their manager and mentor, in which he was never short of bright ideas.

The son of a Church of Scotland minister, Drummond (b. 29 April 1953) is now probably most famous for burning a million quid in a 1994 act of art terrorism with the K Foundation.[7] He came under the influence of premier eccentric, the prankster, actor, writer and director Ken Campbell, while working as a stagehand on Campbell's Science Fiction Theatre of Liverpool production of Robert Anton Wilson and Robert Shea's *The Illuminatus! Trilogy* in 1976. Ken gave Bill some advice – 'Don't bother doing anything unless it's heroic' – and he never looked back.

Thus, Drummond aimed his protégés skyward, catching the attention of Sire boss Seymour Stein – whose instincts about the

Ramones and Blondie had been so spot on – at a Battle of the Bands contest in London's Tottenham Court Road YMCA. The New York punk veteran nabbed the Bunnymen for his new label, Korova – named after the milk bar in which Alex and his little Droogies go to imbibe in *A Clockwork Orange* – co-founded with Warners' future UK boss, Rob Dickens. It was Dickens who insisted that Echo be replaced by a real drummer. Pete de Freitas, the flat-mate of David Balfe's brother, who had first seen the Bunnymen play at the same YMCA gig, stepped up to the riser in 1979.

Born in Trinidad in 1961, de Freitas was the son of a copyright lawyer who had attended the prestigious Roman Catholic Downside public school near Bath and didn't much fancy a life of further academia – he was far keener on studying the techniques of former Big in Japan drummer Budgie. With their crucial fourth element in place, the band set about establishing themselves as heirs to Joy Division's brooding northern soulscapes and long black overcoats; the more credible rivals of their upwardly mobile Celtic cousins U2 and Simple Minds.

The front cover of their first album, July 1980's *Crocodiles*, cast them as proper Romantics – as opposed to habitués of 69 Dean Street – in a darkened forest setting perfectly framed by photographer Brian Griffin. Inside, Mac wove stories of decadence and derangement, mixing up the medicine and leading the listener on a nocturnal journey through Liverpool's white rabbit holes to 'Villier's Terrace', where the inhabitants are 'rolling round on the carpet/Biting wool and pulling strings'. Along the way, marvel as Mac catches a falling star and cuts his hands to pieces; dodges tricky 'Monkeys' and 'Happy Death Men' and turns the titular reptiles into a pair of footwear superior to a rival's alligator shoes: 'Me I'm all smiles/I've got my crocodiles.'

With psychedelic abandon, the Bunnymen riffed off the rock template and into their own altered states; Sergeant's hypnotic guitar drones, de Freitas' spare, jazzy rhythms and Pattison's anchoring bass enabling the listener to fully trip out on little more than cider and black. *Rolling Stone*'s David Fricke name-checked both Morrison and Bowie in his glowing four-star review, while also comparing the Bunnymen's sound to a winning combination of PiL, Jimmy Page's former beat combo the Yardbirds and acid-fried Texans the 13th Floor Elevators.

Heaven Up Here (May 1981) presented the curious with another compelling cover image, again taken by Brian Griffin, of the band standing on wet sands under darkening skies, hands clenched firmly inside the pockets of their long black coats, seagulls wheeling overhead. Once more, its brooding vista perfectly captured the mood of the music within – dark eddies and keening cries of doom surround our protagonists, who nonetheless turn their faces to the pale-yellow glimmer of light on the horizon. Some perennial live favourites first surfaced on this spectral beauty of a record – 'All My Colours', 'A Promise' and the epic 'Over the Wall', all painted in shades of blue with McCulloch's Impressionistic references to 'light on the waves' and Sergeant's layers of choppy, foaming guitars. *NME* awarded it not just Best Album of the year, but Best Dressed LP, too.

However, none of this was getting the Bunnymen as far up the charts as their corporate masters desired. Between *Heaven Up Here* and *Porcupine* (February 1983), they struggled to come up with new material and sought diversions elsewhere – de Freitas with the Wild Swans, whose debut single, 'Revolutionary Spirit' (Zoo, 1982), he produced and played on; Sergeant with his imaginary film soundtrack album, *Themes for GRIND* (92 Happy Customers, 1982). Brian Griffin's next cover image, the most dramatic yet, was taken at the frozen Gulfoss waterfall near Reykjavìk in Iceland – and, along with the record's title, provided another clear visual clue to the band's state of mind.

Their first attempt at *Porcupine*, material that was recorded at Rockfield Studios, where *Heaven Up Here* had poured out of them, was deemed too uncommercial and the Bunnymen were forced to re-record their difficult third on orders from Korova's parents, WEA. The trip to Iceland was part of Drummond's endeavours to get the band to focus, as only he knew how. Like Jaz Coleman, Bill was well aware of the importance of Iceland's psychogeography.

The waterfall, he told his charges, was on an 'interstellar leyline' that connected Mathew Street in Liverpool to Papua New Guinea, infinity and beyond.[8] More practically, when the band commenced re-recording at Trident in London, he brought in virtuoso Indian violinist Lakshminarayana Shankar to add strings, which lifted the January 1983 single 'The Cutter' to number eight in the charts.

But the album's strains were obvious to its reviewers. *NME*'s Barney Hoskyns, who had considered *Heaven Up Here* to be 'one of the most superior articulations of the "rock" form in living memory', found its successor uncomfortably treading old ground, in a state of 'non-stop anxiety'. His diagnosis was spot on. The man who had asked himself 'Am I the worthy cross?' on 'The Cutter' later admitted *Porcupine* was 'a classic autobiographical album, the most honest thing that I'd ever written or sung' – and therefore he found it uncomfortable to perform: 'A lot of the songs are about coming to terms with the opposites in me.'[9]

No Dark Things

But all those anxieties vanished when the heavens shone down on the singer, blessing his vivid imagination with the gift of 'The Killing Moon'. Once those lyrics had arrived, McCulloch began working out the chords, using the magical trick of playing 'Space Oddity' backwards. The band divined the rest on a four-track recorder at Mac's Sefton Park home, in preparation for what would be their fifth Peel *Session*, first broadcast on 6 September 1983.

Will Sergeant had recently acquired a pristine vintage, teardrop-shaped 1965 Vox twelve-string from a shop in Denmark Street, Soho. It's the same type of guitar that Brian Jones used – and the sense of transcultural experimentation that was the trademark of his best work with the Rolling Stones came with it. Sergeant and Pattison had recently been on one of their field trips, to the wilds of Kazam in Russia, where they had discovered a tractor factory, still functioning Bri-Nylon flares and the evocative, rumbling sound of the balalaika, reproduced here on Pattison's bass. Happy with what they came up with for Peel, the band recorded 'The Killing Moon' in Bath's Crescent Studios with producer David Lord, whose recent work on Peter Gabriel's fourth solo album had explored similarly enchanted landscapes. Lord lifted a 'twangy' part from a rehearsal tape by Sergeant and turned it into 'the best-known guitar line in our entire back catalogue.'[10] Inspired by Dave Brubeck's cool jazz *Take Five* album (1959), de Freitas played his drums with brushes. The ascendant 'The Killing Moon' shone its perfect light down on troubled Blighty for the first time on 20 January 1984, a prelude to what McCullouch would not unreasonably describe as 'the greatest album ever made'.

Their next destination was Paris, where a 35-piece orchestra awaited in Studio des Dames to help turn the Bunnymen's songs into the kind of baroque scores that could accompany the twisted torch songs of Jacques Brel and Serge Gainsbourg. 'The songs are good, they've got dynamics and proper chord sequences,' Mac told *The Face*'s Max Bell.[11] '*Ocean Rain* is kissing music, songs to fall in love to. I liked Bowie for the same magical reasons . . . music has got to have that sex thing, we all liked copping off, but you should never miss out on the spiritual aspects, the stuff you can play and suddenly you're on Mars.'

Once again, photographer Brian Griffin captured a succinct cover image of them, aboard a rowing boat, inside the stunning, turquoise environs of Carnglaze Caverns in Liskeard, Cornwall. The lunar, seafaring themes of its nine tracks gave *Ocean Rain* the feel of an epic novel, the Bunnymen's own *Treasure Island*, opening with their next single, 'Silver', a joyous ode to carnal delights in the moonlight plucked out on effervescent strings; and floating away into a sea mist on the bittersweet symphony of the closing title track: 'All at sea again/And now my hurricanes have brought down this ocean rain . . .'

This time, the process of recording in Paris had reawakened the band's sense of joyful experimentation, as if they'd dived into the city's famous flea market and come back with all kinds of new things to try out. De Freitas used xylophones and glockenspiels, Pattison attached an old reverb machine to his bass and Sergeant achieved his distinctive solo on 'My Kingdom' by distorting an acoustic Washburn guitar through a valve radio. Back in Liverpool, they held A Crystal Day of events for fans in May 1984. Broadcast on *The Tube*, the day began with the Bunnymen and their admirers enjoying a café breakfast, followed by a bike tour and ferry across the Mersey, culminating in a gig at St George's Hall, where the Beatles once trod. No longer stowaways, the Bunnymen were now steering their own proud galleon to the toppermost of the poppermost. And so was another artist from further up the shores of the Mersey, who had come crashing back down from his Room at the Top, dusted himself and his Jacques Brel records down and started all over again.

The Boy Who Came Back

In February 1984, as a prelude to the release of Soft Cell's third album, Marc Almond issued a dramatic statement: he was retiring from the music business at the age of twenty-seven. The duo's final valediction in blood, tears and seminal fluid, *This Last Night in Sodom* hit the racks a month later, brimming with images of rape, murder and madness set to the dirtiest, amphetamine-and-amyl-nitrate grooves the duo had ever committed to vinyl. 'I'm going down in the subway,' raved Almond on their final, Bloody Valentine of a single, a cover of Jack Hammer's 1968 Northern Soul belter, 'Jump on that train track and die.'

Their great adventure had burned itself out on the capricious demands of fame. 'There was a lot of unhappiness in myself, between Dave and I and the record company,' he recalled. 'And all this came to an accumulation in me: three years of travelling and touring and having a lot of experiences crammed into such a short time.' Almond and Ball had gone from defining a new meaning for cabaret disco on *Non-Stop Erotic Cabaret* and pioneering the art of the remix on *Non Stop Ecstatic Dancing* (June 1982) to a state of full-blown depression and drug-fuelled paranoia, their once spry Mod groove turning Hammond heavy.

All of which fed into 1983's autobiographical free-fall, *The Art of Falling Apart*, in which Marc soul-mined a lifetime's worth of alienation and Ball pushed the limits of his tech wizardry. The snarling kitchen sink drama enacted on the single 'Where the Heart Is' – 'Fathers never understand/When children have the upper hand' – turned fully psychotic on the staggering 'Martin'. This ten-minute séance on the theme of George A. Romero's titular vampire movie came on a free 12-inch included with initial pressings. Like UK Decay's 'Werewolf', it sounded as if it contained field recordings made by psychical researchers, in this case of violent poltergeist activity, culminating in Almond's abduction into another dimension.

At the same time, Marc also unleashed his second fandango with an expanded line-up of Mambas. In many ways, *Torment and Toreros* (August 1983) picked up where the Immaculate Consumptive had left off, with contributions from Steven Severin and Robert Smith on 'Torment' and Jim Thirlwell – in his Frank Want persona – who played drums and reprised 'A Million Manias' from their cracked cabarets in New York. Thirlwell had experienced firsthand some of the hysteria that had blown up around the Soft Cell singer since 'Tainted Love'.

'I think he probably felt like he'd done a deal with the Devil,' he recalled. 'Up at the Some Bizzare offices, which was on St Anne's Court,[12] there would be a group of sometimes ten or twenty little mock clones hanging out there, just waiting for him to drop by and going "Oh Marc, *Marc*!" and wanting his autograph. He found himself on the cover of *Smash Hits* and those teenybopper magazines and viewed like that, instead of as a serious artist. I think he felt he had more to say and I think that made him go back the other way.'

In an echo of the Bunnymen, it was to Europe that Marc's heart was headed: 'I'd always loved flamenco. I love to listen to songs about life and its sorrows and the cruelty of romance and love. With Spanish singing, there's always a rough edge.' To this end, his song choices mixed covers of Chilean balladeer Joaquin Prieto's 'In My Room', an instrumental reworking of the traditional

Spanish 'Blood Wedding', Jacques Brel's 'The Bulls', George Bizet and Oscar Hammerstein Jr's 'Beat Out That Rhythm on a Drum' and, inspired by Lydia Lunch's *Queen of Siam* cover, his own take on Billie Holliday's 'Gloomy Sunday'. To expand the sound palette, he put together a bunch of classically trained musicians, dubbed the Venomettes: Billy McGee on double bass, Martin McCarrick on cello and on violin, Anne Stephenson and Ginny Hewes – the future Mrs David Ball.

The core Mambas – Annie Hogan on piano, Matt Johnson on guitar, Peter Ashworth on percussion and drums and Flood in the producer's chair – were further augmented by multi-instrumentalist Lee Jenkinson and Steve Sherlock on flute and saxophone. With eleven original compositions on top of the covers, this was both an ambitious project and, as Annie recalls, a difficult one.

'I'd been a tour DJ during the *Art of Falling Apart* tour and it had been a positive and happy experience, despite the inevitable arguments of being a touring band. However, the pressure of being a big act was starting to take a toll and none of it was helped by Stevo, who could make a tense situation impossible. He seemed to live off the drama – but to be fair, he was only nineteen years old. Lots of this tension carried over into the recording of *Torment*. All of a sudden it was no longer just me, Marc and Flood but a whole new lot of faces and all vying for Marc's attention. Looking back, I suppose I was a bit jealous and intimidated by these trained Guildhall musicians. We recorded it at the famous Trident Studios, it was all done mainly at night. Really long hours and it really tested us all.'

'It was an album about a nervous breakdown,' Almond concurred.

Shining Sinners

Which was perhaps not what Some Bizzare's corporate sponsor Phonogram had been hoping for. But Soft Cell's exit was nothing if not defiant. 'We were very rebellious with the last album,' Marc recalled. 'We deliberately recorded a lot of it in mono, going back to punk in a way, and, I suppose, reflecting the drugs that we were taking at the time – it was very speedy!'

He certainly kept up his momentum. Having waved goodbye to Soft Cell at the beginning of the year, Almond's 'retirement' was brief. He had formed a new band, the Willing Sinners, from core Mambas Hogan, McCarrick and McGee, guitarist Richard Riley and drummer Stephen Humphreys[13] and created the album *Vermin in Ermine* by October 1984. Its cover, designed by Marc and longtime artistic collaborator Huw Feather with a photograph by Peter Ashworth, depicted the devilishly horned singer perched atop a dustbin. 'It came from a Spanish interview I'd done that ran with the headline: *The Judy Garland of the Garbage Heap*,' he explained. 'It was my favourite description of me, and the themes of glitter and dirt, the tarnished glamour.'

The songs – recorded in suitably fairytale surrounds at Hartmann Digital Studios in the Bavarian Alps, with Banshees' producer Mike Hedges – were wonderful orchestrations of these themes. A reinvigorated Almond rapidly reconnected to his songwriting muse, turning out all twelve tracks[14] in one fell swoop. With a supporting cast of supremely talented musicians – saxophonist Gary Barnacle (the Clash, the Ruts, Spear of Destiny), brass ace Enrico Tomasso, Gini Ball (as she now was), former Orange Juice drummer Zeke Manyika, percussionist Martin Ditcham and bouzouki maestro Spiros – the Sinners hit epic soundtrack mode. Hedges, recalls Hogan, 'loved the piano and used his own version of the Phil Spector "Wall of Sound" with the piano doing well in the mix.'

For Marc, collaborating with the producer was a revelation: 'He was perfect to work with because he loved all the experimentation and he had strange ways of recording things – but at the same time, he brought all the ideas together into something coherent, and started to bring out a really good sound in my voice. People always said I was a really out-of-tune singer and there was an uncontrolability about it – I'd just go in and sing the song straight off and that would be it. But Mike brought a lot more out of me.'

With their adventures in the sounds and styles of Europe and the orchestrations of the film score and dramatic balladeer, Almond and the Bunnymen were signalling a way forward, a solace to be found after the carnage of the Miners' Strike in the more optimistic past. The sounds of the bittersweet summer of 1984 vividly evoke a turning point for the country, which had once had so much belief in trade unionism. After the Battle of Orgreave, the reckoning was swift.

No Time to Cry

The most visceral firsthand account of that confrontation I read at the time came from the *NME*, by then my chief source of information on political matters. Though the paper contained as many vociferous factions as the Left itself, all agreed on fundamental issues: the events of Orgreave, described by their correspondent as 'the most important struggle that any of us have seen in our lifetimes', were given front-cover status. That on-the-spot reporter was X Moore, otherwise known as Chris Dean, lead singer and guitarist of York's only revolutionary Marxist skinhead band, the Redskins.

While in no shape or form a Goth – the Tamla-mad Redskins were more like the Style Council's more belligerent yet groovesome little brothers – Dean was an energising figure. Possessed of a fierce intelligence, he had won a scholarship to public school, so, like Justin Sullivan, had seen both sides of the British education system. Dean blazed a trail through the Miners' Strike then disappeared so completely that, when the Redskins' sole LP, *Neither Washington Nor Moscow*, was re-released in 2022, even his former manager had no idea where he was. All of which has subsequently lent him the mystique of a folk hero.

'Chris was very, very bright,' his friend Jon Langford recalled. 'So motivated, and he had it all worked out. He knew exactly how it was going to happen. How when the Redskins got a hit single there would then follow a socialist revolution and capitalism would be destroyed – that's all it needed.' Jon did his best to assist the cause, producing and putting out the first Redskins' singles on CNT – 'Lev Bronstein', a paean to Trotsky with a refrain of 'Moscow is like Leeds', and a timely appropriation of Bill Withers' 'Lean on Me' – which was enough to get them a high-profile deal with Decca/London Records.

'It was funny, knowing him and Eldritch,' Langford mused from a forty-year distance. 'They were very similar in the fact that they both had their masterplans. They'd closely observed what everybody else was doing and they were going to be the biggest and best they could possibly be.'

Eldritch's schemes were coming on apace. Ben Gunn was cast adrift in September 1983, shortly after the Sisters' first tour of America. In a tenuous analogy with his fictional alter ego's stealing away of pirate treasure, he returned to study Economics at Liverpool University. And it was from Liverpool that his replacement was found. Another Eric's graduate, Wayne Hussey (b. 26 May 1958) was recruited for his abilities on electric twelve-string and acoustic guitar – which in itself was suggestive of the direction Eldritch wished to travel.

Born in Bristol, Hussey was brought up in the Church of Jesus Christ of Latter-day Saints, but found his true salvation in punk. Instead of going out into the world as a missionary for his parents' faith, at the age of eighteen he relocated to Liverpool to serve a musical apprenticeship with the Walkie Talkies. Wayne briefly made contact with the shade of Ian Curtis, when recruited by Martin Hannett's Invisible Girls to play in a live ensemble with former Penetration singer Pauline Murray in 1980. He made one single with them, 'Searching for Heaven' in 1981, before switching allegiance to a former member of the Mystery Girls.

Liverpool's most outrageous dresser, Pete Burns (1959–2016), first traded under that name during another improbable threesome with Pete Wylie and Julian Cope. After the Mystery Girls' legendary one-night stand at Eric's in 1977, Burns assembled the proto-Goth danceband, Nightmares in Wax, going through over thirty line-ups in three years before changing their name to Dead or Alive in 1983. Hussey played on their breakthrough *Sophisticated Boom Boom* album of 1984,[15] but he left before Burns startled a nation that had only just warmed to Boy George when he appeared on *Top of the Pops* resplendent in off-the-shoulder, bright yellow playsuit and vast mane of hair, performing KC & the Sunshine Band's 'That's the Way I Like It'.

Buccaneer Wayne was not happy with DOA's poptastic direction and sold his Jimmy Page skills to the Sisters in April 1984. It was a canny move on his part – before the month was out, the Sisters had signed a deal with WEA, and as he would later tell the *Irish Independent*: 'I didn't have to schlep up the motorway in a Transit van with the Sisters. The first gig I did with them was a warm-up show in Birmingham and then we went off to America to tour.'[16]

With major label heft behind the Sisters' label Merciful Release, the single 'Body and Soul' reached the outer limits of the top forty in June. But the sombre track, backed with the Suicide-esque 'Train', was something of a disappointment compared to its illustrious forebears. Its video – though never actually aired in Britain at the time – signalled more ill omens. While Eldritch and Marx played its post-apocalyptic scenario straight, Hussey and Adams appeared to think they might actually be members of Spinal Tap. As Ben Gunn would tell *ZigZag*'s Jayne Houghton later that year: 'They were always taking the piss out of the system, which is why I was in the band, until they started taking themselves more seriously. Now they're no better than anyone else. Worse, in fact.'

Another crucial anchor to the Sisters' success up to this point would also be weighed after the Warners' deal: 'When the Sisters suddenly became quite big, I was replaced,' recalled Claire Shearsby.

Towards the end of June 1984 the band began the lengthy process of committing their first album to vinyl with producer Dave Allen (the Cure, Human League – sadly not the Irish comedian). Work began at Joy Division's old haunt, Strawberry Studios in Stockport, with in-house engineer Chris Nagle – Martin Hannett's right-hand man on *Unknown Pleasures* and *Closer* – at hand.[17] Slated for release four months later, its working title was *Black October*.

The Damage Done

Just before 3 a.m. on 12 October, a 100-pound bomb ripped through the seafront Grand Hotel that was hosting the Conservative delegates for their party conference. Its blast brought down a five-tonne chimney stack, which, as it crashed through the floors, took the lives of Deputy Chief Whip Sir Anthony Berry, North West Conservatives Chairman Eric Taylor, the wives of two other regional chairs (Lady Shattock and Lady Maclean), and Roberta Wakeham, wife of Chief Whip John. Margaret Tebbit fell four floors alongside her husband, Secretary of State, Norman, and would spend the rest of her life in a wheelchair. Still working on her speech for the next day, the bomb's intended target, Margaret Thatcher, escaped unscathed.

This device had a long fuse. Patrick Magee, head of the IRA team that planted it, checked into the Grand in September 1984 and hid the explosive, with its delayed timer, in the room he had taken on the sixth floor. But he had originally conceived of the plan way back in October 1977 – payback for Labour removing the Special Category Status for Northern Irish paramilitary prisoners and sending them all into the Maze – when he had combative Northern Ireland Secretary Roy Mason in his sights. As he revealed in his 2021 memoir, *Where Grieving Begins*: 'We stood on the top floor of a shopping mall overlooking the rear of the Brighton Centre during the British Labour Party's annual conference and imagined Mason's reaction if he knew how close we were.'[18]

But what did not kill Mrs Thatcher only made her stronger. At 4 a.m., from the steps of Brighton police station, she told the BBC's political editor, Ulsterman John Cole, the conference would go ahead as scheduled. Duly, she appeared at 9.30 a.m., rose to a standing ovation and described the night's events as 'an attempt not only to disrupt and terminate our conference, it was an attempt to cripple Her Majesty's democratically elected government'.

Although she toned down some of the content she had intended to deliver before the night's dramatic events, Thatcher returned later in her 47-minute address to others who, she said, shared the same aims as the IRA. 'What we have seen in this country is the emergence of an organised revolutionary minority who are prepared to exploit industrial disputes, but whose real aim is the breakdown of law and order and the destruction of democratic parliamentary government,' she declared.[19]

With this awesome display of nerve and purpose, Thatcher was once again able to feast on those who would destroy her. In the aftermath of the Brighton bomb, the Tories' spiralling poll ratings dramatically reversed, while the miners' fortunes plummeted along with the seasonal temperatures. NUM funds of £2.75 million were frozen by the High Court and by the time Bob Geldof's Band Aid single had begun its festive season at the top of the charts, the government had deducted supplementary benefits from the families of striking miners, too.

'The Mekons made a record during the Miners' Strike, "Beer and Whisky",' recalled Jon Langford, now a resident of Chicago, 'and it seemed to resonate more in the States than it did in England. We didn't know where the records were going, but talking to the distributors they said: New York, Chicago, San Francisco. Okay, we better go there, then. So we got an agent and then we went every year until I moved here.' Langford continued to keep an eye on things back home – as Chuck Death, his *Great Pop Things* satirical cartoon strip made in collaboration with old Newport buddy Carlton B. Morgan, that appeared in *Record Mirror* and *NME* throughout the '80s and '90s.[20] But he would never move back – 'That was the end of it, the Miners' Strike.'

The only way of making the future look rosier now was by donning the pink-tinted glasses of an earlier generation.

Gothfather: Jacques Brel

'He was a big influence on my songwriting, as a person writing about sex and death and real life and grit,' said Marc Almond. 'Life in the streets, prostitutes, outsiders, characters. But at the same time, he was very romantic.'

The author of 'My Death', 'Amsterdam', 'If You Go Away' and 'Next' – the iconic songs that, as performed by David Bowie, Scott Walker and Alex Harvey, lit the black touchpaper for Goth – Jacques Brel was born in Brussels on 8 April 1929. His father was the director of a cardboard manufacturing company and his childhood was austere, dominated by his family's Catholic faith – which would also provide the outlet for his artistic inclinations. Having evinced talents for songwriting and acting at school, it was via the Catholic youth organisation La Franche Cordée that he got to escape his planned future in packaging, meet his wife Thérèse 'Miche' Michielsen and begin performing his songs on the Brussels cabaret circuit. Perhaps it was because he had so much faith to lose that his lyrics – and his very physical, sweat-and-nicotine-stained delivery of them – packed such power. If they are comparable to the work of any other artists, it is the Weimar world of Dadaists Otto Dix and George Grosz, both of whom had seen for real the world described in 'Next' and painted their harsh experiences without sentimentality, but instead a heady mix of satire and surrealism.

Though Brel's military service as a corporal in the Belgian airforce came after the end of the Second World War in 1948, he was able to process the shocking and absurd extremes of that conflict and its aftermath just as successfully into his work. The death that waits 'like a Bible truth/At the funeral of my youth', a constant, grinning companion in the twilit bar and brothel rooms of his existence.

It didn't take long before his name became known in Paris and in 1953, at the age of twenty-four, he signed a contract with Philips Records and moved to the French capital. Living in the grotty confines of the oxymoronic Hôtel Idéal, he took to the circuit of Montmartre and Montparnasse music halls, impressing archetypal existentialist Juliette Greco with his song 'Le Diable (Ça va)' – 'The

Devil Is Okay'. With his fortunes on the up, Brel's wife and two daughters joined him in Paris in 1955, but, unable to cope with his itinerant lifestyle, returned to Brussels three years later, where his third daughter was born. By the end of the decade, Jacques was a massive star in France, sharing bills with fellow roué Serge Gainsbourg and smoothie Charles Aznavour and becoming synonymous with his favourite l'Olympia music hall in Paris, where he recorded two albums.

As the '60s dawned, Brel laid down his guitar to concentrate on his increasingly theatrical vocal performances, leaving Philips Records for Barclay. His reputation spread in a cult-like manner to Britain and America, where he was able to command performances at the Royal Albert Hall and Carnegie Hall respectively by 1965. The latter gig was witnessed by songwriter Mort Shuman, who was so intrigued by Brel's idiosyncrasies that he began translating those mysterious lyrics. It was his version of 'La Chanson de Jacky' that Scott Walker released as 'Jackie', his first post-Walker Brothers single in 1967.

Scott's exuberantly expressed desire to 'join the social whirl/Become procurer of young girls' and be 'cute cute, in a stupid-ass way' became the Swinging Pop world's portal to Brel's darker European expressionism. Shuman was also responsible for the translation of 'My Death' as performed by David Bowie. But other interpreters were not so astute – perhaps the best-known Brel cover is Terry Jacks' 1973 version of 'Le Moribund', translated by poet Rod McKuen into the cloyingly sentimental 'Seasons in the Sun'. Jacks swiftly followed his pop smash with another McKuen translation, 'If You Go Away' – originally 'Ne Me Quitte Pas' – subsequently recorded by Frank Sinatra, Dusty Springfield and Marc Almond.

'I've always understood why Brel has a very big gay audience, even though he was a womaniser,' said Almond. 'His songs were about women, there was no suggestion that he was gay. But his settings are so often the brothel, the bedroom and the bar, settings a lot of gay people know very well. So I related to his work and I felt I had a right, it was part of my roots, to sing his songs.'

When he came to record his album of Brel covers, Jacques *(Some Bizzare, 1989), Marc worked with translator Paul Buck to tune the lyrics back into more faithful renderings of the originals. 'We did have to contact Madame Brel, who owned all the estate, and we had to submit all the lyrics to her for approval. Paul translated them and I did some adaptations to make them scan. And she wrote back and said she loved the translations. She thought it was one of the best interpretations of her husband's work that she'd heard for a very long time.'*

Brel's own season lasted not much longer than his discovery by Walker. After his dramatic exit from the l'Olympia stage in 1966 – as mimicked by David Bowie at Hammersmith Odeon – he spent the final decade of his life acting, recording four more albums and indulging a passion for sailing, heading to sadder shores on 9 October 1978, at the age of forty-nine.

Gothmother: Juliette Gréco

With her shining black curtain of hair, smoldering dark eyes and gravelly ravine of a voice, Juliette Gréco was the female embodiment of French Left Bank existentialism. All dressed in black, she would stand before a microphone like a goddess before an altar to make solemn sacrifice of whatever poem or song she was offering up to her disciples. At Les Deux Magots café she entranced the writers Boris Vian and Jacques Prévert, along with philosophy's glamour couple, Simone de Beauvoir and Jean-Paul Sartre, the latter, who co-wrote her first record, noting: 'Gréco has a million poems in her voice.' Visiting American jazzers Quincy Jones and Miles Davis both fell in love with her – at the same time – and she had a long relationship with Hollywood producer Darryl F. Zanuck, appearing in some of his classic movies: The Sun Also Rises *(Henry King, 1957),* The Roots of Heaven *(John Huston, 1958) and opposite Orson Welles in* Crack in the Mirror *(Richard Fleisher, 1960). Noir writer Derek Raymond delighted in recalling a dance he once had with her, when he was a dashing young art smuggler about Paris in the early '60s.*

Gréco was born on 7 February 1927 in Montpelier in the south of France, to an absent father, Gérard, a Corsican who gave her only his surname. She and her elder sister Charlotte were brought up by their maternal grandparents in Bordeaux until she was seven, when her mother Juliette Lafeychine reappeared and took them to live in Saint-Germain-des-Prés, Paris – the district with which she would always be associated. When the city fell to the Nazis in 1940, the sisters were sent to school in Bergerac while their mother joined the French Resistance. On a visit to meet her in 1943, Juliette and Charlotte were arrested by the Gestapo. Gréco recalled in her 1982 memoir, Jujube*: 'A French Gestapo officer humiliated me. I became so upset that I punched him on the nose. Well, that cost me!'*

Aged just fifteen, Juliette was sent to a brutal women's jail in Fresnes. Released a few months later, she walked the eight miles back to Paris in the blue summer dress and sandals she had been arrested in, during the coldest winter on record. She would not discover the rest of her family's fate until after the war, when, miraculously, she found her skeletally thin mother and sister at the Hôtel Lutétia, where survivors of the Ravensbrück concentration camp were taken: 'We held each other tight, in silence. There were no words for what I felt at that instant.'

Back in Saint-Germain-des-Prés, Juliette made ends meet singing in cafés. She and Charlotte frequented the Hôtel Pont Royal, where they fell in with de Beauvoir, Sartre and his younger rival, Albert Camus. Sartre introduced Juliette to composer Joseph Kosma, who had written scores for Jean Renoir and Marcel Carné. Kosma changed the tune to Sartre's song 'La Rue des Blancs-Manteaux', giving her the material for her first single, and also the song he and Jacques Prévert had written for Carnés' 1945 film, Les Enfants du Paradis. *Photographed on stage at La Rose Rouge, the image of 'the black muse of Saint-Germain-des-Prés' was made.*

At the famous cellar club Le Tabu, Juliette would sing to an audience that included Picasso, Orson Welles, Marlene Dietrich and Marlon Brando, who would give her a lift home on his motorbike. Jean Cocteau invited her to star in his film Orpheus *(1950), Robert Doisneau and Henri Cartier-Bresson snapped immortal images of her and she had this to say on the subject of her monochrome look: 'Black provides space for the imaginary' – manna for every subsequent Goth.*

Gréco lived a long life, marrying three times and becoming emblematic as the last of the great chanteuses, touring the world with an ever-changing repertoire of songs that had largely been written just for her, by the likes of Brel, Gainsbourg, Georges Brassens and rapper/slam poet Abd al Malik. When asked to perform to Chilean dictator Augusto Pinochet in 1981, this survivor of the Nazis walked on to rapturous applause and let rip with a set consisting entirely of songs he had banned. 'I went off to dead silence,' she recalled. 'It was the greatest triumph of my career.'

She became the president of the association to preserve Saint-Germain-des-Prés and carried on releasing albums, including Gréco Chante Brel *in 2013 and a further volume of autobiography,* Je Suis Faite Comme Ça

(I Am What I Am) *in 2012. She also made her final live appearance at l'Olympia in May 2017, and took her final leave of Paris on 23 September 2020 at the age of ninety-three.*

As she wrote in Jujube: *'I know that I myself will fight until the last day of my life, against oppression, against intellectual terrorism, indifference and the denial of the only treasure that is worth preserving at all costs: the right to live as we choose, to think, to laugh, to give, to change, to love without fear whatever and whoever we love.'*

CHAPTER 10

Psychedelic Jungle

Further down the rabbit hole: Siouxsie and the Banshees, the Cure, the Glove, the Creatures, the Cult, Doctor and the Medics and the Damned meet Alice in Wonderland

Warlock: Hey man, where d'you get that gear from?
Neil: Oh, er, down the police station.
Warlock: Well, you had me fooled, I've just eaten half my stash.
Neil: Look, Warlock, this is very heavy.
Warlock: No, it's not, man, we got plenty more inside. Come on in, take the tit off your head.

– *The Young Ones*, 'Cash', first broadcast on BBC Two, 15 May 1984

Despite Johnny Rotten's punk ultimatum 'Never trust a hippy',[1] it could be argued that the Banshees went straight into the '60s medicine cabinet by putting 'Helter Skelter' onto *The Scream*. It didn't take long for them to return to the more controversial corners of the Lennon–McCartney songbook, as encapsulated on the era-defining *The White Album*, which, said Steven Severin, 'has always been an influence on the way we work'.

A Kiss in the Dreamhouse (1982) was conceived under the influence of the Beatles' ninth and most enigmatic album.[2] Just as John and

Paul worked the loss of Brian Epstein, the influence of the Maharishi and the entrance of Yoko Ono into the *White Album*'s grooves, so the Banshees unfurled their own psychedelic masterpiece as an aural oil projection of their inner dark materials.

With a string section comprising violinist Venomettes Anne Stephenson and Ginni Hewes, plus Alison Briggs and Caroline Lavelle on cello, producer Mike Hedges created a wall of strings Hitchcock would have been proud of. He also supplied Siouxsie with the same kind of California Sunshine acid that had opened the fourteen-year-old Poison Ivy's third eye, sending Sioux into a reverie in which she confronted the mother-shaped demons of her past, writing the autobiographical 'Cocoon' and 'Circle' as a result. 'When we were doing these sessions and I first took acid, I remember thinking, "I wonder if I should go and see my mum and just say, "Here, Mum, let's take some acid together,"' she told *Uncut*'s Garry Mulholland. 'I remember thinking, "Is that a good idea, or could she die from it?" I really wanted to understand everything about where she came from and my childhood.'[3]

The intensity of the nocturnal sessions and accompanying mood enhancers made magic: midway through the epic single 'Slowdive' – itself a lyrical riff on Fats Waller's euphemistic 'Honeysuckle Rose' – Anne Stephenson lets out a shuddering: 'Oh my God!' This was not an expression of ecstasy but exhaustion: 'I wanted the string players to slow down and get tired,' Sioux remembered. 'That is the sound of her wrists falling off!' But that gasp was exactly what the song required. Fortune had even permitted the Banshees to record it in Abbey Road. When a mixing desk at Hedges' Playground Studios was put out of action by Budgie inadvertently dousing it in champagne, band and producer moved into Studio 2 of EMI's in-house complex instead. Acknowledging its parallels with *The White Album*, *NME*'s Richard Cook called *A Kiss in the Dreamhouse* 'a feat of imagination scarcely ever recorded,' surmising: 'It will take your breath away.'

But all of this was not achieved without a major casualty – John McGeoch, whose guitars settled 'a shattered beauty on the tattooed skin of the songs' as Cook so eloquently put it – had wrought similar desolation on his own psyche. His alcoholism had reached such a point that his wife had him sectioned. Sent for rehabilitation treatment at specialist clinic the Priory, he promptly absconded to the pub a week before the band were due to go on tour.[4] Tragically, it was a pattern he would repeat for the remainder of his short life. After being sacked from the Banshees, he went on to work with PiL until 1992, when the rock 'n' roll lifestyle caught up with him again and he quit to retrain as a nurse. But he never completely conquered his addictions, dying in his sleep at the age of forty-eight in 2002.

Back in 1982, there was only one person the Banshees could rely on for emergency cover. One phone call later, Robert Smith was back in the band.

The Continuing Story of Bungalow Bob

The Cure's singer-guitarist had done substantial work on his own creative progression in the intervening three years, shifting band members and mood sets as he worked through his own sources of existential despair. When Michael Dempsey left the band that recorded *Three Imaginary Boys* to join Fiction labelmates the Associates, Crawley punk veterans Simon Gallup and Matthieu Hartley – who had previously lent their talents to the 1979 Cure side-project single 'I'm a Cult Hero' – joined forces with Smith and Lol Tolhurst on bass and keyboards respectively.

The resulting *Seventeen Seconds* (April 1980) was, said Smith, a more collaborative affair, which benefitted from the expansion into Hartley's eerie synthscapes. 'Early on,' he told *Trouser Press*'s Jim Green, 'the songs were credited to the group even if I'd written them, so there wouldn't be any jealousy over my getting more money; I didn't want that to be a factor. Now the songs are group compositions. I couldn't just say, "Here, we're gonna do this song," 'cause if everybody's unhappy with it, they wouldn't play it. Though it's down to compromise, we all do tend to think along the same lines.'[5]

Co-produced by Smith with Mike Hedges, *Seventeen Seconds* was, by Robert's admission, hugely influenced by his stint as a Banshee, watching Severin and Budgie instinctively working up a song from scratch together. You can also hear echoes of Nick Drake's melancholy debut, *Five Leaves Left* (Island, 1969) – in particular the haunting riddle of a song 'Riverman'. Its broodingly sinister, edge-world atmosphere permeated *Seventeen Seconds*, especially on the album's most successful and enduring track, 'A Forest', which gave the Cure their first top-forty success when released in April 1980. It was, said Smith – who remained the sole lyricist – an album about the loss of innocence, 'learning you can't trust people as implicitly as you'd thought when you were younger'.[6]

Though the band subsequently also lost Hartley to the hardy perennial of musical direction, they continued to work with Hedges on the following *Faith* (April 1981). Smith used this album to further interrogate his place in the world by testing his religious convictions alongside those relationships that had floundered along the path of his 22 year-long existence. All of which was reflected in Porl Thompson's ghostly cover image of the Gothic ruins of Bolton Abbey in North Yorkshire and Robert's reading of Mervyn Peake's similarly intricately constructed *Gormenghast* novels.

'I kneel and wait in silence/As one by one the people slip away,' he keens on 'The Holy Hour'. The sense of dread reaches its peak on the concluding title track, a Ouija board connection with the unquiet spirit of John George Haigh: 'Hold you close and hear you cry/Kiss your eyes and finish your life.' A majestic gloom had settled over these inhabitants of Creepy Crawley, whose output was now frequently – and not kindly – being compared to the work of Pink Floyd.

But *Faith* was merely a prelude to the third in the Cure's triptych of terror, *Pornography* (May 1982), this time produced by Phil Thornally and recorded, largely at night, during a freezing winter at Mickie Most's RAK studios with accompanying blizzards of cocaine. According to band biographer Jeff Aptead, £1,600 of the recording budget was spent on that kind of snow[7] – and when the supply ran out, 'Doctor' Robert began dropping acid instead.

'I was incredibly obnoxious, appalling, self-centred,' he admitted. But: 'I channelled all the self-destructive elements of my personality into doing something.'

What he thought he was ultimately achieving was sloughing off the Cure entirely with 'the ultimate fuck-off album'. As well as creating mood-altering chemical states, he was also driven by a desire to experiment with found sounds, prompted by a recent immersion in David Byrne and Brian Eno's *My Life in the Bush of Ghosts* (EG, 1981). Flicking between TV channels to record random snatches of dialogue they could layer into the séance-like atmosphere of the recordings, Smith and Thornally chanced upon a debate between Monty Python's Graham Chapman and Germaine Greer on the subject of pornography, which gave the album its title. It was one that met with the stern disapproval of Fiction's parent, Polydor.

Now reappraised as the Cure's uncompromising dark masterpiece, *Pornography* was also given a hard time in the press on its release, and its sole single, 'Hanging Garden', only crept as far as number thirty-two in the charts. It came laden with disquieting imagery: 'Cover my face as the animals die,' shrieks Smith, the lyric, according to Tolhurst, stemming from a hallucinatory encounter with some imagined wildlife in his family's back garden.[8]

All of which took a toll on its creators. After recording his most cavernous of drum roles on *Pornography*, Tolhurst lost faith in his John Bonham abilities and switched to playing keyboards. While, since Simon Gallup's relationship with Smith had deteriorated into fisticuffs, his first tenure as Cure bassist would be over once they completed their next tour. Down to a duo, they released two starkly contrasting singles – the synth-led pop of 'Let's Go to Bed' and 'The Walk', both surprise hits. But with his band in disarray, Robert's Banshees' call-up papers couldn't have been served at a better time.

Glass Onion

Once they'd been reunited, it didn't take long for Severin and Smith to sneak off to the studio together. With touring commitments delivered, they booked themselves in to work on a song whose title Steve had filched from a pulp paperback. 'Punish Me with Kisses' began as an experiment for a project the Banshees' bassist was nurturing, 'just to see if we could work together,' as he recalled. 'By the end of the second day, our secret session had been invaded by most of Fiction records, the Associates, the remnants of the Cure and some of Marc and the Mambas.'[9] This delirious party of a session spontaneously created a psychedelic supergroup, which further comprised Anne Stephenson, Ginni Hewes, Martin McCarrick and drummer Clifford Leon 'Andy' Anderson (1951–2019), who had already done serious time with Nik Turner's Sphinx, Gong's Steve Hillage and Hawkwind. Named the Glove – after the flying appendage of the Chief Blue Meanie in the Beatles' film *Yellow Submarine* (1968) – the band became a means for Severin and Smith to explore and extrapolate their love for all of punk's forbidden fruit. Though, their task was not made easy. Although Severin had struck a solo deal with Polydor that allowed him a Banshees' side project, Smith's contract with Fiction – and Chris Parry's determination that he shouldn't abandon the Cure – meant he was restricted on the amount of singing he was allowed to do elsewhere. 'In reality,' Steve noted, 'there was a lot of pressure for this not to work.'[10]

They surmounted this problem by employing Liverpudlian Jeanette Landray – a dancer from the *Top of the Pops*' troupe Zoo and the former girlfriend of Budgie – to sing on most of the tracks that came out of the twelve-week-long sessions that produced the *Blue Sunshine* LP. '[Robert and Steven] never suffocated me, they let me experiment,' Landray told Post-Punk.com. 'There was a time when my singing of "Like an Animal" was not getting crazy enough, and all of a sudden, I hear this soft voice singing from behind a couch. I walk over towards the voice and it's Robert on all fours, singing "Diamonds Are a Girl's Best Friend!"'[11]

The album's title came from Jeff Lieberman's 1978 horror film about a batch of acid that turned its users into homicidal maniacs – an influential video nasty of the time, it also inspired the Meteors' song of the same name from their 1983 *Wreckin' Crew* LP. Further splattercore classics informed Severin and Smith's songwriting, in particular the stylish Giallo oeuvre of Italian maestro Dario Argento, soundtracked by diabolical progsters Goblin, which were consumed by the pair in vast quantities as the album took shape. Along with a mind-bending amount of stimulants: 'After that period with Steve, I was physically incapable of cleaning my teeth,' Smith recalled at a safe distance. 'The whole thing was unreal – a dream – and not something I'm likely to repeat in a hurry.'[12]

For Severin – who once harboured the ambition of getting Pink Floyd producer and Abbey Road Beatles' engineer Norman 'Hurricane' Smith to produce a Banshees' version of 'Arnold Lane' – this was a chance to indulge his love of '60s-style eccentricity while, at the same time, he made playful use of his pastiche lyrics to poke fun at the recording industry: 'Here comes the book/The book of rules,' went one of Robert's few permitted vocals, on 'Mr Alphabet Says', conceived as 'the track that Ringo would sing'. 'Robert and I knew we stood a good chance of a critical drubbing no matter what the Glove sounded like. Rather than play down the "self-indulgent card" we used it as our Joker! There is no artifice on this record, it's just a reflection of our chemistry, our shared sense of humour.'[13]

Smith staggered off blinking into the daylight, arm in arm with Andy Anderson – an inspired choice of new drummer for the Cure. With Phil Thornally lending his talents on double bass, the revitalised band hit swing jazz gold with 'The Love Cats' in October 1983. With its accompanying, Tim Pope-directed video full of felines, this was the single that sealed the image of Smith as the polka-dot-shirted, smudged-lipsticked, tousle-haired dream prince of Goth. 'Composed drunk, video filmed drunk, promotion made drunk. It was a joke,' he would later mewl. It reached number seven in the charts.

Honey Pie

Leaving the Glove to their revels, Siouxsie and Budgie went on their own search for Bali Ha'i, decamping to Hawaii to fashion their next work as the Creatures in a shack in the middle of a jungle. 'We wanted to go somewhere which was really isolated,' Budgie explained to *NME*'s Richard Cook. 'We found one drum kit on the island and only one marimba. So it was like we had to find all the stuff and just do it all for ourselves.'

The resultant *Feast* album was an exploration of the forces of voice and rhythm that, said Budgie, owed more to the detachment the couple found on their island hideaway than any surrounding musical influences. 'There's no real cultural crossover . . . Just us out there.'[14] Despite this assertion, Siouxsie does appear on the album's cover in a feathered headdress, and learned something of the mysteries of native Hawaiian musical traditions from the singers of the Lamalani Hula Academy, who lent their voices to 'Morning Dawning', 'Inoa 'Ole' and 'A Strutting Rooster'. 'We knew the chants were special to them,' was Sioux's response to Richard Cook's questioning on the subject. 'They guard their language and customs very carefully. We were told what they mean.' She declined to elaborate further.[15]

The first single from *Feast*, the plaintive 'Miss the Girl', had lyrics inspired not by the island's tropical rainforests, but the asphalt jungle of J. G. Ballard's *Crash*. It was the first Banshees' side recording to be released on their Wonderland offshoot label, in April 1983, followed by the Glove's 'Like an Animal' and *Blue Sunshine* in August. The Creatures created a potent chaser for their *Feast* with a fresh recording of Herbie Mann's 'Right Now', previously a hit for Mel Tormé off his *Comin' Home Baby!* album (Atlantic, 1962). Recorded back in London with Mike Hedges and a brass section comprising Gary Barnacle on sax, Peter Thoms on trombone and Luke Tunney on trumpet, Budgie's channelling of Buddy Rich and Siouxsie's finger-snapping vamp as a jazzer reached a heady number fourteen.

After all this outpouring of relentless creativity, what else could the reunited Banshees do? Record an opulent version of *The White Album*'s most spare and tender moment, 'Dear Prudence', which John Lennon had written after learning a country-style finger-picking technique from Donovan.[16] With a vastly more ornate harpsichord part played by Smith's sister Janet, the hallucinogenic Banshees' cut would soar to number three in September 1983, giving them their highest-ever chart placing.

'One of the main reasons we chose it was that John Lennon's version sounds a bit unfinished,' said Severin. 'There's also the background behind why he wrote it – that it was supposedly about the attempted rape on Mia Farrow's sister by the Maharishi. It's the same as why we do "Helter Skelter" – because there is a context to it, the influence it had on Charles Manson. There are always misinterpretations. Songs like that are more than just pop music.'

Yer Blues

This line-up of the Banshees was captured in peak live form at the Royal Albert Hall a few weeks later. The resultant *Nocturne*, filmed for BBC Two's *The Old Grey Whistle Test* and released as an album in November 1983, is a jewelled collection of songs from their back catalogue, including 'Dear Prudence' and a fearsome 'Helter Skelter'. Shortly afterwards, Robert Smith fans were treated to a new compilation of Cure singles, *Japanese Whispers*, to stick in their Christmas fishnet stockings. They wouldn't have long to wait before he came out with yet more original goods either – the Cure's next album, *The Top*, beat the Banshees' *Hyæna* into the schedules by two months. Clearly, there hadn't been very much curling up by the fire to sleep for a while for Smith that winter – and the Blue Sunshine was kicking in.

The Top opens in furious opposition to the frolics of 'The Love Cats' with the glowering 'Shake Dog Shake', the serial killer inside Robert bursting out to 'Tear your red hair by the roots . . . Hold you cherished in the dead electric light,' accompanied by screes of metallic guitar. Referencing the porcine beasts from George Harrison's *White Album* tune that also inspired Manson, 'Give Me It' and 'Piggy in the Mirror' continue in this vein, the former adding a further horror twist. The cats in this song are 'Slit . . . like cheese', leaving sticky entrails all over the carpet and 'Blood thick swimming round your feet'. *Mee-ow*!

There was only one single to be found on *The Top* and it could have come straight out of the Syd Barrett songbook. Like 'The Love Cats', 'The Caterpillar' was a charming, oddball nursery rhyme, on which Robert picked up his violin to pluck out the patter of larval feet. Decorated with a grinning Blue Meanie-style creature on its Porl Thompson/Andy Vella-designed sleeve and picture disc, it came wrapped up in another dreamlike Pope video, shot in the Great Conservatory of Syon Park in west London. 'Dust my lemon lies/With powder pink and sweet,' sighs Smith, an enticement to lure innocents into the charnel house of the rest of the album.

Two months later came the Banshees' sixth LP, *Hyæna*. This time, a 27-piece ensemble, the Chandos Players, from the ranks of the London Symphony Orchestra, illuminated Siouxsie's vocals on the outstanding singles 'Dazzle' and 'Swimming Horses'. 'This,' she said of the latter, 'is based on a programme I saw about a female version of Amnesty International called Les Sentinelles. They rescue women who are trapped in certain religious climates in the Middle East, religions that view any kind of pre-marital sexual aspiration as punishable by death – either by the hand of the eldest brother in the family, or by public stoning. And there was this instance of a woman whose daughter had developed a tumour, and of course, gossip abounded that she was pregnant. The doctor who removed the tumour allowed her to take it back to her village to prove that no, it wasn't a baby – but they wouldn't believe her. The woman knew her daughter would have to be stoned to death so she poisoned her, out of kindness, to save her from a worse fate.

'Now this organisation has all these escape routes for women like her, mainly through the elder brother, who pretends to have killed them. But, once they've been saved, they can never go back. So the song starts: 'Kinder than with poison . . .' I also used the imagery of 'He gives birth to swimming horses,' from the fact that male sea horses give birth to the children, so they're the only species that have a maternal feel for the young. It was, I suppose, an abstract way of linking it all together, without being sensationalist. I remember just being really moved by that programme and wanting to get the sorrow out of me.'

Contrastingly, 'Dazzle' was written on a toy piano, Sioux fondly recalled. 'The sentiment behind it is of laying in the gutter but still looking up at the stars. I'd seen *Marathon Man* and I was really intrigued by the guy swallowing diamonds to keep them and then realising it was like swallowing glass – that they would pass through his system and tear him apart. So that's the line: 'Swallowing diamonds, cutting throats.' Quite a lot of this, and 'Swimming Horses', comes from visiting Israel for the first time. 'The sea of fluid mercury' in the lyric is the Dead Sea. We did this crazy thing and hired a car to go to the Dead Sea – Robert had to be the chauffeur, he was the only one who could drive. But, when we got there, it was like *The Hills Have Eyes* – all barbed wire and tanks and flags with skull and crossbones on them! In Tel Aviv, most of the audience were on acid – which was available after the show, so we took it too! We ended up on the beach, having a party until sunrise, and of course, we ended up swimming. The sea was very clear but there were all these little fish flying about. It wasn't the drugs, honest!'

But something was definitely expanding in Goth's collective unconscious.

Don't Pass Me By

'What is upsetting,' said Billy Duffy to *NME*'s Cynthia Rose, 'is that they're now trying to manipulate the average working-class person in this country into believing that they're middle class. It's just horrible illusionism, like people in council houses are made to feel "Oooh, you're really quite well off, y' know . . . you got a *video.*"' It was September 1984, three months since the Battle of Orgreave and three weeks after the release, on Beggars Banquet, of *Dreamtime*, the Cult's first album under their newly trimmed name.

Along with Ian Astbury and bassist Jamie Stewart, the guitarist was expounding on why he thought his band's substantial following might put more faith in Astbury's interpretations of Native American belief than the UK's prevailing political mood. At this point, Duffy believed, punk was dead 'and it's sad. Because I was involved with punk at fifteen and it was a wonderful, energetic time.' He yearned to be able to 'feel a great solidarity with other bands' again.[17]

Perhaps this was why the Cult would shortly undergo their own psychedelic transformation. *Dreamtime* gathered up all of Astbury's studies into the cultures of Senecas, Mohawks, Hopi and Dakota, along with the beliefs of Australian aboriginals that its title alludes to. It contained songs begun with Southern Death Cult – 'A Flower in the Desert' was SDC's 'Flowers in the Forest' reworked, 'Horse Nation' continued Astbury's *Bury My Heart at Wounded Knee* dialogue and the single 'Spiritwalker' is about shamanism – while Duffy's epic riffology was not a million miles removed from that of U2's the Edge. Like Echo and the Bunnymen, the Cult had ambitions to create soundscapes that might eventually fill up an arena – but for now they were sticking to their punk principles.

They'd also been going to a new nightclub at 69 Dean Street. Alice in Wonderland was the brainchild of former mortician Christian Paris and DJ Clive Jackson (b. 7 July 1961), better known as 'The Doctor', who, despite hailing from Ken Dodd's corner of Liverpool, Knotty Ash, was far from being a Diddy Man. The towering Clive, whose lean, Lux-like frame was further emphasised by a veritable horn of hair sprouting from the top of his head, fronted his own psychedelic combo, Doctor and the Medics. He and Paris were veterans of the earlier '80s Psychedelic Revival, during which they had started their first club, the Clinic.

'Originally the Doctor persona was a tribute to the likes of Dr John and Screamin' Jay Hawkins – I wanted a voodoo sort of image. During that time, I had a friend who bet me a fiver I couldn't set up a band to support his,' Clive told *Wales Online*.[18] He put together a bunch of friends: guitarist Steve McGuire, drummer Steve 'Vom' Ritchie, bassist Richard Searle and singers Wendi West and Colette Appleby, aka the Anadin Brothers, who made themselves up to look like identical twins. 'We supported the band but not only that, we blew them off stage. I decided that was what I wanted and I have never looked back. I never got paid the fiver.'

The Medics' first single 'The Druids Are Here' was released on their own Whaam label in 1982. They didn't get around to releasing anything else until 1985. Clive and Christian were too busy creating their own crushed velvet underground from the former roost of the Batcave. From 1983, Alice's was held every Monday night and became the Goth enclave's natural successor, a place to hear what was in Dr Clive's bag of vinyl gris-gris and watch a new mushrooming of Nuggets-style garage psych bands – at least one of whom were infamous punk rockers in disguise. They started doing their own Magical Mystery Trips, ferrying the Alice crowd on coaches from Speakers' Corner in Hyde Park to inspired destinations where gigs would take place – literally beneath the pavements on their first excursion, to Chislehurst Caves in Kent on 27 October 1984. This venue's pop culture heritage goes back to the '50s, when scenes from Edmond T. Greville's 1959 juvenile delinquent classic *Beat Girl* were filmed there. It was rediscovered as a venue later in the '60s, when Jimi Hendrix, Pink Floyd and the Yardbirds filled the man-made labyrinth with freaks. Unsurprisingly, the Medics had come to the attention of Floyd's former managers, Peter Jenner and Andrew King.

After being medicined at Alice's, the Cult's next, chart-cracking breakthrough album would be full of the spirit of 1967 and labelled with *Love*. But that wasn't the vibe being felt by the actual counter-culture. Members of the travelling community who had travelled to Stonehenge to celebrate the Solstice of 1985 found themselves cornered by police in a bean field instead.

What followed on the hot summer morning of 1 June were scenes of brutality more shocking even than those meted out to the miners, as members of what was known as the Peace Convoy – including pregnant women – were attacked with batons and had their homes destroyed in front of their eyes during the biggest mass arrest in Great Britain since the Second World War.

As *The Young Ones*' resident hippy Neil had predicted just over a year before, it was going to get 'very heavy'.

Helter Skelter

The final defeat of the NUM was the prelude to the second 'Battle' of Thatcher's civil wars. Throughout the winter of 1984–85, more miners had been lured back to work as the TUC attempted to restart talks with the NCB, the ugly divisions in the affected communities worst illustrated by the actions of two striking miners in south Wales, who dropped a concrete block from a footbridge onto a taxi transporting a strike-breaker to work. The driver, 35-year-old David Wilkie, was killed on the spot, just outside Rhymney en route to the Merthyr Vale mine, on 30 November 1984. Three days after one last rally in London, the NUM blew the final whistle on the strike on 3 March 1985. For a further week, Kent miners stayed out, continuing to picket other pits in an attempt to get amnesty for miners who had been sacked as a result of new legislation. But the longest industrial dispute in British history was over, the honourable working-class population of the coalfields its losers.

Like the miners, the Peace Convoy – so-called for their allegiance to the Campaign for Nuclear Disarmament (CND) and the Greenham Common camp that had been evicted four months' earlier by 1,500 police and soldiers in the largest peacetime operation of its kind – were portrayed as 'the enemy within'. In this case, villainous drop-outs, whose determination to live outside mainstream society was presenting a threat to democracy. Their purpose in converging upon Stonehenge was to carry out heathen rites that, it was claimed, cost Wiltshire Council tens of thousands of pounds to clean up after, endangered archeological sites and caused the wilful destruction of landowners' property.

After the 1984 Stonehenge Free Festival had attracted an estimated 10,000 such revellers, the Department of the Environment passed the management of the site onto English Heritage. A High Court injunction was obtained to stop the Festival and a four-mile exclusion zone set up around the stones, with tonnes of gravel and rings of barbed wire positioned as roadblocks. The Peace Convoy – about 600 people in 140 vehicles – had spent the previous night in the Savernake Forest at the invitation of landowner David Brudenell-Bruce, the Earl of Cardigan. They approached the site from the A338, the Earl riding shotgun on his motorbike to observe their progress.

Like the miners being directed by police into the enclosed topside at Orgreave, the travellers found themselves diverted into a field of broad beans and stranded, seven miles from the stones. Here, numbers of officers, equipped with the same kind of riot gear they had faced off the miners with, swelled to 1,300 – easily doubling the ranks of those they pursued. Surrounding the vehicles, they began pulling women – some of them heavily pregnant, some of them carrying babies and young children – out of their vans.

'The police formed up and attacked absolutely everything in sight – smashing windows, dragging people out by their hair through broken glass,' eyewitness Alan Lodge told the BBC. As with Orgreave, the idea that this event – later dubbed the Battle of the Beanfield – was a case of 'two opposing armies having a pitched battle in a field in medieval style is completely false,' continued Mr Lodge. 'This was an ambush that happened on a small, mild mannered bunch of people – hippies, for God's sake.'[19]

In total, 537 people were arrested. Once all the vehicles had been forcibly emptied, the police systematically smashed them up and set several on fire. Seven dogs belonging to the travellers were removed to be put down by the RSPCA, while their owners were transported across the country to prison cells as far away as the Midlands and the North, with no concern for keeping parents and children together.[20]

Very few people in positions of power spoke up in the Peace Convoy's defence. One who did was the Earl of Cardigan, who testified for the twenty-four travellers, who later sued Wiltshire Police for wrongful arrest, assault and criminal damage. He described seeing a heavily pregnant woman 'repeatedly clubbed on the head' by police, who illegally covered up their ID numbers and methodically smashed up vehicles with batons and hammers. For speaking out, he was labelled a class traitor by *Daily Telegraph* editor Bill Deedes, whom he subsequently successfully sued for defamation.[21] 'I got a BMW off them,' the Earl recalled to *The Independent* in 2013.

While My Guitar Gently Weeps

The travellers' whole way of life had been deliberately destroyed and from this point on, the anarchist voice in popular music was pretty much sidelined, too. Having played their last gig as a benefit for striking miners at Aberdare in the Cynon Valley, an exhausted Crass called it a day in July 1984. 'We found ourselves in a strange and frightening arena. We had wanted to make our views public, had wanted to share them with like-minded people, but now those views were being analysed by those dark shadows who inhabited the corridors of power,' Penny Rimbaud would explain in the sleeve notes to their posthumous *Best Before 1984* compilation album (Crass, 1986).

There was one exception: New Model Army signed a deal with EMI. Though it was one that gave them 'complete artistic control' and included the former employer of both the Beatles and Sex Pistols making a large donation to a miners' fund, the fact that they had pledged allegiance to one of the UK's largest defence companies – with divisions involved in radar, electronic warfare and communications – did not go down entirely well. NMA would make their sole *Top of the Pops* appearance in May 1985, performing the single 'No Rest', with sentiments that echoed Penny Rimbaud's words. They all wore T-shirts that proclaimed: *Only stupid bastards take heroin*, with lines of masking tape protecting viewers from seeing the rude word. Enraged Crass affiliates Conflict created their own live album and corresponding T-shirt: *Only Stupid Bastards Help EMI* on their own New Army Records.[22]

But in the parallel universe of Wonderland, the Mystery trips went on – on 6 July, Magic buses pulled up at a disused Butlin's in Clacton, Essex, disgorging the Medics and a veritable rainbow nation of new groups with such names as the Magic Mushroom Band and Bad Acid & the Spooks. Another Alice's regular turn were Naz Nomad & the Nightmares, who had released a curious album entitled *Give Daddy the Knife, Cindy* on Ace subsidiary Big Beat in 1984, packaged to look like the soundtrack from a lost '60s horror film. It contained covers of a host of *Nuggets/Pebbles* psych-outs; The Seeds' 'The Wind Blows Your Hair', the Electric Prunes' 'I Had Too Much to Dream Last Night' and some much rarer cuts – like 'Cold Turkey' by Pete 'Big Boy' Miller – that suggested the band were cult connoisseurs. In fact, Naz Nomad, Sphinx Svenson, Nick Detroit and Buddy Lee Junior turned out to be original punks the Damned in convincing masquerade.

And Naz – aka Dave Vanian – was having so much fun with Dr Clive that they wrote a smash hit single together. 'Grimly Fiendish' gave the Damned their biggest seller since 1979 and marked a new era for the band, following the departure of founder member and major songwriter, Captain Sensible. Vanian (b. David Lett, 12 October 1956), who took his band's name from the 1963 Hammer classic, had always looked like the son and heir of Screaming Lord Sutch and the Damned had never paid much attention to Johnny Rotten's advice. They attempted to get Syd Barrett to produce their second LP, *Music for Pleasure* (Stiff, 1977), and when they couldn't lure the recluse out of his Cambridgeshire lair, went with Floyd drummer Nick Mason instead. *Machine Gun Etiquette*, which followed for Chiswick in 1979, contained a cover of Jefferson Airplane's 'White Rabbit' and lashings of Farfisa organ, as Vanian's vocals developed from punk yelp to (murder) ballad singer baritone.

Since their inception, band members had chopped and changed in rapid succession around the core of Vanian, multi-instrumentalist Sensible (b. Raymond Burns, 24 April 1954) and drummer Rat Scabies (b. Christopher Miller, 30 July 1955). These core components reached a creative high on 1980's *The Black Album* (Chiswick) – often cited as a precursor to Goth and not just for the Inverse Beatles title. With its dramatic seventeen-minute 'Curtain

Call' centrepiece, the Damned fashioned a theatrical epic cut from the black velvet cloth of Scott doing Brel, *Nancy and Lee Again* and the mysterious Barry Ryan, a windswept late-'60s lost boy to whom Vanian would return in 1986.

The following *Strawberries* (Bronze, 1982) was made while Sensible was topping the charts with his delightful rendering of Rodgers & Hammerstein's 1949 *South Pacific* showtune 'Happy Talk'. It marked the first appearance of Roman Jugg on keyboards and further introduced sitar and cello to the band's sound. Prog giant – and one of Bowie's most crucial collaborators – King Crimson's demented genius guitarist Robert Fripp joined them in the studio during the recording.[23] Though it received some of the best reviews of the Damned's career – nine out of ten in *Smash Hits* from no less a sage than Fred Dellar, who called it 'the kind of pop Paul McCartney would be pleased to have his moniker on' – newfound solo star Sensible's commitments left the band without their songwriting genius. His last stand (for now) was a heartfelt tribute to Mary Whitehouse's bête noir, 'I Fell in Love with a Video Nasty', performed inside *The Young Ones*' house alongside new bassist Bryn Merrick (1958–2015) and Jugg on lead guitar. After the amusing diversion of Naz Nomad, 'Grimly Fiendish' – which sounded like something Madness could equally well have come up with – was a career tonic.

As the name suggests, parent album *Phantasmagoria* (MCA, July 1985) marked the point where the band came out as full-on Goth, appearing on *Top of the Pops* in clothing Peter Cushing and Christopher Lee would have been proud to duel in – all designed by Vanian's ace seamstress wife Laurie, the Morticia to his Gomez Addams.[24] Six months after its release, they reached their highest-ever chart position with a lavish – but faithful – cover of Barry Ryan's 1968 epic, 'Eloise'.

And it was around the same time that 'Grimly Fiendish' was rising up the greasy Gallup pole, alongside the Cult's shimmering, lightbulb-changing masterpiece 'She Sells Sanctuary', that I first began to hear the word 'Goth' being used as a pejorative term.

As the amount of chart hits listed in this chapter indicates, at the midpoint of the decade, and with all our protagonists giving and receiving a little help from their friends, the Dark Arts went mainstream. '*Goth*' – delivered with as much lip-curling disdain as the 1985 equivalent of Matthew Hopkins could muster – was a barb aimed at those whose carriages had only just pulled up at the crumbling castle gates. And like the residents of seventeenth-century East Anglia or Salem, those accused would quickly turn to point the finger at others who may not previously have been aware of the Banshees, the Damned, the Cult, Killing Joke – who also broke into the 1985 charts with the epic 'Love Like Blood' single – or the Cure, en route for superstardom with their *Head on the Door* album that August. The implied crimes here were not putting in enough hours on the graveyard shift with John Peel; not being able to produce any evidence of gig tickets, a stack of old music papers, or a collection of rare flexidiscs; not having the ability to name every previous member of the Damned off the top of your head and possessing a wardrobe that revealed an absence of flaking band T-shirts with their sleeves cut out, Johnson's boots, winklepickers, Victorian nightshirts, paisley silk dressing gowns (worn as jackets), paisley shirts, rosary beads, leather jackets, crimpers or stocks of Boots Extra Strong hairspray – just a single pair of brand new fishnet tights.

'I'm not a . . .' would from now on be the three little words on every Goth's lips.

Gothfather: Dr John the Night Tripper

Doctor Clive's guru of the New Orleans night was born Malcolm John Rebennack Jr in Louisiana's most enchanted enclave on 20 November 1941. He became better known as Dr John the Night Tripper, a Bayou Baron Samedi decked out in feathers, robes and towering headdresses, who played piano with a human skull atop his keyboard; his signature tune, the haunting, seven-minute-long incantation 'I Walk on Gilded Splinters', a fervid swamp funk fever dream. While Screamin' Jay Hawkins howled and gibbered out his curses, spells dropped softly from the Night Tripper's lips – and were all the more chilling for it: 'I walk through the fire and I fly through the smoke/See my enemy at the end of my rope.'

Growing up in the Third Ward of New Orleans, Rebennack was a hugely gifted musician from an early age and his veins ran with the blood of many nationalities: 'In New Orleans, in religion, as in food or race or music, you can't separate nothing from nothing. Everything mingles into each other,' he wrote in his autobiography Under a Hoodoo Moon *(St Martin's Press, 1995). 'Everything mingles each into the other – Catholic saint worship with gris-gris spirits, evangelical tent meetings with spiritual-church ceremonies – until nothing is purely itself but becomes part of one fonky gumbo.'*

His father ran a business selling and repairing PA systems, so Mac Jr would tag along with him to nightclubs, catching performances by all the local legends. Fats Domino's guitar player Walter 'Papoose' Nelson tutored him on that instrument; his piano idol was Professor Longhair, who played a captivating mix of blues, boogie woogie and rhumba rhythms. Dressed up to the max in outré stage adornments, Longhair would spin strange stories of bald-headed girls and Mardi Gras queens in his distinctive, gravelly vocals. Rebennack began accompanying him live on guitar at the age of thirteen, disappearing into a night world of strip joints and speakeasies where he could play for eighteen hours a day all week and for which the Jesuit brothers at his high school educationally excommunicated him. But by then, Mac couldn't care less – he was already playing both guitar and piano on sessions for Joe Tex, Allen Toussaint and Art Neville. By sixteen, he was the original Ace Records in-house A&R man, but after a gunfight at a nightclub in Jackson, Mississippi left him minus the use of the ring finger on his left hand, he was forced to stop playing guitar. Rebennack was by now living a dangerous double life, dealing and taking heroin, the hellhound forever on his trail.

Following a jail sentence for possession in 1965, he relocated to Los Angeles and soon became a premiere session guy, playing on records by everyone from Aretha Franklin to Bob Dylan, working with Phil Spector but coming a cropper again when counter-culture icon Frank Zappa fired him for his extra-curricular narcotic activities. He saved himself this time through the power of all his talents.

On studio time borrowed from Sonny & Cher, he summoned up all the Bayou magic he'd learned from Professor Longhair and those long nights in the Big Easy to recreate himself as Dr John the Night Tripper – a title taken from a real nineteenth-century voodoo priest. The resultant album Gris-Gris *– the Creole French word for a magic powder, talisman or amulet – was like nothing Atlantic Records boss Ahmet Ertegun had ever heard before. 'What is this album you gave me?' the man who had previously signed Ray Charles, Otis Redding, Aretha and the Rolling Stones asked. But he still put it out on his Atco label and the love generation promptly fell under its powerful conjuration.*

Dr John gained more influential friends with the following Babylon *(1969) and* Remedies *(1970) – Mick Jagger appeared on the 1971 album* The Sun, the Moon and Herbs, *and his then girlfriend,* Hair *actress Marsha Hunt, recorded her own deeply groovy version of 'Walk on Gilded Splinters'. Mac paid tribute to Professor Longhair on* Dr John's Gumbo *(1971) and had his greatest success getting fonky with fellow New Orleans stalwarts Allen Toussaint and the Meters on* In the Right Place *(1973). This spawned the* Billboard *top-ten single 'Right Place, Wrong Time', whose lyric gave the world the memorable phrase 'brain salad surgery' – as in the Emerson, Lake & Palmer album that no bargain bin is ever without. Around the same time, Mac's doppelgänger Dr Teeth began fronting the Muppets' Electric Mayhem band.*

In 1989, he finally kicked his heroin habit, signed to Warners and had a further string of hits with In a Sentimental Mood *– a collection of standards* *for which he earned a Grammy singing 'Makin' Whoopee' with Rickie Lee Jones – and* Goin' Back to New Orleans *(1992). When Hurricane Katrina devastated his home city, he rallied to the cause, releasing the fundraising* Sippiana Hericane *EP in 2005, then pouring his anger, grief and subsequent reflections on the tragedy into* The City that Care Forgot *(2008).*

Like Allen Toussaint, Rebennack found a kind of home from home in Manhattan, where he had a pad in Washington Heights, taking to the streets with a walking stick adorned with voodoo beads, a yak bone, an alligator tooth and a Narcotics Anonymous key ring. He told the New York Times *in 2010: 'I relate to people up there that kind of hangs on the streets.' Asked if he could speak Spanish with the largely Dominican American population there, he replied: 'No, I don't even speak English.'*

He walked on through the veil at dawn on 6 June 2019, aged seventy-seven.

Gothmother: Fenella Fielding

England's answer to Juliette Gréco, the girl with the hair, the voice and the spider's legs eyelashes, was born Fenella Marion Feldman in London on 17 November 1927. Though more than capable of carrying a tune, it was for acting rather than singing that she made her name. As well as sharing a penchant for wearing black – but always with an accompanying huge white collar – Fenella's mellifluous vocal delivery was every bit as ravishing as her Gallic opposite number; she was a famed raconteur and second to none in the art of the double entendre. 'Do you mind if I smoke?' – the line she is most famous for and the title of her 2017 autobiography – was uttered in the guise of Valeria the Vampire in Carry on Screaming *(Gerald Thomas, 1966).*

The finest and most enduring of all the franchise's comedies, this Edwardian-era horror pastiche cast Fenella's offstage arch enemy Kenneth Williams as her Frankencidal brother Dr Orlando Watt, Bernard Bresslaw as Lurchalike butler Sockett and Harry H. Corbett as Detective Sergeant Sidney Bung, investigating a spate of strange happenings in the woods around her Gothic mansion-cum-retirement home. After Valeria receives DS Bung into her drawing room with these words, she reclines on a chaise longue, her entire, red-velvet-clad body exhaling a mist of billowing vapour into his astonished face. Fenella played every role of her life to similar, delightfully devastating effect.

The daughter of Jewish émigré parents, Lithuanian Philip and Romanian Tilly, she grew up in Clapham, where her father was a cinema manager, boss of a ladies' underwear firm and prominent Freemason – in her memoir, she describes him as a tyrant: 'Home life was horrid. Daddy used to knock me about with his fists, and my mother would egg him on.' Though she won a scholarship to RADA, her parents made it impossible for her to complete her studies. When she tried to go to university instead, her father's response was: 'I'd rather see you dead at my feet.'

So Fenella escaped to London's Theatreland, taking a flat in Mayfair shared with a prostitute and supporting herself by working in beauty parlours and taking to the cabaret circuit in such early '50s hotspots as Churchill's in Bond Street, the Don Juan in Brook Street and the Washington Mayfair Hotel. Talent-spotted by English thesp Ron Moody, who signed her up for her first West End stage role in Cockles and Champagne *at the Saville in 1954, by the end of the decade she was appearing for the first time with Williams in* Pieces of Eight *(1959), written by Harold Pinter and Peter Cook, at the Apollo. Here, the seeds of envy were sown: 'He wanted me to be good,' she noted, 'but not too good.' When she got a review that praised her as a 'beautiful butterfly of comedy', he blew his top: 'I used to be innocent. I used to be trusting. But after eighteen months of that . . .'*

Her early big-screen appearances were in comedies, starring opposite young heartthrob 'Dark' Dirk Bogarde and old roué James Robertson Justice in Doctor in Distress *(Ralph Thomas, 1963). Norman Wisdom was less fun: 'Hand up your skirt first thing in the morning. Not exactly a lovely way to start a day's filming,' she recalled in her memoir.*

Using her natural wit as her armour, Fielding was a female comedy pioneer, performing her own material, sketches and musical revues at Cook's Establishment Club in Soho. But she was a serious actress – her turn as Ibsen's Hedda Gabler in 1969 being described by The Times *as 'the experience of a lifetime.' This was the sort of role she most wanted to make her own.*

Others could see how deep her talent ran. The great Italian director Federico Fellini begged her to star in a film he wanted to make as the incarnation of six different men's desires. 'It was thrilling. I had to meet him at a hotel. It was a fascinating time; full of secret telegrams and so on. He was gorgeous,' she told The Independent's *Robert Chalmers in 2008. But fate had other ideas. She was booked to play Chichester Theatre at the time and: 'I thought it would be dishonourable to let them down. I would say that's the thing that I really regret.' Fellini's instinct was spot on – Fenella never married but kept up affairs with two different men for over twenty years without either finding out about his rival. Well, smoke* does *get in your eyes.*

In her fifties she fell upon hard times, losing everything to a swindling agent. But she still had the gift of the golden voice – lending it to audiobook versions of everything from T. S. Eliot's Four Quartets *to J. G. Ballard's* Crash *– and this led her to the role that most haunted me as a child. In Eric Thompson's unnervingly prophetic* Dougal and the Blue Cat *she played a maleficent, unseen entity poised to take over the happy, flowery world of* The Magic Roundabout *and turn all its colours into one deeply Conservative hue. From a sinister old treacle factory, up on the hills above the Magic Garden, the Blue Voice and her feline enforcer, Buxton the Blue Cat, plotted their dictatorship: 'All must be blue!' she thundered. 'No other colours will be tolerated! I'm blue! I'm beautiful! I'm best!'*

Ironically, Fenella's older brother Basil, Baron Feldman of Frognal (1923–2019) was an ex-Conservative member of the House of Lords. When asked by The Guardian's *Simon Hattenstone if she had ever considered becoming a Tory herself, she replied: 'It never occurred to me to touch them with a bargepole.'*

Fenella published her memoir, written with Simon McKay, at the age of ninety and continued to take to the stage to promote it. I was lucky enough to see her in action in London in May 2018, part of an audience that also included another Goth icon – Magenta, aka Patricia Quinn, who didn't disappoint either, having hair the same shade as her Rocky Horror Picture Show *alter ego's name. Fenella talked for over an hour, with particularly hilarious impersonations of her former Mayfair flatmate – 'a PROPER prostitute' – wearing her trademark black suit and white collar, still looking as magnificent as she sounded.*

Four months later, she was gone in a puff of smoke.

CHAPTER 11

Born Under a Bad Sign

The Outlaws: Einstürzende Neubauten, J. G. Thirlwell, Nick Cave and the Bad Seeds, Crime and the City Solution

'Now I got a reason to be waiting/The Berlin Wall'
– Sex Pistols, 'Holidays in the Sun',
released 14 October 1977

If there was one bunch of Batcave regulars who were not to be found flicking peace signs at Alice's, it was Nick Cave, Lydia Lunch, Jim Thirlwell, Blixa Bargeld and Barry Adamson. Not simply because the wearing of flares was anathema to these perennially sharp dressers, but because by 1984 they had all flittered off elsewhere – to the West Berlin district of Kreuzberg, for the most part.

The Birthday Party had put the finishing touches to *Junkyard* in 1982. They wrapped this fearsome album up in a worthy sleeve – courtesy of custom car commando artist Ed 'Big Daddy' Roth – and, as Rowland S. Howard put it, 'the whole rock 'n' roll monster thing that we had put forth came out of our control'. Certainly, reviewers didn't quite know what to make of it. Were the band parodying their own Stooges-like swagger on such grand guignol fare as 'Dim Locator', 'Hamlet (Pow, Pow, Pow)' and 'Big-Jesus-Trashcan'? Or simply gunning their garbage-pail hotrod through the decomposing corpse of post-punk? 'Big Jesus soulmates trashcan,' Cave offered a cryptic clue: 'He's got greasy hair wears a suit of gold.'

They were certainly severing ties: they had parted company with manager Keith Glass, 4AD could no longer afford to fund them and they had long run out of patience with their drummer. All these things considered, the band made the decision to relocate to Berlin. Along the road in Europe they had made friends not just with Einstürzende Neubauten but also fellow Kreuzberg residents, the darkly psychedelic instrumental outfit Die Haut and electronic experimentalists Malaria!, fronted by Neubauten comrade, Gudrun Gut. These were the people – and not the multifarious Sex Fiends now hatching from the Batcave's bowels with alarming rapidity – with whom they shared common cultural ground. 'For the first time since we left Australia we felt part of some kind of scene,' Howard recalled.[1] More alluringly still, in the funkiest part of old West Berlin, rents were cheap, artists thrived and – unlike London – the city stayed open twenty-four hours a day.

Relocating also gave them the excuse to ditch Phill Calvert, metaphorically left standing on the tarmac in a perplexed state. 'People are talking about me like I've died or something!' he told *Sounds*' Helen Fitzgerald, another Pete Best on his way. Following a brief stint drumming for the Psychedelic Furs on a tour of America, Calvert returned to Melbourne, where he joined up with former members of Camberwell's Scrap Museum. They changed their name to Blue Ruin – slang for bathtub gin – and commenced pedalling their potent distillation of post-punk blues for twelve years and five albums.

Night of the Hunter

With Mick Harvey taking over on drums, the Birthday Party's next recordings reflected their new sense of freedom. *The Bad Seed* EP (4AD, February 1983) was recorded at David Bowie's old Berlin haunt, Hansa Studios on Köthener Straße, adjacent to the Wall.

But it spoke of a landscape very similar to the haunted backwoods Jeffrey Lee Pierce had been staking out in *Miami*. It begins with Nick screaming 'Hands up who wants to die!' on the pulverising 'Sonny's Burning' and ends, in grim humour, with 'Deep in the Woods', a song whose creation began on the road through the epicentre of Germany's Gothic imagination, the Black Forest. It's a slavering beast, slouching along to notes plucked like screams from Howard's fretboard and Cave's onerous vocals. 'This knife feels like a knife that feels like it's feed,' he intones, a Robert Mitchum-style nightstalker full of diabolical retribution. 'Baby, tonight we sleep in separate ditches'. As the killer closes in, Howard whirls up a tornado of feedback and we're not in Kreuzberg any more. 'The songs on this record,' *NME*'s Barney Hoskyns appraised, 'are charged with an appalling, almost absurd power . . . If this is the bad seed, then what is the healthy soil?'

The EP's Cave-designed sleeve offered further provocation: photographic portraits of the four band members within a swastika, an enormous sacred heart flaming in the middle – the equivalent of having LOVE tattooed across one knuckle, HATE across the other. 'It always amazed me that people didn't understand that,' Mick Harvey said. 'Hansa Studios used to be a Nazi ballroom. The ghost of the Nazi era was so powerful in Berlin in the early '80s. The swastika was an obvious reference to that.[2]

The Bad Seed was the Birthday Party's finest work to date and their last with 4AD. But by now, Daniel Miller's canny championing of Depeche Mode had put the Mute founder in a position where he was able to offer the band he had first seen at the Moonlight Club in 1980 the deal that would secure Nick Cave's future. And no sooner had they signed it than the outfit fell apart at the Cave–Howard seams.

Memories of events differ, but essentially, in Blixa Bargeld, the singer had found a guitarist he preferred working with. 'Nick's a lot more innocent than he looks,' Rowland told Ian Johnston. 'He gets really impressed by things and people. He's almost a fan of certain people, particularly people who look slightly dilapidated, people who look like they've lived.'[3] In Berlin, Cave had been living close with Blixa in the bars and clubs of Schöneberg, where the Neubauten singer tended at a bar called Risiko and life was one long George Grosz out. And so the final BP release, the aptly named *Mutiny!* EP, was the sound of Nick and Rowland's relationship being thrown overboard.

The Speaker Cabinets of Dr Caligari

If any one figure in '80s Berlin commanded the attention, it was Blixa Bargeld (b. Christian Emmerich, 12 January 1959 in Tempelhof, Berlin), whose very appearance distilled the essence of German Expressionist cinema into astoundingly gaunt humanoid form, somewhere betwixt Max Schreck's Count Orlok and Conrad Veidt's Cesare. A self-taught musical alchemist, Christian rebaptised himself, taking his first name from a brand of felt-tip pen and his surname from Dada artist Johannes Theodor Baargeld, another pseudonym that is a variation on the German 'Bargeld', meaning 'cash money'[4]. He first began his experiments in sound at the age of thirteen and in true Joe Meek style, dissecting and reassembling tape recorders at the kitchen table while using the utensils around him to make the noises he captured on tape. It wasn't long before he dropped out of school to seek his fortune in the squats around Schöneberg – close to David Bowie's former Hauptstraße residence – where the Berlin post-punkers were making good use of deserted buildings in the same way as their counterparts on Ladbroke Grove and No Wave New York. He found a home in a flat above Eisengrau, a shop on Goltzstraße. Below him, musicians Gudrun Gut, Bettina Köster and designer Claudia Skoda were selling clothes in an environment painted a very Bauhaus shade of grey and beneath them was an enticing cellar. Here, Blixa and schoolfriend NU Unruh (b. Andrew Chudy, 9 June 1957, in New York) continued to experiment musically, using salvaged items and Blixa's body as percussion instruments, selling tapes of the resultant recordings from the shop.

'I didn't start being a musician to provoke anything, or to be intentionally different,' Bargeld told *The Quietus*'s Luke Turner.[5] 'The starting point for Neubauten was more that we didn't have anything, so I didn't really have the choice to say: "I am doing this, I am doing that, or maybe I should play organ." I didn't have any of these things, and I could not afford any of these things, and neither could anybody else in the group.'

The first Einstürzende Neuabauten gig was on April Fool's Day 1980 at the Moon Club in Wilmersdorf, with a band composed of Blixa on vocals, Beate Bartel and Gudrun Gut – both then members of Mania D – on bass and Korg MS-20 respectively and NU Unruh on drums. But the performance that has gone into legend was the June 1980 recording made by Bargeld and Unruh of 'Stahlversion', the B-side of their first single 'Für den Untergang' made in a 1.4 x 5 x 50-metre steel-lined room located beneath the north-eastern pillar of a motorway bridge.[6] The image of the skeletal Blixa and burly Unruh hammering away at the sound of Collapsing New Buildings – as their band's name translates into English – beneath the bowels of the autobahn is the one sealed into public imagination. The pair recreated the session for an accompanying 'Stahlmusik' video at the same location in April 1981.

The two principal architects were joined that year by sound technician and multi-instrumentalist Alexander Hacke (aka Alexander von Borsig, b. 11 October 1965, in West Berlin) and percussionist F. M. Einheit (aka Mufti, b. Frank-Martin Strauß, 18 December 1958, in Dortmund). They recorded their first LP *Kollaps* (*Collapse*, October 1981, Zick Zack), a collision of found sounds, found instruments and industrial noise presented in a sleeve stamped with the band's logo: an archaic-looking drawing of a stick man with a circled dot for a head. As enigmatic as the album's contents, it resembles the *Monas Hieroglyphica* created by Elizabeth I's court magician Dr John Dee in 1564.[7] Shortly after *Kollaps*' release, bassist Mark Chung (b. 3 June 1957, in Leeds) – who had previously played with Mufti in Hamburg punk band Abwärts – completed the Neubauten line-up, which remained consistent for the next fifteen years.

Strategies Against Architecture

It was Jim Thirlwell who first brought them to London in 1982. The thrusting young Foetus was at that time living in Ladbroke Grove, part of the west London squat scene that socialised in the ZigZag club and Centro Iberico – where he witnessed a revelatory gig by Throbbing Gristle – and working at the Virgin Records shop on Oxford Street. Nothing perhaps better illustrates the links between the Batcave habitués and those who shared the space of 69 Dean Street at the Comedy Store than the source of Jim's first Ladbroke Grove squat: '[Actor] Keith Allen found this block of flats on Westbourne Grove,' he recalled. 'They had just been built, but I think they had skimped on the construction materials and they were cracking a little bit, so they were uninhabitable, despite being new.' He also shared this Health and Safety-free zone with his friend, the Swell Maps/Jacobites singer-songwriter Nikki Sudden, who he remembered 'living in an alcove' somewhere in these flats.

Like Blixa in Berlin, Thirlwell was a teenage bedroom producer. Though he had been taught cello and percussion at school, the experience of learning by rote and then being plonked straight into an orchestra was not a comfortable one for Jim: 'It was so intimidating, I was like a deer in the headlights. Sight-reading and learning paradiddles was just not what I wanted to do. Then punk rock came along and you didn't have to be a virtuoso, just pick it up. I bought a bass and I would just sit in my bedroom playing it. Then I bought my first synthesizers, a Wasp then a Korg MS20. I started making tapes using these very primitive things.'

It was Keith Allen who encouraged him to get out a bit more: 'Keith kept saying, "Look, you've got to get out there and play with other people, you're not going anywhere making tapes in your room! My friends Sue and John from pragVEC are looking for people to play with – why don't you go and hang out with them?" Keith was dating Barbara Gogan, the singer for the Passions, and Barbara was the sister of Sue, pragVEC's singer. So I started playing keyboard and hanging out with them and we made some recordings. That was my first time in a multi-track studio and the engineer was Gerry Shephard, who was in the Glitter Band – so I also got to learn the secrets of the Glitter Band's album.'

Armed with such Eldritch-envy-engendering insight, with prag-VEC and their Spec records label, Thirlwell rode fast and hard along the experimental frontiers, both as a musician and producer, putting out his first Foetus records on his own Self-Immolation label with help from Geoff Travis. 'I was lucky to be there at the dawn of the explosion of independent labels, which Rough Trade was the hub. Punk rock had already democratised things by saying just play three chords. Then with No Wave, you don't even need to play the instrument conventionally, you can invent your own language.' Then came Nurse with Wound, whose founder, Steve Stapleton, was a regular customer at Jim's Virgin day job and with whom he continued his rapid education in the unorthodox.[8]

'With Steve, it was – you don't even have to have an instrument at all, you can just use a chair. Or you can use tape loops, you can take anything that makes a sound and that's your palette right there. Then it's using the studio and manipulating sounds – so not only did you have the democratisation of being a musician, you also had the democratisation of production; all the old rules were off. If punk rock was the big bang, then everything that happened after was like the expansion of the universe.'

Nurse with Wound, Coil – whose 1983 *Scatology* album Thirlwell also produced – and Throbbing Gristle all shared aesthetics with the inhabitants of Kruezberg. T. G.'s Genesis P-Orridge and Cosey Fanni Tutti had created their band from a visual art background and always used mixed media to put across their vision of music as confrontational conceptual art. Which – along with the influence of key Kosmische bands Can and Neu!, whose music also impacted on the Banshees and PiL – was very much in line with Blixa's thinking. Thirlwell saw Neubauten playing in Berlin in 1982, at a time when they had introduced the use of drills, jackhammers and other power tools into their sets, 'and they just totally blew me away'.

Acting as a one-man British A&R department, Jim set about compiling the *Stratagien Gegen Architekturen* (*Strategies Against Architecture*) album of rare cuts and outtakes with Mark Chung, originally intending to release it himself. But when he signed Foetus to Some Bizzare in 1983, Stevo was happy to offer the Brutalist Berliners a place on his roster too – although he wanted new, original material from them. So they recorded their second album, *Zeichnungen des Patienten O. T.* (*Drawings of Patient O. T.*), in London for him in 1983 and – fittingly for the man who began his record label with alter ego the Normal's homage to *Crash*, 'Warm Leatherette' – Daniel Miller took *Strategies Against Architecture*'s sonic Situationism to Mute.

Jim, who had trained as an artist in Australia and always presents his records in striking, Constructivism-inspired sleeves, designed its jacket with Blixa: 'I was obsessed by Sergey Marchenko, Klee and Kandinsky and people like that. It crystallised a sort of socialist manifesto about what they were doing and why they were doing it, and in some of my early records, like *Finely Honed Machine*, there's a lot of this kind of Constructivism. The first line, "This body is a machine for living in", is a riff from Leo Tolstoy, and there's other stuff from Surrealism and DaDa-ism that were infused in my work, and from reading about those people, and working at the record store.' It was the first in what would become a series of *Strategies* . . . LPs, the latest of which, volume four, appeared in 2010.

Prior to going into Trident Studios to make *Zeichnungen des Patienten O.T.* – a homage to the Austrian institutionalised schizophrenic artist Oswald Tschirtner – Neubauten played their first UK gig with the Birthday Party and Malaria! on 7 March 1983. By August – having forged a DIY shop industrial subgenre alongside London's Test Dept and expat Aussies, SPK – they had their first and only Peel *Session*. Back in London again, on 3 January 1984, Neubauten staged their most infamous of all gigs at the Institute of Contemporary Art (ICA), performing *A Concerto for Machinery and Voice* – a one-off arrangement for cement mixers, chainsaws and pneumatic drills with vocals by fellow Mute artist Fad Gadget. The ultimate in what you might call Musique Concrète, this spectacle was called off after twenty-one minutes as Mufti, Chung and Hacke, assisted by Gadget, Genesis P-Orridge, Stevo and a late-coming Blixa, attempted to drill through the stage and into the alleged secret passages that link the building on the Mall to nearby Buckingham Palace. In the ensuing carnage – with audience members hurling debris around the hall and at intervening ICA staff – witness for the *NME* Biba Kopf reported: 'Damage to bodies and the building was, surprisingly, minimal.' Little wonder that Cave had nothing but admiration for Neubauten's chisel-cheekboned Lord of Misrule. Who just so happened to be in London for that Peel *Session* while the Birthday Party were concluding the recording of their final EP at Britannia Row Studios in Fulham.

Nick's lyrics for 'Mutiny in Heaven' make explicit his desire for more radical change: 'Well ah jumped!/And fled this fuckin' heap on doctored wings!' As if to underline his point, it was Blixa playing guitar on this track, not Rowland. The Birthday Party's founder guitarist had not even been aware there was any more studio time booked when the rest of his band recorded it without him. As well as a severance with Howard – whose extraordinarily expressive playing had reached a creative peak only five months prior on *The Bad Seed* – the *Mutiny!* EP marked the crossroads from whence Cave's musical direction would meet with the revenant Robert Johnson.

Its four tracks teemed with more Southern Gothic imagery from a novel Cave had begun working on, one of which shared its tentative title, 'Swampland'. The song told the tale of a hunted man sinking into a bog while a lynch mob pursue him through 'trees veiled in fog', equipped 'With boots of blood/With pitchfork and with club'. And thus, with the primordial murk closing over his eyes, the Party was finally over.

If Howard was dismayed at being cast out of his brotherhood, there were no hard feelings from Tracy Pew. Cave's old sparring partner returned to Melbourne, where he happily dived back into academia, studying literature and philosophy at Monash University. Unhappily, he began suffering from epilepsy not long after his return home – and, just like Ian Curtis, struggled to find an effective treatment. Despite giving up alcohol and the rest of his wild ways, Pew's life was cut short on 7 November 1986 by a violent fit, during which he smashed his head against a bathtub at his girlfriend's house in Melbourne. The Birthday Party's fearless bass-slinger was just twenty-eight years old. 'Tracy is the one male genius I've ever met,' Nick reflected. 'I think up until he died what was going on in his head was beyond anything anyone was capable of understanding.'[9]

Ghost on the Highway

And what of that wayward son of the Gun Club, Jeffrey Lee Pierce? Perhaps not entirely surprisingly, the band broke up again before the year 1982 was out, Jeffrey Lee's frequent onstage drunkenness and offstage consorting with the likes of William S. Burroughs, Allen Ginsberg and Billy Idol all being contributory factors. Ward Dotson quit for good, while Terry Graham went on gardening leave and Patricia Morrison stayed in LA as Pierce recorded the sombre *Death Party* EP in New York in December 1982.

For this, he hooked up with drummer Dee Pop (Dimitri Constantin Papadopoulos), whose previous band Bush Tetras had supported the Gun Club on that last, disastrous Gun Club tour, and Dee's bassist friend, Joe Uliana. Completing the line-up came veteran guitarist Jim Duckworth, who had played alongside Alex Chilton in the legendary Memphis band, Tav Falco's Panther Burns – for whom former Jerk Jim Sclavunos has also served serious time.[10] None of them would stick around for too long – Patricia Morrison returned to active duty in February 1983, in time for the UK tour with the Sisters, and Terry Graham made a tentative return in September, only to bail again, alongside Jim Duckworth, right before the band's first tour of Australia.

Averting disaster by the skin of his well-worn knuckles, Jeffrey Lee wasn't short-handed for long. Within a day of landing in Melbourne, he had recruited drummer Billy Pommer and guitarist Spencer P. Jones from local band the Johnnys, the latter of whom filled in until Kid Congo could be summoned back from the Cramps to his longed-for return at Pierce's side. Having made his point – for now – Graham came back to the fold in November. Morrison later reflected on the constant tour dramas and the fact that Duckworth and Graham had no compunction about dropping Pierce right in the kangaroo do rather than follow him across Australia: 'That is what he could drive you to. It's hard to explain unless you've put up with it, but I've seen him get people to tears.'[11] Yet, despite all these distractions, the Gun Club's travelling medicine show made a similar impact on Australia as it had in the UK – it wouldn't be long before bands there were retuning their guitars to a blues setting and learning some country-style picking.[12] For now, reunited with Terry Graham, they continued as a four-piece and, shortly after the March 1984 release of their live *Birth, The Death, The Ghost* album on ID records, they began recording again at Ocean Way Studios in LA. Here, they mingled with some vastly different – yet equally storied – interpreters of American music.

'It was a big studio, but we had the cheaper "off hours" time, so we'd go in at like midnight until six in the morning and record,' Kid recalled. 'Ry Cooder was recording the *Paris, Texas* soundtrack during the day and he had all these vintage amps there and all these crazy noisemaker things. So we poked around his stuff and used some percussion. Also, Stevie Nicks was recording in the next studio and she was the one that didn't come in until three in the morning . . . this big white limousine would roll up and like 18 people would fall out and immediately go into the bathrooms and block the doors – both the men's and the women's.'[13]

Within two weeks they came up with *The Las Vegas Story* (Animal/Chrysalis), a sonic road trip across the Reagan nation, during which Pierce followed his jazz muse all the way to a stunning cover of George Gershwin's 'My Man is Gone'. 'Jazz is my main preoccupation. Dolphy, Mingus and Coltrane are my favourites plus a lot of late-'50s jazz,' he told *ZigZag*'s Richard Kick (aka North aka Cabut) – although in his restless quest for new musical forms, he was also exploring 'South American music, stuff from

Bali, Ecuador and Peru.'[14] On 'Walkin' with the Beast', 'Bad America' and with the album's title, he aimed his lyrical shotgun towards everything he detested about his mother country, using the sham Shangri La in the middle of the Mojave Desert as the most potent symbol of its malaise.

By the end of 1984, as Ronald Reagan was re-elected to the White House by the largest electoral vote in US history, Jeffrey, Kid and Patricia relocated to London while Terry Graham left them for the last time. He may have consulted a crystal ball. For only days after their arrival, when Jeffrey Lee met Romi Mori at a pre-Christmas Gun Club show in Dingwalls, it all went pear-shaped yet again. Ditching Powers and Morrison, Pierce refashioned a band around her and set off on his ill-fated 1985 solo project, *Wildweed*, recruiting Nick Sanderson and Dean Dennis from Sheffield electro-industrialists Clock DVA as his rhythm section. For Romi, it was hardly the most romantic of new beginnings: 'He was incredibly drunk, very lonely I thought,' she recalled of their initial meeting to Sylvie Simmons at a twenty-year distance. 'He came to talk to me after the show, kissed me and slipped some acid in my mouth without my knowledge. We went clubbing, out of my mind, and I woke up in his bed.'[15]

If You're Looking for Trouble . . .

London was also the place where Nick Cave, Mick Harvey and Blixa Bargeld had ended up, back in September 1983, to record fresh material for Mute. Initially, they brought in Jim Thirlwell to work with them on 'A Box for Black Paul' – a song from the Immaculate Consumptive shows that Cave had never managed to quite finish off – plus new compositions, 'Saint Huck', 'Wings Off Flies' and 'From Her to Eternity'. Sketches for these songs had also come via *Swampland*, the manuscript that Cave was almost constantly working on, carrying it wherever he went and sometimes losing chunks of it to the back seats of cabs in the process.

His lyrics were accordingly growing in ambition and scope – the abstract impressionism of *Junkyard* morphing into linear narrative, a journey begun on 'Six-Inch Gold Blade' that gathered its strength on 'Deep in the Woods' and would, in the Mississippi Delta of 'Saint Huck', arrive at its final destination. Nick and his hungry knife had gone hunting for the blues and now he was going to fill him some pot. Only, before he could carry home that kill, he needed to be certain he was running with the right pack. Things began promisingly enough with Thirlwell: 'Nick and I had written the music to "Wings Off Flies" on the piano at Lydia's place,' Jim recalled. 'Then I played guitar on an early version of "From Her to Eternity" with Blixa.'[16] But this song of murderous desire, written with Anita Lane and destined to become the title and dramatic centrepiece of the first Bad Seeds' album, went through many incarnations, as Jim and Nick's relationship then also turned tricky. 'It was a turbulent time back then,' Jim told Ian Johnston, citing 'some tension with the Lydia connection' as one of the possible root causes.

What eventually surfaced from Jim's end was the track 'Sick Man' from Scraping Foetus Off the Wheel's extraordinary *Hole* album of September 1984. Thirlwell, no lyrical slouch himself, penned a portrait of Cave as the Byronic Man – a lurching bar-room brawler and intimidating braggart, his typewriter clattering, his fists flying, his life 'taking notes off toilet walls', a black novel in progress 'written in his own blood'. The line 'Rends and mends companion's tights' chimes unnervingly with 'From Her to Eternity''s erotic prelude to homicide: 'She's wearing those blue stockings, I bet'. It was Cave's own methodology of writing songs in character that inspired Jim, he said: '[Nick] knew about ["Sick Man"] and when I first played it to him, I remember him listening to it with great scrutiny . . . he said, "That's really nasty!"'[17]

The bad vibes certainly made for great art – 'Sick Man' is one of the stand-out tracks on *Hole*'s inspired mash-up of extreme industrial noise with sublime pop, berserk big-band swing and cutting-edge invective. Further down Thirlwell's astonishing neural pathways, 'I'll Meet You in Poland, Baby' was an imagined dialogue between

Hitler and Stalin that moved Biba Kopf to remark: 'Of all the sad songs emerging from this sad world, [this is] the saddest song I've ever heard.' While 'Satan Place' was a blissful pastiche of the Beach Boys, despite the fact: 'I had never owned a Beach Boys' record before in my life when I made it. I just thought: Wouldn't it be cool if it sounded like this? And not because I had even heard *Pet Sounds* at that point.' By the time it came out, he and Lydia had escaped to New York, where they would continue to commit and record their audacious adventures for some time yet.

Back in the aftermath of Jim's immediate departure, Nick took a breather down the Portobello Road, where he bumped into Barry Adamson.

I Got a Right to Sing the Blues

Their paths hadn't crossed since 1982, when Barry had stood in for Tracy Pew during the *Junkyard* sessions, staying on to play some gigs and TV appearances with the Birthday Party and lending his double bass to Lydia and Rowland's 'Some Velvet Morning'. Back then, as well as 'taking over from the big man' on bass, Adamson had also become romantically involved with Tracy Pew's former girlfriend Caitlin, who by now had just given birth to their daughter, Christina.

His musical luck hadn't been so hot – despite providing the bassline that propelled Visage's biggest hit single 'Fade to Grey', he had been contractually cut off from any fiscal credit for the Steve Strange-fronted combo's resultant chart action and was now living back in Manchester, scraping money together to get married. There was another reason for his perpetual lack of funds – by now he had a heroin habit to rival Cave's own, so the sudden reappearance of Nick with an invitation to join him, Mick and Blixa in the studio could not have come at a better time.

It was also downright uncanny. Cave had just managed to replace one genius guitarist with another equally audacious one. Now he was also getting the benefit of a bassist with musical abilities every bit as profound as Thirlwell's. If anyone else knows how hot jazz and Cold War philosophy, Dr No and No Wave and Count Basie and the Count Five all connect, it's Wythenshawe's own Swinging Detective.[18] And as soon as he stepped into the Garden, the studios owned by John Foxx where the trio had been rehearsing, Adamson could feel alchemical forces at work. He recalled in his memoir: 'There's Mick Harvey on the drums. His unbalanced aggression alone is worth the price of admission. During "Wings Off Flies" he smashes the kit so hard I wait for it to fall apart while I scratch around looking for a bass line. Blixa is in and out of time with a deconsecrated blues guitar. My insides light up at the fuck-off of it all.'[19]

All the crucial elements were now in place. The three new Bad Seeds rapidly fell in with each other as they began to flesh out 'Saint Huck', an epic yarn of Mark Twain's Huckleberry friend, heading down on a Mississippi riverboat for a date with destiny – and Elvis. Adamson instantly picked up the 'Old Man River' tempo on his bass and with Blixa extracting 'never-heard-before noises from the guitar . . . the most brutal of landscapes is created from nothing.'[20]

They would complete the process in March 1984, in Trident Studios with Mute's in-house producer Flood (aka Mark Ellis, b. 16 August 1960), the band having picked up additional guitarist Hugo Race from Melbourne's Plays with Marionettes along the way. The finished album would credit one further Bad Seed, Anita Lane – although she didn't play on it, her role as co-songwriter and closest accomplice in all Cave's matters of the heart were nonetheless pivotal to the album's creation. Identifying that she had appeared in his songs right back to 'Six-Inch Gold Blade', Ian Johnston asked Anita how it felt to be murdered over and over in song by her beau. 'I didn't know anything else,' she replied. 'I didn't know my rights. I always felt fine about it. You live with what you know. To other people it may have been really shocking, but I liked the idea of how shocking it was. I didn't take it completely literally.'[21]

If the song 'From Her to Eternity' – with Harvey's crashing piano chords echoing Bernard Herrmann's *Vertigo* theme – marked the turbulent culmination of Cave and Lane's obsessive love story, then 'Saint Huck' saw the singer petitioning for a higher purpose. Unlike the penitent Jeffrey Lee, though, Nick did not come to prostrate himself at the feet of the Burger King and beg deliverance. No. As also previously alluded to in a Birthday Party song, it was the greasy-haired, swivel-hipped Sun God that Cave called upon – through thunder, lightning, the mighty roar of the Mississippi and all its sinner saints – to make him his Gold-suited heir. And his prayer would be answered. Released in June 1984, *From Her to Eternity* was greeted in the pages of the *NME* as 'one of the greatest rock albums ever made'.

Cave, his hair pomaded with the same Black and White balm the young Elvis used into a magnificent greaser quiff, a pair of Vegas-style sunglasses shading his eyes and some good ol' boy-style tattoos on his shoulder, returned to Berlin with his Wild Bunch, ready to unleash a series of albums – and the best-selling results of his novelistic endeavours – that would see him crowned the Black Crow King.

Only, one of the Kruezberg Kowboys had already taken something that Cave said in song literally. A poisoned barb was working its way towards Barry Adamson's heart.

Just South of Heaven

'Australia is a hot country and it's geared towards sport and macho things. And if you're not into that, you have to go a long way up the road to find someone else like you. It's a very extreme culture and it's very hard to grow up in the shade.' Singer Simon Bonney (b. 1961) was part of the same Melbourne music scene that produced the Young Charlatans and the Boys Next Door. A tall, dark handsome man, he was often said to have been the singer that the young Nick Cave most wanted to be. Yet, passing physical similarities aside, they couldn't have been more different: while Cave's music and persona brimmed with swaggering menace, Bonney's songs internalised their violence and he delivered them looking like an elegantly wasted Bryan Ferry in the sonorous, bruised baritone of Karen Dalton's friend, Fred Neil.

He began to perform in 1977 with the Particles, the punk band of drummer Don McLennan, who morphed into Crime and the City Solution that year. Taking their name, UK Decay-style, from a newspaper headline they were, said witness Mick Harvey, 'in a world of their own. Kind of like sludge with a saxophone and singing. It was quite extraordinary.'

By 1978, Bonney had moved to Sydney, where, according to the Australian Music Database, 'his more arty pretentions were better accepted'.[22] Here, he and McLennan were joined by Chris Astley on keyboards, Kim Beissel on sax, Lindsay O'Meara on bass and Dan Wallace-Crabbe on guitar. But things fell apart. Diagnosed with what was then called manic depression, Bonney was hospitalised for seven months.

In 1978, fortune sent him a soulmate in the strikingly beautiful, red-haired artist, writer and violinist Bronwyn Adams, a former schoolmate of Rowland Howard's. 'There are very few individuals in Australia,' she said of their meeting, 'so when you do find someone like you it's an immense relief.' Together, they began to write songs, Bronwyn acting as an editor on the reams of material pouring out of Simon, and they followed their friends over to London in 1985. Here, where the weather suited their clothes, they would be reunited with both Harvey and Howard and offered a new home on Mute.

'The earlier Crime and the City Solution were very different, but both were to me really great,' Mick told Biba Kopf. 'Something special carried over into both groups and that was obviously Simon. I'd been friends with him for a long time, but I was too busy with the Birthday Party to pull him out of the mire he'd slipped into when his group split.'[23] Now, with former Swell Maps drummer Epic Soundtracks (b. Kevin Godfrey, 1959–97, the brother of Foetus' old squatmate Nikki Sudden) and Howard's brother Harry on bass, they built a band that could summon up the necessary thunder and consolation to do Simon and Bronwyn's lyrics justice.

They recorded the four tracks of their first EP, *The Dangling Man*, with Flood at Music Works in London in February 1985. It was the first proper musical engagement Rowland had had since *Mutiny!* and he was delighted to be back and working with another story-teller of such power: 'I'd lost a lot of confidence, I'd written all these songs, but nothing had happened to them. My life had become totally dull,' he told Biba Kopf. 'When you're happy, you have no reason to write. Just so with Simon. He writes about the less pleasant side of human nature.'

'The Dangling Man', 'The Last Day', 'At the Crossroads', 'Shakin' Chill' – all these songs mined trauma and transmogrified it, using the language of the blues. But Bonney was always adamant he should not be taken for a poet of despair, telling *Sounds*' Jack Barron: 'Manic depression is about as interesting as gout or diabetes . . . if you make a big deal out of my illness you immediately put me into a category separate from other human beings, and so my observations will be seen as mad as opposed to normal. The truth is, I think my lyrics are closer to what many people feel than banal pop lyrics. There is no copy value in an illness like manic depression, I want my work to stand on its own legs.'[24]

And so it did. Both *The Dangling Man* and the following, six-track *Just South of Heaven* EP of July 1985 proved an aural catharsis for Crime and the City Solution, through which all their communal ghosts were summoned and then exorcised: Bonney's impassioned howl surfing Rowland's retributive wail of weird sound, preacher's son Mick pounding on the tabernacle keyboards, Harry and Epic's dense, drum and bass. The wild cover painting by Bronwyn expressed the terrain the songs traversed – stormy skies bluster over a ridge of hills, with a rim of golden light that glows and crackles beneath them. It could either be a wildfire or the dramatic exit of the sun. Whatever it is, it rages against the dying of the light.

Though initially they suffered from dim journalistic comparisons to the Birthday Party and that band's more craven copyists, the power of these records echoed down the decades, impacting on those residents of Seattle who would, some five years hence, find themselves part of another youth culture labelled with a G word. The late lamented Screaming Trees/Queens of the Stone Age singer Mark Lanegan (1964–2022) was a fan and friend, who would play some of his last gigs alongside Simon Bonney – and also the Mekons, their barstools all lined up along the lounge of Heartbreak Hotel. 'I'm not big on gimmicks,' as Mick Harvey put it back in July 1985. 'The only thing that gives you longevity is your own depth of emotion.'

Despite Harvey's modest appraisal that 'I've got no talent, no technique, I'm a total musical moron in fact. I'm really surprised I've got the audacity to get up and play!', he was at the epicentre of some of the greatest music to be made in the '80s. Between recording and live dates with Crime, he was also going back to Berlin to record 'Tupelo' with the Bad Seeds – a song that grew from under a bassline he'd begun fashioning on 'Saint Huck' into another of Cave's Elvine epics: one that told of the birth of the King and the death of his twin brother, Jesse Garon Presley, and was the beginnings of the next album to be recorded at Hansa, *The Firstborn Is Dead*.

Trouble Came This Morning

Cave had by now found a publisher for his manuscript in Simon Pettifer of London-based Black Spring Press and within the fertile bayou of his mind had fashioned new songs around its setting. 'Blind Lemon Jefferson' drew on the life of the Father of the Texas Blues, 'Knockin' On Joe' came from US prison slang and 'Train Long-Sufferin'' offered further Sun Studios' kinship with Johnny Cash that was sealed with a cover of his 'Wanted Man', a song written by Bob Dylan. Nick got so carried away with creating a 'Ride This Train'-style Cash travelogue that he added a further fourteen verses of his own to 'Wanted Man''s original lyric. Now also in collaborations with Australian film-maker friend John Hillcoat on what would become the *Ghosts . . . of the Civil Dead* prison movie (1988), Cave was on a creative roll.

Conversely, Barry Adamson was emotionally bleeding out. As he recalls in his memoir, his relationship with Caitlin was not saved by marriage and fatherhood – heroin addiction took it all. Then there was that word. The word he hadn't been able to get out of his head all the time he'd been playing with Nick. A word, still twisting its knife, from a line in 'Saint Huck': 'A bad, blind *nigger* at the piano'. Summoning unbidden memories of past torments suffered in the playground, shot by both sides for being neither black nor white but both, he felt Cave was taunting him by talking about John Lee Hooker's songs 'My First Wife Left Me' and 'It Serve You Right to Suffer', and with his probing of the blues in general. Adamson's alienated feelings crystallised along with the rain through the freezing Berlin winter of 1984. As the Bad Seeds commenced recording at Hansa, he began shooting up a type of synthetic cocaine in lieu of heroin, stopped sleeping and steamed off the rails towards a nervous breakdown. When he got home to Manchester that Christmas, there was no respite. His older sister Carol was dying, the result of a succession of routine operations that had gone horrifically wrong.

Barry was in no fit state to rejoin the Bad Seeds when they began touring in early 1985 – and they had no album to promote yet, since Bob Dylan was taking his time in approving Nick's additions to 'Wanted Man', ultimately delaying *The Firstborn Is Dead*'s release until June. Blixa was also absent, touring America with Neubauten, so bassist Christoph Dreher and drummer Thomas Wydler were recruited from Die Haut. Then, in circumstances close to farce, Rowland was asked to come back on guitar. This was not a great social success. 'Someone in Leeds came up to me and said: "I thought you were dead",' Howard recalled.[25] However, Wydler would stay on behind the drumkit for the next Bad Seeds' album, *Kicking Against the Pricks*, a collection of covers that had shaped Cave's musical outlook, which followed in July 1986. Twelve tracks, including Alex Harvey's 'The Hammer Song', Johnny Cash's 'The Singer', the Velvet Underground's 'All Tomorrow's Parties', Gene Pitney's 'Something's Gotten Hold of My Heart' and the Seekers' definitive Australian anthem 'The Carnival Is Over' were recorded in AAV

Studios in Melbourne, bringing about reunions with Blixa, Barry, Rowland, Tracy Pew, Hugo Race and producer Tony Cohen.

Adamson enjoyed that recording, especially working with Cohen, whom he remembers as being 'brilliant'; and he was further delighted to play a handful of Bad Seeds shows with Screamin' Jay Hawkins in Australia.[26] But his spell of cursed luck was far from over. Between the mixing of *Kicking Against the Pricks* with Flood in Berlin and the recording of the next Bad Seeds LP, *Your Funeral . . . My Trial*, his mother had also suddenly died and his father had been diagnosed with terminal cancer. The last recording Barry made for this incarnation of the Bad Seeds was the album's title track, at Hansa, in March 1986. He described the process: 'I come up with a descending line that takes the verse to the chorus, picturing a metaphorical lowering into the ground, into darkness.'[27]

It was time for Barry to leave the Bad Seeds and heroin behind, to make his own painful journey back to himself and address the question of his own identity.

Walking with the Beast

Another funeral featuring a prominent Australian had also begun in the early months of 1986, as the death knell was sounded for the Fleet Street print unions at Rupert Murdoch's new, high-tech fortress in the old dockyards of Wapping, east London.

Print unions had been around since the dawn of Fleet Street and the foundation of the London Society of Compositors in 1834. By 1986, this and other unions representing typographers, proofreaders, designers, engravers and news agency staff had been amalgamated into the National Graphical Association (NGA). It ran a closed shop and, as a result, many generations of the same families had worked the hot presses of the great newspaper officers.

Rapid advances in technology meant that by the mid-'80s, most of this work could be done by a fraction of the staff on modern offset litho technology, as Murdoch's papers in Australia and America already were. But the NGA were still powerful – a day's strike put paid to an entire, non-returnable day's edition of their product – so proprietors were reluctant to take them on. Not so Murdoch.

First, he watched as provincial publisher Eddy Shah took on the NGA, installing new desktop publishing equipment at his Messenger Group plant in Warrington, Cheshire. Shah refused to hire unionised workers and sacked members who took action in protest. Thanks to the new union laws passed during the Miners' Strike, he emerged victorious, launching his own national daily *Today* from Wapping on 4 March 1986, with Murdoch cheering him on, while urging Thatcher to 'crack down on [the British trades unions] hard'.[28]

By this time, Murdoch had already invested £100 million in his new premises and struck a deal with the Electrical, Electronic, Telecommunications and Plumbing Union (EETPU) to enter business with him on a no-strike agreement. He made the NGU a similar proposal: accept flexible working hours, agree to a no-strike clause, adopt new technology and abandon their closed shop. As he anticipated, the printers voted to strike and were immediately served with notices of dismissal. The National Union of Journalists (NUJ) urged its members not to accept Murdoch's new employment conditions but, faced with their proprietor's incentives – individual payments of £2,000 to cross the picket line or the sack – the majority of *Times*, *Sunday Times*, *Sun* and *News of the World* staff stayed on.[29] Of the refuseniks, many found jobs on a different kind of newspaper also launched on 7 October that year, *The Independent*.

As protesters assembled, a clandestine unit within the Met's Special Branch reconnoitered.[30] The News International HQ is situated in an isolated area, far from the heart of London, where demonstrators could easily be contained, and, as Tony Benn observed and recorded in his diary for 3 May 1986, 'charged' upon by mounted police.[31]

By the dispute's end, on 5 January 1987, 1,262 people had been arrested and 410 police injured. The NGA was virtually bankrupt and facing court action, its members on their uppers.[32] News International had not lost one single day of production. Thatcher's victory over the forces of subversion outlined in the Ridley Plan, the unions, the social drop-outs, the anarchists and the working class itself was just about complete, while Murdoch had made himself unassailable. Here in his pocket, the Story of the Blues.

Six Bells Chime

Some succour came through the autumnal mists of 1986, in two Halloween-straddling Mute LPs, Crime and the City Solution's *Room of Lights* on 27 October and Nick Cave and the Bad Seeds' *Your Funeral . . . My Trial* on 3 November. On the former, Bronwyn Adams picked up her bow and commenced as a full-time member of the band, while the album's sleeve was once again adorned by her painting of the titular bedsit chamber, emitting glowing, ecto-plasmic manifestations. 'For me, the inspiration is only ever there when you're making something truly new,' said Mick Harvey. 'I'm interested in people making a personal expression and with Crime, the perfect understanding Simon and Bronwyn have is the reason I'm so interested.'

Meanwhile, after Adamson's departure, the remaining Bad Seeds had recommenced work on *Your Funeral . . .* while searching out possible replacements. Cave, still working at his draft manuscript, had been mainlining novels by the American noirist Jim Thompson, author of such hardboiled gems as *The Killer Inside Me* and *A Hell of a Woman*, which were definitely scribbled in the author's own blood. As a result, Nick was able to pull off such narrative feats as 'The Carny' – a warm-up for his impending novel with a full freakshow cast – and the lycanthrope lament of the album's title track. Anita Lane made her own devastating testimony on 'Stranger Than Kindness', detailing scenes from her fragmenting relationship with Cave, played out in anonymous hotel rooms lit by 'Bottled light'. 'It was just how I felt one day,' she told Ian Johnston, 'I had this sadness a lot, like it was raining in my chest. We never really stopped seeing each other, but we weren't together at the time.'[33] Nick sang her blues to music composed by Bargeld, with Harvey furnishing a complete funerary repertoire of piano, organ, glockenspiel and xylophone. By both Blixa and Mick's accounts, the making of this album was hard, but Cave would later call it a favourite: 'There are songs on that record that, as far as I'm concerned, are about as perfect as we can get: "The Carny", "Stranger Than Kindness" and "Your Funeral . . . My Trial".'[34]

By the time they came to tour it, the Kreuzberg Kowboys had their new recruit – another friend met along the Lost Highway. It was Kid Congo Powers' destiny to play alongside the most formidable frontmen of the '80s: Lux Interior, Jeffrey Lee Pierce and now Nick Cave. 'A like-mindedness of aesthetics and personality secured my place in the Bad Seeds,' their new guitarist considered, 'and an affinity for the darkness in the songs, which was something I had been drawn to, over and over, whether through the Cramps or the Gun Club.' He styled himself perfectly for his new job, like 'a killer lesbian Mexican mobster,' as he recalled in his memoir. 'A good shirt, good shoes, good hair – and you're off.'[35]

Gothfather: Johnny Cash

One of Johnny Cash's first memories was of sitting on the back of a flatback truck with his two brothers and two sisters, singing the gospel song 'I Am Bound for the Promised Land' while his father Ray drove them to their new home, a sharecropper plot two miles outside Dyess, Arkansas. It was 1935 and he was three years old. From the age of five until he reached eighteen, he would be out there picking cotton every day after school, singing songs he had learned from the family's wireless by Hank Williams, Sister Rosetta Tharpe, Jimmie Rodgers and the Carter Family. He told his friend, the biographer Sylvie Simmons: 'Songs were my magic to take me through the dark places.' His own composition, 'Five Feet High and Rising' (1959), about a flood, spoke directly of the Cash family's hardship during those Depression years.

In 1944, when he was twelve, three pivotal incidents shaped the future course of his life. He saw the Louvin Brothers play a travelling show in Dyess, wrote his first song and watched his older brother and best friend Jack Cash die in horrendous circumstances. Sliced almost in two by a power saw while out cutting wood, Jack lingered for days in his hospital bed while his family sang hymns. Before he finally passed, he sat up and told them he could hear the angels calling.

When he was seventeen, Johnny's voice broke into the most distinctive baritone in country music history. At eighteen he was working a car assembly line in Detroit, which he would later recall in the song that gave the world 'psychobilly', 'One Piece at a Time' (1976). He didn't last long in such menial work, enlisting instead with the US Air Force, where he became a radio interception operator. Posted to Landsberg, West Germany, he bought his first guitar and formed a band, the Landsberg Barbarians, performing songs he'd learned and written along the way. At his airbase, he watched the documentary Inside the Walls of Folsom Prison *and afterwards, mesmerised by what he'd seen, worked his way inside an inmate's head by writing 'Folsom Prison Blues'.*

His four years' service up, Cash rode the rails to Memphis in 1954 – the year of Elvis Presley's breakthrough hit 'That's All Right Mama' – and went knocking on Sam Phillips' door. He described himself as a gospel singer but the Sun boss thought otherwise – he knew an outlaw when he saw one. Johnny's first recording, the stark, country style 'Cry! Cry! Cry!' was released in June 1955, the day after his wife Vivian had given birth to their first child, Rosanne. 'Folsom Prison Blues' followed, then, in 1956, 'I Walk the Line' crossed the 24-year-old, fresh from a tour with Elvis, from topping the country charts into the national top twenty.

In 1958, Cash left Sun for Columbia, wanting to spread his wings into other musical spheres. He moved his family to California and spent most of the next decade on the road. Here, he learned to love amphetamines, at one point taking more than 100 pills in a day, his body thinning, his eyes taking on a psychotic stare. 'For me, it was deeper, darker. It was violence,' he said of their allure. He kicked out the footlights of country's holiest of holies, the Grand Ole Opry, in 1965, was arrested for starting a forest fire and tried to commit suicide by driving a tractor off a cliff. By 1966, as Vivian filed for divorce, he was apprehended by a sheriff who was also a fan. Duty-bound to search the singer, he found a stash of amphetamines. Disgusted, he handed the drugs back, telling Cash to go ahead and kill himself.

But Johnny had an angel waiting in the wings. June Carter, whose family's songs he had sung to keep himself sane working in the cottonfields, took him in and cleaned him up. With her at his side, he returned to that place of formative inspiration and made his classic At Folsom Prison *album of 1968; then as a newly sobered-up and married man,* At San Quentin *the year after. Within the two penitentiaries, his audience members included future country star Merle Haggard and the writer and actor Eddie Bunker, later to become* Reservoir Dogs' *Mr Blue. When, in protest against the Vietnam War, Cash said he would wear no other colour, a generation of draft-dodgers and revolutionaries took the Man in Black to their hearts. On his TV show, which ran from 1969–71, he played alongside his esteemed peers Ray Charles, the Carter Family, Roy Orbison and Kris Kristofferson and introduced such talents as Bobbie Gentry, Tony Joe White and Neil Diamond.*

Cash lost his way again in the '80s, tested this time by his record company's doubt and loss of faith, sliding from Columbia to Mercury and back on the

Road to God Knows Where, where he ended up on a circuit, playing old hits to a similarly ageing audience. This time, deliverance came in the form of a different kind of record-producing outsider, the thirty-year-old New Yorker and rap/metal mogul, Def Jam co-founder Rick Rubin, who could still see the Beast in Johnny. Signing Cash to his American Recordings label, he worked with him on an album of the same name, a collection of stripped-back songs penned by Cash, son-in-law Nick Lowe, Leonard Cohen, Tom Waits and black metaller Glen Danzig, that brimmed with Old Testament fire and the wisdom of a sage. Its sleeve gave the 62-year-old back to the world in April 1994 as his country's cowboy preacher conscience, framed in stark black and white and complete with not one but two hellhounds on his trail.

The series of six albums Cash subsequently produced with Rubin brought him four consecutive Grammys and enabled him to work on through his grief when June died, aged seventy-three, on 15 May 2003 and his own battles with ill-health, up to and beyond their reunion on the other side, four months later on 12 September 2003.

'The thing about Johnny was the man,' Rubin told Sylvie Simmons. 'His strength wasn't in being a musician, it was bigger than music. He was such a great man that anything he did would have been great, and we get a glimpse of him through the prism of music.'

Gothmother: Billie Holiday

No one had more right to sing the blues than the woman born Eleanora Fagan on 7 April 1915 in Baltimore, Maryland. In the opening lines of her autobiography, Lady Sings the Blues, *written with activist William Dufty in 1956, she said: 'Mom and Pop were just a couple of kids when they got married. He was 18, she was 16, and I was three.' The truth – as detailed in John Szwed's* Billie Holiday: The Musician and the Myth *(Viking, 2015) – was that she was born when Pop Clarence Halliday was seventeen, and Mom Julia 'Sandy' Fagan was nineteen, and they never married. Julia was turned out of her home for getting pregnant out of wedlock and little Eleanora became a burden to everyone subsequently tasked with taking care of her. Nobody ever really would.*

She was first brought before a juvenile court at the age of nine for truanting and was sent to a Catholic reform school, the House of the Good Shepherd, for nine months' hard penitence. She would be back there again by the age of eleven, after having been raped. By the time she was twelve she was working in a brothel, where she first heard the songs of Louis Armstrong and Bessie Smith being played, and in them caught hold of something powerful. Something she could do, too.

When Julia Fagan moved to Harlem at the end of the '20s, her wayward daughter followed her, renaming herself at the age of fourteen after Billie Dove, an actress she admired, and her absentee father, a guitarist with the Fletcher Henderson band. Big-band leader Benny 'King of Swing' Goodman recalled first seeing her at the Bright Spot in 1931 and when his producer, John Hammond, caught the seventeen-year-old at Covan's on West 42nd Street in early 1933, he thought he'd seen Armstrong reborn in slight and youthful female form: 'Her singing almost changed my music tastes and my musical life, because she was the first girl singer I'd come across who actually sang like an improvising jazz genius.'

He brought her in to record with Goodman, cutting her first records, 'Your Mother's Son in Law' and 'Riffin' the Scotch'. Two years later, with the growing jukebox trade in mind, Hammond signed her to Brunswick to record with pianist Teddy Wilson. The resultant 'What a Little Moonlight Can Do' was so successful she made her next recordings as a solo artist in her own name, often accompanied by the saxophonist Lester Young (1909–59), whom she nicknamed 'Prez'. He returned the compliment, rebaptising her as the immortal 'Lady Day'.

The musical conversations these two engaged in bordered on the psychic and forged a platonic creative love that ran deeper and stronger than any she was capable of expressing with the stream of abusive men – and sometimes women – she shared her bed with, whose number included the omnipresent Orson Welles. Prez and the Lady recorded together, with Wilson, Count Basie and the Billie Holiday Orchestra up until 1941. She always chose her material and had a hand in its arrangements, so that her recordings of 'I Must Have That Man', 'Trav'lin' All Alone' and Gershwin's 'Summertime' from Porgy and Bess *are among the most arresting vocalisations of the era. As one of her sidemen once put it: 'When Ella [Fitzgerald] sings "My man he's left me", you think the guy went down the street for a loaf of bread. But when Lady sings, you can see he ain't never coming back.'*

The song she is perhaps best known for, 'Strange Fruit', has had entire books written about it. In it she utilises all her unique, mediumistic skill to create popular music's most affecting channelling of the horror that is lynching and the endemic racism of American society. She came across the song in 1939. It started life as a poem by Jewish schoolteacher Abel Meeropol – who used the pseudonym Lewis Allan – and was turned into a song through the folk clubs of Greenwich Village. The first time she performed it, at the integrated Café Society club in the Village, she feared she might end up hanging from a tree herself. Instead, the awe that her performance engendered in its witnesses paved the way for her greatest commercial success. Not that she got to enjoy any of the fruits of her own labours – her mother, three consecutive husbands and multifarious lovers were all busily spending it for her. It was hardly surprising she chose to record the notoriously cursed 'Gloomy Sunday' in 1941.

When not lost in her music, Billie dealt with the painful realities of existence the way most American musicians learned to – with drugs and alcohol. The end of her short life was clouded in a haze of arrests and acrimony. After losing her licence to perform in venues selling alcohol in New York, she went to London in February 1959 to appear on a television show, giving Melody Maker's *Max Jones an interview while she was over. 'Singing's the only thing I know how to do,' she said, 'and they won't let me do it. Do they expect me to go back to scrubbing steps – the way I started out?' It seemed they did. Lester Young died on 15 March 1959, his exit bloody and brutal – varicose veins in his oesophagus split on a transatlantic flight and the only treatment he got came out of the bottom of a bottle. Denied by his widow the chance to sing at his funeral, a devastated Lady Day predicted: 'I'll be next.'*

On 12 June, after having collapsed unconscious, she was arrested for the last time for possession of heroin, fingerprinted and photographed in a bed at New York's Metropolitan Hospital. Her lawyer Don Wilkes had the cops removed from her bedside but there was nothing more he could do. Billie suffered a relapse and died in the early hours of 17 June. She was forty-four and had less than $1,000 to her name.

'There's no damn business like show business,' as Lady Day herself surmised, 'you have to laugh to keep from throwing up.'

CHAPTER 12

Something Wicked This Way Comes

Saints of the Pit: Diamanda Galás, These Immortal Souls, Metallic KO: Zodiac Mindwarp, the Sisters of Mercy, the Cult

Grim Reaper: Silence! I have come for you!
Angela: You mean to . . .
Grim Reaper: Take you away. That is my purpose. I am Death.
Geoffrey: Well, that's cast rather a gloom over the evening, hasn't it?
– Monty Python's *The Meaning of Life*, released 31 March 1983

All the time Thatcher's civil wars had been raging, a Pale Horseman had arrived on our shores, carrying a mysterious new disease. The first case was diagnosed in Britain in December 1981, but few outside of the *Gay News* were then concerned enough to ask whether, as their headline put it, this was: 'Gay cancer or mass media scare?'

Their confusion was caused in no small measure by the way the American press had reported on how gay communities in New York and San Francisco had been hit by an invisible killer in their midst. The first article about an immune system disorder, which had so far taken the lives of 136, was published on the front page of the *New York Times* on 11 May 1982, under the headline: 'New Homosexual Disorder Worries Health Officials'.[1] They called it

GRID – Gay-Related Immune Deficiency. Other, more right-wing and religiously biased publications, who seized upon the news as a sign of righteous retribution, translated this into 'the gay plague'.

Most of its victims died very shortly after diagnosis as an array of opportunist diseases, such as pneumonia, took advantage of their weakened immune systems. Terrence Higgins was among the first British victims to succumb, on 4 July 1982. After getting no clear answer as to what had happened from the doctors who had been treating him, Higgins' partner Rupert Whitaker and friends set up the Terrence Higgins Trust to try to raise funds for research and awareness into what was then called 'the American disease'.[2] It was only after US researchers had discovered it was also affecting women – and children – who were receiving treatment for haemophilia, the partners of afflicted men and drug users sharing needles that the Centers for Disease Control and Prevention (CDC) gave it the name Acquired Immune Deficiency Syndrome (AIDS), in September 1982.

It took until 1984 before researchers identified its cause as the HIV virus and a test was approved for use in the UK – with alarming results. As many as 1,200 haemophilia patients who had received blood transfusions had been infected with HIV. But the vast majority testing positive were gay men and intravenous drug users. Which gave the media here the opportunity to grade sufferers from the disease either 'innocent' or 'guilty' – just as they had once divided up the Yorkshire Ripper's victims between those who were sex workers and those who were not.

By 1985, when actor Rock Hudson became the first high-profile victim and over 20,000 cases had been reported worldwide, the panic had set in. Although research showed the disease could not be passed on by casual contact, stories abounded in the tabloids about people contracting AIDS from toilet seats and coffee cups. 'I'd shoot my son if he had AIDS, says vicar' ran a typical *Sun* headline from October 1985. Manchester's controversial Christian Chief Constable James Anderton added his opinion that sufferers – by then, an estimated 7,500 – were 'swirling in a cesspit of their own making' in December 1986. Condemned by his Chief of Constabulary, Lawrence Byford, as 'his own worst enemy' for this remark, in the ensuing clamour, the UK government finally decided to act. Secretary of State for Health, Norman Fowler commissioned ad agency TBWA to come up with the 'Don't Die of Ignorance' advert to spearhead a public information campaign. Directed by Nicolas Roeg, it came on like a trailer for a horror movie, featuring a three-ton giant black granite tombstone and the ominous tones of actor John Hurt – who, fittingly enough, had recently played Winston Smith in Michael Radford's big-screen adaptation of *Nineteen Eighty-Four*. 'Some people thought anyone with HIV should be left to their own fate, and there were certainly people in government who felt uneasy about homosexuality. I thought – this is unjust,' the now Lord Fowler told *The Guardian*, forty years after the ad's initial screening in September 2017, adding: 'Margaret Thatcher was not a natural supporter.'[3] It was instead Princess Diana who publicly exposed the myth of transmission through touch, as she opened the country's first AIDS Unit at the Middlesex Hospital on 9 April 1987, by shaking the hand of a terminally ill patient for the benefit of the world's TV cameras.

By then, the Greek-American soprano sfogato and 'Black Rose of the Avant-Garde', Diamanda Galás, had already personally witnessed the worst of the disease. While she was working on her *Masque of the Red Death* triptych of albums, which aimed to address every aspect of the subject, her brother, the playwright Philip-Dimitri Galás, contracted HIV. He died in his sister's arms in the autumn of 1986.

An Instrument of Truth

'My voice was given to me as an instrument of inspiration for my friends, and a tool of torture and destruction to my enemies,' was Diamanda's mission statement when Mute re-released her debut recording, 1982's *The Litanies of Satan*, in the UK in 1986. 'An instrument of truth.' As anyone who witnessed her New Year's Day

1989 performance of *Masque of the Red Death* at London's Queen Elizabeth Hall could testify, this voice was nothing short of hair-raising and Diamanda herself a Maria Callas of the Underworld, channelling all its demons. One who did, and was able to find adequate words, was *Melody Maker*'s Simon Reynolds. 'Her first "piece" is like a Moslem widow's prayer wail, a fathomless abyss of grief,' he wrote. 'She bucks and writhes as though struggling to unwind, work out and expel via her throat a giant tapeworm of ectoplasm. She cuts between this laser-searing scream and a verminous babble of multiple voices, like a horde of vindictive goblins.' Her intention, Reynolds correctly perceived, was to 'show us, by induction, how deeply embedded in our souls is the mediaeval mindset'.[4] Diamanda performed her Crimson Mass for all of us sinners.

Galás was born in San Diego on 29 August 1955, to agnostic American-Greek Orthodox parents with roots in Smyrna, Sparta and Egypt; regions of the world beset by centuries of wars, religious conflict and blood feud, and whose musical and devotional traditions she would continually draw upon. 'A lot of Greeks would agree with me when I say to be a Greek Orthodox atheist is to have the certainty of the Devil with no hope in God,' she said of her background. 'I look at religion more as geography of a mentality, of laws.'[5] And she looked upon the Devil not as 'some abstract, Gothic figure. He is, in my definition, the coward, the man who is spiritually impotent, the homophobe, the willfully blind, the deserter.'

Her parents were both teachers and her father, James – the director of a gospel choir and a massive fan of jazz – began teaching her piano as soon as she could sit at a keyboard, 'almost from the beginning of life. Beethoven, Brahms, Fats Waller, Greek music, Arabic music – everything. It seems stupid when people limit themselves to one type of music.' But he didn't want her to sing. 'Only idiots and hookers are singers,' he told her.[6] Perhaps he was thinking of Billie Holiday's cruel fate when he said this. It would be ironic if he were.

While TV and radio were forbidden in the Galás household, literature was not and Diamanda and Philip-Dimitri developed a taste for the dark stuff that would also continue to inform her songbook: Edgar Allan Poe, Friedrich Nietzsche, the Marquis de Sade and Charles Baudelaire, from whose *Les Fleurs du Mal* she would draw text for *The Litanies of Satan*. Diamanda began performing piano publicly by the age of twelve and at fourteen was playing with the San Diego Symphonic Orchestra.

With an intellect as ferocious as her artistic abilities – and sense of humour – Diamanda went to study biochemistry at the University of Southern California, specialising in immunology and haematology, subjects that would also be useful to her future musical career. At the same time, she took her own walk on the wild side on the streets of Oakland, taking up with three black drag queens and working on the streets. 'I was known as Miss Zina,' she told the *Pink Paper*'s Liz Naylor in 1988, reflecting that: 'I got out of it because I realised I was probably a better piano player than I was capable of being a good criminal. I think I've found a successful interface between the two.'

Her post-graduate work took her to Paris, where she met the French-Slovenian avant-garde composer Vinko Globokar. It was he who initiated her singing career by inviting her to perform the lead in his opera *Un Jour Comme Un Autre* (A Day Like Any Other), based on Amnesty International documentation of the arrest and torture of a Turkish woman for alleged treason. As she recalled: 'The kind of stuff I do with my voice really did come out of the blue. People have assumed I was an opera singer who decided to move into the avant-garde. But I developed the opera technique with a teacher because I wanted to have a gigantic expression.'

The Litanies of Satan, first released by ZE in February 1982, was sung in French. 'It's not my first language, so it allows me to be committed to the sound, not the meaning. Foreign languages belong to a part of me that English can't inhabit.' She returned to Paris for performances of her solo works, *Wild Women with Steak Knives* and Τραγούδια από το Αίμα Εχούν Φονός (Song from the Blood of Those Murdered) at the Théâtre Gérard Philipe, Saint-Denis. The former drew on Diamanda's experiences of ghetto life in America to portray a woman whose mental health has been destroyed by physical depravation. The latter was an invocation and malediction sung in Greek, directed against the military junta that ruled the country between 1967 and 1974, and was dedicated to its victims. The roots of this piece lay in the *demotiki* tradition of Diamanda's forebears in the Mani Hills near Sparta, the spontaneous dirges of Maniatic women for men killed in blood feuds.

She followed this with an eponymous album released by Metalanguage in 1984, which contained *Song from the Blood of Those Murdered* and *Panoptikon* – Diamanda's own 'Folsom Prison Blues' – or, perhaps more accurately, '25 Minutes to Go', the Johnny Cash song she would later incorporate into her repertoire. Written from the perspective of an inmate on death row, it was inspired by both Jeremy Bentham's 1843 design for a maximum-security prison and Jack Henry Abbott's 1981 prison memoir *In the Belly of the Beast.*[7] The same book – and its author – was simultaneously informing the *Ghosts . . . of the Civil Dead* film project Nick Cave and John Hillcoat were working on. Or perhaps there is no such thing as coincidence – it would not be long before Diamanda was herself drawn to Berlin.

For now, though, she began work on her *Masque of the Red Death* trilogy from San Francisco, unaware at the time that her brother was ill. The first of these albums, *The Divine Punishment* (Mute, June 1986) – its title a reference to 'the gay plague' – centred on texts taken from the Old Testament: *Leviticus* (The Law of the Plague), *Psalm 22* ('My God, why hast thou forsaken me?') and *Lamentations*. 'I started the work in San Francisco and there's suffering there due to the AIDS epidemic, which couldn't but inform the work,' she reflected. '*The Divine Punishment* isn't about AIDS but AIDS is a manifestation of a basic dilemma – the feeling of powerlessness, the concept of quarantine and scapegoating, the mystery of why one should be given life and have it taken away.'[8] *The Saint of the Pit* (Mute) followed only three months later. Between the two recordings, she lost Philip-Dimitri.

The Ninth Circle

'My brother was one of the finest and most prolific writers I ever met in my life,' she said. 'It was important that *Masque* should not sound pathetic but strong and sardonic like him.' *Saint of the Pit* was filled with apprehension, Diamanda's vocals expressing the physicality of prostration and torture as she returned to the books that had sustained herself and her sibling through childhood and adolescence. Along with her own 'Εξελόυμε' (Deliver Me), texts came from Baudelaire's *L'Héautontimorouménos* (The Self-Tormentor), Gérard de Nerval's *Artémis* and Bréton poet Édouard-Joachim (aka Tristan) Corbière's astonishing evocation of the Crucifixion, *Blind Man's Cries*, which in translation reads: 'I see circles of gold/The white sun bites me/I've two holes pierced by an iron bar/Reddened in the forge of hell/I see a circle of gold/The sky's fire bites me'.

On this recording, Diamanda began working with producer Gareth Jones, a close friend of Daniel Miller's, who had recently worked with both Depeche Mode and Einstürzende Neubauten on their *Halber Mensch* (Half a Man) album of September 1985, introducing the band to the technique of sampling.

Diamanda was getting ever closer to Berlin and, after the album's completion she was awarded a bursary to work there. Here, she commenced the final part of the *Masque* triptych, *You Must Be Certain of the Devil* (Mute, May 1988) with Gareth Jones at Hansa, the producer's preferred rabbit hole of sound: 'At that time Hansa was one of the most high-tech studios I'd ever been in. It had a very big Solid State Logic mixing console and Universal Audio compressors in the racks.'[9] Jones called in the expertise of Neubauten's F. M. Einheit (aka Mufti) as percussionist as Diamanda turned gospel singer, mining traditional spirituals for inspiration both in the covers she chose and her own writing. 'The paradox is that gospel music was once the music of the black slaves, used for prayer and in desperation by people who were threatened by death,' she said. 'So it can express the fears and needs of victims as well as persecutors, just as the Old

Testament language that I used on earlier albums can be a tool of bigots but can also be an eloquent language of despair.'

During her time in Berlin, Diamanda also became romantically involved with Blixa Bargeld – perhaps Goth's ultimate Terror Couple.

After *The Masque of the Red Death*'s premiere at the South Bank, London, and simultaneous release as a three-album boxed CD set on Mute, Galás's work went beyond performance. She was arrested in New York on 10 December 1989 during a demonstration by AIDS Coalition To Unleash Power (ACT UP) at St Patrick's Cathedral and charged with disorderly conduct, disrupting a religious service, resisting arrest and criminal trespass. In her affidavit, Diamanda stated: 'This "House of Compassion" impedes the work of people who, as modern-day saints, are trying to work together to find a solution to this epidemic . . . Let us pray in word and deed for the afflicted.'

Part of that prayer became *There Are No More Tickets to the Funeral*, in which Diamanda took the approach that: 'Jesus was an outlaw. That's the whole position of people I know who have AIDS. They are outlaws and fighting until they can't stand up.' In October 1990, she performed an expanded version of *The Masque of the Red Death* incorporating this new segment at the Cathedral Saint John the Divine in New York, stripped to the waist and covered in blood. The event was recorded and released by Mute as *Plague Mass* in April 1991. She performed the work again at the 1990 International AIDS Conference in San Francisco, the 1990 Olympic Festival in Barcelona and the Festival delle Colline in Tuscany, where she was denounced for committing blasphemy against the Roman Catholic Church.

'When I began the trilogy, most of my so-called artistic and business associates tried to discourage me,' she would later reveal. 'They said it would be a bad direction. I guess they were hoping that I'd get soft and do something more polite. Well, the music world is full of cowards, idiots, impotence and homophobia. In the face of that level of resistance to my intuition, that attempt to sabotage my vision, I've had to say: The Mike Tyson of the voice does not waste time talking about bullshit.'

Paradise Lost

Hansa Tonstudio now stood at the centre of the '80s Gothic imagination – and on the cusp of momentous times. After recording *Room of Lights* there with Tony Cohen and Flood, Crime and the City Solution's Simon Bonney and Bronwyn Adams stayed on in Berlin with Mick Harvey. Here, they recruited DAF's Chrislo Haas on synths and Neubauten's Alexander Hacke on guitar, and made Berliner Ring's Thomas Stern a permanent member.

Ahead of them lay a hat-trick of inspired albums for Mute: *Shine* (1988), *The Bride Ship* (1989) and *Paradise Discotheque* (1990). The last of these, which arrived after the fall of the Berlin Wall on 9 December 1989, saw this incarnation of the band reach a sublime songwriting peak. The second side of the album looked out on the emerging new world of a reunified Germany with the four-song story of 'The Last Dictator'. This Miltonesque meditation on the impulses of tyrants reflected not only on Europe's recent history but also the shared delusions of rock stars: 'Why power is to truth what history is to song/It all depends on what you're looking for and where you're looking from.'

Meanwhile, back in London, the songwriter inside Rowland S. Howard had been quietly amassing new material while he lived a life of crime – and now had sufficient to make an album's worth of words he wanted to sing himself. With Epic Soundtracks, his brother Harry and partner Genevieve McGuckin on keyboards, he conjured up a new configuration to carry these tunes, These Immortal Souls.

'I had lots of songs I really liked,' he told *Sounds*' Ralph Traitor, 'songs that would never have been done if I hadn't said, "Right, I'm going to sing them." Because you just can't give somebody a set of lyrics and tell them what to sing if you want any kind of sincerity.' The resultant *Get Lost (Don't Lie)!* was released by Mute in October

1987, an album of ragged glories. Rowland had been working just as hard on his beloved Fender Jaguar as he had on his words. The title track was a full-blooded barroom blues, howling at the moon over Kilburn High Road, where Howard had made his home, in the bosom of London's Irish community. Indeed, Rowland's vocals suggested a further kinship with Irish Rover supreme Shane MacGowan, evoking as they did a sense of dangerous intoxication, teetering on the brink between laughter and despair; while McGuckin's keyboards flooded his songs with stained-glass hues of light.

'It's really important to have some kind of irreverence about things, to have a sense of your own enthusiasm,' Howard expounded. 'One of the most important things about rock music, as clichéd as it is, is the sense of rebellion against something, particularly what's expected of you.'[10]

It would be five years before this band made their next album, October 1992's *I'm Never Gonna Die Again* (Mute). Produced by Paul 'PK' Kendall, it marked another creative high for Howard, who had been honing a killer noir style in his preceding projects. He was reunited with his Nancy Sinatra muse Lydia Lunch, both on the eventual release of the Birthday Party-era *Honeymoon in Red* album in 1987 and for the *Shotgun Wedding* (Triple X) album of May 1991. This, the pair's ultimate slice of Southern Gothic, came on the heels of Lydia's Harry Crews project (see 'Further Tales from the Crypt' appendix, Chapter 4, 'Building a Gothic Library') and after she had relocated to New Orleans. In the heat of the Night Tripper's fonky bayou, Lydia and Rowland walked on gilded splinters.

Between *Shotgun Wedding* and *I'm Never Gonna Die Again*, Rowland returned to Australia, which, he would confide in *Option*'s Susan Compo, was perhaps not the wisest of moves. 'Melbourne has an incredibly big urban sprawl and it's fairly well-off and it's sunny and it's nice. But it's boring. Unfortunately, people take a lot of drugs and it's really depressing. A large percentage of the people I know always seem to be that much worse off than when I was there before. And a great percentage of them seem to have died.'[11] Back in the relative safety of Kilburn High Road, he ended the interview returning to the long gap between his band's recorded releases and cursing his writer's block: 'I'm sick of being stuck at a halfway point.'

Heavy Metal Thunder

There was another Rider on the horizon now and he sat astride an Iron Horse, filling the air with the sound of Marshall stack thunder and Led-heavy petrol fumes. Just as the Hells Angels had ruined it for the Peace Generation when they cut their murderous swathe through the Rolling Stones' audience at Altamont Speedway in December 1969, so too did a bunch of leather-clad marauders invade Alice in Wonderland, bringing pillage and disruption in their wake.

Zodiac Mindwarp and the Love Reaction were the brainchild of Bradford-born graphic designer Mark Manning. While working as art editor for *Flexipop!* magazine,[12] Manning developed a fascination with the decadent lifestyles led by those pop stars who would often visit their office and determined to find a way of sampling this for himself. After *Flexipop!* bit the dust in 1983, he joined *Metal Fury* magazine. By day he continued to toil as a graphic artist, but by night he transformed into Zodiac Mindwarp – a name taken from the title of an underground magazine created in mid-'60s New York by fellow graphic artist Spain Rodriguez. Through the power of Manning's fertile imagination, he would be made flesh as a would-be rock messiah.

This transformation was initially achieved with a little help from Youth, following his exit from Killing Joke under a black cloud in 1982, when he launched his next musical move, Brilliant, with Jimmy Cauty.[13] Brilliant were managed by Bunnymen Svengali Bill Drummond, who would eventually get them signed to Warners and then beckon Cauty to join him in the JAMMs and the KLF. Back in 1982, Manning had designed the sleeve for the second Brilliant single 'Colours' and recruited Cauty himself into the gonzoid ranks of his dream metal band. The first incarnation of

Zodiac Mindwarp and the Love Reaction comprised Manning as Zodiac, Cauty on guitar, Stephen 'Kid Chaos' Harris on bass and drummer Boom Boom Kaboomski – actually Jake Le Mesurier, son of John and Hattie Jacques.

With his canny designer's eye, Manning styled them in the threads of degenerate B-movie bikers: well-worn, patched leathers adorned with Iron Crosses, and in his case, the pelt of what looked like a skinned wolf tossed over one shoulder – an image that made the prevailing heroes of Heavy Metal, NWOBHM stalwarts Judas Priest and Def Leppard, look like a bunch of wimps who cleaned their teeth and always told their parents what time they were coming home.

Musically, too, the Love Reaction only stole from the hardest and best, drinking deep from the pint pots of Motörhead, AC/DC, Black Sabbath and Steppenwolf, whose cosmic lyrics Manning effortlessly parodied – all chased with shots of T. Rex jitterbug boogie. Sensing the dawning of a new Zodiac zeitgeist, Drummond's old prankster partner Dave Balfe signed them to Food, his new Phonogram subsidiary, in 1986. By which time – and with Cobalt Stargazer (formerly, philosophy student Geoff Bird) replacing Cauty on guitar and Slam Thunderhide (aka Stephen Landrum from Vancouver) taking over on drums – they were touring with Doctor and the Medics and going down a treat with the Alice's crowd.

The Medics had got themselves a deal with Illegal/IRS Records in 1985, their *Happy but Twisted* EP with its cover of Hawkwind's 'Silver Machine' grazing the top of the indie charts. By June 1986, they had reached the top of the actual charts with a version of Norman Greenbaum's 1969 'Spirit in the Sky' that was maybe just *too* inspired. Keeping its number-one position for three weeks, the song and its accompanying Op Art video effectively jumped the psychedelic shark. What had mushroomed so spectacularly in the darkness of Dean Street – creating not just their clubs and mystery tours but even their own Portobello Road-based boutique – would all rapidly shrivel in the glare of fame's headlights, turning the Medics' cult cool into novelty fare.

While they floundered in its wake, releasing a less inspired but perhaps more apt follow-up cover of ABBA's 'Waterloo' to rapidly diminishing returns, the Love Reaction thundered on past with their 'Wild Child' and 'High Priest of Love' EPs, topping the indie charts with the latter in August 1986. After converting the masses at the 1986 Reading Festival, by May 1987, with a rejigged version of 'High Priest' called 'Prime Mover' – sample lyrics: 'I'm a napalm god/Your lipstick flickers round my lightning rod' – the triumphant Love Reaction were roaring up the actual charts too.

As well as initiating a look that would be rapidly purloined by rebel Americans Al Jourgensen and Rob Zombie – as well as others, much closer to home – it helped that Manning was so witty. And that the music press was in on the joke: 'This is the Dawning of the Age of Hilarious' proclaimed the same *NME* that had cringed at Killing Joke's grebo proclivities five years before. Throwing down his biker guantlet, Manning had done the unthinkable and made Metal cool – and now it was time for everyone else to Smell the Glove.

There would be no shortage of rival messiahs.

A Rock and a Hard Place

After months of toil and trouble, the Sisters of Mercy's *First and Last and Always* album was eventually released not in Black October 1984, but March 1985. It contained some durable classics – the haunting 'Marian', a Wayne Hussey composition with magnificently doom-laden lyrics by an Eldritch imperiled by the sea and praying to a siren; the Morricone-esque twang of 'First and Last and Always' itself, the harrowing 'Nine While Nine' and plaintive closer, 'Some Kind of Stranger' – all written by Marx with Eldritch lyrics. But despite all the time and money lavished on its creation, the fretting over perfecting the lyrics and making the whole thing sound epic, something had gone missing. A spark, a divination – or perhaps a hunger – left in a garage in Bridlington.

Donning his black Stetson, Eldritch pushed his rock star persona: 'We are the children of Altamont,' he told *NME*'s Paul du Noyer in March 1985. 'We regard ourselves as having sprung from pre-Seventies rock music, as the inheritors of that tradition and the only people with any chance of propagating it further.' But all the time he had been delaying recording by indulging himself to the point of collapse, Hussey and Adams had only deepened their bonds – while Marx was headed for the door. The Sisters' totemic founding guitarist didn't make the final gig of the ensuing tour, at the Royal Albert Hall on 18 June 1985 – a grandiose curtain call for this version of the band. Billed as *Altamont: A Festival of Remembrance* and filmed for a memorial video *Wake*, the assembled were first treated to a screening of Godfrey Reggio's 1982 experimental film *Koyaanisquatsi*, with its Philip Glass soundtrack, then an organist playing a medley of Messiaen and Lynyrd Skynyrd, rather than a support act.[14]

By this time, Eldritch had departed Leeds Station, his wintry outward journey recorded on 'Nine While Nine', a requiem for his relationship with Claire Shearsby. As heralded by 'Marian''s *deutsche* verses, he crossed the water to Germany. Not to Berlin, though: he made his new base amid the fleshpots of Hamburg's Reeperbahn, where the teenage Beatles had their baptism in speed and endurance.

After attempts to record material for a new album – tentatively titled *Left on Mission and Revenge* – from Eldritch's new lair proved futile, the split between the singer and the remaining Sisters rapidly turned acrimonious.[15] Recruiting ex-Artery guitarist Simon Hinkler and ex-Red Lorry Yellow Lorry drummer Mick Brown, Hussey and Adams announced they had formed a new band: the Sisterhood. Lining up a Radio 1 *Session* for Janice Long, they played their first gig under this provocative moniker at Alice's on 20 January 1986, before heading off for a tour of Europe in support of their new friends from 69 Dean Street, the Cult.

Naturally, Von Eldritch did not let this affront go past unnoticed. Firing a warning shot via Merciful Release about the use of this name, he registered the Sisterhood for himself and released a single under the name 'Giving Ground' on the same day as Wayne and

Craig's Alice's debut. Initially packaged in a plain black sleeve, it jumped to the top of the indie charts, giving Eldritch the moral – and legal – high ground.

A strange artefact, 'Giving Ground' was sung by soundalike – or Eldrone[16] – James Ray, who fronted the Performance, a band named after Nicolas Roeg and Donald Cammell's canonical 1970 film. Its title did not, as could have been interpreted, signify that Eldritch was giving his ex-bandmates any quarter but a Bradford one – the lyrics refer to a quicksand into which he casts his memories of them: 'What you have lost can never be found . . . Everything is lost in the giving ground'.

He would go on to create the equally enigmatic *The Gift* album with Ray, multi-instrumentalist/producer Lucas Fox and, apparently, Suicide's Alan Vega. Though he had won this skirmish, it was Hussey and Adams' newly rechristened the Mission who would run off with the audience, turning the pair's Led Zeppelin dreams into a bare-chested, tight-trousered, stadium-filling reality by the end of the decade – Wayne wearing Andrew's trademark black cowboy hat all the way to the bank.

But, as any fule kno, Mick Jagger's celluloid Turner had already decreed: 'The only performance that makes it, that makes it all the way, is the one that achieves madness, right?' On the Mekons' 1987 album *Honky Tonkin'* (Quarterstick), Jon Langford painted two very different portraits of his old friend. In 'Charlie Cake Park', we see the Andy and Claire of old, 'dressing to kill' in preparation for a Leeds night out to come. But in 'Prince of Darkness', the Hamburg Eldritch broods: 'Well he said to me, "I've waited seven years/And I am a very patient man/After all those things that we've gone and done/I still need someone to tell"/His pleasures were a mystery to us all/You'd never see him out after dawn/In a German seaport town he takes his coffee in the red-light/He is the Prince of Darkness'.[17]

Eldritch's move, when it came, would be to chase the Gods of Excess like a *Bat Out of Hell* – and with a new Bride of the Night riding pillion. While Kid Congo Powers joined the Bad Seeds, Patricia

Morrison became Eldritch's new consort on the Sisters' bombastic return, September 1987's 'This Corrosion' single. Together with the forty-piece New York Choral Society, a video directed by Ridley Scott and set amid the upwards thrust of the redeveloping London Docklands, lyrics that evoked the Great Beast – 'Kill the king with love is the law' – and Meat Loaf's mate Jim Steinman in the producer's chair. A suitably Wagnerian prelude to the November release of the second Sisters album, *Floodland*, recorded with Steinman between Suicide's favourite the Power Station in New York, Joy Division's Strawberry Studios in Stockport and the Wool Hall in Bath, where the Smiths recorded their swansong *Strangeways Here We Come* (Rough Trade, 1987).

Had Eldritch sorted his head out in the intervening two years? This was the question asked by *Sounds*' Neil Perry – a journalist who was also a close confidante of the Mission. 'I hesitate to call it sorted. I feel more together,' Andrew said, later adding: 'It's okay for me, I'm used to being called a raving madman. But for Patricia . . . she's been an awesome tower of patience during all this. It's all very well being the idiot, but being the idiot's lieutenant is no fun at all.' As we have seen, Patricia had had quite some experience of this. 'One of the main reasons Patricia and I get on so well is that we've both been through the same trials,' Eldritch elucidated. 'We both despise musicians for their ability to let things happen to them and for their total inability, generally, to understand that equation between power and responsibility.'

The *Floodland*-era Sisters would never play a single gig, instead creating an opulent series of videos to portray the album's epic constructions. 'Dominion', inspired by Shelley's *Ozymandias* – the ode of a traveller who comes across the legs of a statue standing in a desert, all that remains of the once-mighty kingdom of the titular king now lost in 'the lone and level sands' – was filmed in the ancient city of Petra in Jordan, with Eldritch in full T. E. Lawrence mode. 'Lucretia, My Reflection' – the singer's ode to his new accomplice – was a similarly epic, Indiana Jones-style production, this time filmed in India.

'This Corrosion', originally written for the scrapped *Left on Mission and Revenge*, was certainly a dish best served cold. When played an advance version of it, alongside the elegiac album track '1959', an impressed Perry concluded: 'If, when and how he and Wayne settle their differences is for them to know and for us to find out – if we care. But as long as both continue to make great music, it's of little consequence.' Eldritch, 'the man who unwittingly launched a million black cowboy hats on to the streets' was 'an underground hero soon to break out'.[18]

King Contrary Man

Not to be outdone by any of this, Wayne's new friends, Billy Duffy and Ian Astbury, had already got their motors running and headed quite some distance down the highway. An abrupt change of mood overcame the Cult between *Love* and sessions for its follow-up, which was once to have been called *Peace*, in the Zodiac summer of 1986. Dissatisfied with what they had recorded with *Love* producer Steve Brown at the Manor in Oxfordshire, they turned instead to a man known for his love of AC/DC and expertise with outlaws, outsiders and Men in Black in general – Rick Rubin.

They sought him out in New York, where the Def Jam supremo remixed the first, tellingly titled single 'Love Removal Machine' with its confessional lyric 'Having trouble with my direction/Upside down psychotic reaction', sonically tailoring it a Full Metal Jacket. Using this to convince Beggars Banquet they should re-record the entire album, Rubin returned with Billy and Ian to leafy middle England, where, according to Manor studio engineer Tony Platt: 'A snatch of *Highway to Hell* would get played, and then a snatch of *Back in Black* . . . Literally, as he was mixing, he was getting a guitar sound on the Cult and then comparing it directly from the guitar sound he wanted to get from *Back in Black*.'[19]

His results turned *Peace* into *Electric* (Beggars Banquet, April 1987), which, like its predecessor, would reach number four in the charts and go on to outsell *Love*. Swiftly jettisoning their psychedelic garb into the dustbin of history, the Cult re-emerged in denim and leather, adorned with Iron Crosses, Texas flags, Lynyrd Skynyrd T-shirts and, atop of Ian's flowing tresses, what looked suspiciously like the entire carcass of a beaver, pinned into place with a massive Panzer Totenkopf. Duffy even customised his trademark white guitar, turning it into 'The Black Falcon'. Take that, Zodiac Mindwarp!

And in fact, they did – moving Jamie Stewart back to his original instrument, rhythm guitar, Astbury and Duffy deftly purloined the Love Reaction's Kid Chaos to play bass for them on the Electric tour, in front of drummer Les Warner, the eventual replacement for Nigel Preston, whose erratic, drug-dependent behaviour had long since got him the sack.[20] Warner had previous with Johnny Thunders – so he knew all too well the consequences of failing to understand the relationship between power and responsibility. Despite all these warning signs – and the inclusion of what *Trouser Press* described as 'one of history's worst versions of "Born to Be Wild"' – *Electric* opened up America to the Cult the way none of their previous recordings could have done. So began a full-throttle ride into Excess All Areas, or as Ian put it on second single 'Lil' Devil' – 'Trying to get to heaven 'fore the sun goes down/Lizard in a bottle, yeah!'[21]

Before the year was out, Billy and Ian had sold 3 million copies of *Electric*, wrecked £30,000's worth of equipment, swallowed an ocean of Jack Daniel's, fallen out with each other, sacked their management and Warner, been dumped by Kid Chaos and relocated to Los Angeles, where Duffy commenced a life riding high on the Harley hog with fellow punk exiles Billy Idol and Steve Jones.

Catching up with them again in the pages of *NME* in 1992, Steven Wells catalogued for the uninitiated what had befallen his former flatmate Astbury in the 'Post-*Electric* blowout: 35lbs overweight, lost those cheekbones, banned from *Vogue*, didn't wash his hair as often as he should, pissed in his boots at parties to garner attention from the rock cognoscenti, his breath stank of tabs and Jack and he was chased away from the Dakota Building, where Lennon met a warm gun, by an irate caretaker and slept in Central Park and generally went rock pig doo-lally . . .' Which was, he posited after catching his breath, all a long way from the Poison Girls.

Ian agreed. 'My father got sick, cancer,' he said. 'As I was going to see him I realised how pathetic I was. I saw him deteriorating and I knew how he was going to go because I'd seen it happen to my mother and I felt ashamed of what I was doing . . . I felt I'd been given a gift and I'd been abusing the power I'd been given . . . I'd become everything I used to hate. If I was seventeen years old and I'd seen myself walking down the street at twenty-seven, I would probably have crossed the street and spat on myself.'[22]

Riders on the Storm

After the 11 June 1987 general election, Margaret Thatcher became the first Prime Minister in 160 years to win a third consecutive term in office, beating Labour by 376 to 229 votes. Neil Kinnock insisted that Labour morale remained high, telling the BBC: 'Any feeling that we have of depression is outweighed by the feeling of enormous concern about what the consequences of the re-election of a Conservative government will mean.' He subsequently put his shoulder to the wheel of reuniting his party from the inside.

The triumphant Thatcher, speaking at the Tory Party Conference in Blackpool on 9 October, crowed: 'That makes it three wins in a row. Just like Lord Liverpool. And he was prime minister for fifteen years. It's rather encouraging.'

Yes, history fans, her illustrious Georgian Tory forebear was Robert Banks Jenkinson, second Earl of Liverpool, who served from 1812–27 and was in office when the 1819 Peterloo Massacre, of which Shelley wrote in *The Mask of Anarchy*, was carried out. For the Iron Lady to equal his achievement, she would have to stay put until 1994, when she would be sixty-nine. She was confident of being up to this task. 'Our third election victory was only a staging post on a much longer journey,' she said. 'Soon there will be more shareholders than trade unionists in this country. Of course, not all trade unionists are shareholders – yet. But I hope that before long they will be . . . it is our passionate belief that free enterprise and competition are the engines of prosperity and the guardians of liberty.'[23]

But perhaps she had just reached the high-water mark of her own hubris.

Just under a week later, on the night of 15–16 October, the Great Storm hit southern England. A violent, extratropical cyclone with hurricane-force winds, it killed twenty-two people as it raged its way up from the Bay of Biscay, into Cornwall and eastward through the counties, to exit via the Wash in Norfolk. The National Grid was imperiled as crashing cables short-circuited, overheating the main system. A crisis decision was made to shut down all the south-east systems, leaving hundreds of thousands without power, in order to avert the destruction of the entire network. As the morning news was broadcast from emergency facilities, most of the southern transport network was out of order and Londoners were advised not to try to get to work. An estimated 15 million trees had been felled across the storm's swathe, including the titular ring at Sevenoaks, Kent; the ancient specimens clustered around the Iron Age hillfort of Chanctonbury Ring in West Sussex; and all the old willows that had tap-tap-tapped on my childhood window pane around my parents' house. The Met Office were excoriated for not accurately predicting the scale of the tempest's destructive power and having advised viewers the previous day not to be worried about wild rumours of an approaching hurricane, their public mouthpiece, BBC weatherman Michael Fish, would never recover his cred.[24]

The Great Storm was an ominous portent from Mother Nature that was swiftly followed by man-made catastrophe. On 9 October, Thatcher had boasted to her conference audience: 'Just look at what we have achieved – low inflation, tax cuts, wider ownership, a revival of enterprise and, over the last year, unemployment has fallen at record speed by 400,000 . . . We are now the second biggest investor in the world, and the very model of a stable economy.'

Three days after the hurricane, partially abetted by the suspension in trading caused by the Great Storm, an unprecedented Wall Street crash wiped £50 billion off the Stock Exchange in London.

They called it Black Monday.

Gothfather: Edgar Allan Poe

> Once upon a midnight dreary, while I pondered, weak and weary,
> Over many a quaint and curious volume of forgotten lore –
> While I nodded, nearly napping, suddenly there came a tapping,
> As of some one gently rapping, rapping at my chamber door.
> ''Tis some visitor,' I muttered, 'tapping at my chamber door
> Only this and nothing more.'

Orphaned at the age of three, he was dead by forty, in circumstances as mysterious and appalling as one of his fictions. As we have seen, Edgar Allan Poe has inspired every Gothic thinker from Baudelaire to the Banshees, Joseph Conrad to Roger Corman, since his untimely passing in 1849. During his short span on Earth, Poe pioneered the art of the short story, earning his crust at the coalface of nineteenth-century American literary journals and periodicals, his fervid imagination conjuring myriad tales of mystery and the macabre. As well as fashioning the first detective stories, he made significant contributions to the emergent science-fiction form, while maintaining a sideline as a poet of genius, authoring the never-bettered chiller The Raven *in 1845.*

He was born in Boston, Massachusetts, on 19 January 1809, the second child of actors David and Eliza Poe, who, it is said, named him after the oldest son in Shakespeare's King Lear, *which they had been performing that year. David, the grandson of an Irishman who had emigrated from County Cavan in 1750, abandoned Edgar, his older brother William and infant sister Rosalie in 1810. When English-born Eliza succumbed to tuberculosis a year later, Edgar was taken into the home of Virginian merchant John Allan, who baptised his charge into the Episcopal faith and gave him the name Edgar Allan Poe, without ever formally adopting him. As a child, Edgar travelled with his new family to Scotland and England, studying for a time in Irvine, North Ayrshire, then Chelsea and Stoke Newington in London, before returning to Richmond, Virginia, in 1820. Something of the atmosphere of these places came back with him.*

Evincing extraordinary literary prowess from an early age, he was enrolled at the Thomas Jefferson-founded University of Virginia in Charlottesville in 1826 to study ancient and modern languages. But, striking out against his strict upbringing, the young Poe spent more time at the gaming tables and pursing a fruitless engagement with his childhood sweetheart Sarah Elmira Royster – thus incurring the wrath of his benefactor. Dumped by Royster and unable to sustain his student lifestyle, Poe left university and took his first job, as a newspaperman in Boston, under the pseudonym Henri le Rennet.

Such endeavours still did not furnish him enough for a living, so Edgar enlisted in the army in 1827, using the alias Edgar A. Perry. The same year, he published his first collection, Tamerlane and Other Poems, *as 'A Bostonian'. After serving two years and attaining the rank of sergeant major for Artillery, he revealed his true identity to his commanding officer, who allowed his discharge on the condition that he reconcile with Allan. Following a brief rapprochement, Poe published a second collection,* Al Aaraaf, Tamerlane, and Minor Poems, *in 1829 and went to study at the US Military Academy at West Point, New York. But it wasn't long before he fell out again with his guardian and got himself court-martialled for disobeying regulations and ignoring his duties.*

Edgar left for New York with money raised from his student peers to publish a third volume, entitled simply Poems *in 1831. He found a new home with his widowed aunt, Maria Clemm – his mother's sister – and her daughter, Virginia, seven at the time he moved in. It was from Virginia that Poe's most tormented fictions would spring, after she first became his wife at the age of thirteen in 1836; and then his most tragic muse, following her death from tuberculosis aged twenty-four in 1842. Given their familial background and her extreme youth, Poe biographers continue to argue about the nature of their relationship. Was it a platonic marriage, engineered to protect Clemm and her mother from financial hardship after Edgar had got himself a steady job, editing* The Southern Literary Messenger*? Was it a torrid passion or did Virginia die a virgin? Whatever was the truth, his wife's death from the same disease that had laid waste to his mother opened up a chasm in Poe and haunted him to the end – through the short story* Ligeia *(1838),* The Raven *(1845) itself and his final, posthumously published poem,* Annabel Lee *(1849).*

Poe never got his hands on any of the fortune possessed by John Allan after his estranged guardian's death in 1834 but instead supported himself with earnings from the editorship of a succession of literary journals, including Burton's Gentleman's Magazine, *where he first published* The Fall of the House of Usher *in 1839, leading to his first short story collection,* Tales of the Grotesque and Arabesque, *in 1840. For this, publisher Lea & Blanchard declined to pay him any advance or royalties, merely twenty free copies of the book. He moved to New York in 1842, as Virginia began to show the first signs of her disease, editing the* Broadway Journal *and publishing* The Raven, *which made him a household name – he received $9 for that. After his wife's death, his life became an unsteady blur of torrid affairs and drink, neither of which he could handle well. Returning to Richmond, he picked up the pieces of his teenage relationship with Sarah Elmira Royster Shelton – now a wealthy widow – and set a wedding date.*

Poe was on his way from a round-trip that was supposed to have included an editing job in Philadelphia, then a return to New York to pick up Aunt Clara for his wedding in Richmond, when he met instead his strange fate, along the road at Baltimore. On the morning of 3 October 1849 – Election Day – Joseph W. Walker, a compositor for the Baltimore Sun, *was making his way to the Gunner's Hall public house, which was serving as a polling station. Lying in the gutter outside, dressed in dirty, tattered clothes, was a semiconscious Poe. Walker got Edgar to the house of his friend, magazine editor Joseph Snodgrass, but in his four remaining days, the author never fully recovered consciousness. Like a character in one of his own fictions, he was trapped in a state of hallucinogenic delirium, calling out for 'Reynolds' – whose identity remains a mystery.*

There has been no shortage of theories as to what befell the author of The Masque of the Red Death *(1842),* The Cask of Amontillado *(1846), and the first modern detective story,* Murders in the Rue Morgue *(1841). Some say he was abducted and beaten by ruffians who had first got him drunk – an easy matter, since he was known to get intoxicated on a single glass of wine. In other versions, the ruffians were pursuing a form of voter fraud known as 'cooping', whereby a pressgang would select a victim, disguise him and force him to vote for the same candidate multiple times. A common interpretation of his delirium and ragged appearance was that they were down to the demon drink.*

However, Poe had become a vocal member of the Temperance movement before his death, after a doctor warned that he might not survive another bout with alcohol, and other theories suggest some form of poisoning – carbon monoxide from coal gas-fired indoor lighting, or mercury from a cholera cure he had undertaken in 1849. Still others proposed rabies from an animal bite, flu, encephalitis, meningitis and a brain tumour. In echoes of Shelley's indestructible heart, witnesses to Poe's exhumation – when he was moved in 1875 from the unmarked grave of his immediate burial in Baltimore to a plot beneath a statue later erected in his honour – reported seeing a strange mass in his skull, which could have been a calcified tumour. It has even been suggested, in the 2000 book Midnight Dreary *(St Martin's Press) by John Evangelist Walsh, that Poe was murdered by his intended's three brothers . . .*

And the Raven, never flitting, still is sitting, *still* is sitting
On the pallid bust of Pallas just above my chamber door;
And his eyes have all the seeming of a demon's that is dreaming,
And the lamp-light o'er him streaming throws his shadow on the floor;
And my soul from out that shadow that lies floating on the floor
Shall be lifted – nevermore!

Gothmother: Maria Callas

Hailed as 'La Divinia' and 'The God-Given', the soprano Maria Callas was, according to general manager of the New York Metropolitan Opera Rudolph Bing, 'the most difficult artist I have ever worked with. Because she was so much more intelligent. Other artists, you could get around. But Callas, you could not get around. She knew exactly what she wanted, and why she wanted it.'

The Greek Goddess, who starred as the titular Medea *in Pier Paolo Pasolini's 1969 film about Jason and the Argonauts, achieved her own mythical status following a life as full of drama as any of the characters she portrayed onstage. In her only film outing, Callas' Queen Medea kills her brother and leaves her homeland for the love of Jason, who swiftly grows tired of her, abandoning her for a political marriage and thus stoking her homicidal and infanticidal rage. In real life, it was Maria's husband, Giovanni Battista Meneghini, and her mother, Litsa, whom she would have cheerfully murdered; while the love that poisoned her soul was for the shipping magnate Aristotle Onassis, who left her for the US President's widow, Jackie Kennedy, in 1968.*

The child born Maria Anna Cecilia Sofia Kalogeropoulos in Queens, New York City, on 2 December 1923 was to leave her place of birth for her parents' homeland after Litsa's marriage to George, who had subsequently shortened their surname to Callas, broke down. Maria was fourteen when Litsa took her and her sister Yakinthi (later called Jackie) back to Athens. A frustrated artist herself, Litsa had noticed young Maria's singing talent early and sent her for lessons from the age of five. At the Greek National Conservatoire in Athens, said tutor Maria Trivella, her progress was 'phenomenal. She studied five or six hours a day. Within six months, she was singing the most difficult arias in the international opera repertoire with the utmost musicality.' She made her public debut in 1938, singing from Puccini's Tosca.

But the Second World War was looming and after Germany invaded Greece in 1941, Maria's homelife became unbearable. Litsa entertained the occupying soldiers and tried to force her daughters to follow suit. At the same time, she secured Maria a place at the most prestigious opera house in Greece, the Athens Conservatoire, where her studies continued apace under Spanish coloratura soprano Elvira de Hidalgo, who taught her the secrets of the real bel canto *– as Callas described it – 'not just beautiful singing. It is a very hard training; it is a sort of a strait-jacket that you're supposed to put on, whether you like it or not.' She studied for ten hours a day, 'devouring music', perfecting her technique to command a three-octave range – and staying away from home as long as she possibly could.*

In 1941, she made her professional stage debut; a year later she was singing the lead in Tosca *and going on to play Marta in Eugen d'Albert's* Tiefland, *a performance over which critic Vangelis Mangliveras rhapsodised the arrival of 'a new star in the Greek firmament, with a matchless depth of feeling'. Even her detractors began referring to her talent as 'God-given' after this.*

Following the liberation of Greece, at the suggestion of de Hidalgo, Callas based herself in Italy. Here, she dazzed La Scala's musical director Tullio Serafin and, in 1949, got married to Giovanni Meneghini, who assumed control of her career until their divorce ten years later. Her breakthrough Italian performance came in Venice, when she was a last-minute replacement for Elvira in Bellini's I puritani, *switching to that role from the one she had been studying, Brünnhilde in Wagner's* Die Walküre. *It was a feat described by the film-maker Franco Zeffirelli, who thus fell under her spell, as 'incredible. You need to be familiar with opera to realise the size of her achievement. It was as if someone asked Birgit Nilsson, who is famous for her great Wagnerian voice, to substitute overnight for Beverly Sills, who is one of the great coloratura sopranos of our time.'*

La Scala became her base throughout the '50s and Italy's great directors were drawn to her flame – Zeffirelli himself and, most importantly, Luchino Visconti, who mounted lavish new productions of Verdi's La traviata, *Bellini's* La sonnambula *and Donizetti's* Anna Bolena, *later saying that he only began directing opera because of Callas. She made her London debut at the Royal Opera House in 1952 and appeared at New York's Metropolitan in 1956 – her return to the place of her birth preceded by a damning* TIME *magazine cover story about her volcanic temper, her antipathy towards her estranged mother and her rivalry with Renata Tebaldi, the Italian soprano being cast as Bette Davis to Maria's Joan Crawford.*

It wasn't just her personality that was continually dissected in the press; it was her weight, too. Between 1953 and 1954 Callas lost nearly six stone, transforming herself from what Rudolph Bing charitably described as 'monstrously overweight' in 1951 to his revised opinion of 'an astonishing, svelte, striking woman', who 'showed none of the signs one usually finds in a fat woman who has lost weight'.

It was this dramatic weight loss that was often cited as a reason for her voice beginning to fail her – however, her recent biographer Lyndsy Spence tracked down the neurologist who treated her before her death. 'Callas suffered from a neuromuscular disorder whose symptoms began in the '50s, but she was dismissed by doctors as "crazy",' she said. 'It also explains the loss of her singing voice, which cut her career short.'

Maria made her last Royal Opera House performance on 5 July 1965, completing the circle back to the lead role in Tosca. *By this time, she had ditched the husband she described as 'a louse' who had 'robbed me of more than half my money by putting everything in his name since we were married' and taken up instead with the wealthy Greek shipping tycoon Aristotle Onassis, whom she met in 1957.*

Spence's biography Cast a Diva *(The History Press, 2021) uncovered correspondence about their relationship that revealed Onassis as a brutal bully who repeatedly threatened her life and drugged her for sexual kicks. An earlier tome,* Greek Fire *by Nicholas Gage (Alfred A. Knopf, 2000), contended the couple had conceived a child, a boy who died hours after his birth on 30 March 1960. In ex-husband Meneghini's version of events,* My Wife Maria Callas *(Farrar Straus Giroux, 1982), he states that Maria was unable to bear children. But if that were true, it would make a sad echo of an earlier tragedy – the reason her parents left Greece for America in the first place was Callas' father's dismay at the early death of his son Vassilis from meningitis at the age of two, before Maria was conceived. Just like the mythical Jason, Aristotle grew weary of his Medea and, as soon as the prospect of political advancement came along in the shape of Jackie Kennedy, he abruptly and publicly dropped Maria.*

Retreating to Paris, subsisting on sedatives, Callas thereon lived a lonely existence. She made a brief comeback tour of Europe in 1973, appearing one final time on stage in Paris, before being felled by a heart attack on 16 September 1977 at the age of fifty-three.

Playwright Terrence McNally, who authored the 1997 play Master Class *in her honour, recalled the great diva's courage in the face of tremendous hostility, facing a New York audience fired up by that* TIME *article, who had queued around the block to throw vegetables at her when she played Bellini's Norma at her 1956 debut at the Met.*

'I remember Callas being bombarded with vegetables as she took her bows after her second New York Norma, a Saturday matinee. Bunches of carrots and heads of cabbage are not sold at the refreshments bar at the Metropolitan.' But what he, then a seventeen-year-old music student, had witnessed was a woman who 'made opera live. She made the notes and words of the great nineteenth-century Italian Romantic composers and poets sound spontaneous, inevitable, even natural . . . Other sopranos only sing "Vissi d'arte" in Tosca. *Only Callas talks to God.'*

CHAPTER 13

The Last Enchantment

Off to Never Never Land: the Cocteau Twins, the Virgin Prunes, Danielle Dax, Cardiacs

> 'The days of our kind are numbered. The one God comes to drive out the many gods. The spirits of wood and stream grow silent. It's the way of things'
>
> – Merlin (Nicol Williamson), *Excalibur* (directed John Boorman, released 10 April 1981)

Just as Bauhaus and Killing Joke imbued their work with serious magical intent, so, too, were there musicians who conjured up a sense of 'the other' as they slipped through punk's open door and out into imaginative landscapes beyond. Musicians whose creativity was stirred by the inaugural three-chord challenge and, as the decade progressed, were able to turn those base materials into something entirely more rich and strange. Inspired outsiders, you might call them, these were individuals whose creativity had not been nurtured in any art school but sprang instead from some deep, driving force within. By strange fate, as the remade, remodelled '80s of shareholders, credit cards and deregulated conspicuous consumption swaggered boorishly towards their end, these wild talents were also reaching creative peaks – suggesting that the forces of monetarism had not yet swept all of the magic from these isles.

Blue Bell Knoll

The Cocteau Twins came from a particularly unloved and unlovely place to make music that was once described as the 'Voice of God'. Grangemouth, Falkirk, lies where the Firth of Forth pours into the North Sea and was founded in 1768 around the construction of the Forth and Clyde Canal. Industry has always been the town's raison d'être, and though business was booming in the days of the Empire, by the '60s, in another example of that era's planning madness, the Georgian old town had been almost completely demolished. From the time Elizabeth Fraser (b. 29 August 1963) and Robin Guthrie (b. 4 January 1962) were growing up and into teenagers, the town was dominated by the cooling towers of Grangemouth Refinery, established in 1924 to process crude oils and developed by British Petroleum (BP) into a massive petrochemical complex from 1964–75.

The 1975 discovery of North Sea Oil in the '40s oil field, 110 miles off the coast of Aberdeen, brought to Grangemouth the Kinneil crude oil stabilisation terminal, which connected directly to BP's '40s pipeline. From 1979 onwards, profits from North Sea Oil made black gold for the British economy, delivering 10 per cent of Treasury revenues by the mid-'80s. Flares could be seen rising from multiple oil platforms along the eastern shoreline, from Grangemouth down to Great Yarmouth, like the candles of Thatcher's own Black Mass. The men who worked these rigs were flown in by helicopter from across the United Kingdom and with wages averaging £64,000 a year,[1] the brass to be made from this muck was a great deal better rewarded than the £9,300 the average miner was making in 1983.[2] The Piper Alpha disaster on the Occidental Petroleum (Caledonia) Limited rig that exploded and sank on 6 July 1988, killing 165 of the men on board and two rescue crewmen, came as a stark reminder of who the country owed this prosperity to, though. Piper Alpha accounted for nearly 10 per cent of North Sea oil and gas production.[3]

Elizabeth Fraser's parents did not work in the oil industry but at other manual toil – her mother as a seamstress at Racke's sewing factory, her father as a tool-grinder in a wood yard. They loved music, playing drums and accordion respectively, and passed this passion on to their six children. 'We used to sing along to charty pop stuff, along with traditional Scottish music,' Elizabeth told *Mojo*'s Barney Hoskyns, 'and we'd have talent competitions in the bedroom. I didn't think I was necessarily going to be a singer. I always thought I would draw or paint or dance.'[4]

Nonetheless, it was through music she would escape 'horrendous' Grangemouth – and both the forgotten man of the Birthday Party and John Peel would play vital roles in her liberation. Back in 1980, as a seventeen-year-old who had learned the gospels of Johnny and Siouxsie via Peel's radio show, Elizabeth went out to 'The Nash' – a hotel that was the only place in Grangemouth to host a weekly punk disco. The resident DJ was the eighteen-year-old Robin, a guitarist and budding bedroom producer, who had just formed a band with his bass-playing friend, Will Heggie, named the Cocteau Twins after a 1979 song by Simple Minds. When he spotted Fraser on the dancefloor, he knew he'd found his singer.

Elizabeth, who had no reason to want to stay around Grangemouth, ran away with Robin to Falkirk and the music she began making with him there 'flowed from the chemistry between us'.[5] In 1981, they fashioned two demo tapes – recording each separately, as they didn't realise they could simply have copied the first – and took them down to London, where their favourite new band was playing.

Because of Peel's championing of the Birthday Party, they assumed – correctly – that the DJ would be in the audience and Robin gave one of their precious C90 cassettes to him. Buoyed by this triumph, he then 'decided to wheedle us all backstage,' as Elizabeth explained to their earliest music press champion, *Sounds*' Helen Fitzgerald, a few months later, 'and sat himself down next to Phill [Calvert]. I was bloody terrified at the audacity of it, but Phill was genuinely interested and helpful, he gave us the address of 4AD and told us to write, and of course Rob being Rob, he did.'[6] Despite the rough quality of these demos, Peel immediately offered the Cocteaus a *Session*, which they recorded for him in June 1982. Meanwhile, the second tape passed through the hands of Simon Raymonde (b. Simon Pomerance, 3 April 1962), then working in the record shop beneath Beggars Banquet, from where Ivo Watts-Russell also ran 4AD. Ivo put the tape in his car 'and drove 50 miles playing it over and over.'[7]

Neither of them had heard anything quite like this before.

Head over Heels

Watts-Russell installed the Cocteaus in Blackwing Studios – a deconsecrated church in Southwark, where Depeche Mode and Yazoo had previously recorded – upstairs with founding producer/engineer Eric Radcliffe. They made their debut 4AD album, *Garlands* (July 1982), with Ivo producing, in nine days flat. Guthrie and Fraser had already written the material, two of the tracks being ones they'd recorded for their Peel *Session*, 'Wax and Wane' and 'Garlands' itself. On his car ride with their C90, Watts-Russell had been hypnotised by the waves of distorted sound Guthrie managed to get out of his guitar. Now, in the studio, he was at last able to properly listen to the voice that had been buried deep in the demo's murk.

To do Elizabeth Fraser's talents justice without sounding unbearably pretentious is one of the hardest challenges any music writer can face. Like Diamanda Galás, what comes out of this tiny woman's mouth is nothing short of astonishing. In Fraser's case, it wasn't simply the sound she could create, but the words she chose to express herself with: opaque conjurations, with such mystical titles as 'Grail Overfloweth' and 'The Hollow Men'. Lyrics that seem to have been carefully constructed for the impression they make as they are sung, the feelings they evoke. Any more direct meaning is almost always impossible to discern.

Then there is the matter of *how* they are sung. Fraser's voice can be the most heart-stoppingly beautiful thing you have ever heard. She seems to draw from elemental forces that connect with her listeners in a secret language of dreams and deeply encoded DNA. As if she really is conversing in the ancient tongue of the fairies – and we somehow dimly remember what it means.

Helen Fitzgerald had a better stab at it: 'Putting a needle to songs like "Wax and Wane" and "Shallow Then Halo" is to follow Elizabeth through a circuitous tunnel,' she wrote in *Sounds*, marvelling at how the 'lilting colloquial inflexions' of Fraser's speech 'lose themselves when she sings'. The journalist detected a vulnerability in the Cocteaus' singer that made her want to cook her a proper meal and protect her from those in the music press who dismissed her as a second-rate Siouxsie – and there were plenty who did. 'Step closer, worm!' was Fitzgerald's warning to such writers. 'I fight to the death!'

Fraser did love Siouxsie, so much so that she had her name tattooed on her arm, something she would subsequently be at pains to keep covered, lest it be construed as camouflage for other sorts of needle work. The cover of *Garlands* was originally conceived by designer Nigel Grierson as an alternative to the Banshees' *The Scream*, for an art college project he was working on. Like all subsequent Cocteau Twins releases, *Garlands*' sleeve art purposefully did not depict the band at all – and Helen Fitzgerald was the first in a long stream of interviewers to recognise how little either Fraser or Guthrie wanted to give away of themselves.

The mystery only deepened the affections of their listeners. The Twins released successive EPs, *Lullabies* in 1982 and *Peppermint Pig* the following year, the latter being the only time they ever used an 'outside' producer, the Associates' Alan Rankine – and Guthrie was not happy with the results. From then on, he would be in complete control of their recordings. This collection of songs – particularly 'Hazel', with its heavy McGeoch mannerisms – was the last time anyone would mistake them for Banshees' copyists. It was also the final record to be made with Will Heggie, who left during an arduous tour supporting Orchestral Manoeuvres in the Dark in Germany. Returning to Scotland with him, Robin and Elizabeth took time off to write new material, and while they did so, Ivo also enlisted them in a project he'd been working on.

This Mortal Coil was the name he gave to a collective of 4AD musicians, drawn together to record new versions of songs Watts-Russell held dear. The one he gave the Cocteau Twins was Tim Buckley's 'Song to the Siren', from his 1970 album, *Star Sailor*. Buckley, who had moved in the same Greenwich Village circles as Fred Neil,[8] was a tragic figure: a singer and guitarist of rare genius who had burned too fast and died at the age of twenty-eight, the result of a heroin OD. Tim had a voice, many said – and few who heard it could deny – that was heaven-sent.

This song, inspired by the Homeric myth of the enchantresses who lured sailors to their deaths on the rocks of their island domain, had lyrics by Buckley's writing partner, Larry Beckett. Fraser and Guthrie recorded it together, her vocals coursing over a simple guitar line, turning transcendent: 'Did I dream, you dreamed about me?/Were you here when I was full sail?' Raising the shipwreck of Buckley's talent, they immortalised his song, which became their best-known and most revered recording, even before fate dealt it another, deeper level of tragedy.

'We never thought about it seriously,' Elizabeth told *ZigZag*'s Jonh Wilde, 'never imagined it would come out at all. I'm not really pleased with my vocals. I really like the song itself though, I thought the words were beautiful.'[9]

Head Over Heels, recorded and produced as a two-piece in Edinburgh's Palladium Studios, followed in October 1983. With his multiple layers of shimmering guitar, Guthrie was finally getting closer to the sound he craved, while Fraser's lyrics became still more oblique, but all the more potent for their powers of suggestion. Spells entitled 'Sugar Hiccup', 'Glass Candle Grenades', 'When Mama was Moth' duly summoned a new 'third Twin', a catalytic presence and the man they had passed their original demo tape on to in the Beggars Banquet shop: Simon Raymonde.

In Our Angelhood

Simon was a man with music in his blood, the son of legendary '60s producer and arranger Ivor Raymonde, who wrote 'I Only Want to Be with You' for Dusty Springfield, produced the Walker Brothers and Billy Fury and regularly appeared on the BBC radio comedy *Hancock's Half Hour*.[10] He brought more than just his bass guitar to the Cocteau Twins. The first EP recorded with him, April 1984's *The Spangle Maker*, contained the exquisite 'Pearly Dewdrops Drop', which, when released as a single, reached number twenty-nine in the charts. But the band turned down a request for *Top of the Pops*: 'I don't want to be a freak show,' said Guthrie. 'Why try to be a part of something that so obviously has nothing to do with you?'[11]

The aptly named *Treasure* album cast its jewels in November 1984 and the Cocteaus continued to deliver their bedazzling wares throughout the '80s, each release a reminder that, however bleak things looked in real life, there was always an escape to be found through their black vinyl magic. The EPs *Echoes in a Shallow Bay* and *Aikea-Guinea* – a Scots term for seashells bleached and smoothed by the waves – continued their maritime explorations in 1985. They forged as far afield as Antarctica for their 1986 LP *Victorialand*, named after a region of the frozen continent and recorded as a duo while Raymonde lent his talents to a further This Mortal Coil album, *Filigree and Shadow*. The full Twins trio teamed up with American minimalist composer Harold Budd to create *The Moon and Melodies* album in November of that year, before returning with the fifth Cocteaus album proper – and the definitive record of the height of their unearthly powers – *Blue Bell Knoll* in September 1988.

By now, Guthrie's policy of ploughing all their earnings back into their own studio had paid dividends. They were renting space from the Who's Pete Townshend on his idyllic Thames eyot, Eel Pie Island, and living close by, in an area of London where J. M. W. Turner often painted and William Hogarth, Horace Walpole, William Morris and Gustav Holst had all once called home: along the stretches of the river west of Hammersmith, where you can easily forget you are in London at all. As a result of their autonomy, on *Blue Bell Knoll*, wrote David Stubbs, every track was 'a sheer supernova, dreamily cinematic yet electrically alive'.[12] Between this album and the next, September 1990's *Heaven or Las Vegas*, their most commercially successful record to date and the one that broke them in America, attracting the attentions of Madonna and Prince – who both wanted to sign them – Guthrie and Fraser had a daughter, Lucy Belle.

Besides the music itself, the story of the Cocteau Twins has many elements of a fairy tale: of Robin realising how special Elizabeth was before he even heard her sing a note and rescuing her from a life of unrequited obscurity in Grangemouth; of John Peel and Ivo facilitating their wondrous talents no sooner than they had recorded their first demo; of Raymonde completing their creative curve and the romantic couple casting off the miasmas of the commonplace in the dingy Falkirk and London bedsits of their early days to create their own sonic cathedral in the sunlit uplands of the Surrey borders.

But those who know their fairy tale also realise that such fictions are spun to snare the unwary: to deceive, trick and manipulate – and that to spend any time in the fairies' land is to risk your mortal soul. *Heaven or Las Vegas* was the last album the Cocteau Twins recorded for 4AD. The reason for the souring of relations with their mentor, Ivo, would only be revealed in the aftermath of their split: Guthrie was a long-term alcoholic who had latterly become addicted to cocaine. The record industry's fatal powdered charisma fuelled his already obsessive and controlling nature and he spiralled completely out of control after the birth of his daughter, ultimately landing in rehab – a process the by-then equally addicted Raymonde went through with him, loyal lieutenant to the last.

Fraser attempted to write their wrongs in the uncharacteristically blunt lyrics to their next album, 1993's *Four-Calendar Café* (Fontana). 'I'm not real and I deny, I won't heal unless I cry,' she sang on 'Know Who You Are at Every Age', 'I can't grieve, so I won't grow, I won't heal 'til I let it go.' Still more explicit was 'Bluebeard' – named after the pirate from Charles Perrault's 1679 French folktale collection:

'Are you the right man for me?/Are you safe?' she asked. In the process of penning this confessional, she suffered a breakdown.

During therapy, buried memories of childhood sexual abuse at the hands of her brother-in-law, and possibly even her father, came to the surface.[13] Elizabeth had run from one abusive situation straight into the arms of another domineering man, and her 'magic' lyrics had been a means of coping with Robin all along. This revelation makes reading old interviews with the Cocteau Twins a deeply uncomfortable experience – let alone the realisation that comes with this knowledge: that what all her listeners mistook for heaven was actually Fraser's personal hell.

And it wasn't over yet. Elizabeth was not long out of therapy before she fell in love with another man, one whose vocal gifts were every bit as extraordinary as her own. To make this story even more like a work of Oscar Wilde's imagination, that man was Jeff Buckley – the son of 'Song to the Siren''s Tim – who had arrived from out of nowhere to floor the music world with his 1993 debut album, *Grace*. This uncanny echo of his father's lost gifts heralded the arrival of a major talent – and one whose lifespan was almost as brief as Tim's. His eighteen-month affair with Fraser was over by the time Buckley drowned in the Wolf River Harbour of the Mississippi River on the evening of 29 May 1997, at the age of thirty.[14] Elizabeth thought she had written 'my last goodbye, as it were' to him on the songs of Cocteau Twins' 1995 *Twinlights* EP. But how could anything prepare anyone for this? Her earthbound sailor to meet the fate of the lover she had breathed back to life in his father's tune, only for him to walk out into the breakers and take Death as his bride: 'Hear me sing/Swim to me, swim to me'.

There really is no Mystery so great as Misery.

Fraser found a less perilous love with Damon Reece, formerly the drummer of Echo and the Bunnymen, Spiritualized and, latterly, Massive Attack, the Bristol band with sonic markers of the Cocteaus in their trip-hop genes. He provided her with the title of the final Twins' album, 1996's *Milk and Kisses* (Fontana), and she settled with him in Bristol, where they had a daughter, Lily, in 1998. At the time of writing, the pair had released music as Sun's Signature,[15] a record that gives her listeners fresh hope in the redemptive magic of music.

Village People

Dublin does not appear to be as remote a starting point as Grangemouth – it is, after all, the capital city of Ireland. But making his first visit there in his capacity as a *Sounds* journalist in 1979, Belfast native Dave McCullough admitted to his readers that he thought of the place as a rural backwater. 'Travelling south from Belfast, you can't but help notice the hazy, subtle change of most aspects physical and spiritual, which reveals itself in the transition from a louder, snarling land into an altogether more tranquil, withdrawn countryside,' he wrote. While his Troubles-strewn old manor had given the world premier punks Stiff Little Fingers, John Peel's favourite band the Undertones and Terri Hooley's Good Vibrations shop and record label, Dublin and the Ireland beyond remained, he considered 'quietly uninvolved, content only to throw forth the odd [Boomtown] Rats [or] Horslips freak.'[16]

But what had brought him to Dublin was the concerted efforts of a group of friends who, as punk's clarion sounded across the waters in 1976, realised that although London might be Calling, it surely wasn't going to come to them. Instead they created their own, alternative society, which they called Lypton Village. A place where they could study notions of art, literature and beauty, using Wilde, Yeats, Brendan Behan, James Joyce and Northumbrian imp Lindsay Kemp – who taught Bowie the art of mime – as their spirit guides. Thus enriched, they would create from their endeavours something so powerful it could not be ignored. At school, those friends were known as Fionan Hanvey, Paul Hewson and Derek Rowan. In the Village they became Gavin Friday, Bono Vox and Guggi.

With the help of other friends and siblings, they created two distinctly different bands to play the Village Social Club. The one that snagged McCullough was, of course, U2 – and you know what happened to them. The other, and the one he would describe as the only band to rival 'the genius of the Sex Pistols', were the Virgin Prunes, the outfit fronted by Friday and Guggi. This most gender- and genre-fluid of all bands, their name a self-invented slang for 'outsiders', were possessed of even more front than John Lydon facing off the combined ranks of the King's Road Teds and Bill Grundy's incensed and tooled-up viewers. They had recently come under onstage attack while supporting the Clash, an event that Gavin Friday – 'called so because that name reflects the way he looks' – reminisced about with amusement: 'The punks were quite relaxed while the Clash were on, but they went bananas over us!' McCullough was able to see this epitome of effrontery in action at the Baggott Inn, a venue the Villagers had seized as their own for the night, in the hope that they might establish a regular event there.

'Sometimes [Guggi and I] go transvestite on stage,' Friday told him. 'Sometimes we wear suits. We shock. If the audience doesn't want to listen to us, if they can't stand what we're doing, then we tell them to fuck off . . .' Confronting them with songs called 'Caucasian Walk', 'Greylight' and 'Art Fuck', Gavin held up a challenge to his audience: 'To look in that mirror or turn away is your choice.' And the kids, as McCullough observed, readily came through the looking glass to him – with the beneficial result that 'their sizeable following readily protected the band from any would-be tough boy assailants'.

Which didn't prevent them getting regularly banned from other venues, another pitfall of life in such a heavily Christ-haunted country. But the numbers of their tribe increased as all the little weirdos from the remotest villages of Ireland realised they were no longer alone.

The first Virgin Prunes line-up consisted of Friday and Guggi alongside third vocalist Dave-id Busaras Scott (David Watson), bassist Strongman (Trevor Rowen), guitarist Dik Evans (brother of U2's the Edge) and drummer Pod (Anthony Murphy). By the time of their show-stealing appearance with pigs' heads at Futurama 2,[17]

Pod had left the band. His replacement on percussion and keyboards was Haa Lacka Binttii (Daniel Figgis), a former child actor who had once appeared in a 1969 stage production of *Waiting for Godot* with Peter O'Toole and, after his brief tenure in the Virgin Prunes, would go on to record as outré diva Princess Tinymeat, before embarking on his current career as Daniel Figgis, composer.[18]

He appeared on their debut single, January 1981's 'Twenty Tens' – an ode to chain-smoking, a practice Friday would artfully return to on his 1995 album, *Shag Tobacco*. Released on their own Baby Records via Rough Trade, this led to a deal with Geoff Travis' label, through which the following single 'Moments and Mine (Despite Straight Lines)' came out in June of that year.

Beauty and the Beast

Virgin Prunes' songs did not settle into any distinct form but came spontaneously onstage and were either worked out further from there or abandoned completely. Within them could be found traces of *The Velvet Underground & Nico*, *Metal Machine Music* and *Low*; a smudge of Marc Bolan's glitter; hints of Foetus Art Terrorism; some McGeoch guitar shards; the outer reaches of experimental early PiL, when Keith Levene was painting from a similar palette; and some older, Montparnasse echoes of Gréco and Brel. The Virgin Prunes summoned their own, native Banshee by singing in the style of the *Sean nós*, a traditional Irish vocal form.

While U2, who had all attended the multi-denominational Mount Temple Comprehensive school, were unabashedly Christian and sang of their faith on debut album *Boy* (Island, October 1980), Friday, who was educated at the hands of Catholic Christian Brothers, was determined to shake up the hierarchy and reawaken older, heathen spirits in his land. 'Pagan Lovesong' (1982) would be a hit at every Goth Disco across Ireland and Britain, but before that, the Virgin Prunes set themselves a task of Wildeian proportions – a multi-part project given the overall title 'A New Form of Beauty'.

Part 1 came in the form of a 7-inch single featuring the dreamlike 'Sandpaper Lullabye'. 'A New Form of Beauty 2' was its 10-inch nightmare reverse, wherein the harrowing 'Come to Daddy' tackled the subject of incest. Then, the shade of Yeats' least favourite Golden Dawn contemporary was summoned on the demonic 12-inch 'A New Form of Beauty 3' in the form of 'Beast (Seven Bastard Suck)'. All three releases had been strewn throughout 1981 and were followed in early 1982 by Part 4, a cassette release featuring extracts from the band's live performance, 'A New Form of Beauty 5' at Douglas Hyde Gallery, Trinity College Dublin, on 8 November 1981. Called 'Din Glorious', this caustic collage mixed songs from the three previous 'Form's with a variety of taped sounds, spliced together to engender a distinctly uneasy listening experience. Somewhere still out there are Parts 6, an unpublished book, and 7, an unreleased film.

Their next, slightly more conventional album . . . *If I Die, I Die* (Rough Trade, November 1982) was produced by kindred spirit, Wire's Colin Newman, at Windmill Lane Studios in Dublin. It continued the band's aesthetic quest. 'Ballad of the Man' was said by Friday to be a satire on Bruce Springsteen's storytelling style, something often emulated by fellow Dubliners the Boomtown Rats and parodied perfectly here: 'Spanish Johnny came in from the underworld last night/Looking for a gang to rob a bank.' Meanwhile, the album's title is taken from the 'Bau-dachöng' in which Friday details the criticisms of his detractors: 'You're mad, you're mad, you're a weirdo/You've gone too far, too far, too soon'. Newman captured a peak Prunes' performance on . . . *If I Die, I Die*, and one that reached out across Great Britain to touch the hearts of other Irish exiles. The best review I found of it came from Karl O'Connor, aka techno musician and label owner Regis, who described its impact on him as a teenager in early '80s Birmingham in *The Quietus*. This record, he said, 'hit me at the core of who I was . . . They were the Catholics at the underbelly of Irish culture, they were this amalgamation of the disfigured beauty of Joyce and the perversity of the Church.'[19]

Something this intense could not last forever. Following 'Pagan Lovesong' came *Hérésie*, a boxed double-pack of 10-inch singles and art booklets on the subject of insanity and its connections to art and filth, made for French label L'Invitation au Suicide. Its sonic material was recorded during a three-night session in Dublin, when the band went without sleep for three days to fashion songs while fully immersed in their artistic brief. Long tours around Europe both deepened Friday's thirst for the chanson style and fractured the nerves of the overworked Prunes. Things began to fracture – disenchanted with the music industry, Guggi and Dik left the frame, leading to Mary D'Nellon taking up guitar and Pod returning on drums.

The Moon Looked Down and Laughed – recorded in 1984 but not released until 1986 – brought them into orbit with kindred spirits, producer Dave Ball, just stepping out of the Soft Cell wreckage, and guest vocalist Jim Thirlwell. Inspired by much the same sources, Friday's songwriting was by now moving in a similar direction to Marc Almond and his Willing Sinners' nocturnal demi monde, and Gavin followed Guggi and Dik out of the Exit door in 1986. With multi-instrumentalist Maurice 'The Man' Seezer as his Mick Harvey, he would record three beautiful albums in this vein – *Each Man Kills the Thing He Loves* (1989), *Adam 'n' Eve* (1992) and *Shag Tobacco*, all on Island Records – as well as running a cabaret club in Dublin, from where he found a further cast of characters to fuel his fertile imagination. Proving himself to be perhaps this book's ultimate Gothfather, Daniel Miller gathered up and re-released all the Virgin Prunes' recorded output for his Grey Area of Mute archive in 2004, with Friday overseeing all remastering and repackaging.[20]

Never Forever

What of other fellow travellers we have lost sight of along the way? While we linger in a realm where time can be suspended, let's catch up with some of them. Starting with Marc Almond, who had been summoning ghosts on the title track of his second Willing Sinners' album, *Stories of Johnny* (1985), 'about a young guy I knew who smoked heroin and later died, hence the lyric 'My smoky lover will take me away forever'.' Shortly after its release in 1985, he was back in the upper reaches of the charts, covering Donna Summer's 'I Feel Love' with Bronski Beat – the trio fronted by angel-voiced Glaswegian Jimmy Somerville, who spoke so eloquently and hauntingly of being a gay runaway on 1984's 'Smalltown Boy'; and on the album it came from, *Age of Consent* (London, 1984). In Scotland, it remained illegal to be gay until 1980, which was why so many young men followed the trajectory Somerville's song described. He and bandmate Steve Bronski met Southend native Larry Steinbachek in London, where they shared a flat in Brixton. Their choice of song was a form of rebuke to anti-gay statements that Born Again disco diva Summer, revered as a gay icon, was widely reported to have made at a 1983 concert;[21] and they wanted Almond, whom they saw as a guiding light, to join them in 'camping it up on *Top of the Pops*.'

Marc continued to peruse his extensive record collection for the 1986 EP *A Woman's Story*, plucking out songs by Lee Hazlewood ('For One Moment'), Johnnie Ray ('The Little White Cloud That Cried') and the Nino Tempo-April Stevens title track; while the same year's *Violent Silence* EP grew out of a tribute festival to transgressive French writer Georges Bataille that Almond had taken part in, and pursued the theme of internal damage caused by external repression.

Keeping with those subversive literary voices, the title of 1987's *Mother Fist and Her Five Daughters* came from Truman Capote's 1980 short story *Nocturnal Turnings or How Siamese Twins Have Sex* and referred to the joys of solo sex. An Almond favourite, the album contained, he said, 'the most personal lyrics I'd written since *Torment and Toreros*' – although, conversely, these were songs of joy, not pain. It came packaged in imagery that echoed German director Rainer Werner Fassbinder's fantastical final film, 1982's *Querelle*, itself based on Jean Genet's 1947 novel *Querelle de Brest*.[22]

A homoerotic epic, *Mother Fist* arrived just before legislation to 'prohibit the promotion of homosexuality' by schools and councils was made legal by the implementation of Section 28 of the Local Government Act, enacted in May 1988. Almond's briney jolly rogerings, thick with the sound of Martin McCarrick's poop deck accordion, did not wash so well with his record company though. Virgin terminated their dealings with Some Bizzare after the album failed to knock out any chart hits.

Marc's revenge was sweet. With a slimmed-down Willing Sinners reborn as La Magia – Annie Hogan, Billy McGee and Steve Humphreys – and a new sponsor in Parlophone, on 1998's *The Stars We Are*, he cast a glamour for global domination on his duet with Gene Pitney, 'Something's Gotten Hold of My Heart'. Pitney, who had originally recorded his hit version of the Roger Greenaway-Roger Cook song in 1967, was touring the UK while La Magia were in the studio. On a whim, they sent a demo of Hogan's new arrangement to Marc's vocal and the venerable silver fox loved it so much he agreed to a duet. 'Often the thing of getting away with it is just the doing of it,' Marc recalled. His experience with Gene would more than make up for the crushing disappointment of working with Nico on the same album even if, because their vocals were recorded separately, they didn't get to meet until they made the video. 'But it was perfect. He had his limo, I had mine and we recorded at 3 o'clock in the morning, in the freezing cold, in a neon junkyard in Las Vegas!'

Act of Contrition

Elsewhere in 1988, Barry Adamson had managed to channel all of his ghosts into a miraculous reinvention. Inspired by a tape of movie music given to him by F. M. Einheit in Berlin, he took in a midnight Scala screening of Otto Preminger's 1955 adaptation of Nelson Algren's 1949 novel, *The Man with the Golden Arm*, in which Frank Sinatra superbly portrays drug-addicted jazz drummer and poker dealer Frankie Machine. Deciding he would like to remake

Elmer Bernstein's scorching theme as an epic ode to his own battles against heroin, he did so in spectacular style and company. Using an Ensoniq Mirage sampler, Barry channelled Sinatra's cinemanic drum sequence to lay down a foundation track. He then had it enhanced by former Magazine colleague John Doyle, brought in Seamus Beaghen on piano and Hammond, the multitalented Annie Hogan on violin, Enrico Tommaso on trumpet and Terry Edwards on sax, with himself providing bass, in an orchestration pulled together by Billy McGee, produced by Paul Kendall and released by Mute as his dramatic debut solo single.

Around this track, and while, unlike Frankie Machine, he finally kicked his habit, Adamson fashioned the 1989 album that had begun in his child's spy-obsessed mind. *Moss Side Story*, an enquiry into time, place and race, opens with the banshee screams of Diamanda Galás in 'On the Other Side of Relaxation'; pulls in a ferocious guitar salvo from Rowland S. Howard on 'Autodestruction'; elicits the perfect car chase sax solo from Gary Barnacle on 'Sounds from the Big House' and throws into its cells Mick Harvey, Kid Congo and Anita Lane as a choir of back-up singers. Foley sounds and snatches of dialogue interspersed these musical reveries, layering in the tension and *Sweeney*-style menace. In a sleeve portraying grainy, black-and-white location shots of Moss Side by Lawrence Watson – including Leech's Funeral Home, whose services Adamson was by now all too familiar with – it was packaged like a soundtrack album, with liner notes in the form of a detective story, penned by former Moodists' mainman and Australian raconteur supreme, Dave Graney. On the cover, Barry stands under his brolly in the Mancunian rain, with the strapline: 'In a black and white world, murder brings a touch of colour'. Hell is a city, indeed.

With this perfectly executed artefact, Barry had fully alchemised his dark materials. This opened up his own fruitful career in film, which began on a commission for Derek Jarman's *The Last of England* (1987) and would lead all the way to David Lynch's *Lost Highway* (1997) – as well as a two-decades-long trail of captivating musical investigations to follow. As he records in his memoir, his best review came from no less a personal hero than Hubert Selby Jr, who wrote his sorcerer's apprentice a letter of approval when he received *Moss Side Story*: 'It sounds like a shoot-'em-up, and I love shoot-'em-ups.'[23]

Valleys of Green and Grey

On the other side of the Pennines, there was more conflict for our men in clogs and their flame-haired enchantress to overcome. In the aftermath of their controversial signing to EMI, Stuart Morrow upped and left New Model Army, midway through the 'No Rest' tour. It was the same fateful day – 11 May 1985 – that 56 Bradford FC fans were tragically killed when fire engulfed the wooden roof of the Valley Parade stadium during a match with Lincoln City.[24] NMA's first gig with their new bassist, seventeen-year-old Jason 'Moose' Harris, would be a benefit for the families of those who died in the disaster.

A different style of songwriting would begin to emerge from the Justin Sullivan-Rob Heaton axis after the recording of 1986's *The Ghost of Cain*, made with Rolling Stones' producer Glyn Johns. This experience was a 'steep learning curve' for the argumentative singer, who later admitted Johns had, at one point, taken him 'by the scruff of the neck, led me round the back of his studio, pointed to all these gold discs he had on the wall and said, "How many of these have *you* got?" A sobering experience.'[25]

But they found their own Avalon while recording Joolz' first album, 1987's *Hex*, at Sawmills: a remote studio set on a tidal creek on the River Fowey at Golant in Cornwall, reachable only by boat at high tide. 'Robert and I had a golden year together that began with *Hex*,' Justin recalled, 'everything that I wrote that he touched turned to gold; and everything he wrote that I touched turned to gold.'

In their cabin accommodation, deep in the surrounding woodland, they fashioned the richly atmospheric scores for Joolz's tales of pride, ambition, lust and love, as she had seen it played out from toilet circuit to the amphitheatres of rock 'n' roll. Like Barry Adamson, Sullivan and Heaton were now discovering the possibilities of synthesisers in broadening the horizons of their compositions. They made full use of new technology to create soundscapes for 'Protection', 'House of Dreams' and stand-out single 'Love is (Sweet Romance)' and then the next New Model Army single, the eerie 'White Coats', which remains one of the most haunting Cold War-era warnings of impending ecological disaster.

The formation of Red Sky Coven[26] – a travelling troubadour show comprising Justin, Joolz, fellow poet Rev Hammer and multi-instrumentalist Brett Selby – helped hone the lyrics for NMA's second great album of the Thatcher years, 1989's *Thunder and Consolation*. The band returned to Sawmills with producer Tom Dowd – a still more distinguished veteran, who had cut his teeth at Atlantic, recording and producing everyone from Ray Charles to Willie Nelson and inventing the multi-track recording system while he was about it. The supremely gifted Dowd had also been a White Coat himself: before he began his career in music, he served his Second World War military draft as a physics scientist, working on the Manhattan Project, which developed America's first atomic bomb.

Taking its title from a 1663 book by revolutionary Quaker Edward Burroughs, *Thunder and Consolation* was very much the spiritual flipside of *Vengeance*, a portrait of all that had been lost in the years since NMA's debut. In '225', Sullivan predicts the coming era of CCTV and covert computer surveillance, while in 'Archway Towers' – which also records the band's short-lived and miserable existence in London, queuing at the dole office in the grim surrounds of its title – he watches with impotent rage as: 'The conference hall rings to the standing ovation/The people in blue ties rise from the podium/Crazy with power, blinded by vision/The mass-chosen leaders for a brutalised nation'.[27] Most elegiac of all, those desires of escape expressed in 'Smalltown England' are put into the rear-view window of a bus travelling back through the West Yorkshire valleys of 'Green and Grey', the story of those left behind.

Yet after the thunder comes the consolation: beside these laments sat 'Vagabonds', their most uplifting ode to a lifestyle suppressed at the Battle of the Beanfield – yet nurtured still beneath the tatterdemalion cloak New Model Army's travelling Family. To violinist Ed Alleyne-Johnson's delirious jig, Sullivan watches his audience 'follow the tail lights out of the city/Moving in a river of red'.

The Celtic knot drawn by Joolz on the album's front cover offered a shield boss of protection to anyone who'd chosen an alternative way of life. 'The rest of the rock 'n' roll circus – all the lingerie models, the Jack Daniel's behaviour – we would find tedious,' was her surmise. 'The magic part of it is that moment when you get onstage and you can command 2,000 people to be silent. When you become the conduit for the gods.'

Which sounds still more poignant now, in the wake of Robert Heaton's untimely death in 2004 from pancreatic cancer, aged only forty-three.

Ill-Met by Moonlight

One of the most enchanting images of the '80s was captured by director Neil Jordan in his 1984 adaptation with author Angela Carter of her story, *The Company of Wolves*. An exploration of lycanthropy and the themes of the fairy tale, *Little Red Riding Hood*, Carter's original short story first appeared in her 1979 collection, *The Bloody Chamber* (Penguin). Working for the first time in film, the author expounded on her work's allegorical and folkloric links by creating with Jordan a series of connecting fables about the beasts within.

The film begins in a country house in the present day, where a pubescent girl, Rosaleen (Sarah Paterson), dreams she lives in one of the enchanted forests of pre-seventeenth-century Europe from whence Red Riding Hood emerged. She was first recorded by Frenchman Charles Perrault in 1697 and then the Brothers Grimm, who believed her tale to be German in origin, in their folktale collections of the early 1800s. Jordan transports us back through the mists and into the trees, giving Rosaleen a red-shawl-knitting grandmother in the redoubtable '80s form of Angela *Murder She Wrote* Lansbury, who spins a series of cautionary tales. 'Never stray from the path,' she begins – just as Brian Glover's recalcitrant Slaughtered Lamb patron had also advised the unwary in John Landis' *An American Werewolf in London* in 1981. 'Never eat a windfall apple and never trust a man whose eyebrows meet in the middle.'

After hearing about examples of such proto-Gallagher brothers and coming face to face with Brian Glover – here also present as the father of her would-be sweetheart – Rosaleen then spins her own tale of a she-wolf, who comes up from a well in the middle of the night to take a look at the world of men. Shot and injured by a villager, she is saved by the old priest (Graham Crowden), who recognises her innocence and tends to her wounds, offering her his sanctuary. But the creature has seen enough to know she will never be safe and slips back down the well by nightfall, returning to her mysterious realm beyond our sight.

The woman who so movingly portrayed the vulnerable wolfchild, with her huge saucer eyes and wild mane of hair, was a singer who came up from the most Matthew Hopkins-haunted county of Essex. Danielle Dax (b. Danielle Gardner, 23 September 1958 in Southend-on-Sea) also had a grandma who was what some locals might call a wise woman, others a witch. 'She was considered quite eccentric,' she recalled. 'But when I was very young and living with her, she was a medium, who believed in the crystal ball and divination.'

Dax's granny used to call the manifestations she routinely saw gliding past her 'Inky Bloaters' – a title her infant charge later gave to her pivotal album of 1987. To further her granddaughter's education: 'She gave me her crystal and all her occult books.' Brought up between two worlds, 'I just thought it was all great. At the age of three, you don't question it, you just think it's all real – and why not? There are many strange types of energy, occult or other wise, which various theories in particle physics bear out. Woe betide foolish human hubris for thinking we have all the answers.'

Time spent in Granny's enchanted realm was a welcome diversion for the miasmas of Danielle's childhood. 'I came from an extremely dysfunctional family and, as a coping strategy, I developed a rich and creative inner world,' she recalled. 'I devoured books voraciously and began my quest for alternative meanings and an explanation for the world around me.' As well as Granny's bequest, these included: 'Jungian psychology, Carlos Castaneda, mysticism, astronomy and Erich von Däniken's UFO books. I used to pray for a flying saucer to land on the playing field and take me away!'

Danielle learned dance from the age of three, tap dancing to Shirley Temple and, as a prelude to the she-wolf, she played one of the Wicked Witch of the West's flying monkeys in a stage version of *The Wizard of Oz*. She learned flute and tenor sax at school and in her early teens, developed a penchant for Captain Beefheart, early Brian Eno – 'the feather-boa-wearing, post-Roxy period' – and Robert Wyatt. 'These artists felt like my "real" family and I often fantasised about being some sort of weird hybrid of all three.'

Practical Cats

Dax was first encouraged to do so in 1979, by the singer and multi-instrumentalist Karl Blake (b. 1956) for his avant-garde ensemble, Lemon Kittens. Moving to his base in Reading, she initially signed up to do artwork for the record sleeve of their first release, the *Spoonfed and Writhing* EP (Step Forward, 1979). 'I hadn't even thought of doing music. I wanted to make stage designs and costumes; that whole 3D movement-sculpture-instillation-based events – like Actionism, a kind of performance-based art. Karl had a large collection of instruments, which, with his encouragement, I began to experiment with.' Dax, who had the most prodigious and eclectic record collection Blake had ever seen, would go on to make three more Lemon Kittens recordings, with titles that sounded like unpublished Edward Gorey fictions: *We Buy a Hammer for Daddy* (United Dairies, 1980, LP), *Cake Beast* (United Dairies, 1980, EP) and *Those who bite the hand that feeds them sooner or later must meet . . . The Big Dentist* (Illuminated, 1981, LP). They performed with acts as diverse as Killing Joke and Divine, in arts centres and Soho strip joints.

Along the way, Danielle got to record with Robert Fripp, on his 1981 League of Gentleman production,[28] for which she also supplied the cover art, and to work with her teenage inspiration Robert Wyatt, recording a duet with him for fellow United Dairies' artists the Bombay Ducks, which sadly remains unreleased. Then, out fly-postering one night, a conversation with a friend about the autonomy of women in the music business sparked a revelation. Dax created her *Pop Eyes* album (Initial, 1983) in its entirety, playing every instrument, producing and wrapping it in a sleeve that the packaging company initially refused to handle: a collage called *Meat Harvest* that gave the startling impression of a skinned cadaver, its eyeballs sticking out on stalks.[29]

She hit her stride with the following *Jesus Egg That Wept* (Awesome, 1984), another self-produced and authored work, although she ushered Karl Blake back into the musical groove on 'Ostritch'. His musical partner in Shock Headed Peters – and Danielle's romantic partner from 1984–89 – David Knight (b. 1958 in London) lent his distinctive rocking guitar groove to 'Evil-Honkey Stomp'. Dax was another Batcave regular, her appearance in those days not so different from her lupine celluloid self, fashioned from the accoutrements of a Soho lifestyle: 'I used to go and stay with Olli Wisdom from the Batcave in Old Compton Street. We knew all the locals, the Soho edge-worlds. We would go to the Whore's Wig Shop, as Olli called it. The clothes I used to wear, with all the red hair and white make-up, I used to wear all the time, for everything, going for milk at the corner shop, whatever. Olli and I went to Phonogram to try to get me a record deal and Musical Youth were there. They were terrified when we walked in. They looked up at us and said: "Are those guys for real?"'

Inky Bloaters cemented her creative partnership with Knight, who shared musical writing and arrangement credits. It also spawned a surprise hit single, 'Bad Miss M' – Dax's hex on Margaret Thatcher, which somehow managed to bypass the usual Radio 1 filters and get onto the playlists of the poptabulous Steve Wright and Simon Bates – despite lyrics that looked wistfully forward to dancing on the PM's grave. 'I can't say I was politically aware,' she reflected, 'but I could see how society had been affected by her policies. I was disappointed that a woman who had reached such a pinnacle of success could be so ghastly a person. She wasn't good for women, she didn't help other women in politics and as an entity I found her repugnant.'

All of these gifts from Grandma in turn caught the ear of Seymour Stein, who signed Danielle to his discerning Sire roster in 1988. She scored two more mutoid rockabilly hits with 'Cathouse' and 'White Knuckle Ride', culled from her *Dark Adapted Eye* compilation of that year,[30] then created her own potent psychedelia – including a hypnotic take on the Beatles' 'Tomorrow Never Knows' – on *Blast the Human Flower* (Sire, 1990) with producer Stephen Street.

Which all might sound like the makings of another fairy tale. 'I had so many bizarre experiences with Seymour,' Dax recalled. 'One minute I'd be signing on in Brixton, the next I'd be at a Dover Street art gallery watching him buying Francis Bacons.' But inevitably, a major label was no Magic Garden. Danielle wanted 'Id Parade' to be a single; Sire thought its references to political warmongering were a little too risky for their market. 'So they released "Big Blue '82" instead. Which is ironic, considering a BLU 82 is actually a bomb' – and one that was used by the US Army in Vietnam, the Gulf War and Afghanistan. 'They told me to shut up, that I was too political and might get into trouble and be at risk from the public.'

So Danielle went back down the well, where she exists to this day in the new parallel universe of the internet. Occasionally, she pops back up under the cover of darkness to record disturbingly witchy little lullabies, like 'Hate on Sight' and 'Son of Thumbs of a Murderer', for Shock Headed Peters' *Fear Engine II* (Cyclops Prod, 1993) and, more recently, 'Jack Sorrow' – 'a creaky folk-tale about a mythical character' – on UnicaZürn's *Temporal Bends* (uZu Music, 2009), alongside Knight and Coil's Stephen Thrower.[31] Then, not wishing to linger longer than is safe to do so in the world of men, she slips from our sight again.

Is This the Life?

In *Excalibur*, John Boorman's 1981 epic cinematic retelling of Thomas Malory's *Le Morte d'Arthur*, Nicol Williamson's Merlin describes himself as 'A dream to some – a nightmare to others!' This was also the general view of the last band I wish to introduce to this story.

While not exactly Gothic, Cardiacs took from everything that was odd and eccentric in British music – from music hall to punk, prog rock to pop, sea shanties to psychedelia, folk and choral music – drawing out the euphoric charge from centuries of song through the Merlin-like channel of singer/guitarist Tim Smith. Goths certainly comprised a large part of the audience drawn in by word-of-mouth to their astonishing live shows.

Cardiacs faced their audience dressed in brass-buttoned maroon Salvation Army uniforms, wielding guitars, drums and a plethora of keyboards and percussion. Their faces were smeared in greasepaint: white, black and scarlet gashes of colour that horribly distorted their features. Only saxophonist Sarah Smith diverged from the dress code, twirling across the stage in a ripped-up ballgown, an expression of demented glee on her similarly scarily made-up face.

Their backdrop depicted a blown-up image of a daisy – also the emblem of their record company, the Alphabet Business Concern – and, as their sets reached a climax with a floridly emotive song called 'The Whole World Window', a man in a tail suit and a woman who resembled a Victorian governess came onto the stage bearing a tray of Champagne for the band, letting off streamers and showering the stage with glitter.

'What we try to do is soak up the feelings and atmospheres,' Tim told me in 1993. 'There's whole worlds of things in there that hit you all at once so it takes time to get it all in. You won't get it all on the first listen.'

Cardiacs fans within the music press were a rare commodity. As Tim put it: 'A barrage of things all hitting you at the same time puts a lot of people off.' Most of their critics gave them a merciless time, but in a way that said more about their own prejudices and hang-ups than accurately portraying either Cardiacs' music or their background – just as Gavin Friday had done, Tim Smith held a mirror up to his audience.

In 1987 Cardiacs were on the verge of releasing their extraordinary *A Little Man and a House and the Whole World Window* LP (The Alphabet Business Concern, 1988), which would push the sounds Tim had been crafting for the best part of a decade out from his bedroom into widescreen, high-tech studio-assisted sound. 'I think people should give it another chance and forget everything they've ever known in the past or might do in the future,' Smith surmised. 'It's a big bag of sweets, you know.'

A Little Man and a House

Cardiacs' story begins in Chessington, an outer suburb of west London, then geographically located in Surrey, still further down the banks of the Thames than the Cocteaus' Eel Pie Island base. Here, in a little house shared with their mother Eileen, Tim and Jim Smith created their own world of adventures. They attended local state schools and their musical bent came from their father, a trumpeter in a swing dance band, who died suddenly when Jim was six and Tim still a toddler – an experience his former wife Sarah considered he was always trying to come to terms with through his music: 'Tim was holding his father's hand when he died. He was always so close to death, all the time. And most of his songs are about death, really.'

Teenager Jim bought his first bass in 1972, to play along with a neighbour, Geoff Shelton, who had a guitar. His precocious eleven-year-old brother insisted on joining in, banging on a snare drum as they rehearsed in their garage and generally annoying them. By the age of thirteen, Tim had got his hands on Geoff's guitar and his LP of instructions on how to play it, learned 'Frankie and Johnny' and started to fashion his own compositions. By fourteen, he had started a series of bands with school friends, including drummer Mark Cawthra, keyboard player Colvin Mayers and Jim, which became first Cardiac Arrest in 1977, then Cardiacs in 1979.

Smith Jr began recording songs with titles like 'Icky Qualms', 'Jibber and Twitch' – not so far removed from Elizabeth Fraser's parallel universe of 'Feathers-Oars-Blades' and 'Alas Dies Laughing'. With no formal training at all, Tim taught himself to read and write music by following the printed score to the Who's *Tommy* while listening to the LP. He wrote out every Cardiacs' composition by hand, working out the arrangements for each instrument as he could hear them in his head. Not just those instruments the group played, but strings and woodwind parts, too. As drummer Dominic Luckman recalled: 'He knew how something was going to sound before he'd written it and before he'd played a note.'

Their cassette-only productions *The Obvious Identity* (as Cardiac Arrest, 1980) and *Toy World* (1981) were constructed on primitive equipment in his bedroom. By 1984, they had budget enough to hire a real studio to record *The Seaside* (1984) at Crow Studios: 'A tiny basement in a Victorian house in Surbiton,' according to Luckman. The drummer and his friend, percussionist Tim Quy, hailed from the neighbouring suburb of Tolworth and became first roadies and then Cardiacs themselves as Cawthra and Mayers departed. This also coincided with Sarah, an art student who had been classically trained on sax, joining the band. Cardiacs set up the Alphabet Business Concern, maintaining complete autonomy over their recordings and how they were presented.

The final element of the line-up was Luckman's flatmate, William D. Drake, a child prodigy on harmonium and piano, and a distant cousin of Nick Drake's. Bill's comprehensive classical training enabled him to keep up with Tim's wildfire talents, which he described as being akin to simultaneously working with 'all four Beatles and George Martin as well.' Cardiacs created their own videos to accompany their singles releases, which give a flavour of what their live shows were like. The two figures that joined them onstage, the Consultant and Miss Swift, were said to be representatives of the Alphabet Business Concern and sometimes also appear in these promotional films.

All were heavily influenced by cinema's darkest adapted eye, David Lynch, who found in white-picket-fence American suburbia the same undercurrents Tim was simultaneously picking up in the Metroland of London's commuter sprawl: '*Eraserhead* (1977) and *Blue Velvet* (1986) and their soundtracks, in particular,' said Sarah. 'Cardiacs had a kind of visual sense that wasn't separate from the sound, which is what David Lynch did so brilliantly.'

When they acquired a manager in Mark Walmesley, an associate of extreme Brummie metallers Napalm Death, they got to open up the whole world window. Their very own Arthur Daley, Walmesley cut them a deal to record their first album at Manfred Mann's state-of-the-art Workhouse Studios on the Old Kent Road. In 'dead time' – from dusk until dawn – they pieced together their first album proper over three years. During which Smith learned how to use all of Workhouse's equipment – mixing desks and consoles that were, at the same time, being used by Stock Aitken Waterman (SAW) on their production line of hits. 'Kylie Minogue would be wandering around every now and again,' recalled Jim.

Their finished album could not have sounded further from the soap star's bubble-thin pop. *A Little Man and a House and the Whole World Window* is a flickering nocturne of gaslight on cobbles. Mournful brass notes seemed to serenade the departing miners, while strange, industrial sounds of factories and Tim's lyrical 'immense machines' echoed the now-stilled Fleet Street presses. These special effects were either improvised in the studio or culled from a huge collection of foley sounds the two Tims had previously amassed. The sumptuous sound of a borrowed Mellotron, a fairground organ's whirligig patter, a violin ascending and the hiss of a bottle of underarm deodorant all collaged together in the same hallucinatory manner as one of Lynch's equally carefully constructed films. In this case, his 1980 masterpiece about the ultimate outsider – and John Hurt's most astonishingly affecting role – *The Elephant Man* – springs to mind.

Cardiacs almost had a hit record off it, with the single 'Is This the Life?', one of their most musically straightforward, heart-swelling moments, which hid its darker questions in Tim's lyrics: 'Following around to see a life that's never in/Always calling itself on its own phone/Though it's never quite at home in the world today.'[32] 'That was the only one that got any radio play,' as Jim recalled. 'And, ironically, it was ruined by Kylie Minogue. They didn't print enough copies to sell, because all the presses were taken up with "I Should Be So Lucky".'

This line-up of the band recorded one more album together, 1989's *On Land and in the Sea*, an equally mind-expanding collection, described by *MM*'s Andrew Smith as 'one continuous, sweeping collection of sawn-off epic joy . . . a deeply satisfying album' and by me in *Sounds* as 'a veritable masterpiece that stands alone in demented ingenuity'. An opinion I stand by.

I would like to leave Cardiacs basking in this sunlit glade. Those who know the end of this fairy tale will already be aware it is perhaps the saddest of all those I have told in these pages and that Tim's life deserves a wider and more thorough appreciation than can be allowed here. So let's leave the last words to him.

'I don't see why music has to be such a little thing. Why can't it be several big things? What we do musically is a fantasy, not to be muddled up with the fantasy that is goblins and all that shite. Fantasy is the infinite world which is your own head. You can do anything there that you want.'[33]

Gothfather: Aubrey Beardsley

Our final tragic male genius is one whose work has come to define the Decadent era, tapping in, as it does, to all the obsessions and repressions of the Victorian age. His stunningly sinuous black-and-white drawings formed a link between the Pre-Raphaelites, the Symbolists and the Art Nouveau movement – and then came back for more in the Psychedelic Sixties. A cadaverous and sickly young man, he was aware from the age of nine just how time was pressing upon him and invented his arrestingly original style from his sickbed, battling the tuberculosis that would eventually kill him at twenty-five. But Aubrey Vincent Beardsley did not go gently into that good night – he was determined to make a lasting sensation.

Born in Brighton on 21 August 1872, he grew up in genteel poverty, alongside his devoted sister, the beautiful Mabel, one year his senior. Their mother, Ellen, was the daughter of Surgeon-Major William Pitt of the Indian Army, a cultured woman who taught her children piano every evening and opened the mind of the largely bedbound Aubrey with the possibilities of literature. She married beneath her status when she took up with feckless Vincent Beardsley, the son of a Clerkenwell jeweller with no trade of his own and a fondess for women and drink. He had managed to blow all of his grand-maternal inheritance by the time Aubrey was born.

Beardsley's long fingers were ever restless, both at the easel and on the piano keyboard; drawing and playing became the conduits through which his active mind could evade and transcend his sickly body. He and Mabel inhabited hugely imaginative worlds, loving to act, dress up and play music together. Further drama was provided by their conversion to Roman Catholicism, initiated by Mabel, when she was sixteen. Attending Mass with all its rituals and Mysteries was as keen a spur on Aubrey's imagination as the wealth of exotica he perused in the Oriental Rooms of Brighton Pavilion, naughty George IV's Xanadu-by-the-sea. The collection of Japanese woodcuts Beardsley studied there left an indelible mark on the style he developed. Not just the fine, precise lines, but in the bestiary of fantastic creatures that inhabited his drawings – there were always dragons.

After his sporadic attendance at Brighton, Hove and Sussex Grammar, where his drawings were first published in school magazine Past and Present, *Aubrey got a job as an insurance clerk in London, while amassing a portfolio of drawings. He was inspired by the work of the Pre-Raphaelite Brotherhood, who had re-enchanted the Industrialist's landscape with their glowing visions of Medieval Arcadia. Assisted by Mabel – who cast a glamour on the artist with her striking red locks – he showed this work to one of their clan, Edward Burne-Jones (1833–98), who immediately recommended Beardsley to Westminster School of Art.*

Within a year, Aubrey had received his first commission, from publisher Joseph Dent – the epic task of illustrating a reprint of Mallory's Le Morte d'Arthur *(1893). With over 300 images, the work contained elements of William Morris's decorative art, the Pre-Raphaelites' Romantic view of history and Japanese-style erotica revealing the beastly outer reaches of his own imagination. Under the ivy could be found all manner of weirdness: hermaphroditic fauns, spouting phallic mushrooms, imps that resembled miniature versions of the Great Beast. 'A strange boy,' Dent described his young protégé, who he felt was 'not long for this world.'*

The book's publication was the Beardsley siblings' entrée to the world of Decadent London. Wilde and Yeats fell upon them with relish, the former describing Mabel as 'a daisy', while her brother, he said, resembled 'a monstrous orchid'; the latter admired Aubrey's quick-witted, cross-dressing sister as 'practically one of us'. The association with Wilde would, however, be a double-edged sword. Beardsley produced perhaps his finest work for Oscar's 1893 Salome *and his depiction of Herod's daughter lasciviously kissing the severed head of John the Baptist created all the outrage the artist craved.*

Punch *dubbed him 'Daubrey Weirdsley' and 'Awfully Weirdly' and society's attention was drawn to the young aesthete's meticulous appearance – his neatly tailored morning jacket and polished patent shoes – as evidence of homosexuality. His drawings, of course, could still more easily be read for signs of further 'depravity': transvestitism and incest with Mabel, the latter a notion picked up on by Brian Reade, who curated the 1966 V&A exhibition that turned the Love Generation on to Beardsley. As the artist himself said: 'People hate to see their darting vices depicted [but] vice is terrible and it should be depicted.' Wilde soon became afraid that Aubrey's talent might outshine his own and a feud began to simmer. 'I invented Aubrey Beardsley!' Oscar pronounced. The artist's riposte, the caricature 'Oscar Wilde at Work' (1895), depicted the author merrily plagiarising the Bible and Swinburne, with a copy of* French Verbs at a Glance *to hand.*

Beardsley loved creating posters for theatrical productions and his scrying eye saw the possibilities of advertising. In his 1894 essay 'The Art of Hoarding', Aubrey wrote of a London 'resplendent with advertisements' idealistically envisaging: 'Beauty has laid siege to the city, and telegraph wires shall no longer be the sole joy of our aesthetic perceptions.'

At the height of his powers, he became the art editor of aesthetes' bible The Yellow Book *in 1894, providing its sumptuous covers in the same daffodil shade that the fictions of Baudelaire had been published in France. Inside could be found poetry and literature by Yeats, George Gissing, Arnold Bennett and Henry James, with illustrations from Walter Sickert, John Singer Sargent and William Rothstein. But this tenure coincided with Wilde's very public downfall in 1895. Arrested for indecency and sodomy, Wilde was reported being taken into custody carrying 'a yellow book' under his arm. Although this was, in fact, a reference to Dorian Gray's reading matter, the public came to believe it meant Beardsley's journal and so his publisher, John Lane, gave Aubrey the sack.*

He was not out of sensation's spotlight for long though. Leonard Smithers was a clandestine purveyor of upmarket erotica, who immediately moved in on Beardsley, setting up the rival Savoy *magazine with him and commissioning new versions of Pope's* The Rape of the Lock *and Aristophanes'* Lysistrata, *which Aubrey managed to complete despite an exhausting bout of tuberculosis in 1896. The former work moved the previously sceptical James Abbott McNeill Whistler to tell Beardsley: 'Aubrey, I have made a very great mistake – you are a very great artist.' The latter's depictions of gigantic phalluses and female masturbation marked the apex of Beardsley's transgressive fantasies, of which he would later repent and beg Smithers 'by all that is holy' to destroy these works. Naturally, the pornographer declined this request and went on to publish more of Beardsley's work before and after his death.*

With his health in steep decline, Aubrey moved to the French Riviera in the spring of 1897, where he died a year later. Mabel would outlive her brother by eighteen years, succumbing to cancer at the age of forty-four, a grief-stricken Yeats at her bedside. She lives on in his verse 'Upon a Dying Lady', while her brother had his latest reawakening at Tate Britain in March 2020, just before the world also retired to its sickbed.

Gothmothers: The Brontës

As previously mentioned, before the coming of Andrew Eldritch, there were three sisters who first claimed Yorkshire as Goth's Own County. Charlotte, Emily and Anne Brontë were born in Thornton, near Bradford, in 1816, 1818 and 1820 respectively. Together with their brother Branwell (b. 1817), they moved to the hilltop town of Haworth when Charlotte was five as their father, the Reverend Patrick Brontë, was appointed parish priest. The Parsonage sat on the very edge of the surrounding, dramatic moorland, firing the imaginations of the children, who created their own secret worlds there.

Angria and Gondal were the names they gave to their Lypton Villages and from whence their stories grew: heavily populated realms with intricate histories that they would record and sew into tiny books in script that looked like it had been taken down by fairy hand. Like Aubrey and Mabel Beardsley, they created and performed plays and read voraciously from their father's well-stocked library, newspapers and periodicals – everything they could lay hands on.

Death was never far from them either. Their mother Maria, who had lost her first two daughters, Maria and Elizabeth, in infancy, died herself in 1821. Thereafter the children were brought up by their maternal aunt, Elizabeth Branwell, and a maid, Tabitha Aykroyd – 'Tabby' – who taught them all the local folklore, delivered in authentic dialect; tales eagerly soaked up by Emily in particular.

The townsfolk around them toiled in the textile industry, typically either farming a few acres, combined with hearthside wool combing or hand-loom weaving. The new, water-powered mills that had begun to appear along the River Worth from 1790 signalled the end of such cottage industry and the start of mechanised factory production. The average life expectancy among workers was just twenty-four.

The sisters' prospects were slightly less daunting, but still a far cry from the lifestyles enjoyed by the wealthy landowners or newly moneyed industrialists, with whom their father envisoned a more fruitful future for his daughters. Charlotte trained as a teacher, which she cursed as 'wretched bondage', quitting her post after three days. She spent two months working as a governess, the 'wearisome duties' of which she hated still more. Casting around for other options, she persuaded Aunt Elizabeth to pay for her and her sisters to study in Brussels, so they could improve their French and open their own school. There, she fell disastrously in love with her married tutor, Constantin Heger, who recognised her talent – offering her a dizzying glimpse of being treated as an intellectual equal – but did not reciprocate her affections. Returning to the Parsonage in 1843, she determined to write her way out of heartbreak.

Emily, who lasted only months in Brussels, had long returned to Haworth by then, settling in as housekeeper after the death of Aunt Elizabeth, a position that suited her just fine. The most enigmatic sister, she preferred the company of Tabby and the blustery surrounds of the moors – both the raw materials for her ultimate Gothic fiction, Wuthering Heights *(1847). Anne, who suffered the worst health and had the least in the way of formal training, also endured the travails of governessing with a heavy heart. Yet the oldest and youngest sisters' forays into the worlds of thankless semi-servitude would provide the blazing heart of their fictions.*

A proto-Svengali, Charlotte persuaded her sisters to self-publish a book of verse, entitled simply Poems, *under the male pseudonyms Currer, Ellis and Acton Bell in 1846. Though a commercial disaster – selling all of two copies – it cast the spell of publicity and by the end of the next year, all three sisters would have novels published under these names. Charlotte's* Jane Eyre *was an immediate and resounding success. 'Currer Bell' had spoken through her titular literary governess to a world of women stuck in the same predicament and cleft between the classes, whose mores she brilliantly observed. Following the publication of* Shirley *in 1849, Charlotte was able to come out under her own name and enjoy some celebrity in literary circles, going on to further success with the fictionalisation of her formative experiences in Belgium with* Villette *(1853).*

Emily used her own formidable observational powers to electrify her saga of wealthy and impetuous Catherine Earnshaw and her changeling adopted brother-turned-demonic-lover-spurned, Heathcliff, by relating their star-crossed story via lowly servant, Nelly Dean – who may be neither as dull nor reliable as she seems. Wuthering Heights *got a worthily dramatic new lease of life 131 years later, when Kate Bush, who shares Emily's 30 July birthday, became the first woman to top the British charts with a song she had written herself, at the age of eighteen. Emily, who never revealed Ellis Bell's true identity in her lifetime, died from tuberculosis at the age of thirty, a year after her book's publication. Not that anyone suspected this wildly amoral tale could possibly have been written by a woman, let alone a vicar's daughter, when, as G. K. Chesterton once put it, 'it could have been written by an eagle.'*

Anne's two novels, Agnes Grey *(1847) and* The Tenant of Wildfell Hall *(1848), also detail the lives of women trapped, the former as a governess, the latter as a mysterious woman fleeing her marriage to a Byronic debauch – which, by then, her brother Branwell was closely resembling. In September 1848, he succumbed to tuberculosis aged thirty-one, followed three months later by Emily. Anne herself was diagnosed with the disease a fortnight later and died in Scarborough on 28 May 1849, having fulfilled her last wish to see the sea one more time.*

Charlotte, who married her father's curate, Arthur Bell Nicholls, in 1854, died in the early stages of pregnancy on 31 March the next year. The sisters' father cooperated with Elizabeth Gaskell in her Life of Charlotte Brontë, *published in 1857, which sealed the image of the tragic yet heroic sisters that has since spawned an industry as fevered as any religious cult. Poor Patrick stayed on in the Parsonage, his wife and six children tapping on the other side of life's window, until his death in 1861 at the age of eighty-four.*

EPILOGUE

The Black Mass

The Witch in Winter: The last days of Margaret Thatcher and the afterlife of Goth

Duc de Richleau: Time itself has been reversed for us. Tanith's death, Peggy's abduction, the ride to Chilbury; the ritual in the cellar . . . all these things happened. But now they have not happened. We're back. We are all safe again.
Simon Aron: And is Mocata also safe?
Duc de Richleau: You will also remember what I said to you about the Angel of Death once being summoned . . .
Simon Aron: Cannot return empty-handed!

– *The Devil Rides Out* (Directed Terence Fisher), first released 20 July 1968

On 3 January 1988, Margaret Thatcher became the longest-serving PM of the twentieth century, having been in office for eight years and 244 days. Since the release of 'Hong King Garden', Siouxsie's reign as the Ice Queen already had a 257-day start on the PM's and would continue for a good while yet. While Thatcher had divided the nation, the kids who had first been united by punk continued to form new alliances from within their musical parallel universe. Some of these proved yet more fruitful, others the denouement of mutually assured destruction.

After Robert Smith left the Banshees for the last time in 1984, they returned to their own beginnings. With new guitarist John Valentine Carruthers (b. 1958 in Wortley, West Yorkshire) – formerly of Clock DVA – and Martin McCarrick, Billy McGee, Gini Ball and Anne Stephenson returning as the Chandos Players, they made sumptuous reworkings of 'Overground' from *The Scream*, 'Placebo Effect' from *Join Hands* and B-sides 'Voices' ('Hong Kong Garden') and 'Red Over White' ('Israel') as *The Thorn* EP. Carruthers stayed on for 1986's full-length *Tinderbox*, released as the Banshees reached their first decade; and the 1987 covers album *Through the Looking Glass*, which tipped its feather boa to Julie Driscoll ('This Wheel's on Fire'), Iggy Pop ('The Passenger'), Kraftwerk ('Hall of Mirrors') and the Doors ('You're Lost Little Girl') among other inventive reworks.

By 1988, there had been another reshuffle – in came Martin McCarrick on a permanent basis, out went Carruthers, to be replaced by Specimen's Jon Klein – and a dramatic change of image. Sick of looking out over an audience of spiky-haired clones, Siouxsie had her raven locks chopped into a sleek, Louise Brooks-style bob. With McCarrick's seadog concertina to the fore, their 'Peepshow' single wore a complementary, twisted jazz vibe, Sioux's refrain 'Golly jeepers, where'd you get those peepers?', a glam echo of Johnny Mercer's 1938 'Jeepers Creepers'.

Sioux and Budgie continued their Creatures' explorations further afield on 1989's *Boomerang*, recorded with Mike Hedges in rural Andalusia and picking up on Iberian and flamenco sounds, blues, jazz and, on 'Pity', Jamaican steel drums. Jeff Buckley covered its 'Killing Time' frequently in his live sets, including the 1993 London Astoria show that marked the release of *Grace*. The influence of the Banshees on an upcoming generation of American artists – the new G-word – was underlined by the band's inclusion on the first Lollapallooza, the travelling alternative festival masterminded by Jane's Addiction's Perry Farrell, in 1991, alongside Ice T, the Butthole Surfers and Nine Inch Nails.

After the thorough exorcism of *The Top*, Robert Smith took full command of a revitalised Cure in 1985. Simon Gallup returned on bass, Porl Thompson came in on guitars and keyboards, while Boris Williams (b. 24 April 1957, in Versailles) replaced Andy Anderson on drums. Sacked after a fracas with a security guard on an American tour in 1984, Anderson was thereafter picked up by a passing Jeffrey Lee Pierce to put down the beats on his solo album, 1985's *Wildweed.*

Smith crafted the lavish pop hooks of *The Head on the Door*, co-produced with Dave Allen and spearheaded by the 'In Between Days' single, which succeeded in breaking the band in America. The subsequent *Kiss Me, Kiss Me, Kiss Me* (1987) and *Disintegration* (1989), together with the singles compilations *Standing on the Sea* (1986) that marked the Cure's first decade and remixed cuts *Mixed Up* (1990), saw the Crawley Creepshow conquer all by the end of the decade. Cure songs are now the very fabric of alienated teenage life, webbed into the soundtrack of countless movies, television shows and computer games,[1] with Smith's ever more effusive tarantula locks, crumpled black suits and big white trainers their global fashion template.

Grunge pioneers Dinosaur Jr, whose lead singer J. Mascis cultivated a similar reclusive eccentric persona to Smith's, perhaps offered the greatest tribute to the Cure with their 'Just Like Heaven' cover of 1989, released by Blast First. At the time he wrote the song, Robert told his bandmates: 'I'll never write something as good as this again.' To date, and following many subsequent line-up reshuffles – including the acrimonious departure of Lol Tolhurst in 1989 – the Cure have sold over 30 million albums worldwide.

Andy Anderson, who enjoyed a long and varied subsequent career – working with such notables as Peter Gabriel, Edwyn Collins, Zeke Manyika, Youth and Mike Oldfield – died from cancer on 26 February 2019, at the age of sixty-eight.

Portrait of the Artist in Hell

Kid Congo's arrival in the Bad Seeds in 1986 coincided with the fruition of Nick Cave's immersion in Americana and his involvement in *Ghosts . . . Of the Civil Dead. Tender Prey*, recorded between

London and Berlin with Flood and Tony Cohen and released in June 1988, crystallised all those obsessions into the seven-minute fever of 'The Mercy Seat', Cave's Biblical electric chair epic. Here, we join a felon very much like Preacher Powell as he is strapped into the death chamber, protesting his innocence until the very last line. In fatherly old lag sympathy, Johnny Cash recorded it on his *American III: Solitary Man* album of 2003.

Cave's onscreen portrayal of psychotic inmate Maynard, in the screenplay he co-scripted of John Hillcoat's film about life and death in the Big House, followed in December 1988. Meanwhile, the bundle of scribblings the singer had been carrying around was finally published as *And the Ass Saw the Angel* in 1989, by Black Spring Press in the UK and the Murdoch-owned HarperCollins in the States.

Nick did not exactly enjoy the fruits of these labours at the time, though. As chronicled in LP *Bad Seed*, his chaotic private life was on a downwards spiral that would land him in rehab and precipitate his retreat from Berlin and relocation to São Paulo in 1990. His former Birthday Party cohort Rowland S. Howard also threw in the tourniquet, moving back to Melbourne in 1995, where the 'gentleman junky', as brother Harry described him, managed to get clean. Epic Soundtracks stayed in London and was found dead at his flat on 6 November 1997, aged only thirty-eight. An autopsy never established the cause of his death.

Rowland's songwriting gifts returned to him in Melbourne, where he forged his masterpiece, *Teenage Snuff Film* (Cooking Vinyl, 1999), an album that Lee Hazlewood would have been proud of. Mick Harvey came back into orbit, contributing drums, organ and rhythm guitar to the album's blissful mix of '60s girl group sizzle and way-out western style. 'He really believed in that album,' Harry Howard reflected, 'that it was the best thing he'd ever done.'[2]

Ten more years passed before Rowland's *Pop Crimes* album, recorded with Mick Harvey and J. P. Shilo, by which time a new generation of bands – Savages and the Yeah Yeah Yeahs – had got hip to Howard. The latter invited him to tour with them in

Australia, but by then he was already in the advanced stages of liver cancer. Like John McGeoch, his only rival for the most inventive, expressive and influential guitar sound of the '80s, the Shelley of the Melbourne suburbs Rowland S. Howard left the stage far too early, on 30 December 2009, at the age of fifty. His epitaph already written in song: 'These immortal souls of ours, scratching the window pane/Leave a ghost blood calling card.'[3]

Before rejoining the Bad Seeds for 1990's *The Good Son* – his last release with them to date – Kid Congo was called back to the Gun Club one last time, to bear witness and testimony to the final resurrection of Jeffrey Lee Pierce.

In 1986, *Sounds*' Jack Barron caught up with the singer on the road in Rotterdam with the Jeffrey Lee Pierce Quartet – himself, girlfriend Romi Mori and more ex-Clock DVA personnel, bassist Dean Dennis and drummer Nick Sanderson. They had just released the *Flamingo* mini-album of outtakes from *Wildweed* (1985, both Statik) and the self-explanatory *Love & Desperation* EP. Jeffrey Lee's personality appeared to be fracturing, just as his music was going off at stark tangents – into free jazz improvs ignited by his explorations of Albert Ayler and Archie Shepp, which he knew he could never reconcile with his blues impulses, either to himself or his audience. He was trying not to drink because he knew how it would end – he explained the song 'Portrait of the Artist in Hell' as: 'An eternal tour with no days off and an excruciating Jack Daniel's hangover every day. Always sitting with that hangover alone at breakfast and looking out of a window.'[4]

Pierce went on to demonstrate the reality of his predicament to the journalist, who witnessed the effects that the whisky he could not, finally, resist had on Jeffrey Lee. Hours later: 'The Jekyll in him is possessed by the monster Hyde. Full moon, bottle in hand, and flat on his face.'[5] A portrait of the artist in the grip of depression and self-medication doesn't get much bleaker than this.

However, while he had still been sober, Jeffrey Lee told Barron of his plans to break out of the Ninth Ring. He had some new songs written – 'drifting off more into dreamsville' territory – which he planned to record with the Cocteau Twins' Robin Guthrie. 'I want to spend a long time doing it, filling it with idiosyncrasies and being meticulous over details. With the meeting of Robin's frame of mind and my own, at the very least it'll be interesting . . . I've chosen to record with Robin because the Cocteaus' songs are always in dreamsville.'

For this, he needed his Sundance Kid back in the saddle beside him. Powers duly returned to record *Mother Juno*, besides Romi on bass and Sanderson on drums, with Blixa Bargeld making a stylish guest incursion, playing slide guitar on 'Yellow Eyes', as they recorded the songs over six days at Hansa. The album was mixed in London by Guthrie, who – despite all possible alternate outcomes of these two great minds getting together – wove gossamer-winged magic over these lean and hungry songs, matching Pierce's every expectation. It was released in October 1987 on Red Rhino, a triumphant return to form; openers 'Bill Bailey' and 'Thunderhead' as magnificent in their rawboned swagger as 'The Breaking Hands' was glisteningly delicate. 'Roll out the blue velvet, try not to bleed too much on the carpet,' wrote *Sounds*' Robin Gibson, 'comeback of the year.'

But it proved only a short parole for Jeffrey Lee, who could never evade the demands of his alcoholic day-release tag. Cirrhosis of the liver, with which he was first diagnosed five years earlier, came back on the eve of his thirtieth birthday. Without his liquid courage, the sober Pierce's confidence suffered. Though Kid would intermittently return to play with his old companion, 1990's *Pastoral Hide & Seek* and 1993's *Lucky Jim* (both Fire) were the simmering embers of *Mother Juno*'s flames. Medicine prescribed for a throat condition while recording the former reawoke other dark habits and Jeffrey Lee went out hunting heroin again. At which point Romi called time on their relationship, leaving with Nick Sanderson. She would remain with the drummer – having a daughter together and forming a new band, Free Heat, with Jim Reid and Ben Lurie of the Jesus and Mary Chain – until his death from lung cancer in June 2008. By May 1990, previous Gun Club bass player Rob Ritter had already cooked up his own accidental last fix. After serving the sentence for armed robbery pre-empted his sacking from the Cult, Nigel Preston would also briefly occupy the Gun Club's drum stool, a tenure curtailed by his own fatal overdose in 1992.

Pierce attempted to bring his greatest disciple, Mark Lanegan, in to harmonise with him on *Lucky Jim*'s title track, recorded at Banana Studios, Haarlam, the Netherlands, in February 1993. But the then Screaming Trees' lead singer – a frequent visitor to Jeffrey Lee's Holland Park crashpad in London – found that his vocals were shot from recently performing with his own band. In his *Sing Backwards and Weep* memoir (Orion, 2020), Lanegan recorded his utter regret that he never ended up on vinyl with his hero: 'It was simply one of the greatest songs he'd ever written and the recording was pristine, the words completely evocative. As I realised the missed opportunity, I was crushed.'

Between tours, Jeffrey Lee lingered in Holland Park, recording new material with fellow west Londoner, Tony Chmelik – aka Cypress Grove, the multi-instrumentalist and production wizard – which became their *Ramblin' Jeffrey Lee & Cypress Grove with Willie Love* album (New Rose, 1992).[6] The Gun Club played their final British show at the Mean Fiddler, Harlesden, on 6 May 1993 and the last time Jeffrey Lee appeared on a London stage was at the Bad Seeds' Shepherd's Bush Empire show on 20 May 1994.

In November 1994, Pierce was arrested in a pub near his London flat, after trying to settle an argument by using a samurai sword. Deported thereafter, he returned to his mother's house in LA. There, he began working on a memoir, *Go Tell It to the Mountain*, for Henry Rollins' 2.13.61 publishing house and drifted between periods of hopeful creativity – playing sets at the Viper Room with Steve Jones and Blondie's Clem Burke – and alcoholic self-destruction. While staying at his father's house in Salt Lake City on 25 March 1996, he collapsed into a coma. The hospital diagnosed a blood clot to the brain, a complication caused by cirrhosis. Jeffrey Lee was thirty-seven. He had lasted a whole eight years longer than Hank Williams did, plying his trade on the Lost Highway. Ten years earlier, he had said to Jack Barron: 'When the body is finished then good, it's used up like an old car. Into the breakers' yard with it and on to the next one.'

Unaware, Kid Congo had been trying to get a new Gun Club together, with bassist Peter Aaron and drummer Bob Bert of New Yorkers Chrome Cranks. He rang Jeffrey Lee's mother and, as he recalled to *Mojo*'s Sylvie Simmons: 'She said, "Oh, you've heard?" I said, No, but I knew what was coming, even though I couldn't believe he would die. After all he had lived through before, I thought he would last forever. He was my brother and I'd lost him.'[7]

All at Sea Again

There would be other premature burials. After the triumph of *Ocean Rain*, a hurricane came down on Echo and the Bunnymen when their manager, Bill Drummond, departed them for Mu Mu Land in 1984. For a year the band treaded water, with only the lacklustre 'Bring on the Dancing Horses' single and a compilation album, *Songs to Learn and Sing*, to offer in 1985. Restless drummer Pete de Freitas was the first to jump ship. He headed to New Orleans with a group of friends and hangers-on he dubbed 'The Sex Gods' and got involved in some seriously bad gris-gris.

The band struggled on without him, hiring a string of drummers and producers, none of whom could open the old spell book for them. Cleaned up and with a new wife and baby to anchor him, de Freitas returned to the fold in 1987 – but, distrustful of his stability, the others only let him back in as a hired hand. New manager Duran Duran's handler Mick Hancock could not connect his commercial purpose to the Bunnymen's anarchic ways. Without Drummond to keep them on one leyline, they recorded their next, eponymous album all over the place – Conny's in Cologne, ICP in Brussels, the Workhouse in London and Amazon in Liverpool – first with Gil Norton, then with Laurie Latham, whose work with the Stranglers on their 'Skin Deep' single Mac had admired.

There were a few more high points to come. After meeting him while recording a cover of the Doors' 'People are Strange' for stylish vampire flick *The Lost Boys* (Joel Schumacher, 1987), the Bunnymen enticed an admiring Ray Manzarek to play keyboards on the stand-out single 'Bedbugs and Ballyhoo'. But their fifth album reflected both their dislocation from each other and disenchantment with their label's impatience for them to finally attain U2's sales figures.

After a particularly unfestive Christmas drink in 1987, McCulloch got his raincoat. Rather than splitting the band, Will Sergeant and Les Pattison replaced him with Noel Burke, formerly of Liverpool band St Vitus Dance. 'It felt like I was cuckolded or something,' Mac surmised. 'It was like suicide.'[8]

If the Bunnymen's fortunes were mixed, then at least they were not so cursed as their beloved Liverpool FC, whose professional achievements with new manager, former star striker Kenny Dalglish, were eclipsed by the horrors vested on them in the remainder of the decade. An hour before the European Cup final on 29 May 1985, when the Reds were due to take on Juventus at the Heysel Stadium in Brussels, a stand collapsed, killing thirty-nine and injuring 600, mainly fans of the Italian team. The disaster – which came only eighteen days after the Bradford stand fire – was blamed on rampaging Liverpool supporters, who had cornered their rival fans up against a concrete wall that subsequently collapsed. UEFA then banned all other British clubs from further fixtures until the 1990/91 season, Liverpool's exclusion lasting a further year. A horrified John Peel was eyewitness to the carnage. As the shaken DJ reflected to his listeners on 3 June 1985: 'As a boy, I never understood why my dad wouldn't tell us about his experiences in north Africa and Italy during the war . . . and now I do.'[9]

Worse was to follow, four years later. The Hillsborough disaster of 15 April 1989 was English football's darkest hour. Ninety-seven Liverpool supporters were crushed to death after being funnelled through tunnels into overcrowded enclosed 'pens' before an FA Cup semi-final between Liverpool and Nottingham Forest at Sheffield Wednesday's home ground. South Yorkshire Police Chief Superintendent David Duckenfield – appointed to his post by Peter Wright, the Chief Constable who had overseen operations at

Orgreave – initially told the FA that Liverpool fans were to blame. He said they had pushed their way through a large exit gate that he had, in fact, ordered to be opened – but the truth of that would take twenty-seven years to come out.[10]

In the immediate aftermath, Liverpool fans were vilified on the front cover of *The Sun*. Under the headline 'The Truth', Kelvin MacKenzie told his readers that LFC supporters had picked the pockets of the dead, urinated on police and beaten up one officer, who was attempting to resuscitate a dying victim. Yet when this was finally proved to be A Lie, neither *The Sun* nor *The Times* would deign to report the findings of the 2016 Hillsborough Report on their respective front covers.

Two months after Hillsborough, in 14 June 1989, Pete de Freitas was involved in a head-on collision on the A51 road in Longdon Green, Staffordshire, riding his motorcycle to the Bunnymen's first rehearsal with Noel Burke. The 27-year-old was killed instantly.

The band carried on, finding a replacement in Elizabeth Fraser's partner, Damon Reece. McCulloch released a solo album, *Candleland* (Sire), in 1990, a meditation on the deaths of both de Freitas and his beloved father. He was joined on the title track by Fraser, singing his lyric: 'Get your handful of remembrance/For you to sprinkle through your life . . .'

These Days Are Gone

Another charismatic frontman who burned his brightest in 1984 was Kirk Brandon. Back then the singer had worked up a new collection of songs and a new alignment of musicians to render his most cinematic vision yet, named after Marlon Brando's 1961 directorial debut, *One-Eyed Jacks* (Burning Rome, 1984). Brandon continued to needle at the same subjects that occupied Justin Sullivan on 1985's similarly epic *World Service* (Burning Rome). 'Harlan County' described an American mining dispute that was settled by force. 'The man who instigated it,' Brandon told *Melody Maker*'s Martin Aston, 'I believe I'm right in saying, was Ian

MacGregor, who we've all come to know and love . . .'[11] Taken up by the now globe-straddling U2 to play stadium supports, SoD's time appeared to have come.

In 1987 – right after the single 'Never Take Me Alive' from their fourth album *Outland* had launched them into the upper echelons of the charts – a legion of fans waited for Spear of Destiny to appear at Reading Festival. But instead, Kirk was 'in hospital, screaming my head off.' He had contracted reactive arthritis, which caused his joints and muscles to swell to twice their size and kept him bedbound for almost a year. After which, SoD never managed to pick up their lost momentum.

Worse fortune still awaited Brandon. When Boy George published his memoir *Take It Like a Man* (Sidgwick & Jackson) in July 1995, he wrote of the intimate relationship he'd had with Kirk, back in those clubbing/squatting days of the early '80s, when the Theatre of Hate singer had first penned his tortured lyrics to 'Original Sin'. George followed his revelations with a song called 'Unfinished Business' on his *Cheapness and Beauty* album of the same year (Virgin), which appeared to refer to Brandon's recent marriage to his Danish wife, Christina.

'Hey, don't you know that secrets kill?' sang George.

In response, Brandon sued for malicious falsehood, claiming that his career had been damaged. Receiving legal aid – he had been declared bankrupt the year before – he represented himself in court. It was not the wisest of moves.

The Brandon of 1984 had good reason to want to keep his private life to himself – as we have seen, homosexuals throughout the '80s were brutally discriminated and even legislated against. His: 'I'm not gay' *Tube* statement may well have been heartfelt – as George had written in the pertinent passages, Kirk 'denied being gay, preferring to think of me as a girl. I tried to live up to the role, telling everyone I was having a sex change.' Brandon's three-word denial certainly illuminated the nasty strain of homophobia implicit in Amrik Rai's *NME* interrogation of him. You can't help who you fall in love with. Presiding at the 1997 trial, Justice Douglas Brown surmised: 'Mr Brandon is a decent man,' who had convinced him that he was, 'heterosexual, or, in the current phrase, straight.'[12]

But the past is a foreign country – thanks to the efforts of such brave souls as the Terrence Higgins Trust, OutRage!, ACT-UP, Stonewall, Diamanda Galás, Jimmy Somerville and Boy George in changing public attitudes. Though Section 28 of the Local Government Act 1988 would not be repealed until 18 November 2003, eleven years on from *The Tube*, his actions are more difficult to defend.

The seven-day hearing at the High Court in London generated worse and more glaring tabloid headlines for Brandon than anything ever published in *NME*, as George revealed far more under cross-questioning than he had in the book. The plaintiff did not convince the judge he had 'been truthful about his physical relationship with Mr O'Dowd'. By contrast, Boy George came across as 'a truthful' and 'impressive witness'. Brandon lost the action and was ordered to pay £250,000 in costs. The singer who had always put himself on the side of the oppressed now appeared intolerant and hateful – as well as foolish. As that earlier libel loser Oscar Wilde could have advised Kirk: 'The truth is rarely pure and never simple.'

Such Power Is Dangerous

Mrs Thatcher herself was also unheeding of those 1987 portents of tempest and financial devastation and would not be halted in her tracks by the 8 November 1987 Remembrance Day IRA bombing of Enniskillen, County Fermanagh, which killed twelve and injured sixty-eight; nor the fire in London's King's Cross Station that followed ten days later, killing thirteen. She also survived her junior health minister Edwina Currie's December 1988 attempts to convince the public that their breakfast eggs were all infected with salmonella and the furore of protests by Bradford Muslims over the publication of Salman Rushdie's *The Satanic Verses* that led to the leader of the Islamic Republic of Iran, Ayatollah Khomeini, placing a fatwa on the author on Valentine's Day, 1989. Britain broke off diplomatic relations with Iran shortly after and the repercussions go on to this day – at time of writing, Rushdie had recovered from an attack on his life at Chautauqua Institution in New York State on 12 August 2022 that left him without the sight in his right eye and the use of his left hand; while his publisher, Vintage, ordered a reprint of *The Satanic Verses* to keep up with the public's demand to re-read it.

In fact, the most surprising thing about the end of Thatcher's term in office was that it didn't finish in the total nuclear annihilation of the planet, as most of us '80s kids feared it would. Instead, the Thatcher–Reagan affair brought about Perestroika, the fall of the Berlin Wall and the end – for the time being – of the Cold War. All of which was instigated by the PM herself, when she made her move on the architect of Soviet reform, Third Man Mikhail Gorbachev, in December 1984, three months before he became President of the USSR. She came back purring: 'I like Mr Gorbachev, we can do business together.'

In his 2022 BBC documentary series, *Thatcher & Reagan: A Very Special Relationship*,[13] Thatcher biographer Charles Moore was told by aides to the president that, after surviving his assassination attempt in 1981, Reagan divined he had been saved for a purpose. And that purpose, as Gil Scott-Heron had said all along, was to get back in the saddle, ride out and save the planet. So perhaps the woman described by France's President Mitterrand as having 'the eyes of Stalin and the mouth of Marilyn Monroe'[14] was uniquely able to act as a bridge between the two superpowers. As Thatcher's foreign policy adviser Sir Percy Cradock put it, she was 'an agent of influence in both directions', smoothing misunderstandings between the two men – who both admired and, in Reagan's case, adored her – and advisors on both sides.[15] Could a male politician in her position have achieved such a skilled level of diplomacy? Perhaps Thatcher's greater purpose was to save us from the apocalyptic nightmare that might have been, and if so, we should at least thank her for that.

But Mrs Thatcher also proved the agent of her own undoing, when she attempted to instigate the Poll Tax, set out in a Green Paper of 1986 and the centrepiece of the Queen's Speech of 1987. Veiled as the Community Charge, it was advocated as a fairer way of collecting revenue for local services: a fixed tax, levelled at every adult resident of Britain – to be trialled in Scotland first – rather than the existing Rates system, paid by home-owners according to the size of their property. It was aimed at high-spending – i.e. Labour-controlled – councils, but it caused immediate problems for all, as local governments struggled to identify every person living in one household – student accommodation, any type of shared housing and those residents not on the electoral roll – a Kafka-esque burden of bureaucracy.

History could have tapped the PM on the shoulder at this point – and perhaps a Sir Humphrey did – to mention the results of previous attempts to impose a Poll Tax. The Peasant's Revolt of 1380, perhaps, or the more recent attempts of Charles I's 1641 Long Parliament and Charles II's Hearth Tax of 1662, at each end of the Civil War – which she certainly should have paid attention to. Because it wasn't just the Lefties and the low-paid who were outraged. Her own supporters were up in arms about the impending April 1990 imposition in England and Wales of the 'Tory Tax' – as former Defence and Environment Secretary Michael Heseltine called it.[16]

In November 1989, she faced a stalking horse challenge to her leadership by Sir Anthony Meyer, which she easily crushed. But Environment Secretary Chris Patten – tasked with the implementation of the tax – warned her in January 1990 that at least eighty-three rebels were mustering behind Heseltine. On 25 March, she consulted her recently appointed chancellor, John Major, about reviewing her policy.[17] But by then it was too late. Central London exploded on Saturday, 31 March 1990, when protestors who flocked to the Capital to demonstrate got a taste of what the miners at Orgreave and Peace Convoy at Stonehenge had experienced when mounted police charged on a group of around 1,500 demonstrators outside the Ministry of Defence in Whitehall, backed up by lines of further officers in riot gear; what stewards described as 'agent provocateurs' were also sent in to provoke Socialist Workers Party and Anarchist groups. They certainly succeeded in turning this rout into a fully fledged battle as the crowd turned on their attackers. One woman, who had attended the protest with her two daughters and become trapped in Trafalgar Square, described 'riot police hitting out indiscriminately with truncheons and trying to push those of us clinging to the railings into the path of police horses'. She admitted that: 'As the riot policeman lifted his truncheon to us, I kicked him in the goolies and he soon retreated.'[18]

It was one thing for this to happen in a field in South Yorkshire, rural Wiltshire or even Fortress Wapping, but this riot rapidly sprawled out of its containment zone in Whitehall and into the tourist areas of the West End and Knightsbridge beyond. Car showrooms were smashed and their contents destroyed; exclusive shops like Burberry, Mappin & Webb and the Scotch House looted. Over 400 protestors and bystanders were injured in the carnage, an almost equal tally this time to the 374 police casualties.[19]

The Poll Tax Bill became law the next day, Patten securing an extra £1.3 billion from the Treasury to try to keep householders' bills down. But it was the previously mild-mannered Sir Geoffrey Howe who would light the touch paper for Heseltine's imminent challenge. Incensed by the PM's blunt response to proposals for closer European integration at an EU Summit in Rome,[20] on 13 November he resigned as leader of the House and deputy prime minister. 'The time has come for others to consider their response to the tragic conflict of loyalties with which I have myself wrestled for so long,' he told Parliament. Heseltine – or 'Tarzan', as he was known on the ITV satirical puppet show *Spitting Image* – made his leadership challenge the next day.

Thatcher won the first Conservative leadership contest of 20 November, but under party rules, her fifty-vote majority was insufficient to avoid a second vote. Speaking at another European summit in Paris that night, she defiantly declared: 'I fight on,

I fight to win.' But upon her return home, her cabinet lined up to tell her that, as far as they were concerned, it was all over. On 22 November, she left Downing Street for the last time. Not with a bang, but a whimper.

The Danse Macabre

I heard the news as I arrived back in London from Leicester, having spent the day there interviewing Crazyhead for *Sounds*. Outriders of the 'Grebo' phenomena instigated by Zodiac Mindwarp, they had been signed to Food records by Dave Balfe's henchman and my fellow *Sounds* scribe Andy Ross (aka Hurt). As I descended an escalator in Euston Station to catch a tube to the office in Blackfriars, I saw ashen-faced City traders crying into their *Evening Standard*s. In wonder, I read headlines that announced Thatcher was stepping down. Could it be true? It seemed almost surreal that the nightmare could finally be over.

Sounds was incongruously housed in Ludgate House, beneath the offices of the *Daily Express*, whose proprietor, Lord Stevens of Ludgate, we referred to as 'Shaky'. Along with *Kerrang!*, *Record Mirror*, *Music Week* and *Select*, we belonged to Punch Publications, inky offspring of the now-defunct satirical Victorian journal, whose figurehead remained, in rather malign, bronze statue form, guarding our reception. As I stepped out of the lift and passed Mr Punch, I could hear the sounds of a party. On the other side of the office doors, tabletop dancing to 'Ding Dong the Witch is Dead', 'Bad Miss M', 'Stand Down Margaret' and 'Tramp the Dirt Down' with attendant cheering and clanking of bottles of ice-cold Sol reassured me – Thatcher was gone.

Things, it seemed, really could only get better. Two days later, I got to see my favourite band for the first time since the Albert Hall 'Festival of Remembrance' in 1985, when the Sisters of Mercy played a sold-out Wembley Arena. 'I'd like to thank everybody,' said Andrew Eldritch from the stage, knowing his audience contained former members of his band and many other cowboy-hat-wearing imitators, 'who's been keeping my seat warm.' It seemed to me then that the sole remaining original Sister, whose visions of 1983 had so unnervingly foretold the coming civil wars, must have planned this outcome all along.

Of course, things didn't stay this cheerful for long. John Major won his party's vote to succeed Margaret Thatcher and, the day after, brought back Michael Heseltine as environment secretary – his first job was to scrap the Poll Tax. Neil Kinnock did not win the 1992 general election that was supposedly his to take, thanks in no small measure to the ceaseless mockery and derision aimed at him by *The Sun*. With a picture of the Labour leader's head inside a lightblub, their 9 April 1992 headline ran: 'If Kinnock wins today will the last person to leave Britain please turn out the lights', followed two days after John Major's 21-seat majority with the crowingly illiterate: 'It was *The Sun* wot won it'.

Before she left office, Thatcher just had time to pass the Broadcasting Act of 1990, which relaxed the regulations on TV and radio stations sufficiently for Murdoch to merge his new Sky Satellite TV company with his only rival, the British Satellite Broadcasting company (BSB) to form BSkyB on 2 November. All subsequent British prime ministers – including successively more repellant Thatcherite homunculi Tony Blair, David Cameron and Boris Johnson – would show the same fealty to Murdoch and not even the 2011 Leveson Inquiry into phone hacking and police bribery at News International did anything to dent his dark power. The Thelemaic teachings of Aleister Crowley may have served Jaz Coleman and Jimmy Page well enough but if anyone in this story has truly lived up to Aiwass' commandment, as delivered through Crowley: 'Do what thou wilt shall be the whole of the Law,' then it has to be Rupert Murdoch.

Not Fade Away

This Aussie Mocata may still rule over us all, but so, too, does the resistance hold. The mortal remains of most of the bands in this book are still out there – touring, making records, writing books, bickering, splitting up and getting back together again. Some have achieved the garlands of fame and recognition that were their heart's desire, others may never get their due, but will continue nonetheless. They will likely as not swap partners in the dance yet to come: as we have seen, every key player, from Ladbroke Grove to Melbourne, from the Lower East Side to West Berlin, knows everybody else.

As was perhaps hinted at by 'Lucretia My Reflection' and its allusion to Lucrezia Borgia, femme fatale of the scheming, mediaeval Papal dynasty,[21] Patricia Morrison did not remain Eldritch's mirror image for long. She was abruptly dismissed, just before recording began on *Floodland*'s follow-up, *Vision Thing* (Merciful Release, October 1990).[22] The band I saw at Wembley featured Hamburg native Andreas Bruhn and Tim Bricheno, formerly of All About Eve, on guitars. Where Morrison should have stood was instead the incongruous form of top-hatted ex-Generation X/Sigue Sigue Sputnik bassist and would-be Malcolm McLaren, Tony James. But he didn't last long either. Webs of intrigue continue to spin around the Prince of Darkness, who returns to bless disciples with gigs every so often, but has not made a new record since *Vision Thing*. Meanwhile, after leaving Floodland, Morrison fetched up at Grimly Fiendish Towers, began playing with the Damned and became the second Mrs Vanian.

As Ace boss Roger Armstrong predicted, her contemporaries from the crypt that burst open in Chapter 4, Lux and Ivy, were not beaten by adversity. Free from their IRS chains, they released *A Date with Elvis* on Big Beat in 1986, saw the Thatcher era out with 1990's *Stay Sick* and stuck to their essential philosophy until there came an unthinkable parting of ways. At 4.30 a.m. on 4 February 2009, Lux Interior suffered an aortic dissection and rocketed into the great beyond at the age of sixty-two. There he would be reunited with best fiend Bryan Gregory, who suffered heart failure on 10 January 2001, at forty-nine, and be joined by beat master Nick Knox, who succumbed to cardiogenic shock on 15 June 2018, aged sixty. Ivy remains behind closed shutters at their Hollywood home, bereft of her soulmate and taking no visitors. Her beloved 1958 Gretsch 6120 lies silent in its case, awaiting the ultimate Cramps' reunion.[23]

Just as saddening was the news that Anita Lane, who had died so many times for Nick Cave's songs, had actually passed away on 21 April 2021 at the age of sixty-one. When she released her first solo EP, *Dirty Sings*, on Mute in 1988, Anita said that her aim was to 'glorify insecurity rather than be confident and successful.' With this statement, she eloquently summed up what lies at the heart of the music that has been celebrated within these pages.

Goth in the time of Thatcher was a form of resistance against stupidity and ignorance. It was, to use the word that Murdoch has attempted to make the dirtiest in our language, elitist. It feasted on high art, challenging literature, sublime cinema and intelligent discourse. But as we have seen, it was also a meritocracy. Those who created the best music of the '80s came from all backgrounds and many of them overcame all manner of abuse, poverty and neglect to climb through punk's portal and make their own opportunities, educating themselves where public policy and/or their own parents had failed them.

I would never have believed that the shy, reclusive eleven-year-old, hiding under her bedclothes with a torch and a Dennis Wheatley paperback in the middle of a field as Thatcher came to power would see out the end of her reign working for a music paper and living in Ladbroke Grove. Nor that I would get the opportunity to meet – and eventually, even work with – so many of those voices that had come through my radio to illuminate those long nights back then.

So if anyone picks on you for being different in any way, please use this book to hit them about the head with the facts and rest assured, you are in good company. Goth has been ridiculed and derided for decades as being miserable, morose and moronic – when in fact, it is anything but. It stands for all the essential forces of creativity, friendship and vision, not to mention humour – it's just that, until things get brighter, it'll still be mostly wearing black. Forty years on, I think it's time for the curse to be lifted and the words spoken in darkness to be heard in the light.

I am a Goth.

APPENDIX

Further Tales from the Crypt

Chapter 2

Midnight Movies

The Manchester into which Joy Division and Magazine were born can be seen in all its monochrome glory in Hammer's British noir classic *Hell Is a City* (Val Guest, 1960), starring 'Manly' Stanley Baker as hardboiled detective Inspector Harry Martineau. Its climactic scene takes placc on the roof of the Principal Hotel, today the host of the Louder Than Words festival of music and grit lit. Further glimpses of the area before the planners moved in can be found in Bryan Forbes' remarkable *The Whisperers*, filmed in Oldham in 1967, and Albert Finney's directorial debut *Charlie Bubbles*, which was made as the demolition of Victorian terraces began in earnest in 1968 and boasts a screenplay by Morrissey's muse, *A Taste of Honey* author Shelagh Delaney.

The scenario across southern Britain in the same era is caught in two films set in Bracknell, Berkshire, that made vivid use of their location to comment on the post-war societal shift. David Greene's *I Start Counting* (1970) maps the traumatising adolescent awakening of Jenny Agutter's Wynne Kinch as her family move from cottage to high-rise. Bond star Sean Connery optioned the rights to John Hopkins' stage play *This Story of Yours* and invited superlative

American director Sidney Lumet to turn it into his performance of a lifetime as conflicted copper Johnson in *The Offence* (1973), running amok across the concrete curves of a Brutalist landscape eerily enchanted by Barry Stoller's electronic score. It's one of Barry Adamson's favourites. And to catch a glimpse of the pre-Magazine Dave Formula in St Louis Union, treat yourself to *The Ghost Goes Gear*, a 1966 musical comedy ghost story directed by Hugh Gladwish, also starring the Spencer Davis Group and *Just a Minute* host Nicholas Parsons as their manager. Yes, really.

Essential classics that inspired this chapter's music also include *Psycho* (Alfred Hitchcock, 1960), *The Spy Who Came in from the Cold* (Martin Ritt, 1965), *Cry of the Banshee* (Gordon Hessler, 1970) and *Cabaret* (Bob Fosse, 1972).

Building a Gothic Library

No Gothic pile could be complete without its library. If you haven't already, line your shelves from this chapter's most influential and controversial reads:

Fyodor Dostoevsky's *Notes from Underground* (1864) – the first existentialist novel that taps the nerves of Russia's increasingly volatile political climate.

Oscar Wilde's *The Happy Prince* (1888) was the story that turned me into a Wilde addict at the age of six, when I first saw the 1974 TV animation with Christopher Plummer voicing the statue and Glynis Johns the swallow. Alongside an earlier adaptation, *The Selfish Giant* (1971), these twenty-five-minute introductions to Wilde's children's classics (collectively published as *The Happy Prince and Other Stories*) were made by Potterdown productions for Reader's Digest and are available to watch on YouTube. I can still cry my heart out to them today.

Joseph Conrad's *Heart of Darkness* (1899) not only inspired Joy Division's 'Colony' but also Francis Ford Coppola's *Apocalypse Now*.

Albert Camus *L'Étranger* (1942) is a novel of the absurd, clandestinely published during the Nazi occupation of France.

Ka-Tzetnik 135633's *House of Dolls* (1953) sees the horrors of the Holocaust rendered as pulp fiction.

Hubert Selby Jr's *Last Exit to Brooklyn* (1964) writes of drug gangs, teenage prostitutes and the secret lives of transgender people, decades before almost anyone else cared to write about them.

J. G. Ballard's *The Atrocity Exhibition* (1970) includes the immortal short story 'Why I Want to Fuck Ronald Reagan'. Perhaps Margaret Thatcher was a fan?

Chapter 3

Midnight Movies

For a taste of what Ladbroke Grove was like before it became Hugh Grant's *Notting Hill*, Horace Ové's *Pressure* (1976) was filmed in Killing Joke's neighbourhood at a time when it was far from a dream destination of bankers. Malcolm Leigh's 1970 documentary about Alex and Maxine Sanders, *Legend of the Witches*, has recently been rereleased on DVD/BluRay by BFI Flipside, accompanied by *Secret Rites*, a 1971 Mondo-style documentary by Derek Ford exploring witchcraft in Notting Hill.

Bela Lugosi's 1931 turn as *Dracula* was a pre-Hays Code rendering of Bram Stoker's story directed by Tod Browning, who would go on to explore the lost world of the American carny freakshow in his 1932 classic, *Freaks*.

Building a Gothic Library

To go with your Alex Sanders DVD, Robert Irwin's superb satirical novel *Satan Wants Me*, now back in print on Dedalus Press, gives a *Withnail and I*-style lowdown from someone who dabbled in all things occult in the Swinging Sixties.

You may have to have the wealth and taste of a Jaz or Jimmy Page to afford much of Aleister Crowley's back catalogue but his vastly entertaining 1922 *Diary of a Drug Fiend* is still relatively cheap to get hold of – at time of writing, available online for less than a fiver. To read more about Aleister's Adventures in Espionage, consult Richard B. Spence's *Secret Agent 666* (Feral House, 2008), Jake Arnott's *The House of Rumour* (Sceptre, 2013) and Richard C. McNeff's *Aleister Crowley MI5* (Mandrake, 2021), all highly entertaining imaginings of what he might have got up to.

The French novelist Joris-Karl Huysmans offers a further portal into the late Victorian Decadent milieu that Crowley inhabited. No Gothic library should be without his 1884 *À Rebours (Against Nature)*, a massive influence on Wilde's *Portrait of Dorian Gray*, or *Là Bas* (*Down There* or *The Damned*), in which protagonist Durtal (a thinly disguised Huysmans, by day a civil servant) is led to a Satanic Parisian sect via his studies into the life of Gilles de Rais. An edition with cover art by Aubrey Beardsley is currently available from Dedalus Press.

The World of Charles Addams is a wonderful collection of his cartoon strips collated from the *New Yorker* by publisher Alfred A. Knopf in 1991 and, at time of writing, still relatively easy to get hold of for a reasonable price. Morticia and her family also inspired the Gothic world of Edward Gorey, whose deadpan comic creations – especially *The Gashlycrumb Tinies* (1963, reprinted by Bloomsbury in 1998), an A to Z of unfortunate infants – are worth keeping a beady eye out for.

Chapter 4

Midnight Movies

Not having anything to watch was never a problem in the Cramps' house. 'We have seven thousand movies on video tape,' Lux estimated when I first interviewed him. 'I do like monster movies and I do like the alien invasion movies of the Fifties. My earliest memories are of horror movies and they have the sexiest girls. *The She-Creature* (Edward L. Cahn, 1956) is one of the best.' '*Fiend Without a Face* (Arthur Crabtree, 1958),' was Ivy's pick. 'Brains with spinal columns and they just fly on people's faces. *Braniac* (aka *El Barón del Terror*, Chano Ureuta, 1962) is a good monster. He's a very suave Spaniard in a tuxedo who turns into a weird monster who sucks people outta blood. But he's always wearing this tux with Spanish cuffs and cufflinks all the time.' '*I Was a Teenage Werewolf* (Gene Fowler Jr, 1957) is one of my favourite movies,' added Lux. 'He had big mental problems, like any teenager does.' Other films the Cramps cited over the years include *The Phantom of Soho* (Franz Josef Gottlieb, 1964), *The World's Greatest Sinner* (Timothy Carey, 1962), *Deranged* (Jeff Gillen/Alan Ormsby, 1974, based on the Wisconsin grave robber and serial killer, Ed Gein), *Love From a Stranger* (Rowland V. Lee, 1937), *Dr Jekyll and Mr Hyde* (Rouben Mamoulian, 1931), 'Godfather of Gore' Herschell Gordon Lewis's *Blood Feast* (1963) and *Two Thousand Maniacs!* (1964), as well as the films of Ray Dennis Steckler, particularly *The Thrill Killers* (1964). The Cramps themselves appear as a New York gang in Amos Poe's *The Foreigner* (1978) and provided the song 'The Surfin' Dead' for *Return of the Living Dead* (Dan O'Bannon, 1985).

Lydia Lunch made her first film, *Guerillere Talks*, when director Vivienne Dick approached her in the street in New York in 1978. The No Wave film scene was as fertile as its musical counterpart and she was soon appearing in other films by young directors: James Nares' *Rome '78* (1978), Beth B and Scott B's *Black Box* (1978), *The Offenders* (1980) and *Vortex* (1982) and three further by Dick: *She Had Her Gun All Ready* (1978), *Beauty Becomes the Beast* (1979) and *Like Dawn to Dust* (1983). Nick Zedd made the documentary *The Wild World of Lydia Lunch* with her in Ireland in 1983 and, back in New York, she made three key collaborations with Richard Kern: *The Right Side of My Brain*, *Submit to Me* (both 1985) and *Fingered* (1986). 'People tend to tag my films as pornography. I have to throw back the pornography of reality. I'm trying to understand and explain why once you've been battered into submission your whole entire life as a feminine entity, there comes a point where you feel nothing else other than that pain so you have to propagate it. Otherwise you turn that pain into someone else's pain.' Her most recent documentary, *The War Is Never Over* (2021), reunites her with director Beth B.

Building a Gothic Library

The world evoked by the Cramps and the Gun Club has much in common with the works of Harry Crews (1935–2012), who brings to mind Mae West's observation: 'A hard man is good to find.' The son of sharecroppers from Bacon County, Georgia, he was a great hulk of an ex-Marine, professional boxer and karate brown belt with a line from an ee cummings poem etched across his bicep: 'How do you like your blue-eyed boy, Mr Death'? His books stand as testament to America's ignored yet defiant underclass, who strive to forge a living from something better than straight life has to offer, from the freaks exhibited in travelling shows (*The Gypsy's Curse*, 1974) – Crews was once a carny barker – to women body builders (*Body*, 1990).

Harry's own upbringing – including the time he caught a disease that made his legs curl up backwards and was cured by the magic of a conjur woman, only to fall into a hog boiler and have all his skin flayed off – is recorded in his masterpiece, *Childhood: Biography of a Place* (1978, republished in the *Classic Crews* compendium, Gorse, 1993). Tom Jones was so enamoured of Crews' debut novel, *The Gospel Singer* (1968), about revival tent evangelism and lynching, that for years, he optioned it in the hope of playing the title role. Sean Penn also tried and failed to make Harry's New Orleans odyssey of sport and sexual fetishism *The Knockout Artist* (1988), but did get a startling cameo from Crews singing 'John Henry' in his directorial debut, *The Crossing Guard* (1995; you can also see Harry make another dramatic turn in Jim White's film *Searching for the Wrong-Eyed Jesus*, 2003). Lydia liked him so much, she formed a band named after him with Sonic Youth's Kim Gordon, releasing an album with the same title as his 1969 novel, *Naked in Garden Hills*, in 1989 on her Widowspeak label.

'I have never written about anything that I haven't been involved in personally,' Crews told me. 'Also, I have never written anything that isn't screaming out of me. If I had been born black in this country, I would be dead or I would be in jail.'

Chapter 5

Midnight Movies

Joanne Woodward won an Oscar for her depiction of Chris Costner Sizemore in *The Three Faces of Eve* (Nunally Johnson, 1957), making her the first woman to win the award for playing three different personalities inhabiting one body. Eve White is a timid, suburban housewife, plagued with headaches and blackouts. After seeing psychiatrist Dr Luther (Lee J. Cobb), a second personality emerges – the manipulative and self-centred Eve Black, the antithesis of her sister under the skin. Eve attempts to slough off her downtrodden domestic self, first by strangling her daughter Bonnie (Terry Ann Ross), but she is caught in the act by husband Ralph (David Wayne) and sent back to Dr Luther. Ralph is not convinced by her diagnosis and ends up divorcing his wife after Eve goes carousing with another man. But her psychiatrist doesn't give up on her, finding a third personality – Jane – who reunites the two Eves when hypnosis reveals the trauma that caused her psyche to fracture. No wonder Siouxsie found such food for thought in this scenario of suburban madness.

Despite being filmed in London, the opening of Tony Scott's *The Hunger* (1983) captures perfectly the sort of upwardly mobile Manhattan nightclub milieu of Warhol and 'All Tomorrow's Parties'. Following the magnetic opening scene with Bauhaus, vampire lovers Miriam (Catherine Deneuve) and John Blaylock (David Bowie) lure home a young couple and feast on their blood. The bodies are disposed of in the basement of their elegant townhouse, where they pose as music teachers. The rest of the film – in which Susan Sarandon's research gerontologist Dr Sarah Roberts first attempts to help John with the sudden onset of ageing that is his vampire's curse, then becomes Miriam's lover and eventually turns the tables on her – doesn't quite live up to its early promise. Although its themes could be read as a telling analogy of the music business Bowie had been striving to conquer for the past three decades – its dependence on the lifeblood of innocent young dreamers, the cynical manipulation involved in securing those resources and the ultimate terror of ageing. Also, Scott's elevation of visual style over coherent storytelling is a summation of the '80s as a whole. As such, it's still very much worth staying up late for.

Building a Gothic Library

The title of *A Kiss in the Dreamhouse* came from a documentary Steven Severin had seen late one night about a brothel in '40s Hollywood, where the girls were all made up – or had surgery – to resemble the film stars of the day. It's the same true story that James Ellroy (b. 4 March 1948) used as the basis of the third volume of his quartet of novels set in that era, 1990's *L.A. Confidential.* That's the one that became Curtis Hanson's classy 1997 movie, starring Kim Basinger as Lynn Bracken, the Veronica Lake of Pierce Patchett (David Strathairn)'s House of Dolls. This was one of those few remarkable movies that didn't mess with its source material, for what Ellroy created with those novels – channeling his own tumultuous past into the secret history of the City of Angels to create what he called 'the public nightmare of private policy' – changed the face of noir fiction. No longer did one man go down the mean streets in search of justice, now the entire city was involved in its cover-up.

Ellroy was born into Holly*weird.* His father was once Rita Hayworth's business manager. His mother was raped and murdered on a night out when he was ten years old, a case that was never solved. His earliest reading comprised Jack Webb's *The Badge*, a casebook of LA's most notorious unsolved crimes, written by the creator and star of the TV series of the same name, who was also the husband of torch singer Julie London. It was from those pages that baby James learned of the unsolved murder of Elizabeth Short, which called to the unanswered mystery of his mother's last hours. Taking the slangy, staccato style of Webb's oeuvre as his authorial voice, Ellroy time-travelled back to the vacant lot on South Norton Avenue, where Short's bisected, mutilated body was left on the morning of 15 January 1947. In writing a valediction for the bit part actress known as 'The Black Dahlia', this literary outsider sealed his own immortality.

The following films – *The Big Nowhere* (1988), *L.A. Confidential* (1990) and *White Jazz* (1992) – continued to fuse social history, unsolved murder and the hallucinogenic power of Ellroy's imagination, to reconstruct 1946–58 Los Angeles. Fictitious characters seamlessly intersect with real-life movie stars, moguls and mobsters as Ellroy divines the truth behind the tabloid headlines, lacing each story with hot leads from Webb's almanac. Taking a trip with these novels is the closest you can come to a moonlight drive in the back of Vampira's Packard.

Chapter 6

Midnight Movies

Hyde Park Picture House in Leeds was a formative influence on Soft Cell, as Dave Ball told the *Yorkshire Post*'s Duncan Seaman in October 2021: 'They'd show John Waters' Divine films and Russ Meyer and Kenneth Anger . . . Arthouse with trashy elements, which fitted us perfectly . . .'

Harris Glenn Milstead (1945–88) was a sixteen-year-old misfit who got beaten up so frequently by his Baltimore schoolmates for being both gay and overweight that he had to be driven home by police car. Unlikely salvation lurked at the end of his road in the form of his physical opposite, but subversive equal: John Waters (b. 22 April 1946), a skinny beatnik looking for a muse. Waters encouraged his neighbour to out his inner Queen, turning Milstead into the superstar Divine: 'John wanted a very large woman because he wanted the exact opposite of what normally would be beautiful.' Together, they pushed the boundaries of taste with stunning ingenuity. Beginning with the shorts *Roman Candles* (1966) and *Eat Your Make-up* (1968), they made their first feature-length statement of intent, *Mondo Trasho*, in 1969.

A succession of cult hits followed, Waters cunningly getting around the censors in their home city by hiring out churches in which to privately screen them: *Multiple Maniacs* (1970), in which Divine runs a travelling freakshow, *Pink Flamingos* (1972), where she legendarily eats freshly minted dog shit – a clear influence on Marc Almond's infamous early performance pieces with cat food – and *Female Trouble* (1974), a transatlantic hit that led to Divine becoming a London theatre star and the toast of the SEX shop crowd. *Polyester* followed in 1981 and, having scored a UK chart hit with the 'You Think You're a Man' single in 1984, Divine triumphantly crossed into mainstream with Waters' hit musical comedy *Hairspray* (1988, based on the teen rituals of their Baltimore teenage years), as Edna Turnblad, boldly beehived mother of hair-hopper heroine Tracey (Ricki Lake). 'His legacy was that he made all drag queens cool,' Waters told *Baltimore* magazine in 2015. 'He broke every rule. And now every drag queen that's successful today is cutting-edge.'

After *Faster, Pussycat! Kill! Kill!*, Russ Meyer's most crucial contribution to film history is the film he made with *Chicago Sun Times*' film critic Roger Ebert, *Beyond the Valley of the Dolls* (1970). Ostensibly a sequel to the 1967 *Valley of the Dolls*' adaptation of Jacqueline Susann's 1966 novel, starring Manson victim Sharon Tate, Meyer was hired by Richard Zanuck of 20th Century Fox. Not bothering to read the original book, he and Ebert came up with what Ebert called 'a satire of Hollywood conventions, genres, situations, dialogue, characters and success formulas, heavily overlaid with shocking violence' in three weeks flat. With deliberate allusions to the Manson murders, it featured homicidal transvestite record producer Ronnie 'Z-Man' Barzell (John LaZar), who was based on 'Wall of Sound' producer Phil Spector; and Muhammad Ali lookalike Randy Black (Blaxploitation star James Iglehart) causing havoc in a flower child community of musos and actors that funhouse mirrored the real Laurel Canyon. Needless to say, Susann was aghast and sued Fox, but died of cancer aged fifty-six before her case was settled for $2 million in 1975. Meyer and Ebert were hired by an impressed Malcolm McLaren to write the first treatment of

The Great Rock 'n' Roll Swindle, then called *Who Killed Bambi?* in 1977. But, though they did begin shooting at Bray Studios, the home of Hammer horror, the plug was pulled on the venture – according to John Tiberi, then working for the impresario's management company Glitterbest, by McLaren himself: 'Malcolm didn't think he was going to be able to control it enough,' he told me in 2016. 'He was really very fickle.'

Child movie star, author of definitive scandal directory *Hollywood Babylon* (1959), follower of the Thelemaic path and film-maker of stunningly beautiful odes to the male body, magick and motorcycles, Kenneth Anger (b. Kenneth Anglemyer, 3 February 1927) is the Wizard of Holly*weird*. His lushly colour-saturated *Inauguration of the Pleasure Dome* (1954), *Scorpio Rising* (1964) and *Kustom Kar Kommandos* (1965) introduced the idea of soundtrack as ironic commentary on the action, a major influence on Martin Scorsese, David Lynch and John Waters' subsequent use of music in movies. In 1966, he cast Bobby Beausoleil as lead in his ill-starred *Lucifer Rising*, just before the musician became involved with the Manson gang and was subsequently jailed for murder. In the London of 1967, Anger found new assistance, from first the Rolling Stones – who starred in his *Invocation of My Demon Brother* (1969) – and then Jimmy Page, who agreed to produce a soundtrack for *Lucifer Rising*. Despite their mutual interests – which included a trip to Boleskine House – Anger fell out with Page, dramatically threatening to curse him. He finally completed the film, which stars Marianne Faithfull and Donald Cammell, with the music composed by the incarcerated Beausoliel, in 1981.

Building a Gothic Library

Born in 1967 and brought up in Ossett, West Yorkshire, David Peace was a child at the time of the Yorkshire Ripper, who, fearing for his family's lives, attempted to run his own investigation from a secret HQ inside his dad's shed. This close observance of the local and national press reports planted the seeds of his eventual

Red Riding Quartet, four novels – *Nineteen Seventy-Four* (1999), *Nineteen Seventy-Seven* (2000), *Nineteen Eighty* (2001) and *Nineteen Eighty-Three* (2002, all Serpent's Tail) – of the crimes both investigated and committed by the West Yorkshire Police during those years. Influenced by noir heavyweights James Ellroy and Derek Raymond, all four books were soundtracked – and influenced by – the music he was listening to at the time: 'The Banshees, Joy Division, Bauhaus, the Birthday Party, Theatre of Hate, the Bunnymen, Southern Death Cult, the Cramps, the Gun Club and, of course, the Sisters. Especially *Nineteen Eighty-Three*, which was the year Goth broke, the great year.'

Through the potent currents captured by these artists, his own diligent research and hypnotic authorial voice, Peace was able to viscerally render back the Britain of the Thatcher years, making *Red Riding* the most significant and influential reworking of history as crime fiction of recent decades. It was made into a three-part TV series, *Red Riding*, by Channel 4 in 2009 – but nothing can recreate the potent dread of the film that spools through your head as you read these books.

And you know what to put on the turntable . . .

Chapter 7

Midnight Movies

Recreate Kirk Brandon's Electric Cinema nights with Martin Scorsese's 1976 masterpiece *Taxi Driver*, which will also give you a good idea of what No Wave New York really looked and felt like. Vietnam vet Travis Bickle, the titular yellow cab operator, cruises a night city of 'whores, skunk pussies, buggers, queens, fairies, dopers, junkies . . .' praying that 'Some day a real rain will come and wash all the scum off the streets.' There are many reasons you might want to watch this film twenty-seven times, including Paul Schrader's insightful script, written while in the grip of profound alienation himself (cf: his directorial debut, 1978's *Blue Collar*, with Richard Pryor and Harvey Keitel and set in the Motor City of Detroit); Bernard Herrmann's elegiac score (his last, written just before his death in December 1975); and Robert De Niro's towering performance as 'God's lonely man' Bickle, America's self-made nightmare, who turns out to be a hero after all.

Then saddle up with Sergio Leone's Spaghetti Westerns – a term coined by Spanish journalist Alfonso Sánchez to describe the low-budget movies made by the Italian director in the mid-'60s – although, just to confuse you, Leone shot his *Dollars* trilogy in Spain. These existentialist epics, *A Fistful of Dollars* (1964), *For a Few Dollars More* (1965) and *The Good, the Bad and the Ugly* (1966), made a star out of Clint Eastwood as the Man with No Name and saw the classically trained Ennio Morricone revolutionise the western score with his unorthodox instrumentation and Musique Concrète techniques. Then watch cinema's most compelling director-composer combo hit their peak of genius with the Hollywood-funded *Once Upon a Time in the West* (1968). Henry Fonda plays against type as blue-eyed killer Frank, stalked by black-clad Charles Bronson as 'Harmonica', a vengeful wraith almost as scary as Old Shuck, whose calling card is a plaintive harmonica dirge – all those who hear it are marked for death.

Though now more familiar through its recent, J. J. Abrams-produced HBO reimagining, author Michael Crichton's original *Westworld* (1973) was a sensational rendering of an interactive Old West-themed amusement park, where patrons paid to face-off against an android gunslinger, played with precision stony-faced cool by Yul Brynner. With a tenacity to match that of the Man with No Name, Crichton battled MGM execs, persuading them that Brynner's Gunslinger character should be based on the role he'd made famous in *The Magnificent Seven*, with an almost identical outfit. The spooky electronic score by Fred Karlin anticipates Soft Cell keyboardist/songwriter David Ball's later adventures in the Grid.

Building a Gothic Library

The book Crass gave the teenage Ian Astbury to study, *Black Elk Speaks* by Nebraska's poet laureate John G. Neihardt, was first published in 1932. One of its earliest champions was psychologist Carl Jung and its 1961 reprint found its way onto the bookshelves of the Beat Generation. It began as part of Neihardt's research into the Ghost Dance movement and took him to the Pine Ridge Reservation, where he met Oglala holy man Black Elk, who had participated in the ritual. At thirteen, Black Elk had fought in the Battle of Little Bighorn and he went on to survive the devastating 1890 Wounded Knee massacre. Through a translator, Flying Hawk, Neihardt recorded Black Elk's visions and prophecies. Although the book proved inspirational to its white/New Age audience, its authenticity has been questioned by Lakota people and academics. Its present edition – *Black Elk Speaks*, as told through John G Neihardt (Nebraska University Press) – seeks to address their concerns.

Dee Brown's epic *Bury My Heart at Wounded Knee: An Indian History of the American West* was first published in 1970, at the time of the Vietnam War and three years after the establishment of the American Indian Movement (AIM), which aimed to reunite the fracturing native Nations. The book details the nineteenth-century expansion of European settlers across the continent and how, from 1860 onwards, the land belonging to the tribes was seized and the native peoples displaced. The history is told through chapters detailing the stories of the Navajo Nation, Santee Dakota, Hunkpapa Lacota, Oglala Lakota, Cheyenne and Apache peoples, drawing comparisons with the atrocities committed at Wounded Knee with the 1968 Mai Lai massacre of unarmed women and children during the Vietnam War – perhaps Astbury and Duffy were doing the same with their otherwise baffling Death Cult stage outfits. It was adapted by HBO as a made-for-TV film in 2007.

Brandon took the tile of his first SoD album, *The Grapes of Wrath*, from John Steinbeck's Pulitzer-, National Book Award- and ultimately Nobel Prize-winning 1939 novel about the Dust Bowl. It tells the story of the Joads, a dirt-poor family of Oklahoma sharecroppers driven off the land they worked by the cumulative effects of the Great Depression, and their journey towards a new life in California – a trajectory that mirrors the passage of the settlers described by Dee Brown. The title comes from the Book of Revelation and the author's intention was to 'put a tag of shame on the greedy bastards who are responsible for this'. While widely studied in American schools, it continues to face attempts at censorship by concerned Christian parents, particularly in Bible Belt states. Joe Strummer's hero Woody Guthrie imagined the future of its protagonist in 'Tom Joad Parts 1 & 2' from his 1940 *Dust Bowl Ballads* album.

Chapter 8

Midnight Movies

Frankenstein's monster has been resurrected so many times at the cinema that it would take a further volume to do the subject adequate justice. Though there were at least three silent film precursors, the first of the talkies, James Whale's magical 1931 *Frankenstein*, which cast Boris Karloff as the Monster, is still reckoned by most aficionados to be definitive. Shortly followed by Mel Brooks' beautiful pastiche *Young Frankenstein* (1974), with Gene Wilder as the mad doctor and Marty Feldman as his hunchbacked assistant. Every Goth girl has envied Elsa Lanchester's electrified beehive, with its white lightning stripes, from Whale's tragicomic sequel, *The Bride of Frankenstein*, which set the high barnet bar as far back as 1935. Meanwhile, Peter Cushing was Baron Frankenstein's most Byronic incarnation, in the Hammer series initiated by *The Curse of Frankenstein* in 1957, which put his eternal rival Christopher Lee in the Monster's role. Andy Warhol collaborator Paul Morrissey offered up a 3D version in camp classic, *Flesh for Frankenstein* (1973), while Tim Curry became the sweetly murderous transvestite Dr Frank-N-Furter – a dead ringer for the youthful Ian Astbury – in Richard O'Brien's *Rocky Horror Picture Show* (1975).

A very '80s horror show, Jeremy Dellar's recreation of *The Battle of Orgreave* was performed at the original site seventeen years after the confrontation, using 800 extras and 200 former miners who had been there in 1984. The event was filmed by director Mike Figgis and the resulting documentary, which combines footage of the reconstruction with interviews from protagonists on both sides, was aired by Channel 4 in 2001. It took Dellar two years to research and win the trust of the local community. 'I've always described it as digging up a corpse and giving it a proper post-mortem,' he said, 'or as a thousand-person crime re-enactment.'

Building a Gothic Library

Alongside *Frankenstein*, Mary Shelley wrote another eerily prophetic work: *The Last Man* (1826), one of the first dystopian novels ever to be published. In its introduction, Shelley tells of finding predictions written by the Cumaean Sibyl on the wall of a cave near Naples, which she then writes up as the narrative of a man living in the twenty-first century as a mysterious pandemic sweeps across the globe. Her semi-autobiographical lead, Lionel Verney, falls in with Adrian, Earl of Windsor, the son of the last king of England and a shoe-in for her late husband; while ambitious Lord Raymond is a thinly disguised Byron, who had died two years before the book's publication. Researching her futuristic Republican society, Mary sat in observance at the House of Commons. By the magic of modern science, you can now download her vision for free at Google Books.

Alongside the works of the Shelleys, Keats and Lord Byron on your shelves, place the poetry of modern Romantic Joolz, collected in *Mad, Bad and Dangerous to Know* (Virgin, 1986), *Emotional Terrorism* (Bloodaxe Books, 1990), *The Pride of Lions* (Bloodaxe Books, 1994), *Errors of the Spirit* (Flambard Press 2000) and *Pray for Us Sinners* (Comma Press, 2005). As Joolz Denby, she forged a concurrent career as a noir novelist whose stories – like those of Hubert Selby Jr and Harry Crews – take place in the unrepresented margins of society. *Stone Baby* (HarperCollins, 2000) is set in the stand-up comedy circuit; *Corazon* (HarperCollins, 2002) the sinister world of cults; and *Borrowed Light* (Serpent's Tail, 2006) amid surfers, peace convoy refugees and incoming London brats on the Cornish coast. She makes great use of the brooding moors above Bradford in 2012's tale of a feral child, *Wild Thing* (Ignite Books), but most brilliant of all is the tale of biker bride *Billie Morgan* (Serpent's Tail) and her terrible secret. It should have won the Orange Prize, for which it was nominated in 2004.

David Peace's *GB84* (Faber & Faber, 2004) is the occult history of the Miners' Strike, in which the author envisages what really went on behind the scenes of the confrontation, as well as providing a harrowing, day-to-day account from the perspective of a striking miner. Martyn Waites' *Born Under Punches* (Simon & Schuster, 2003) tells a compelling northeastern perspective of the strike. For the definitive non-fiction account into what really happened beyond our sight, see Seumas Milne's *The Enemy Within – The Secret War Against the Miners* (Verso, updated edition 2014).

Chapter 9

Midnight Movies

When Tony Hancock went to Paris as a hopeful 'Shapeist' artist in *The Rebel* (Robert Day, 1961) he found an enclave of Juliette Gréco-style black-haired, blue-lipsticked, polo-necked Existentialists on the Left Bank, who deeply dug his *naïf* daubings. Tortured artist Tony begins the film as a commuting office clerk who finds escape by chipping away at a gigantic sculpture in his improbable bedsit – much to the consternation of landlady Mrs Crevatte (Irene Handl). After seeing an alluring poster in a coffee shop, he heads for Paris, going straight to Montmartre to find lodgings with fellow English artist abroad, Paul Ashby (Paul Massie), whose own works are traditionally figurative. Casting a spell over both Paul and the whole of the Left Bank, he becomes the Beatniks' cause célèbre.

The joke at *The Rebel*'s heart is this dichotomy, raging in the British artworld at the time and akin to the Trad versus Mod jazz battles being waged simultaneously across Soho. An even greater joke lies beneath: both Paul's sophisticated wares and Tony's freeform expressions, including the magnificent *Ducks in Flight Around the Eiffel Tower*, were all executed by one artist, Alistair Grant, in his own personal satire on the satire. With a script by Ray Galton and Alan Simpson, *The Rebel* is – according to no less an authority than Lucien Freud – the best film about art ever made.

Canadian horror maestro George A. Romero (1940–2017) was another formative influence on Soft Cell, and his film *Martin* (1978) was the inspiration for one of their finest moments. The titular Martin Mathais (John Amplas, in the role of a lifetime specially tailored for him by the director) is an orphaned nineteen-year-old with a vampire fixation. He has romantic visions of *Dracula*-style seductions and pitchfork-wielding Transylvanians, which he feeds by doping young women and drinking their blood. Following the suicide of his mother, he is sent to live in the boondocks of Pennsylvania with his elderly Great Uncle Tateh Cuda (Lincoln Maazel), an old-school Lithuanian Catholic who believes Martin is a manifestation of an ancient family curse, an actual Nostferatu. Cuda lines his house with crucifixes and garlic, and lays down strict rules to Martin, forbidding him to speak to his cousin Christina (Romero's wife-to-be Christine Forrest).

In flashback we learn how the awkward, friendless Martin has been treated as an unwanted menace by his family his entire life. Christina has a more pragmatic opinion on the geeky teen's otherworldliness: he is not a vampire but a budding psychopath. What does Martin think? He repeatedly phones a late-night radio show, whose host dubs him the Count – just as any sensation-seeking member of the press and entertainment world would. What do you think? Romero never makes explanation easy, leaving you, the viewer, to decide.

The director's exploration into the myths of vampirism and the fantasies of a psychiatrically disturbed young man was, in the age of serial killers like Son of Sam and the Yorkshire Ripper, very pertinent, and was Romero's personal favourite movie. He also appears in it, taking a passing dig at *The Exorcist* by appearing as the new priest in town, come to offer up his demon-ousting skills.

In a 2011 book of interviews with the director published by the University Press of Mississippi, Romero said: '*Martin* is designed to show that all those supernatural monsters that are part of our literary tradition are, in essence, expurgations of ourselves. They are beasts we've created in order to exorcise the monster from within us . . . I tried to show in *Martin* that you can't just slice off this evil part of ourselves and throw it away. It's a permanent part of us, and we'd better try to understand it.'

Building a Gothic Library

Juliette Gréco's friend, the French polymath musician, poet, singer, actor and engineer Boris Vian (1920–59), was most famous during his lifetime for publishing highly unconventional detective stories under the pseudonym Vernon Sullivan, including *I Spit on Your Graves* (1946). However, he also wrote beautiful, surrealist novels, posthumously discovered by the American Beat Generation. One of the few of them to be translated into English is *Froth on the Daydream* (1947) – also known in translation as *Mood Indigo* and *Foam of the Daze* – which contains several simultaneous plotlines, including that of Nicholas, who ages years in a week; his best friend Colin, who is obsessed with philosopher Jean-Pulse Heartre; and newlywed Colin, whose bride Chloe contracts a rare disease called waterlily on the lung. And then some talking mice . . .

Vian's life came to a dramatic end that is a warning to all authors who wish to see their books turned into films: at the 23 June 1959 premiere of Michel Gast's adaptation of *I Spit on Your Graves** he stood up and shouted: 'These guys are supposed to be American? My ass!' before collapsing in his seat and dying from a sudden cardiac arrest on the way to hospital.

The British Beatnik equivalent is Terry Taylor, whose *Baron's Court All Change* charts the Trad versus Mod wars in Soho in the finger-snapping language of its era. Reefer-smoking hepcat Taylor was a friend of the novelist Colin MacInnes and it is upon him that the Teenager in *Absolute Beginners* was based. Buy it in the New

London Editions' *Beats, Bums and Bohemians* series of 2011, alongside Colin Wilson's *Adrift in Soho* and Laura Del-Rivo's exploration of existential madness in bedsit land, *The Furnished Room*, all first published in 1961.

* Not to be confused with the 1978 Mary Whitehouse-baiting, Meir Zarchi-directed video nasty *I Spit on Your Grave.*

Chapter 10

Midnight Movies

As well as giving the grooving flower children a place to dance and be free at Alice's, Christian and Doctor Clive also masterminded a series of All Night Psychedelic Film Festivals at London's premiere Batscreen, the Scala on Pentonville Road, from 1984–87. Here, they showed cult movies – *Barbarella*, *Blue Sunshine*, *Blow Up*, *Danger Diabolik*, *Dougal and the Blue Cat*, *If It's Tuesday This Must Be Belgium*, *The Magic Christian*, *Morgan: A Suitable Case for Treatment*, *The Party*, *Performance*, *Wonderwall*, the Monkees' *Head* and the Stones' *Gimme Shelter* – which were an education in themselves.

Steven Severin's beloved Dario Argento (b. 7 January 1940) pioneered the Italian horror Giallo subgenre, named after the yellow-jacketed pulp fictions from whence most of their plots came. His *Three Mothers* trilogy – *Suspiria* (1977), *Inferno* (1980) and *The Mother of Tears* (2007) – tells the tales of a triumvirate of witches who have enchanted the world since the eleventh century, while *Tenebrae* (1982) concerns a Giallo writer whose work inspires a copycat serial killer. This was itself a reaction to public perceptions of Argento's previous work that had culminated in death threats to the director – in Britain, *Tenebrae* was banned from sale until 1999. A friend of fellow director Sergio Leone, Argento co-wrote the screenplay for the monumental *Once Upon a Time in the West* (1968) and was a script consultant on George A. Romero's *Dawn of the Dead* (1978), for which he also wrote the score with his beloved progsters, Goblin.

As mentioned earlier, Dave Vanian took his band's name from one of Hammer's most overlooked masterpieces, *The Damned* (Joseph Losey, 1963), which manages to combine a proto-*Clockwork Orange* gang led by a bowler-hatted Oliver Reed doing beatnik dance routines in praise of black leather and flick knives on Weymouth seafront with a chilling dystopian Cold War fable. Directed by the blacklisted Hollywood director in exile – thanks, Ronald Reagan – it makes superb use of the eerie Isle of Portland landscape around the Dorset holiday town, where operations of the secretive military kind really have taken place, and the Modernist sculptures of Elisabeth Frink. Not being a straightforward genre picture, it was badly cut on its initial cinematic release, but has since been restored and reassessed as a highpoint in British post-war sci-fi cinema. Oliver Reed takes a more minor – but just as visually arresting – role in Edmund T. Gréville's *Beat Girl* (1959), which also contains scenes that quite possibly inspired Kubrick's vision of the Droogs. With Christopher Lee as a sinister Soho stripclub proprietor and a twangtastic soundtrack from the John Barry Seven, you'd be a square not to dig it.

- Both *The Damned* and *Beat Girl* are currently available on DVD/Blu-ray.
- The Scala's programmer at the time, Jane Giles, has published an epic and lavishly illustrated guide to the cinema's glory years of 1978–93 that no film freak should be without: fabpress.com/scala-cinema-book.html

Building a Gothic Library

Born in a strange place in a strange time, Mervyn Peake (1911–68) had a dislocated childhood that filled his head with visions of complex otherworlds. As gifted a visual artist as he was a storyteller, his imagination brimmed into the epic realm of *Gormenghast*, a sequence of novels about a castle city state teeming with intrigue, into which the teenage imaginations of Robert Smith, Rowland S. Howard,

David Peace, Neil Gaiman and legions more Gothic dreamers were lured and never entirely left.

His life began in an isolated British enclave in Tientsin in the north of China, where his parents worked as Christian missionaries as about them, the old Imperial dynasty began to collapse. He was abruptly transferred from these exotic surrounds to suburban Croydon at the age of twelve, bringing with him a ticking timebomb of encephalitis lethargica – sleeping sickness – incubating within him and an imagination constantly suspended between the words of wakefulness and dream, from which he could conjure fantastic acts of creativity.

Mervyn studied at Croydon School of Art and won a five-year scholarship with the Royal Academy, joining an artist's colony on the tiny Channel Island of Sark in 1933 and becoming entranced by this time-suspended self-governing dependency to the extent that he failed his exams. Returning to London, he worked as an illustrator of children's books, including *Treasure Island* and *Alice in Wonderland*; and taught at Westminster School of Art, where he met the love of his life, the painter Maeve Gilmore, whom he married in 1937. They had three children – the first, Sebastian, born just after the outbreak of the Second World War in 1940.

The creation of his literary parallel universe began in the same year, when Peake – who had joined the Royal Artillery, hoping to become a War artist – began to write *Titus Groan*, the story of the man born to be the 77th Earl of Gormenghast. Drawing characters and scenes from the novel, he sent his manuscripts home for Maeve to edit. In 1942, shortly after the birth of their second son Fabian, he suffered a nervous breakdown, but continued to write from his sickbed, before being invalided out of the army in 1943. Now acting as a War artist, he – like the then serving army intelligence officer Dirk Bogarde – was one of the first to enter the Belsen concentration camp and the Hell on Earth that he witnessed deeply affected him for the rest of his life.

In 1946, the Peake family moved to Sark in the Channel Islands – daughter Clare was born there in 1949, and a second novel, the

Royal Society of Literature Prize-winning *Gormenghast*, followed in 1950. For a time, they lived a blissful life on the island, a rural idyll throwback to a world without cars. But eventually, the need to make money brought them back to London, where Peake taught for a while at St Martin's, and inherited his father's house in Croydon in 1957.

He published *Titus Alone* in 1959, intending to continue the series, but by then was struggling with the onset of the sleeping sickness that had lain dormant since his childhood in China, which, coupled with Parkinson's disease, laid waste to his physical and mental health. He left this world in 1968 at the age of fifty-seven, bequeathing another universe of unrivalled imagination to anyone who cared to pick up where he left off.

- A Folio Society edition of *Gormenghast*, with an introduction by Neil Gaiman and illustrated by David McKean, was published in 2022. To see Peake's own wonderful illustrations, including his incredible *Glass Blowers* sequence from the Second World War, enter the portal here: artuk.org/discover/stories/the-life-and-unsung-art-of-mervyn-peake.

Chapter 11

Midnight Movies

Both Nick Cave and the Bad Seeds and Crime and the City Solution can be seen performing in Wim Wenders' 1987 paean to the old West Berlin, *Wings of Desire*. The story, conceived by the German director and future Nobel laureate Peter Handke, tells of immortal angels Damiel (Bruno Ganz) and Cassiel (Otto Sander), who abide above the walled city but enjoy descending to its streets, listening in to the thoughts of its human inhabitants. Of these mortals, only children are capable of seeing their Heavenly eavesdroppers – except perhaps for one adult. The actor Peter Falk has come to Berlin to play a part in a film about the Second World

War and, with his *Columbo*-honed skills, seems to be able to detect their presence. Through his creations' seraphic abilities, Wenders is able to reveal to the viewer both the geography of Berlin, in stunning aerial shots that traverse the route of the Wall caving the city in two, and its immediate history, with archive footage of the smoking ruins left at the end of the war. In perhaps the most time-capsule moment of all, Damiel and Cassiel wander through what was then still very much the wasteland of Potsdamer Platz, trying to remember what it looked like before 1939. When Damiel witnesses the exquisite artistry of circus trapeze artist Marion (Solveig Dommartin), he learns what it means to fall head over heels – and casts off his wings to be human. Wenders was such a fan of Nick Cave, who he felt embodied the spirit of Berlin, he said it would have been 'inconceivable' to have made the film without him. *Wings of Desire* also marks the last role of the great German actor Curt Bois (1901–91), who appears as the Ancient Greek Homer, now also wandering through Berlin, engaged in a mission to try to capture the city in prose.

An older Berlin – and one at its creative peak – can be seen in the films of Robert Wiene and F. W. Murnau, who worked in the city during the Weimar Republic, the period between the twin terrors of the First World War and the Nazis winning power in 1933. Reflecting the work of the Dada and Expressionist artists, they used sets that tilted at seemingly impossible angles, casting dark shadows and creating what German film critic Lotte Eisner defined as *Helldunkel*: 'A sort of twilight of the German soul, expressing itself in shadowy, enigmatic interiors, or in misty, insubstantial landscapes'. Of the two films that prefigure the coming of Blixa Bargeld, Wiene's *The Cabinet of Dr Caligari* (1920) tells the story of the titular, insane carnival hypnotist (Friedrich Feher) and his somnambulist sideshow attraction Cesare (Conrad Veidt), who may be responsible for a spate of murders while being placed under hypnosis – an unnerving analogy for those soldiers who didn't come back from the Western Front. Meanwhile, in 1922's *Nosferatu*, cinema's most terrifying vampire arose from an unauthorised adaptation of *Dracula* by

Murnau. Set in an imagined future Germany of the late 1930s, it presaged the horrors that awaited that decade in the snaggle-toothed nightmare form of Max Schreck's Count Orlok. Bram Stoker's widow sued for unlawful use of text and the courts decreed the film should be destroyed, but you cannot kill what does not live and copies of this German Expressionist masterpiece had already flittered their way into eternity.

Building a Gothic Library

Nick Cave's literary companion in Berlin, Jim Thompson, was born above a prison cell in 1906. He spent his life wrestling with alcoholism and forcing out through his typewriter desperate visions of men in a similar predicament. Bungling criminal amateurs, hotel clerks, wildcat oilmen, grifters, drifters and sinister sheriffs – all riddled with diseased obsessions, spiralling towards the Hell of their own making and helped along the way by ruthless, venal women. They were all the strands of Jim's own, cold, hard life.

Thompson's father, Big Jim, was the sheriff of Caddo County, Oklahoma, a place described at the turn of the twentieth century as 'the last refuge of cattle thieves, gunfighters and train robbers'. Big Jim's exploits in those wild times, the ruin he brought upon himself by gambling and drinking, the many desertions his family endured and his pitiful end inside an old people's home inspired his son's devastating prose. Most of Jim Jr's childhood was spent in Nebraska, where Big Jim would dump his brood while he was on the run, and West Texas, where he would reappear, prospecting for oil and the big time. These locations provided all the settings – and the fuel of Oedipal rage.

Jim was taking financial care of his family from the age of fifteen, working as a bellboy at the Hotel Texas, an experience that spawned three novels, *A Swell-Looking Babe* (1954), *Wild Town* (1957) and *Texas by the Tail* (1965). The job also served as his baptism in booze: he turned to whisky to get him through the nine-hours-a-night, seven-nights-a-week routine. He then took a job on the West

Texas oilfields, where he began his first serious writing among the hobos and roughnecks in the shadows of the wells. Thompson rode the hard rails of the Depression, drifting through the south in search of work and while he did so, he learned his territory inside out.

Which is why I think Jim Thompson deserves the accolade for the greatest noir novelist of all. Although he is more famous for those works that ended up on the big screen, *The Getaway* (1958, adapted by Sam Peckinpah in 1972) and *The Grifters* (1963, adapted by Stephen Frears in 1990), his masterpiece was his 1952 tale of a hokey West Texan deputy sheriff called Lou Ford. *The Killer Inside Me* lures the unwitting reader in with Ford's corny commentary about his day-to-day run-ins with the folks of his parish; inviting you to empathise, while at the same time, suggesting that you patronise, this obviously not-too-well intellectually endowed lawman. Just when you think you have his measure, Ford drops his bombshell. If you've never read the book – even if you have, for that matter – Michael Winterbottom's 2010 adaptation is best avoided.

Film directors did love Thompson and while the author was in the autumn of his years, young upstart Stanley Kubrick sought Jim out in Musso & Frank's, the LA diner also haunted by Dean Martin and James Ellroy. Kubrick employed Thompson's talents on scripts for *The Killing* (1956) and *Paths of Glory* (1957), although he shivved him out of a co-writer's credit on the former. But his screenwriting career stalled when it ran into boy racer Steve McQueen, who, as *The Getaway*'s leading man, wrested control of the film from Sam Peckinpah, demanding an ending that diverged from the novel's bleak denouement. The great director reputedly pissed all over the screen when he saw the final results.

'Just you wait,' Jim told his wife Alberta as he prepared to take his leave of this world from Los Angeles in 1977, 'I'll become famous as soon as I'm dead.'

- As well as the above titles, Robert Polito's superb biography of Thompson, *Savage Art* (Serpent's Tail, 1995), comes highly recommended.

Chapter 12

Midnight Movies

The most durable artefact of Goth's metal years was assembled by former *Sounds* journalist Edwin Pouncey, from similar source elements to those Zodiac Mindwarp drew his visions from. *Angel Dust (Music for Movie Bikers)* celebrates the stream of lesser-known biker movies that gunned alongside Dennis Hopper's 1969 counter-culture roadtrip, *Easy Rider*, in the Altamont Age. A stunning picture disc, housed in impressive artwork from the man who doubles as satirical cartoonist and illustrator Savage Pencil, it was released in 1988 by Paul Smith's Mute subsidiary, Blast First. A Crampsian selection of B-movie themes traversed demonic Country with Paul Wibier's mournful 'Satan (Theme)' from Al Adamson's 1969 *Satan's Sadists*, the full-throttle psychobilly of Davie Allen & the Arrows' 'Blues Theme' from Roger Corman's 1966 *Wild Angels*, and 'The Stompers and the Souls' from Anthony M. Lanza's 1967 *The Glory Stompers*. Meanwhile, East West Pipeline's brass-heavy theme from Richard Compton's 1970 *Angels Die Hard* and Randy Sparks' and Jim Helms' greaser-groovy 'By Force' from Lee Madden's 1970 *Angel Unchained* injected sizzling '70s funk into its petrol tank. Sav's 'monsterpiece' was constructed by re-recording all of this booty onto tape, cleaning it up and then fitting it together, 'until something that had a certain flow emerged from the scattered bits of broken sound and slurred soundtrack.'

Despite his noble intentions, the artist's appropriation of some biker imagery did not roar past Hells Angels' HQ unchallenged. 'For the cover, I incorporated my original art with video grabs from the VHS biker movies I'd scored. On one side of the picture disc, I used a blurred shot of a Hells Angel flag, a move that would invoke the wrath of the *real* Hells Angels who, after first sending in a letter of complaint, eventually visited the offices of Blast First and insisted the image be removed.'

Fortunately, label manager Smith was able to act the diplomat and after 'a lively session at a local hostelry, some form of pact was made. At the time, though,' Sav recalled, 'this was a scary moment and a reminder that the biker code should not be treated lightly or with any disrespect. Not that I was doing that in the first place, I just wanted to celebrate biker culture in my own weird way. I don't think *Angel Dust* sold too many copies, but I still get people coming up to me and saying how much it changed their life! Wowie zowie, as Frank Zappa used to say.'

Building a Gothic Library

Another supremely gifted and short-lived adept of the short story, Mary Flannery O'Connor spent her life distilling all the 'Christ-haunted' Southern Discomfort of her Georgia surroundings into prose that awoke the fever dreams of Jeffrey Lee Pierce and Nick Cave. A self-described 'pigeon-toed child with a receding chin and a you-leave-me-alone-or-I'll bite-you complex', she was born to Irish Catholic parents in Southern Gothic Savannah on 25 March 1925. Here, at the age of six, she appeared on Pathé News showing off a chicken she had trained to walk backwards: 'It was the high point in my life,' she recalled. 'Everything since has been an anticlimax.' When she was twelve, her father Edward was diagnosed with the autoimmune disease Lupus, which would claim his life in 1941. By then the family had moved to live with her maternal grandparents in the former state capital of Milledgeville.

Attending Peabody High there, she bagged the job as her school newspaper's art editor and later landed the same role on the in-house publication of Georgia State College for Women. Here, she created acerbic cartoons as a sideline to her BA in sociology and English literature. Going on to study journalism at the Iowa Writers' Workshop, she was encouraged by novelist and dramatist Andrew Lytle, who would publish her early short fiction in his *Sewanee Review*, and Workshop director Paul Engle, who read the initial drafts of her first novel, 1952's *Wise Blood*.

This tells the story of Second World War veteran Hazel Motes, who returns from service to find his family home deserted and falls under the spell of street preacher Asa Hawks – a conman of the cloth, who pretends to be blind. Fusing Hawkes' gospel with those of his preacher grandfather in his traumatised imagination, Hazel formulates his own anti-religion. Going forth to evangelise on behalf of the Church of Christ Without Christ, he leads the reader through a netherworld of shills and cons, always trying to outrun 'the wild, ragged figure, who runs from tree to tree in the back of Hazel's mind' – an allusion to T. S. Eliot's *The Waste Land*, which found further echo in Nick Cave's 1988 'The Mercy Seat', his cell-room vision of Christ 'born into a manger' to die upon the cross 'like some ragged stranger'.

John Huston made a blackly comedic cinematic adaptation in 1979 with Brad Dourif as Hazel and Harry Dean Stanton as Asa Hawks. Jim Thirlwell named his ongoing collaboration with Swans' drummer Roli Mosimann – of 'violent macho American [music] made by non-Americans' – Wiseblood. Al Jourgensen's Ministry made the jaw-dropping 'Jesus Built My Hotrod' single with samples of Dourif's Hazel, alongside Dennis Hopper's Frank Booth from David Lynch's *Blue Velvet* (1986) and the crazed babblings of guest singer, the Butthole Surfers' Gibby Haynes, in 1992.

By the time the book was published, Flannery had already been diagnosed with the same ailment that took her father's life. She spent the remainder of her thirty-nine years living on the ground floor of her mother's farm Andalusia, just outside Milledgeville. Here, she produced one other novel, *The Violent Bear It Away* (1960), and two books of short stories, *A Good Man Is Hard to Find* (1955) and *Everything that Rises Must Converge* (published posthumously in 1965).

In hallucinatory prose, shot through with sardonic humour, Flannery continued to tackle the chief bedevilments of her immediate surroundings: religion and race. Both of which she held conflicted views on, publicly supporting Martin Luther King while privately expressing fear of a Black Planet; going to Mass each day and returning to her desk to dissect lives upended by fanatical dogma – the dilemmas of the white liberal, not just in her time. But through the tumult of her existence, she drew often uncomfortable but unforgettable portraiture of a time and place she would define and never escape from. As she put it: 'I think that to know yourself is to know your region, and that it's also to know the world, and in a sense, paradoxically, it's also to be an exile from that world.'

- All Flannery O'Connor's works are currently in print. You can see her equally sharp illustrations here: themarginalian.org/2013/12/12/flannery-oconnor-cartoons

Chapter 13

Midnight Movies

Charles Laughton's sole foray as a director, *Night of the Hunter* (1955), is now regarded as a cinematic masterpiece, yet it was so baffling to critics and moviegoers alike on its initial release that its box-office failure meant the veteran British actor never got the chance to make another film. Laughton did several unthinkable things with his production: he combined mystery and horror with the darkest humour, and set his tale in an Expressionistic black-and-white world, turning the Deep South into the realm of fairy tale with the help of cinematographer Stanley Cortez, who was 'always chosen to do weird things'.

We've caught a few ragged glimpses of Robert Mitchum's preacher Harry Powell in this story – here's the gist of his tale: from inside a prison cell, he learns of a condemned man who has $10,000 hidden in his house. On his release, he assumes the mantle of a righteous preacher and arrives in the hometown of the widowed Willa Harper (Shelley Winters) and her young children John (Billy Chapin) and Pearl (Sally Jane Bruce). The siblings rightfully distrust the bogus cleric, but Willa falls hard. One torturous wedding night later, she is seen sitting at the wheel of her car on the bottom of a lake, while the children are forced to stuff their inheritance inside Pearl's dolly and flee their terrifying new daddy.

They raft down the river in the moonlight, hide out in a haybarn, but never seem to outpace their pursuer, who, like the nightmare he represents, ambles along just behind them, singing his eerie songs. Their fairy godmother, in the form of silent screen icon Lillian Gish, appears, in the words of Roger Ebert, like 'Whistler's mother holding a shotgun'. With her true faith, this frail old woman vanquishes the false prophet and saves the innocents.

From the Deep South to Swinging London for Peter Cook and Dudley Moore's *Bedazzled* (Stanley Donen, 1967), a retelling of *Faust*, and the high-water mark of the duo's genius. Cook, who plays the Devil, worked every literary reference he could find to the Horned One into his script, quoting from Milton to Mussolini and giving his earthbound incarnation of Beelzebub, George Spiggott, a filing cabinet of souls. Over which he has tacked the Egg Marketing Board's classic 'Go to work on an egg' poster, copywritten by Fay '*Life and Loves of a She-Devil*' Weldon, an allusion to the Medieval belief that the egg represents the soul. His former Beyond the Fringe companion Jonathan Miller, who had just ignited the psychedelic imagination with his BBC production of *Alice in Wonderland* (1966), is dutifully filed within. 'I thought up the Seven Deadly Sins in one afternoon,' Spiggott reflects. 'The only thing I've come up with recently is advertising.'

Dudley Moore, who plays Satan's hapless plaything, failed suicide Stanley Moon, composed the score around variations of his elegant theme tune, performed with his jazz Trio. Between them, Cook and Moore willed David Bowie into being with the film's most legendary sequence, in which Stanley is tricked into performing his heart out in a gold lamé suit on a *Ready Steady Go!*-style proto *Top of the Pops*, only to be upstaged by the deadpan Devil. As Drimble Wedge and the Vegetation, Cook uncannily prefigures Bowie's urban spaceman while simultaneously sparking the imagination of young Johnny Rotten with his delivery of the ultimate punk line: 'You fill me with inertia.'

Which just about takes us full circle to the beginning of the Goth cycle of the Thatcher years. But we can't leave this darkened room without a screening of one of the era's greatest works of art, which returned us to a previous epoch of shadows and fog.

Granada TV's adaptation of Sir Arthur Conan Doyle's *Sherlock Holmes* completed the process begun by *Excalibur*'s Pre-Raphaelite vision of reawakening the very best of Victorian aesthetics, just as Mrs Thatcher endeavoured to take us all back to those inglorious days of Dickensian social inequality. Starring Jeremy Brett as Sherlock, David Burke and then Edward Hardwicke as Dr Watson, and Charles Gray – previously the embodiment of Wheatley's Mocata in Hammer's *The Devil Rides Out* and louche narrator of *The Rocky Horror Picture Show* – as Mycroft, the series began in 1984 and spanned ten years and forty-three adaptations of Conan Doyle's original stories. Every one of them rendered in stunning visual Victorian verisimilitude, correct to the last detail of every flower arrangement – us History of Fashion students watched in awe. With such class acts as Alexander Baron writing the screenplays, the stories remained faithful to their source material while also containing a treasury of innuendo, delivered by seasoned character actors who had known life before the Wolfenden Report.

- The Criterion Collection restored *Night of the Hunter* DVD/ Blu-ray comes with a host of documentary goodies. You can find echoes of its visuals on the cover of Cardiacs' *Sing to God* LP (1996) and on the fan-made video for 'Winds and Rains is Cold'. Cardiacs' nemesis Kylie is brutally dispatched by Nick Cave on the video to their single 'The Wild Rose' (taken from *Murder Ballads*, also 1996) in riverine settings close to those seen through Stanley Cortez's lens.
- Johnny Trunk's reissue of the *Bedazzled* soundtrack on vinyl will arouse the Envy of your friends: trunkrecords.greedbag.com/ buy/bedazzled-original-motion-pictur-1. Nick Cave and Anita Lane covered Drimble Wedge's 'Bedazzled' on her wonderful *The World's a Girl* (Mute) EP in 1995 – though, bewilderingly, they left out the best line, quoted in the text above.
- The Complete Collection of Granada's *Sherlock Holmes* is currently available.

Building a Gothic Library

Gavin Friday's frequent collaborator Patrick McCabe (b. 27 March 1955) did for Irish literature what the Virgin Prunes did for music, giving vent to the wildest corners of his country's imagination in the form of *enfant terrible* Francie Brady, the antihero of his Booker Prize-shortlisted *The Butcher Boy* (1992). Neil Jordan turned this into his 1997 film and you can see Pat in cameo as town drunk Jimmy the Skite. Jordan returned to McCabe's *Breakfast on Pluto* (1998, again shortlisted for the Booker Prize) to create a fairy tale of contemporary Ireland and London, with future Peaky Blinder Cillian Murphy as transgender foundling Patrick 'Pussy' Braden and Friday as his romantic interest, glam rocker Billy Hatchett. The author's latest tome, set in the Kilburn of the mid-'70s, is another hauntingly poetic exorcism of Irish ghosts and shares its name with an early incarnation of Shane MacGowan's band, *Poguemahone* (2022). The should-be national treasure author had this published via the crowd-funder Unbound – go figure.

Our last two authors were also men who saw brief youthful success and acclaim dwindle into indifference when they reached middle age but they went on writing anyway, dying with their boots on, face down in their typewriters. Nelson Algren wrote the original *A Walk on the Wild Side* (1956) and knew of whence he spoke. Born Nelson Algren Abraham on 28 March 1909 in Chicago, he rode the rails across the United States at the time of the Great Depression, fought in France during the Second World War, fell in love with Simone de Beauvoir (1908–86) – who was buried wearing his ring – and set all of his books in worlds he knew intimately. He gave voice to hobos, petty criminals, boxers, working girls, card sharps, bar tenders and weary police chiefs – all manner of people at the bottom end of society who would otherwise have vanished into the ether without record.

His most famous work – which won him the first American National Book Award – was the one Barry Adamson picked up on: *The Man with the Golden Arm* (1949), the story of a Second World War veteran who returns to Chicago with a morphine habit from an injury sustained during the conflict in France. The book contained the first usage of the metaphor 'monkey on my back', an expression Nelson had heard from a withdrawing addict. The photographer Art Shay, who accompanied Nelson on his nightly forays through Chicago's skid row hotels, all-night diners, bars and tattoo parlours, described and recorded with his camera what he called 'one of Algren's favorite theaters, the show-up room at police headquarters, where suspects were paraded before victims.' Nelson watched and listened, making sure his dialogue was spot on. Authenticity was key, which was why, when Otto Preminger acquired the rights to Nelson's book and asked him to come to Hollywood and work on a screenplay, the author left after one week. 'How do you know such people?' was the Viennese director's first question to Algren. 'Such animals?'

Despite the film's strengths – Sinatra's performance, Bernstein's score – it's a pale mockery of the story Algren crafted. Do yourself a favour and seek out the original, reprinted by Canongate, alongside *A Walk on the Wild Side*. Anything else you can pick up by the author is money well spent. His brief time in the spotlight over, Nelson lived his last years exiled from his beloved Windy City in Sag Harbour, New York. He was looking forward to meeting a new British author, whose debut novel, *Midnight's Children*, he very much admired. But Nelson never got to the publishing party being thrown for Salman Rushdie – his heart gave out on him on the same day as the event, 9 May 1981.

Finally, to the man who best described the 'vile psychic weather' of the '80s in his 'Factory' series of books, begun with 1984's *He Died with His Eyes Open*. 'The act of becoming a gentleman,' wrote Robin Cook in 1966, 'is one of murder.' The author, who began his career describing the criminal milieu of the '60s and ended it redefining British crime writing, spent a lifetime doing everything in his power to deny himself this fate. Born in 1931, Robert William Arthur Cook was the son of a textile magnate, destined for Eton at the age of sixteen. 'Terrible bloody place. They were trying to make you into a good all-rounder, a cabinet minister, a bastard.' Although Cook did eventually find a use for his Eton tie – fronting long firms for Soho gangster Charles da Silva.

In the London of the early '60s he found that, 'An Eton background is a terrific help if you are into vice of any kind.' Between inveigling funds, running gambling parties and working in a sex shop, Cook penned his debut, *The Crust on its Uppers* (1962). Its glossary of criminal argot was considered by *Dictionary of Slang* compiler Eric Partridge to be his best source in twenty-five years. For reasons never specified but not hard to imagine, Cook moved to Italy shortly after, where he continued to write vicious satires, *Private Parts, Public Places* (1969) and *Bombe Surprise* (1963), ran a vineyard and was made foreign minister for his local Anarchist collective. In 1970's *A State of Denmark* he had a nightmare vision of a future England under the dictatorship of a Labour Party re-branded 'The New Pace'. Cook returned to London, but after trying to make ends meet mini-cabbing, lost his third wife and a house in Holland Park. He retreated to France, where he worked for years as a labourer, until a neighbour goaded him he'd never write a book again. Cook came home, reinvented himself as Derek Raymond and rewrote British crime fiction in a fever of creativity, following *He Died with His Eyes Open* (1984) with *The Devil's Home on Leave* (1985), *How the Dead Live* (1986), *I Was Dora Suarez* (1988) and *Dead Man Upright* (1993, all now in print via Serpent's Tail), before his liver gave up on him on 30 July 1994.

'Nothing else much matters once you have achieved the hardest thing, which is to act out of conviction,' Cook surmised in 1992. 'Even if you have been beaten by evil, in the bitterness of defeat the battle has left a trace for the others, and you can go feeling clean.'

Acknowlegdements and Sources

This journey down the Time Tunnel was instigated by John Williams and Pete Woodhead, who separately – but equally doggedly – convinced me that I had something worth saying on Goth and the '80s. I was further encouraged by Stephen Coates and Travis Elborough, who invited me to do a Walpurgisnacht talk on Gothic music in the crypt of Kensal Green Cemetery in 2020 – an event that was silenced by the scythe of COVID, but not before I had written for it what became the blueprint for this book. Thanks to the efforts of my Gothmother, Caroline Montgomery of Rupert Crew Ltd, and Gothfather, Pete Selby of Nine Eight Books, I was able to continue my excavations in the furtherance of writing this grimoire through the dark days of the pandemic. Paint all your names in black and gold.

The majority of the unattributed quotes in the text are taken from interviews conducted by myself between 1987 and the present day. While I have done my utmost to pick up every stitch of this story and correctly identify all authors quoted from, occasionally I have used material from ancient fanzines and press releases/biographies that cited interviews and reviews without attribution and I look forward to clarifications for future amendments. Much of the archive music press material was gathered from the Rock's Back Pages website, with thanks to Barney Hoskyns and Mark Pringle. I owe snakebite-and-blacks to: Tom Vague for allowing me to quote from his *Vague* archive; Matthew Worley of Subcultures, Popular Culture and Social Change FB site for trading insights and more old copies of the inkies; and Chris Bohn for sharing his Diamada Galàs archive with me.

I am indebted to Richard Cabut, Susan Compo, Bal Croce, Danielle Dax, Joolz Denby, William D. Drake, Sharron Fortnum, Paul Hollins, Annie Hogan, Jennie Godfrey, Jon Langford, Dominic Luckman, Lydia Lunch, Dave Knight, David Peace, the late Tim Quy and dear friends Chris Fowler and Joe McNally, Savage Pencil, Claire Shearsby, Jim Smith, Sarah Smith and J. G. Thirlwell who took the time to look back at the '80s with me again, read, advise and generally inspire. Walking beers for my Kreuzberg tour guides, Max Décharné and Katja Kleir, who helped me get my Berlin/Neubaten facts straight and German spellings right. Ruth Bayer and Caroline Wise were, as always, fonts of magical wisdom. Mocata Glendening was my Frator Superior through the labyrinth of '80s politics; and my teenage Goth guru Marc Fireman and *Sounds* sister Ann Scanlon were my trusted first readers. Every man and woman of you is a star.

Salutations to the writers I have quoted from and those I read as a teenager – some of whom I subsequently got to work with – who caught the times so insightfully: Martin Aston, Jack Barron, Max Bell, Ian Birch, Michael Bracewell, Caroline Coon, Tony Drayton, Mary Harron, Steve Keaton, Nick Kent, Biba Kopf, Andy Gill, Helen Fitzgerald, Jim Green, Robin Gibson, Vivien Goldman, Jayne Houghton, Jim Irwin, Allan Jones, Steve Keaton, Penny Kiley, Greil Marcus, Mick Mercer, Paul Morley, Charles Shaar Murray, Liz Naylor, Richard North, Paul du Noyer, Betty Page, Mark Paytress, Neil Perry, Edwin Pouncey, Push, Paul Rambali, John Robb, Sandy Robertson, Robert Sandall, Jon Savage, Sylvie Simmons, Dave Simpson, Andrew Smith, Black Mat Smith, Mr Spencer, Mike Stand, David Stubbs, the Stud Brothers, Phil Sutcliffe, Adam Sweeting, Simon Reynolds, Dave Rimmer, Chris Roberts, Cynthia Rose, Ralph Traitor and Jonh Wilde. A toast to the departed: *NME*'s Richard Cook, Fred Dellar, Jane Suck/Solanas and Steven Wells; *Melody Maker*'s Carol Clerk; *Sounds*' foremost man in a Mac, Dave McCullough, and my beloved former comrades David Cavanagh, Leo Finlay, Andy

Ross, Penny Reel and the mighty Tommy Udo; and to John Peel, who enabled us all.

I would never have been able to tell this story without the people who helped me get from the flat field to *Sounds*. My mum and dad, for making sure my brother and I grew up with true Addams Family values. My companions in the Belton bus shelter, Great Yarmouth High School art room, art college and the Oakwood: Brian Adcock, Lisa Avis Stannard, Nadine Baldwin, Bugs, Hugh Burbeck, David 'Bully' Bull, Shaun Connon, Tony Crowley, Michelle Daniels, Emma Dufficy, Deanna Fenn, Lyndall Fernie, Jarrod Gamble, Dominic Gray, Dean Julian, Andrew 'Squid' Kidd, Wanjika Kitchiner, Kriss and Lynn Knights, Sally Pittman, Shaun McDermott, Julie Strudwick, Mark Reeve, Gary Walker and Raymond Yates. A bouquet of black roses for Helen Togneri, for all the adventures we have had in the past forty years and all those yet to come.

Michael Tallboys let me into the London College of Fashion, Jackie Hunter helped me chortle my way through it and Lynne Parker opened the door into the music world beyond. *Sounds* editor Tony Stewart gave me my first chance to write and in the company of Kathy Ball, George Berger, Susie Boon, Keith Cameron, Steve Double, Paul Elliott, Hugh Fielder, Kim Fowley, Steve Gullick, John Harris, Mary Anne Hobbs, Alistair Indge, Peter Kane, Sam King, Billy Mann, Robbi Millar, Tony Mitchell, Jon Newey, Cate Nisbet, Andy Peart, Tim Peacock, Shaun Phillips, Leo Regan, Glenn Rickwood, Mary Scanlon, Ed Sirrs, Sue Smith, Andy Stout, Ian T. Tilton, Roy Wilkinson and Damon Wise. Salutations also to: Andy Allen and Ginni Brown of ultimate Gothzine *House of Dolls*; Daniel Miller, who still runs the coolest record company in the world; and all at Mute and associated labels, past and present.

Love to my family: Matt, Yvette, Tommy, William and Sophie Rose Unsworth; Danny, Frances, Paul, Annabelle, Elliott and Lucy Meekin; Danny, Elaine, Eva, Mick and Maureen Snee. And to my extended Addams Family – Raphael and Lucia Abraham,

Jake Arnott, Pete Ayrton and Sarah Martin, Roger K. Burton and everyone at the Horse Hospital, Ali Catterall and Jane Giles, Billy Chainsaw, Geoff Cox, Anna Davis and all at CBC, Michael Dillon, David Fogarty and the Sohemian Society, Pat Gilbert and all at MOJO, Jon and Caroline Glover, Ronnie Hackston, Ken and Rachel Hollings, Stewart Home, Tina Jackson, John King and London Books, Brian O'Neil, Fenris Oswin, Damjana and Predrag Finci, Aidan McManus, Emma Murphy, Benedict Newbery, Richard and Sarah Newson, Mark Pilkington and Strange Attractor Press, Nick Quantrill, the Shend, Chris Simmons, David Sutton and all at *Fortean Times*, Deirdre Ruisling, Nick Triplow, Jo Willingham and Paul Willetts. May all your days be Crystal Days.

Many more thanks to ace editor Melissa Bond and hardboiled PRs Elinor Fewster, Karen Stretch and Mark Wood, and everyone else at Nine Eight Books who helped me finally get this medicine show on the road. You rule, the others drool.

While writing this book, I lost three women very close to my heart – Catherine Meekin, Jordan Mooney and Laura Del-Rivo – and, in its final editing stages, also beloved Cardiacs' percussionist Tim Quy. See you in the Summerland.

First and last and always: Michael Meekin, thank you for so thoroughly supporting me in the creation of this book, supplying humour and thoughtfulness no matter what the odds and being my best fiend forever.

Sic gorgiamus allos subjectatos nunc

Notes

Prologue

1. Last available data showed some improvement – the inner wards of Yarmouth Nelson and Northgate had been relegated to only twenty-fifth in the most deprived areas of the UK by 2019 (Great Yarmouth Borough Council).

Chapter 1: The Rebel Alliance

1. In 1948, NHS founder Aneurin Bevan called the Conservative Party 'lower than vermin'. The Tories embraced the phrase, forming the Vermin Club in response.
2. Mays wrote his article – accompanied by photographs of the shop and its inhabitants – for the adult magazine *Gallery*. In 1974 a lavish photospread of this nature could only be confined to top-shelf publications. Today, this would not seem out of place in any high-end fashion magazine.
3. The Cambridge Rapist turned out to be 47-year-old delivery driver Peter Samuel Cook (1928–2004), who had multiple previous convictions for theft and burglary but had never once set foot inside SEX. He was tried at Norwich Crown Court on 3 October 1975 and pleaded guilty to seven charges of rape, two of wounding and one of gross indecency. Given two life sentences, he died in HMP Winchester at the age of seventy-five.

Chapter 2: The Clock Strikes Thirteen

1. The traditional rhyme states: 'St Swithin's Day, if it does rain/Full forty days, it will remain/St Swithin's Day, if it be fair/For forty days, t'will rain no more'. Swithin (b. circa 800) was a bishop of Winchester who asked not to be buried inside the city's cathedral, but outside, where the rain could fall on him. Against his wishes, he was moved inside, triggering a great storm and a folkloric legend.

2. Ian Brady and Myra Hindley murdered five children aged between ten and seventeen between 1963 and 1965, when Ian Curtis would have been eight to ten years old himself. Their horrible crimes have fascinated musicians ever since – most famously Morrissey, who wrote 'Suffer Little Children' for the Smiths' eponymous debut album of 1984, and Throbbing Gristle, whose chilling 'Very Friendly' appeared on their 1977 *First Annual Report* LP. Both songs were informed by Emlyn Williams' 1967 *In Cold Blood*-style book about the case, *Beyond Belief*. A band called the Moors Murderers was formed by future Visage singer Steve Strange in 1977, with members including Pretenders' frontwoman Chrissie Hynde and Clash drummer Topper Headon. They recorded – but never released – a song called 'Free Hindley' before splitting in early 1978.
3. Jon Savage, 'Someone Take These Dreams Away', *Mojo*, July 1994.
4. David Bowie would perform 'My Death' to its most dramatic effect as a prelude to announcing his retirement from the music industry and killing off Ziggy at Hammersmith Odeon on 3 July 1973. This itself was a tribute to Jacques Brel's own public retirement from performing at the height of his fame in 1966.
5. See Gareth Ashton's *Manchester: It Never Rains . . . A City Primed for Punk Rock* (Empire Publications, 2019) for the full story of the integral role these clubs played in shaping the identity of Manchester's musical history.
6. According to Annik Honoré, the scene was accurately portrayed in Anton Corbijn's 2007 Curtis biopic *Control*, which was itself based on *Touching from a Distance*, although she strongly disputed the rest of the film's portrayal of her. Deborah Curtis recounts smashing her husband's copy of *Low* to pieces when she found out about Honoré's existence. Annik, who spoke to very few people about Curtis, besides Tony Wilson's former wife Lindsay Reade and journalist Mick Middles for their 2006 *Torn Apart* book, died from cancer in 2014.
7. Phillippe Cornet, Ian Curtis and Annik Honoré – 'The Dazzling History of Joy Division', Joy Division/New Order blogspot, retrieved 28 July 2021.
8. For Ebert's full and insightful appraisal of the film see rogerebert.com/reviews/great-movie-stroszek-1977. There is further reference to Stroszek on the run-off groove to the LP *Still*, a compilation of live and unheard studio recordings by Joy Division released by Factory in October 1981 – etched into the run-off grooves: 'The Chicken Won't Stop' (side A), 'Chicken Tracks Across the Grooves' (sides B and C), 'The Chicken Stops Here' (side D). joydiv.org/st.htm
9. Deborah Curtis, *Touching from a Distance* (Faber & Faber, 1995), p. 127.
10. *Still* reviewed 17 October 1981, Biba Kopf, *NME*.
11. Magazine interviewed by Toby Manning, 2005 from Rock's Back Pages.
12. Or so Devoto would claim in a 2009 interview with Ian Shuttleworth in the *Financial Times*: 'It was the sub-editor's piece of pure mischief! But it's nice to play with it mischievously occasionally.' It was a line that would go on to inspire the 1998 Momus affirmation 'The Most Important Man Alive' – for the full, hilarious lyrics, see imomus.com/devoto.html

13. See John L. Williams' *Miss Shirley Bassey* (Quercus, 2011) for the full story of how this remarkable song came into being. Barry Adamson brilliantly describes his cinematic awakening to it on a rainy-day trip to Morecambe in his superb memoir *Up Above the City, Down Beneath the Stars* (Omnibus, 2021).
14. Themselves named after a book, a 1963 non-fiction paperback by Michael Leigh about 'deviant' sexual practices in the US.
15. *John Barry: The Early Years*, Leonard Walker, p. 32, retrieved from johnbarry.org.uk
16. Michael Bracewell, 'Her Dark Materials', *The Guardian*, 24 September 2005.
17. Siouxsie's whip was legendary – Bertie Marshall's *Berlin Bromley* (SAF Publishing, 2007) recounts a party where she scored weals on his parents' ceiling with said accoutrement. While touring with John Cale in the US in 1997, Siouxsie talked him into performing 'Venus in Furs' with her. 'I knew that since the Velvets split John had some bad feelings, like he didn't want to go back to "that fucking band again",' she told Martin Aston for *Mojo* in September 1988, 'but he came around to it. I worked my spell on him.'
18. Ironically, it would be the combination of Steve Lillywhite and Brian Eno who would turn U2 into the biggest global stadium act of this generation, spawning the all-conquering style vacuum of Coldplay in their wake.
19. Members of Charles Manson's California-based cult, known as 'The Family', carried out a string of brutal murders in Hollywood on his behest in 1969, including that of pregnant actress Sharon Tate, wife of film director Roman Polanski, and four others on 8 August; and restaurateurs Leno and Rosemary LaBianca two days later. The words 'Helter Skelter' were written in Leno LaBianca's blood on his living-room walls. Manson's explanation, as told to the court at his subsequent trial, was: 'It's the Beatles, the music they're putting out. The kids listen to this music and pick up the message. It's subliminal . . .'
20. Overview of the Southall demonstration, Investigating officers' reports into the death of Blair Peach and the decision of the then Director of Public Prosecutions (Report), Metropolitan Police, 24 April 1979. After Peach's death was ruled by the coroner as misadventure, the officers likely responsible, one whom was found to be in possession of Nazi regalia, never faced prosecution. The Special Patrol Group (SPG) was disbanded in 1986. For the complete history of RAR, see Daniel Rachel's epic pop oral history *Walls Come Tumbling Down* (Picador, 2016).
21. It has been claimed Bernard Sumner took this name from Prinz Albrecht Strasse, where the Gestapo HQ in Berlin was situated. Questioned about this by his official biographer David Nolan, Sumner responded that it came from a mishearing of the name of playwright Bertolt Brecht as Bernard Albrecht.
22. The star of Johnny Speight's popular BBC sitcom, *Till Death Us Do Part*, which aired from 1965–75. The bigoted Alf Garnett was played by Warren Mitchell, a Jewish Londoner from Malcolm McLaren's old manor, Stoke Newington. It was perhaps a desire on McLaren's part to outrage the non-Scottish half of his family – and 'not be boring' – by including the swastika on items of his design.
23. One of a succession of movie reworkings of Edgar Allan Poe stories invariably starring Vincent Price as a Satanic nobleman that began with Roger Corman's classic

trilogy *The House of Usher* (1960), *The Pit and the Pendulum* (1961) and the visually stunning *Masque of the Red Death* (1964, with Nicolas Roeg as his cinematographer).

24. *Haigh: The Mind of a Murderer* by Arthur La Bern (WH Allen, 1973). La Bern was one journalist covering the case who became obsessed with Haigh. Another was Duncan Webb, the *Sunday People* crime correspondent who set up a sensational scoop with Haigh's wife – whom he had long since deserted – acting as witness to her marriage to her longtime companion the moment Haigh was safely dangling from celebrated hangman Albert Pierrepoint's noose. Haigh's story has been dramatised many times since – loveable Martin Clunes was depicting him in ITV's *A Is for Acid* as recently as 2002.
25. Chris Parry would continue to manage the Cure until 1988 and put out their records until 2001, when he sold Fiction to Universal.
26. Amusingly, Paul Morley's early life is a reverse of Robert Smith's – he was born in Farnham, Surrey, and was but an infant when his parents moved him to Reddish, Stockport, from where he commenced his career as a professional northerner.
27. norselandsrock.com/siouxsie-and-the-banshees-drop-dead-celebration. Retrieved 19 February 2023. John McKay's quote taken from a 'TV interview', for whom and when not stated.

Chapter 3: Magic, Murder and the Weather

1. According to Jaz Colman, interviewed by Andrew Perry in *Mojo*, January 2020. However, in Chris Bryans' *Killing Joke: A Prophecy Fulfilled* (This Day in Music Books, 2020), Geordie relates that the name came from the girlfriend of one of their flatmates, a nurse called Bindi. The Tavistock Institute of Human Relations is a not-for-profit organisation founded in 1947 with the aim to apply social science to issues in the workplace, in order to improve life for all. See tavinstitute.org
2. 'That Primitive Feeling: Killing Joke' by Phil Sutcliffe, *Sounds*, 9 August 1980.
3. The 4 Be 2s – Cockney rhyming slang for Jews – were a band formed by John Lydon's older brother, Jimmy. The intention behind their name may be attributed to football rivalry between the Arsenal-supporting Irish-Catholic Lydons and their biggest rivals, Tottenham Hotspur, who have historically had a strong Jewish fanbase.
4. Despite his reputation for malpractice and the taint of criminality that hangs around the reputation of the Polish-born Jewish refugee, associate of the Kray Twins and consort of Christine Keeler and Mandy Rice-Davies, Peter Rachman was the only landlord in the area willing to house migrant West Indians invited to relocate to the 'Mother Country' after the Second World War.
5. You could write a book on the social and pop cultural history of W11 – and local psychogeographer Tom Vague has. The complete compiled and revised volumes of his fanzine histories *Getting It Straight in Notting Hill Gate* will be published by Strange Attractor Press in 2023.
6. Release was an agency that provided legal representation for young people charged on drugs offences, founded by Caroline Coon and Rufus Harris in 1967.

7. The squatter suburb comprised Freston Road, Bramley Road and Shalfleet Drive, W10, condemned properties owned by the Greater London Council (GLC), whose residents had been rehoused in new tower blocks. A boho mix of artists, musicians, drug dealers, bikers and politicos moved in and when the GLC tried to evict them in 1977, residents took inspiration from the 1949 Ealing comedy *Passport to Pimlico* and moved to secede from the UK and declare themselves the 'Free and Independent Republic of Frestonia'. They submitted a request to the United Nations and issued their own stamps and visas. This forced the GLC into negotiations and the Bramleys Housing Co-operative formed as a result. Though the UN never responded to the application, the notion to form a breakaway republic was never formally dismissed.
8. 'Killing Joke: The Weird, Wild Story of the Industrial Pioneers', Kory Grow, *Revolver*, 1 January 2003.
9. Heavy Manners, Phil Alexander, *Planet Rock*, September 2017.
10. Originally, they called themselves Bauhaus 1919, but dropped the date before the release of their first single.
11. 'Bauhaus', Mike Stand, *The Face*, February 1982.
12. To see just how closely Bauhaus and their fans emulated the style of the original Bauhaus students, take a look at these photos of the class of 1927: reddit.com/r/OldSchoolCool/comments/ahfd7m/these_bauhaus_art_students_in_1927_look_like
13. Thatcher published the report 'Indictment of Margaret Thatcher, Secretary of State for Education 1970–3. In defence of the Education Act 1944, 7 & 8 Geo 6. Ch. 31. On behalf of local education authorities, teachers, parents, children' in September 1973.
14. Margaret Thatcher, *The Downing Street Years* (HarperCollins, 1993), p. 591. In 1985, Thatcher became the first post-war PM who had studied at Oxford to be denied an honorary degree in protest at her policies on education.
15. 'The *Mojo* Interview: Jaz Coleman', Andrew Perry, *Mojo*, January 2020.
16. Phil Sutcliffe, *Sounds*, 9 August 1980.
17. A varna (class) in Hinduism, Brahmin are typically intellectuals, priests, teachers, healers and protectors of sacred knowledge – all of which Jaz could lay fair claim to.
18. The type of figure for whom the word 'maverick' was invented, Bob Pandy remained a councillor and Labour Party member until his death in 2020.
19. Paul Rambali, *NME*, 15 March 1980.
20. Special Category Status was awarded to political prisoners in Northern Ireland by Tory Secretary of State for Northern Ireland William Whitelaw in 1972. It meant they were treated as *de facto* Prisoners of War, not made to wear a uniform and housed within their own factions with privileges not afforded to the criminal peers. It was phased out in 1976 by the incoming Labour government, who, on the recommendations of the 1975 Gardiner Committee, stripped the paramilitaries of this status and moved them all to the specially constructed H-Blocks of the Maze, where protests began immediately. The 1981 hunger strikes were the culmination of the action. After the death of Bobby Sands and ten other co-strikers, he became a martyr and Thatcher a demon to Irish Republicans. IRA recruitment soared, resulting

in a new wave of violence – according to Peter Taylor's *Provos: The IRA & Sinn Féin* (p. 237): 'It was to be one of the bloodiest periods of the "Troubles". In total, 61 people died, 34 of whom were civilians'.

21. Another band founded in 1976 by a British rocker called Mick Jones – but not the same one as the bassist of the Clash.
22. 'The Killing of Brother Paul', Paul Morley, *NME*, 15 November 1980.
23. Something else Killing Joke took seriously. In the same *Mojo* interview of January 2020 – one of his most entertaining – Coleman claimed his band's early career was funded from the proceeds of hashish smuggled from Iceland.
24. 'The Fatal Curse of Killing Joke', Neil Perry, *Sounds*, 22 November 1986.
25. Sinister Ducks comprised Haskins, Moore and 'Pickle' or 'Mr Licquorice' – a local character who ran a 'mad, anarchic surrealist cabaret' (Haskins' words) called the Deadly Fun Cabaret from an Edwardian pavilion on Northampton racecourse. Their sporadic, improvised gigs were part of these entertainments – for more, see bauhausgigguide.wordpress.com/2013/12/03/the-sinister-ducks-1979-1981
26. Not another doppelganger – the journalist is not the same Andy Gill as was the late Gang of Four guitarist.
27. A sly reference to Jethro Tull's *Thick as a Brick*, itself intended to be a parody of the sort of concept album critics of prog were mocking in 1972.
28. Nirvana's 1992 single 'Come as You Are' rode in on an almost identical riff to Geordie's on 'Eighties' and there was talk of a lawsuit. However, animosities between the bands were dropped after the death of Kurt Cobain (8 April 1994). Nirvana drummer Dave Grohl's subsequent band Foo Fighters covered KJ's 'Requiem' and, in 2003, played drums on the second *Killing Joke* album (the band's eleventh).
29. The original seven series featuring Arthur Daley and Terry McCann ran until 1989, when Waterman quit. It was revived for a further three series with Gary Webster as Arthur's nephew Ray with diminishing comedy returns.
30. The surname Cole is likely derived from the Roman Coelius or Coelestius – or perhaps the Latin *colus*, meaning 'bollock'. Coel, purportedly the ancestor of most sixth-century kings of northern Britain, is mentioned in *The Prosopography of the Later Roman Empire*, vols. 2, 3 (J Martindale, 1980), p. 304. In medieval times, he became 'Old King Cole', the merry old soul – so our Arthur has lineage.

Chapter 4: Rocket from the Crypt

1. Memorandum to the UK Ministry of Defence from USAF Lieutenant Colonel Charles Halt. The Rendlesham Incident has spawned four decades' worth of books, dramas, documentaries, websites and sensational newspaper headlines, offering every kind of theory – from secret military aircraft, unidentified atmospheric phenomenon and a deliberate hoax – to no definitive explanation. In 2010, Lt Col. Halt signed a notarised affidavit in which he stated he believed he had witnessed an extraterrestrial event that had been covered up by both the US and UK governments. See UFO researcher Ian Ridpath's in-depth examination of the evidence at ianridpath.com/ufo/sitemap.html

2. To layer on the UFO-Cold War connections in this corner of Suffolk, Orford Ness itself was home to an atomic weapons' testing sight between 1953 and 1972 that left behind dramatic coastal landmarks known as the Pagodas, now in the care of the National Trust. RAF Bentwaters had its own UFO incident at a time of heightened Cold War tension just before the Suez Crisis, on the night of 13/14 August 1956, involving personnel from both the RAF and USAF. See drdavidclarke.co.uk/radar-uaps/lakenheath-bentwaters-ufo
3. 'The Cramps: Basic Instinct', Bill Holdship, *Mojo*, September 2003.
4. Some accounts say nine, others twenty. Ivy was never clear about what her father's job actually was.
5. Eric Anderson (1923–97) was the father of film-maker Paul Thomas Anderson, whose production company is called Ghoulardi Film.
6. Poison Ivy quoted on punkrocker.org.uk/punkscene/OBITcramps.html, retrieved 29 December 2021.
7. 'The Cramps: Rockabilly Retardation', Sandy Robertson, *Sounds*, 9 June 1979.
8. 'The Cramps: *Songs the Lord Taught Us*', Anna Gaca, *Pitchfork*, 25 October 2020.
9. Seth Rosenfeld, 'Part 4: The Governor's Race', *San Francisco Chronicle*, 9 June 2002.
10. Ibid.
11. Elizabeth Cobbs-Hoffman, Edward Blum and Jon Gjerde, *Major Problems in American History, Volume II: Since 1865* (Wadsworth, 2012).
12. The version told in Ian Johnston's *The Wild Wild World of the Cramps* (Omnibus Press, 1991) and repeated in numerous articles written from their perspective. Kid's own wonderful memoir, *Some New Kind of Kick* (Omnibus Press, 2022), recalls how Ivy and Lux sought out and rebaptised Brian Tristan. But both could equally be true – the brick could have been wrapped in a flyer for those Gun Club gigs at the Hong Kong Café, after all.
13. 'The Ballad of Jeffrey Lee Pierce', Sylvie Simmons, *Mojo*, March 2005.
14. Don Snowden, liner notes for the Gun Club: *Six String Sermon*, Bang Records, 2010.
15. 'The Gun Club Part 2', Ward Dotson, Jeff Clark, *Stomp and Stammer*, stompandstammer.com/feature-stories/the-gun-club-part-2-ward-dotson-interview/, retrieved 4 January 2021.
16. 'Gun Club: Calling on Thunder', Edwin Pouncey, *Sounds*, 23 October 1982.
17. Though in a 2016 interview with *Rolling Stone*, author John Fogerty explained that the song was about America's weaponised society: 'I remember reading around that time that there was one gun for every man, woman and child in America, which I found staggering. So somewhere in the song, I think I said, "200 million guns are loaded" . . . I just thought it was disturbing that it was such a jungle for our citizens just to walk around in our own country . . .'
18. 'Gun Club: Calling on Thunder', Edwin Pouncey, *Sounds*, 23 October 1982.
19. Cassandra Peterson (b. 1951) has lived a colourful life, which included a date with Elvis and an appearance on the front cover of Tom Waits' 1976 album *Small Change*, about which she claims to have no memory.
20. stompandstammer.com/feature-stories/the-gun-club-part-3-patricia-morrison-interview/, retrieved 31 January 2022.

21. Richard Cook, *NME*, 16 October 1982.
22. For the whole story on this, and context for those nationwide riots, see the BBC documentary *The Night James Brown Saved Boston*, available at the time of writing at youtube.com/watch?v=JfSayXyqw64
23. *Lydia Lunch: The War Is Never Over* by Nick Soulsby (Jawbone, 2020), p. 30. There is not enough space here to comprehensively document Lydia's career, but fortunately this book, the accompaniment to Beth B's 2021 film of the same name, does the job with admirable attention to detail.
24. 'Welcome to Fear City: The Inside Stories of New York's Civil Wars', Kevin Baker, *The Guardian*, 18 May 2015, retrieved 8 February 2022. President Gerald Ford was encouraged to veto any financial package to reverse New York's rot by his young chief of staff, Donald Rumsfeld.
25. The birth of hip hop can be traced to the mass looting that went on along electrical shops selling turntables and other DJing equipment on Broadway during the two nights of blackout on 13–14 July 1977.
26. Lydia often included Suicide's 'Frankie Teardrop' in live sets and would later stand in as a vocalist for Vega when he became too ill to perform. She continues to perform Suicide/Vega songs live with Marc Hurtado, and they released the album *Suicide or Murder? You Decide* on Lydia's Widowspeak label in November 2022.
27. ZE – aided and abetted by Island's Chris Blackwell – bridged the gap between punk, funk and disco, also bringing the world Was (Not Was), Kid Creole and the Coconuts, Bill Laswell's Material, Richard Strange, John Cale and Suicide.
28. 'The Birthday Party: Abbo the Album', Andy Gill, *NME*, 13 June 1981. NB: the cultural sensitivities of the *NME* sub-editor who came up with that headline.
29. Harry Howard talking to Daniel Dylan Wray, 'A guitar hero when there were none': the fragile life of Rowland S. Howard, *The Guardian*, 20 April 2020.
30. *Bad Seed*, Ian Johnston (Little, Brown, 1994), p. 30. The first biography of Nick Cave covers his early life in detail with illuminating commentary from both Rowland S. Howard and the elusive Anita Lane, both sadly no longer with us.
31. Ibid., p. 60. Opening with the lines: 'I've been contemplating suicide/But it really doesn't suit my style', 'Shivers' came to a wider audience after its inclusion in the 1986 Richard Lowenstein film *Dogs in Space*, set in the Melbourne of the punk era and starring INXS's Michael Hutchence (1960–97) as Sam, the drug-addled frontman of the band from which the film takes its title. While it is clear that Howard's lyrics are very much tongue-in-cheek, Hutchence would die by his own hand in 1997.
32. *Bad Seed*, p. 63.
33. After the Second World War, thousands of 'Ten Pound Poms' took advantage of an Australian government scheme that offered to resettle them from Britain for just a £10 fare.
34. 'The Birthday Party: The Sound and the Fury', Biba Kopf, *NME*, 26 March 1983.
35. 'After the Pope's Blood: Gatecrashing the Birthday Party', Ralph Traitor, *Sounds*, 3 April 1982.
36. *Bad Seed*, p. 71.
37. Ibid., p. 80.

Chapter 5: London After Dark

1. David Tennant sold the Gargoyle in 1952 to caterer John Negus and it remained popular with the Francis Bacon/Colony Room set. In 1955, it was sold to film producer Michael Klinger – the man who funded *Get Carter* – and Jimmy Jacobs, who transformed it into the Nell Gywn Revue. In 1979, the Comedy Store was launched from the upstairs room, starting the careers of Alexi Sayle, Adrian (Ade) Edmondson, Rik Mayall, French & Saunders and the Comic Strip team, who would change the face of popular comedy over the decade to come.
2. *Gothic Rock*, Mick Mercer (Pegasus Publishing, 1991), p. 102. An extremely entertaining A–Z of Goth from the former *ZigZag* and *Siren* editor, who has been Goth's most persistent chronicler and champion. If you feel I have missed some vital band/artist(s) out of this book, rest assured you'll find a corrective in his.
3. During their brief existence, the Spitfire Boys recruited future Frankie Goes To Hollywood star Paul Rutherford as a singer and also had Wah! singer Pete Wylie pass through their ranks.
4. Budgie talking to Danil Volohov, *Peek-a-Boo* magazine, retrieved 28 February 2022 peek-a-boo-magazine.be/en/interviews/peter-budgie-clarke-siouxsie-the-banshees-the-creatures-2019
5. Despite the prominence of his guitar, McGeoch did not appear on the 'Happy House' or 'Christine' videos as he had yet to sign a deal with Polydor. On the *Kaleidoscope* album, Sex Pistol Steve Jones plays guitar on 'Clockface'.
6. Tom Vague, *Vague#10*, June 1981. Though, lyrically, 'Israel' is one of the most obtuse Banshees lyrics. Its opening line ('Little orphans in the snow') mirrors Teenage Jesus's earlier 'Orphans' ('Little orphans running through the bloody snow') and it does seem doubtful that 'In Israel/Will they sing Happy Noel?'
7. Mark Paytress, sleevenotes for the remastered *Ju Ju* (Polydor, 2006).
8. Siouxsie and the Banshees: 'We were losing our minds', Garry Mullholland, *Uncut*, 24 October 2014.
9. *The War Is Never Over*, p. 99.
10. Lydia, Rowland, Genevieve and Mick recorded more material at this time as Honeymoon in Red, which would take another five years to surface.
11. *Bad Seed*, p. 99. Tracy Pew ended up serving only three months of his sentence, which was reduced for good behaviour.
12. The term 'Angry Young Man' was coined by journalist, writer, social commentator and sometime publican Daniel Farson to describe the wave of social realism novels, plays and films begun by *Room at the Top* and John Osborne's *Look Back in Anger* in the period between 1959 and 1963. Farson described his own affliction with Sohoitis in his classic memoir of time and place, *Soho in the Fifties* (Michael Joseph, 1987).
13. Stevo regarded the term 'Futurist' with disdain because of its associations with pop bands like Spandau Ballet.
14. 'Vixo' was recently re-released on Ann Margaret Hogan's silver vinyl-only *Without the Moon* EP of 2021, along with tracks featuring Barry Adamson, Marc Almond, Jim Thirlwell, Kid Congo Powers, Gini Ball and Jarboe.

15. The first Danceteria show on 30 October 1983 opened with Lydia singing 'So Your Heart' and 'Dead River', both of which would later appear on *Honeymoon in Red* (Widowspeak, 1987), with Thirlwell on sax. She and Jim then paid tribute to Alice Cooper on 'Blue Turk'. Marc debuted songs that would variously appear on the Stevo-compiled *If You Can't Please Yourself, You Can't Please Your Soul* (Some Bizzare, 1983) – 'Love Among the Ruins' – and then his 1983 Mambas' album, *Torment and Toreros* – 'You'll Never See Me on a Sunday' and 'A Million Manias'. Thirlwell/Foetus/Clint Ruin followed with 'Hot Horse', which would appear on Scraping Foetus Off the Wheel's 1984 Some Bizzare album *Hole* and 'Halo Flamin' Lead', from a 1983 *NME* compilation tape, *Mad Mix II*, before Nick Cave closed the show with 'A Box for Black Paul', destined for the first Bad Seeds album, *From Her to Eternity* (Mute, 1984), and 'In the Ghetto' (a 7-inch Mute single in 1984). The encore was the full cast singing 'Body Unknown', an Almond–Thirlwell composition that ended up on Marc's 1986 *Violent Silence* LP (Some Bizzare). With thanks to fromthearchives.com/ll/chronology12.html and Biba Kopf.
16. *The War Is Never Over*, p. 110.
17. And, quite possibly, hashish. We never did get to find out what happened to the *You Only Live Twice*-style underwater recording studio.
18. Killing Joke: 'We went into the most savage jam . . . the universe opened', Peter Watts, *Uncut*, 16 November 2018.
19. 'The Hoax That Joke Built: Killing Joke', Barney Hoskyns, *NME*, 27 February 1982.
20. George McKay, *Glastonbury: A Very English Fair* (Victor Gollancz, 2000), pp. 167–8.
21. Although, in a confrontation with *NME*'s Mat Snow in 1983, Coleman claimed: 'We used that whole situation to our advantage. I'm opposed to the CND.'
22. By December 1982 the Conservatives had regained 44 per cent of the vote, ahead of Michael Foot's Labour and the Social Democratic Party (SDP), whose foundation in March 1981 briefly excited the electorate but ended 1982 in an alliance with the Liberals, their novelty popularity slumped for all time.
23. In a sinister coda to the Pope's visit, on 19 June 1982, three days after victory in the Falklands, the body of Roberto Calvi, known as 'God's banker' for his work with the Vatican, was found hanging underneath London's Blackfriars Bridge. In his pockets were bricks and over £10,000 in cash. Swathed in Mafioso and Opus Dei intrigue, the case has never been solved.
24. 'How the US Almost Betrayed Britain', John O'Sullivan, *Wall Street Journal*, 2 April 2012. See also the BBC documentary series *Thatcher & Reagan: A Very Special Relationship*.
25. It was the Soviets themselves who dubbed Thatcher 'The Iron Lady', in an intended propaganda slur that she took full advantage of. See margaretthatcher.org/document/102947
26. The sleeve artwork for *Revelations* is adorned with Masonic imagery, with the square and compass bookending the track list on the back cover.
27. For a retelling of the hearse tale that also provides evidence of Bauhaus's much-questioned sense of humour, see riotfest.org/2018/06/that-one-time-bauhaus-

bought-a-tour-hearse – adapted from Kevin Haskins' fantastic book *Bauhaus Undead* (Cleopatra Books, 2018).

28. *Gothic Rock*, p. 30.
29. Loring Kent, 'Cover Our Tracks', coverourtracks.com/single-post/2018/03/05/kick-in-the-eye-david-j-on-the-visual-art-of-bauhaus-and-love-and-rockets, retrieved 20 March 2022.
30. At time of writing, this was still available to watch on video at youtube.com/watch?v=Bl0vAAjRvvo. Steve Sutherland later proved his Thatcher-like disinclination for turning by defecting from *Melody Maker* to take the editorship of hostile rival *NME* in 1992.
31. Fittingly, 'Goo Goo Muck' appeared on the soundtrack to *Texas Chainsaw Massacre 2* (Tobe Hooper, 1986) and has recently been revived by Tim Burton for his Netflix Addams Family reboot, *Wednesday*, with star Jennifer Ortega seen dancing to the Cramps classic in November 2022. The compilation CD series *Songs We Taught the Cramps* collates the original material Lux and Ivy spent their lives collecting. See cryptrecords.com and find further rarities on the fabulous trashwax.com
32. 'The Cramps: Basic Instinct', Bill Holdship, *Mojo*, September 2003.
33. 'The Cramps: Twisted Tales', *Vive Le Rock!*, July 2011.
34. Dave Edmunds had previously been in a band called the Stray Cats himself – led by David Essex in the 1974 Michael Apted movie *Stardust*.

Chapter 6: Goth's Own County

1. Learn more about Leeds history/heraldry at leedsowltrail.com
2. The Poulson scandal, which implicated ministers in Ted Heath's Conservative government, leading to the resignation of Home Secretary Reginald Maudling and the jailing of Scotland's top civil servant 'Gorgeous' George Pottinger and leader of Newcastle City Council T. Dan Baker, was dramatised in Peter Flannery's 1996 landmark BBC series, *Our Friends in the North*. You will find further shades of Poulson and Baker in David Peace's *Nineteen Seventy-Four* (1999) and Martyn Waites' *The White Room* (2004) respectively.
3. To witness the full glory of proto-Goth Thackray, see the 2022 *Jake Thackray at the BBC* two-DVD collection and read *Beware of the Bull: The Enigmatic Genius of Jake Thackray* by Paul Thompson and John Watterson (Scratching Shed, 2022).
4. 'Life Before Alice: Andrew Eldritch, Leeds & the Birth of the Sisters of Mercy', Mark Andrews, *The Quietus*, 17 November 2016.
5. 'The Mekons: Blows Against Individuation', Mary Harron, *Melody Maker*, 3 February 1979.
6. 'The Sisters of Mercy: The Devil's Floorshow', Adam Sweeting, *Melody Maker*, 15 January 1983.
7. 'Post Punk Leeds', Jane Hector Jones, *Louder Than War*, 12 November 2020. Pearman had his own band, Vicious Circle, before joining the Sisters. They played one 'disastrous' drunken gig at the F Club, witnessed by an amused Craig Adams, before disbanding.

8. Ibid.
9. Read the full account here: thesistersofmercy.com/mek/mekddone.htm
10. The good Doktor has been through several incarnations since and currently responds to readers' letters on the Sisters' official website: thesistersofmercy.com/misc/deardok.htm
11. 'Post Punk Leeds', Jane Hector Jones, *Louder Than War*, 12 November 2020.
12. According to Jon Langford, Eldritch even called his fridge Spiggy.
13. The journalist Andy Gill finally got to meet Gang of Four's Andy Gill in a piece for *The Independent* on 17 September 2009. Gang of Four were active again and having a critical renaissance. Tragically, the musician was an early casualty of Covid-19, dying on 1 February 2020 after returning from a Gang of Four tour in Asia in November 2019. He was just sixty-four.
14. On 28 May 1981.
15. *The Mekons Story*, a compilation of early recordings, released in 1982.
16. Following a falling-out with Red Rhino's Tony 'K' Kostrzewa, Adrian Collins separated from the label, taking the Mekons/Langford/Three Johns with him. CNT was named after the Spanish anarcho-syndicalist party who refused to take orders from the Soviets during the Civil War.
17. Adrenochrome is a chemical byproduct of adrenalin, which scientists in the '50s researched in vain to try to find a link with the cause of schizophrenia. The substance found its way into texts assuredly read by Eldritch: Aldous Huxley's *The Doors of Perception* (1954), Antony Burgess' *A Clockwork Orange* (1962) and Hunter S. Thompson's *Fear and Loathing in Las Vegas* (1971), in which Thompson's attorney, Dr Gonzo, advises him, adrenochrome 'makes pure mescaline seem like ginger beer' and that 'there's only one source for this stuff – the adrenaline gland from a living human body'. This hyperbolic line has lately been seized upon by American adherents of QAnon, as proof of the conspiracy theory that adrenochrome is being harvested by liberal elites from the blood of kidnapped children in the hope of achieving immortality. This has since led them to the YouTube page for the Sisters' single, where its front cover – Francis Bacon's 'Screaming Pope' *Head VI* (1949) with a blood red underlay – may have acted as a further trigger to their beliefs.
18. To see what he means, take a look at this superb footage of one night in Batley's answer to the Batcave – and probably *the* most perfect document of the Goth '80s: youtube.com/watch?v=A9sMZ_5NjM8
19. Weirdly, the live favourite 'Good Things', which was the fourth song recorded with John Ashton at KG Sounds, never appeared on any Sisters vinyl, although it can be acquired on its Peel *Session* form in the *BBC Sessions 1982–84* album (BBC, 2021).
20. A fact that was suppressed until after Thatcher's death (2013) and only came to light in 2015. Former *Times/Sunday Times* editor Harold Evans told the full story here: theguardian.com/uk-news/2015/apr/28/how-margaret-thatcher-and-rupert-murdoch-made-secret-deal
21. From the full and fascinating story told in Ruth Dudley Edwards' *Newspapermen: Hugh Cudlipp, Cecil Harmsworth King and the Glory Days of Fleet Street* (Secker, 2003).

Chapter 7: Cowboys and Indians

1. Michelle, who, inspired by Vivienne Westwood, studied fashion, has her own clothing line, Sexy Hooligans, which also makes reproduction Seditionaries T-shirts. Wear them at your peril! sexyhooligans.com
2. As previously mentioned in Chapter 5, cowpunk was a genre the Gun Club also sometimes got roped into. A crossbreed of country and punk that, along with Jeffrey Lee's combo, began life in late-'70s California with Social Distortion, the Violent Femmes and the Meat Puppets. This sort of thing has subsequently morphed into what is now called 'alt country' or 'Americana'.
3. As told to Colin Liddell of the *International Herald Tribune* in 2010. Astbury's own accounts vary as to whether he came back from Canada at the age of sixteen or eighteen and are vague on how long he was in the British Army for, although he always recalls his tenure in the forces with vehemence. His memory of his Indigenous Canadian schoolmate was told to Adam Wallis of *Global News*, June 2019.
4. The true identities of the 'Thatchergate Tapes' perpetrators were only revealed by the *Observer* in January 1984 and how the paper managed to find out remains a mystery to Crass to this day. For the full story and transcript of the tapes, see killyourpetpuppy.co.uk/news/crass-capital-radio-reagan-thatcher-tape-new-broadcast-270184. For the full story of Crass, see *The Story of Crass* by George Berger (Omnibus, 2008).
5. 'Southern Death Cult: The Last Tribe', Paul Morley, *NME*, 2 October 1982.
6. *Adam and the Ants: Stand and Deliver* documentary (Marco Pirroni, 2006).
7. Sadly, Jaz did not feel the same way. When asked by *NME*'s Mat Snow in August 1983 what he thought about SDC, Coleman responded: 'They're all ex-Killing Joke fans. I don't like their music – it's wimpy, it's not got an edge to it . . . And as for that bloody wossisname, Ian, out of Southern Death Cult, trying to be a Red Indian, well, that really makes me laugh. He looks as if he couldn't skin a rabbit, let alone a buffalo, right?' I think that's what you call getting a Bradford Quarter.
8. 'Southern Death Cult: The Last Tribe', Paul Morley, *NME*, 2 October 1982.
9. Malcolm Wyatt, writewyattuk.com/2019/01/17/the-leader-of-the-pack-theatre-of-hate-spear-of-destiny-the-kirk-brandon-interview/, retrieved 11 May 2022.
10. killyourpetpuppy.co.uk/news/theatre-of-hate-ss-label-1980 and also killyourpetpuppy.co.uk/news/the-pack-ss-label-1979, retrieved 11 May 2022.
11. For the full Rough Trade story, see Neil Taylor's *Document and Eyewitness: An Intimate History of Rough Trade* (Orion, 2010).
12. 'Theatre of Hate live at London University', Andy Gill, *NME*, 16 May 1981.
13. 'Last of the Great Ear-O's! Theatre of Hate live at Woodville Hall, Gravesend', Paul Morley, *NME*, 27 February 1982. Morley was not the only one to find Kirk's ears amusing. At art college, in the mid-'80s, I was introduced to a young man as Kirk and proceeded to call him by that name. Only decades later, I discovered 'Kirk' was a moniker given to him by his peers – the poor chap wore his hair long in a vain attempt to disguise his own prominent auditory organs.
14. As far as I can ascertain, sadly no relation to John Atkinson Grimshaw.

15. 'Theatre of Hate: The National Youth Theatre', Dave Rimmer, *Smash Hits*, 4 March 1982.
16. Who had himself once been in a band called the London SS. 'We hadn't thought at all about the Nazi implications,' he told author Chris Salewicz, for his book *Redemption Song: The Authorised Biography of Joe Strummer* (HarperCollins, 2006). 'It just seemed like a very anarchic, stylish thing to do.' Like Malcolm McLaren, Jones has Jewish heritage on his mother's side, which perhaps goes to illustrate that shock value, rather than racism, was the intent of all the Nazi symbolism that surrounded punk.
17. Kirk and Billy interviewed by Mick Peek for Duffy's website, November 2016; Billy Duffy to Paul Lester, *The Guardian*, 23 August 2010.
18. Southern Death Cult interviewed by Tom Vague, *Vague 14*, 14 February 1983.
19. 'In the Batcave with Mr and Mrs Fiend', Nix Lowery, *The Quietus*, 8 September 2010.
20. There is no apostrophe in Gods Zoo. Read Tom Vague's full memoir of his time as the 'honorary fifth member' of Southern/Death Cult at vaguerants.org.uk/?page_id=266
21. In *Vague 15*, Aki explained how mutual friend Mark Manning, aka Zodiac Mindwarp, saw Bee's picture in *Skin Two* magazine and passed it on to him as a possible replacement for Ian Astbury. Getting the Fear recently released their archive of recorded material and demos, *Death is Bigger 1984–5* (Dias Records).
22. designermagazine.tripod.com/KirkBrandonINT1.html, retrieved 21 May 2022.

Chapter 8: Ranters, Diggers and Levellers

1. Peter Chippindale and Peter Horrie, *Stick It Up Your Punter* (Faber & Faber, 1990).
2. Margaret Thatcher, *The Downing Street Years* (HarperCollins, 1993), p. 341.
3. The equivalent of the total sum the government paid to retain MacGregor's services. Nigel Lawson, *The View from No. 11: Memoirs of a Tory Radical* (Bantam, 1992), p. 157.
4. Downing Street memos released by the National Archives in 2015 revealed that Scargill was not misinformed: there was indeed a clandestine plan to shut down seventy-five mines over three years. See: bbc.co.uk/news/uk-25549596
5. *Gothic Rock*, p. 162.
6. Ibid., p. 164.
7. Ibid., p. 165.
8. The son of a Puritan clergyman, Matthew Hopkins (b. Wenham, Suffolk, c.1620–d. 12 August 1647) first rose to infamy in 1644, two years into the English Civil War, when he claimed to have discovered a coven of six witches in Manningtree, Essex. Assisted by John Stearne of that parish, he subsequently took upon himself the role of witchfinder general. Taking advantage of a country convulsed down both religious and royalist-republican lines, they sallied forth throughout East Anglia between 1644 and 1667, persecuting, torturing and hanging women accused of consorting with the Devil, including those in Great Yarmouth. My history lessons included a school visit to the Tollhouse Museum, where the dungeon in which Hopkins

interrogated victims remains. For the full story, see *Witchfinders* by Malcolm Gaskill (John Murray, 2005).

9. Al Puppy (Alistair Livingston), sleevenotes to *Let the Tribe Increase* re-release on Overground Records, 2010.
10. Ibid.
11. The original Levellers, Ranters and Diggers grew out of the conflict between king and Parliament that triggered the Civil War. They were led by pamphleteers John Liburn, Richard Overton, William Walwyn and Gerald Winstanley, who took advantage of the new technology of the printing press and the freedom of speech afforded them at a time when there were no censorship laws to spread their ideas about democracy. But even Oliver Cromwell could not adopt principles so dangerous to those with a vested interest in property and power. By 1650 these radicals had been forced off their communal land, deported or killed. For more, see their great admirer Tony Benn at bbc.co.uk/history/british/civil_war_revolution/benn_levellers_01.shtml
12. 'Bittersweet' lyrics by Justin Sullivan © Attack Attack Music/Warner Chappell Music Ltd, reproduced by kind permission.
13. Jason Harris, Robert Heaton obituary, mooseharris.com, retrieved 27 May 2022.
14. See jordansvillage.co.uk/about.html for more.
15. Formally known as the Religious Society of Friends, the name 'Quaker' derives from an insult aimed at practitioners of this radical strain of Protestantism, founded during the Civil War by George Fox, who claimed to have had a vision on Pendle Hill in 1652, where God told him to restore a 'pure' Christian faith. Fox became an itinerant preacher and was brought before magistrate Gervase Bennet on a charge of blasphemy in 1650. According to Fox's autobiography, Bennet 'was the first that called us Quakers, because I bade them tremble at the word of the Lord'. The place of Fox's vision had been, in 1612, the site of the most notorious witch trials in British history.
16. Bradford is also the only UK city to have a peace museum, where you can learn about all those involved in the perpetual struggle against war. See peacemuseum.org.uk
17. 'Join the Professionals: New Model Army', Phil Sutcliffe, *Q*, May 1989.
18. 'Justin Sullivan on 40 years of New Model Army', Sebastian Oake, *Yorkshire Post*, 29 January 2020.
19. Steven Wells (1960–2009), aka 'Swells', was a motormouth journalist, poet and comedian, who regularly performed with the Mekons, the Fall and Gang of Four. He first blagged his job on *NME* pretending to be a girl called Susan Williams – when anyone from the paper rang up for him, Joolz did his voice. Swells was not unduly impressed by what he had helped to create in bringing Ian Astbury home: a typically acerbic Susan Williams review of NMA from 6 August 1983 dismisses the Cult as 'sub-Deep Purple parodies [with a] faked affinity with North American aborigines'. Unlike Bee or Steven Rawlings, you would not have easily mistaken this burly skinhead for a woman, so it wasn't too long before his cover was blown. He continued to write as Steven Wells, starting his own pop video company

GobTV; and pulp fiction imprint Attack! with the equally formidable *Sounds/NME* news editor Tommy Udo. He died tragically young at forty-nine from Hodgkin's Lymphoma. Read Joolz's hilarious account of how Steven (as Ed) became Susan (Edwina) here: joolzdenby.co.uk/post/episode-14

20. *Stick It Up Your Punter*, pp. 175–77.
21. A recent report by *The Guardian* states that South Yorkshire Police officially put the figure at 6,000 officers from eighteen different forces. Mark Garnett's social history *From Anger to Apathy: The British Experience since 1975* (Jonathan Cape, 2007) says the number of pickets peaked at 10,000. For more detail, see: theguardian.com/politics/2017/may/18/scandal-of-orgreave-miners-strike-hillsborough-theresa-may. To see the Ridley Plan, go to margaretthatcher.org/document/110795. For more on the Orgreave Truth and Justice Campaign, visit otjc.org.uk
22. After the subsequent trial in July 1985 collapsed, all of the miners arrested at the Battle of Orgreave were acquitted. There was never any inquiry into the conduct of the police. Five years later, South Yorkshire Police agreed to pay nearly £500,000 in damages to thirty-nine of the surviving men, without admitting culpability. The campaign for a full inquiry into Orgreave goes on.
23. Thatcher had previously described the miners as 'the enemy within' in a speech to the 1922 Committee in June 1984, reproduced here: margaretthatcher.org/document/105563. For more on the speech to the 1984 conference, go to cam.ac.uk/research/news/the-speech-that-never-was-thatcher-papers-for-1984-open-to-the-public
24. '1984' lyrics by Justin Sullivan © Attack Attack Music/Warner Chappell Music Ltd, reproduced by kind permission.

Chapter 9: Through the Looking Glass

1. 'Echo and the Bunnymen: The Making of the Killing Moon', Terry Staunton, *Uncut*, November 2008.
2. John Peel was born in Heswall Cottage Hospital, in the village of Heswall on the Wirral Peninsula, not actually in Liverpool. But he always identified as a Scouser and Liverpool were his team.
3. There is another football team in Liverpool, too.
4. See beatlesfaq.com/2019/10/was-john-lennon-born-during-air-raid.html
5. 'Ian McCulloch: This Much I Know', Andrew Harrison, *The Guardian*, 13 April 2003.
6. 'Echo and the Bunnymen', Max Bell, *The Face*, August 1984.
7. See klf.de/home/tag/k-foundation and the 1995 documentary *The K Foundation Burn a Million Quid* if you possibly haven't heard this one before.
8. Echo and the Bunnymen talking to Dave Rimmer, *Smash Hits*, 3 February 1983.
9. *Turquoise Days: The Weird World of Echo & the Bunnymen*, Chris Adams (Soft Skull, 2002), p. 84.
10. 'Ian McCulloch and Will Sergeant: How We Made "The Killing Moon"', Dave Simpson, *The Guardian*, 7 April 2015.

11. 'Echo & the Bunnymen', Max Bell, *The Face*, August 1984.
12. Trident Studios in Soho is also where Marc Bolan recorded his T. Rex albums with Tony Visconti.
13. Stephen Humphreys went on to work with Ian McCulloch on his 1992 *Mysterio* album.
14. Nine of which appeared on the vinyl, the extra five being added to the cassette and newfangled CD versions of the album.
15. Another fan of Lord Byron, Pete Burns wanted that album to be called *Mad, Bad and Dangerous to Know*, but the title was rejected by their record company, Epic. He would get his wicked way with it on the band's third album.
16. Wayne Hussey talking to John Meagher, *Irish Independent*, 30 April 2022.
17. See Robert Cowlin's detailed account of the making of *First and Last and Always* at heavyleatherblog.wordpress.com/tag/the-sisters-of-mercy
18. Magee served nineteen years for the Brighton bombing and was released under the Good Friday Agreement in 1999. Since his release, he has forged a friendship with Jo Berry, the daughter of his victim Sir Anthony Berry, and the pair have given seminars and made documentaries on the subjects of forgiveness and empathy. Jo Berry wrote the forward to *Where Grieving Begins* (Pluto Press, 2021).
19. For the full text of Margaret Thatcher's speech, see britishpoliticalspeech.org/speech-archive.htm?speech=130
20. The collected *Great Pop Things* strips were published in a handsome volume by Verse Chrorus Verse in 1998, with an introduction by Greil Marcus. The strip returned to *Bizarre* magazine while I was its deputy editor between 1998 and 2001.

Chapter 10: Psychedelic Jungle

1. A line also attributed to Malcolm McLaren and Jamie Reid.
2. Which was actually called simply *The Beatles*, but pop artist Richard Hamilton's minimalist cover design – itself a reaction to its ornate predecessor *Sgt Pepper's Lonely Hearts Club Band* by Hamilton's contemporaries, Peter Blake and Jann Haworth – has led to it almost always being referred to colloquially.
3. 'The Making of *A Kiss in the Dreamhouse*', Garry Mulholland, *Uncut*, November 2012.
4. Ibid.
5. Robert Smith talking to Jim Green, *Trouser Press*, 1 November 1981.
6. Ibid.
7. Jeff Aptead, *Never Enough: The Story of the Cure* (Omnibus Press, 2005).
8. Ibid.
9. stevenseverin.com/lyrics2.htm, retrieved 4 July 2022.
10. Ibid.
11. post-punk.com/artwork-of-the-gloves-jeanette-landray-plus-interview, retrieved 5 July 2022.
12. stevenseverin.com/collaborate.htm, retrieved 5 July 2022.
13. stevenseverin.com/lyrics2.htm, retrieved 5 July 2022.

14. 'All Creatures Great and Small', Richard Cook, *NME*, 14 May 1983.
15. Ibid.
16. Donovan, a fellow follower of the Maharishi, taught Lennon the technique during a Transcendental Meditation course in Rishikesh, India, in February 1968. Mr 'Mellow Yellow' in turn said he had learned 'clawhammer picking' by studying the guitar style of the Carter Family's Mother Maybelle. What really went on with the Maharishi, Prudence Farrow et al. in India? Some possibilities shared here: denofgeek.com/books/the-beatles-the-strange-history-of-sexy-sadie
17. 'The Cultivation of a Better Noise', Cynthia Rose, *NME*, 22 September 1984.
18. walesonline.co.uk/news/wales-news/how-lead-singer-doctor-medics-1799843, retrieved 7 July 2022.
19. 'Summer Solstice: How the Stonehenge Battles Faded', Emma Hallett, BBC News, 20 June 2014.
20. counterfire.org/articles/history/21264-the-battle-of-the-beanfield-an-important-anniversary-in-the-history-of-state-brutality, retrieved 8 July 2022.
21. By the time the six-year trial was over, the derisory £24,000 in damages eventually awarded to twenty-one of the travellers was eaten up by their legal fees after the judge declined to award their costs. There has never been any official inquiry into the police's handing of events. For more, see *The Battle of the Beanfield*, edited by Andy Worthington (Enabler Publications, 2005). There is plenty of footage from the Battle to be found on YouTube.
22. Said fashion item is still available at todestrieb.co.uk/products/conflict-only-stupid-bastards-help-emi-t-shirt if you want one – and badges, too. What kind of a bread-head will it make you, though?
23. Although the track they recorded together, 'Fun Factory', would not see the light of day until 1991, when it was released as a Damned single on Deltic.
24. Dave and Laurie Vanian opened their own design company, Symphony of Shadows, in Hyper Hyper on Kensington High Street in 1983. Laurie, who trained at New York's Fashion Institute of Technology and St Martin's in London, continues to run the company. See symphonyofshadowsdesign.wordpress.com. Meanwhile, in one of those eerie coincidences endemic to this book, *Phantasmagoria*'s cover star is the future Mrs Nick Cave, Susie Bick, photographed in Kensal Green cemetery by doomed smudger Bob Carlos Clarke, now a resident of the equally Gothic Old Brompton cemetery.

Chapter 11: Born Under a Bad Sign

1. *Bad Seed*, p. 113.
2. Ibid., pp. 125–6.
3. Ibid., p. 109.
4. Thank you to translator Katja Klier for the intel on Blixa's assumed identity. She notes: 'Blixa has chosen to adopt the correct German spelling of the word Bargeld in his tribute to Mr Baargeld.'

5. '"You Can't Kill the Drill": Einstürzende Neubauten's Blixa Bargeld Interviewed', Luke Turner, *The Quietus*, 18 November, retrieved 18 July 2022.
6. fromthearchives.com/en/chronology1.html, retrieved 18 July 2022.
7. esotericarchives.com/dee/monad.htm, retrieved 18 July 2022.
8. Nurse with Wound, Coil and Current 93 all form part of a Goth parallel universe that has been given its most scrupulous and authoritative chronicle in David Keenan's *England's Hidden Reverse* (Strange Attractor), available in highly collectible formats at strangeattractor.co.uk/shoppe/englands-hidden-reverse
9. *Bad Seed*, p. 207.
10. To properly explain Tav Falco's Panther Burns would take more space than this book allows. You could begin at their Wiki page – despite its flagged-up serious issues – and just see where that rabbit hole takes you.
11. Patricia Morrison talking to Jeff Clark, stompandstammer.com/feature-stories/the-gun-club-part-3-patricia-morrison-interview, retrieved 19 July 2022.
12. Another side project would come out of their cross-pollination with the Melbourne music scene, when the frontman of Spencer P. Jones' next band, the Beasts of Bourbon, the formidable Tex Perkins, joined Patricia, Kid and friends in Fur Bible in 1985 – their 'Plunder the Tombs' EP (New Rose) made in London with J. G. Thirlwell in the producer's seat.
13. Kid Congo Powers, liner notes to *Las Vegas Story* reissue (Blixa Sounds, 2022).
14. 'The Gun Club: I Left My Hat in San Francisco', Richard Kick, *ZigZag*, September 1984.
15. 'The Ballad of Jeffrey Lee Pierce', Sylvie Simmons, *Mojo*, March 2005.
16. *Bad Seed*, p. 142.
17. Ibid., p. 144.
18. My dream gig would be a soundclash between Barry and Jim, using speaker stacks designed by Big Daddy Roth and with the LSO and a gospel choir between them.
19. *Up Above the City, Down Beneath the Stars*, p. 247.
20. Ibid., p. 248. Cave's first post-Birthday Party live performance, in Melbourne on New Year's Eve 1983, was advertised as Nick Cave: Man or Myth? – a reference to the title of a book his father Colin wrote about Ned Kelly. Here, Cave also recruited guitarist Hugo Race, who appears on *From Her to Eternity*. Back in the UK, for their first gig at the Fridge in Brixton on 10 April 1984, the band were going by the Crampsian moniker Nick Cave and the Cavemen, after which they became the more Biblical Bad Seeds.
21. *Bad Seed*, p. 99.
22. Ian McFarlane, *Encyclopedia of Australian Rock and Pop* (Allen & Unwin, 1999), archived at whammo.com.au/encyclopedia.asp?articleid=235
23. 'Crime Wave: Crime and the City Solution', Biba Kopf, *NME*, 6 July 1985.
24. 'Crime and the City Solution: Crime and Punishment', Jack Barron, *Sounds*, 9 November 1985.
25. *Bad Seed*, p. 178.
26. Mick and Nick were not so impressed by Screamin' Jay. 'I had to sit next to him all the way to Perth and he was listening to *Billy Joel's Greatest Hits*!' an outraged

Mick Harvey told Ian Johnston. 'I can't stand Nick Cave!' Jay countered. Ibid., p. 183.

27. *Up Above the City, Down Beneath the Stars*, p. 290.
28. Andrew Neil, *Full Disclosure* (Macmillan, 1996), p. 80.
29. 'The Wapping Dispute 30 Years On', Donald Macintyre, *The Independent*, 21 January 2016. Read the rest of this insider's description of the events of 25–6 January 1986 at independent.co.uk/news/media/press/wapping-dispute-30-years-on-how-rupert-murdoch-changed-labour-relations-and-newspapers-forever-a6826316.html
30. As reported in *Undercover* by Rob Evans and Paul Lewis (Guardian Faber, 2013). For more on Special Branch's involvement at Wapping, see specialbranchfiles.uk/wapping-strike-story
31. 'I couldn't believe it,' Benn wrote of that night when 200 people were injured, 'seeing the police flailing about with their truncheons at people who, a moment earlier had been standing talking, and to know that it was authorised, planned.' Tony Benn, *End of an Era: Diaries 1980–89* (Penguin, 1994), pp. 448–50.
32. Statistics from 'Rupert Murdoch and the Battle of Wapping: 25 Years On,' Jon Henley, *The Guardian*, 27 July 2011.
33. *Bad Seed*, pp. 197–8.
34. Tracee Hutchinson, *Your Name's on the Door* (ABC, 1992), p. 117.
35. Kid Congo Powers, *Some New Kind of Kick* (Omnibus Press, 2022), pp. 198–9.

Chapter 12: Something Wicked This Way Comes

1. nytimes.com/1982/05/11/science/new-homosexual-disorder-worries-health-officials.html, retrieved 31 July 2022
2. tht.org.uk/our-work/about-our-charity/our-history/how-it-all-began, retrieved 31 July 2022
3. theguardian.com/culture/2017/sep/04/how-we-made-dont-die-of-ignorance-aids-campaign, retrieved 31 July 2022
4. Diamanda Galás, Queen Elizabeth Hall London review, Simon Reynolds, *Melody Maker*, 14 January 1989.
5. Diamanda Galás talking to Holly Day, tokafi.com/15questions/interviewdiamandagalas
6. 'Diamanda Galás Diva of the Dispossessed', Michael Barclay, exclaim.ca/music/article/diamanda_galas-diva_of_dispossessed
7. Jack Henry Abbott, a virtual lifelong inmate of such brutal penal institutions, was made a cause célèbre by Norman Mailer, who had used Abbott's unsolicited letters to him as vital information for his Pulitzer Prize-winning book on Gary Gilmore, *The Executioner's Song* (Little, Brown, 1979). Mailer had Abbott's writings published as *In the Belly of the Beast* and campaigned for his correspondent's parole, a move that seriously backfired when, on his release and his book's publication day, Abbott stabbed to death waiter Richard Adan in an East Village diner. John Hillcoat corresponded with Abbott after his return to the Big House, gleaning insider details of life in the maximum-security Inferno to use in his film.

8. Diamanda Galás talking to Biba Kopf for a Mute records artist biography, 1996.
9. Gareth Jones talking to Marsha Vdovin at Audio Webzine: uaudio.com/webzine/2006/may/index3.html
10. 'These Immortal Souls: Lost Souls', Ralph Traitor, *Sounds*, 12 December 1987.
11. 'Soul on Ice: Immortalizing Rowland S Howard', Susan Compo, *Option*, May 1992.
12. A music magazine that came complete with a flexidisc of its contents, *Flexipop*! was launched by former *Record Mirror* journalists Barry Cain and Tim Lott in 1981. Despite technology rapidly overtaking its cover-mounted gimmick, back issues with their wares intact are highly sought after – particularly the 1981 flexidisc with Adam and the Ants performing a version of Village People's 'YMCA' as 'ANTS'.
13. Wirral-born Cauty had previously played guitar in a band called Angels One 5.
14. Returning to Leeds, Marx formed a new band, Ghost Dance, with Anne-Marie Hurst, formerly of Keighley's Skeletal Family, re-employed Claire Shearsby as his sound engineer and took a portion the Sisters' audience with him.
15. Thankfully Doktor Avalanche proved more faithful, consistently keeping Eldritch's back.
16. A variant of 'Eldrone', an 'Eldron' was a derogatory term, on a par with 'Goth', used in Great Yarmouth after one such 'weekend weirdo' inadvisably announced his love for Sisters singer 'Andrew Eldron'.
17. Lyrics to 'Prince of Darkness' by Jon Langford/P. Cooper/M.Connors reproduced by kind permission.
18. 'Sisters of Mercy: The Man Who Told the World', Neil Perry, *Sounds*, 19 September 1987.
19. Tony Platt talking to Murray Engleheart and Arnaud Durieux in *AC/DC: Maximum Rock & Roll: The Ultimate Story of the World's Greatest Rock-and-Roll Band* (HarperCollins, 2009), p. 387.
20. Preston was sacked during the making of *Love*. Big Country's Mark Brzezicki filled in for him at the time and you can see him on the 'She Sells Sanctuary' video. You can see the Anadin Brothers in action as Cult back-up dancers on the video for 'Rain'.
21. Lyrics that are uncannily close to those that open the Rutles' 'Get Back' parody 'Get Up and Go'. Neil Innes's lyrics go: 'Working up a fever in a one-horse town was a jockey by the name of Joe'. However, I don't think that 'Lil' Devil' is intentionally a parody of a parody.
22. 'The Cult: Bill and Ian's Excellent Adventure', Steven Wells, *NME*, 19 January 1992.
23. Read Margaret Thatcher's full speech to the 1987 Conservative Party Conference here: margaretthatcher.org/document/106941
24. Watch Michael Fish's downfall here: youtube.com/watch?v=NnxjZ-aFkjs

Chapter 13: The Last Enchantment

1. Statistics on revenues and oil workers wages from *The Guardian*, theguardian.com/commentisfree/2013/apr/19/north-sea-oil-80s-boom

2. Miners' average wage of 1983 from Hansard, hansard.parliament.uk/Lords/1984-12-03/debates/21bf59fe-d7ed-45cb-9715-5d236dde8577/MinersEarnings
3. For the full story of the safety breaches that led to the Piper Alpha disaster, see pubs.acs.org/doi/10.1021/acs.chas.9b00022
4. 'Cocteau Twins *Milk and Kisses*', Barney Hoskyns, *Mojo*, May 1996.
5. 'Elizabeth Fraser: The Cocteau Twins and Me', Dave Simpson, *The Guardian*, 26 November 2009.
6. 'Cocteau Twins: Cocteau Hour', Helen Fitzgerald, *Sounds*, 11 September 1982.
7. 'Cocteau Twins: None of this should have happened', Mark Cooper, *Q*, April 1987.
8. Tim Buckley covered Fred Neil's 'The Dolphins' and you can see him perform it on *The Old Grey Whistle Test* here: youtube.com/watch?v=spgDTEMraBI
9. 'Cocteau Twins: Two's Company', Jonh Wilde, *ZigZag*, October 1983. You can hear the incredibly moving Radio 4 Soul Music investigation of 'Song to the Siren' here: bbc.co.uk/programmes/m00127bz
10. For more on Ivor Raymonde, see bellaunion.com/artists/ivor-raymonde/
11. 'Cocteau Twins: None of this should have happened', Mark Cooper, *Q*, April 1987.
12. 'Cocteau Twins retrospective', David Stubbs, *Uncut*, October 2000.
13. Elizabeth Fraser told Alternative Press' Val Phoenix about her psychotherapy in a piece subsequently published here: cocteautwins.com/embracing-otherness-alternative-press.html
14. Fraser and Buckley recorded one sublime musical memory, 'All Flowers in Time Bend Towards the Sun', which can be found floating in the internet ether.
15. See partisanrecords.com/artists/Suns_Signature
16. 'Coming up for Eire', Dave McCullough, *Sounds*, 15 September 1979. Subscribe to Rock's Back Pages to read the full, fascinating article here: rocksbackpages.com/Library/Article/u2-iet-ali-coming-up-for-eire
17. Jim Thirlwell – who would appear with Friday at Carnegie Hall in New York to perform Virgin Prunes' songs alongside Guggi and Dik on Gavin's fiftieth birthday in 2011 – also used 'the heads of six to eight freshly slaughtered pigs' as stage adornments on his Scraping Foetus off the Wheel live shows in 1985–86.
18. For more on Princess Tinymeat, see dangerousminds.net/comments/princess_tinymeat_meet_the_obscure_genderbending_trashglam_post-punk_goth_o
19. thequietus.com/articles/28487-karl-o-connor-regis-interview-favourite-music?page=8
20. mute.com/virgin-prunes/virgin-prunes-a-short-history
21. Donna Summer later angrily denied making any such comments, saying that she had lost a lot of friends to AIDS. See advocate.com/arts-entertainment/music/2012/05/17/exclusive-donna-summer-denies-making-antigay-remarks-hurt-her
22. See sensesofcinema.com/2016/cteq/the-betrayals-of-rainer-werner-fassbinders-querelle-1982 for the full and equally fantastical story.
23. *Up Above the City, Down Beneath the Stars*, p. 317. To see Barry's video for 'The Man with the Golden Arm', for which he discovered his co-star, Minnie Driver, go to youtube.com/watch?v=kkl0jkb2zWA

24. The antiquated stand, already assessed as a fire risk, was scheduled to be demolished and replaced at the end of the season. See bradfordcityafc.com/club/valley-parade-fire-disaster
25. 'Join the Professionals: New Model Army', Phil Sutcliffe, *Q*, May 1989.
26. Seeing Red Sky Coven was one of the formative experiences that made me think I could become a writer. See newmodelarmy.org/links/red-sky-coven for more about them and their recorded output.
27. 'Archway Towers' lyric by Justin Sullivan/Robert Heaton © Attack Attack Music/ Warner Chappell Music, reproduced by kind permission.
28. Dax also did the cover art for Fripp's 1981 *Let the Power Fall* LP (EG).
29. On its later rerelease on Awesome records, *Pop-Eyes* came in a sleeve with artwork by Holly Warburton. See hollywarbs.com
30. 'Cathouse' was recently reinvigorated by the Damned. Watch them perform it here: youtu.be/0cFPq72z2F4
31. Investigate UnicaZürn further at unicazrn.bandcamp.com/music and find Danielle's online lair at danielledax.com
32. Lyrics from 'Is This the Life?' by Cardiacs written by Tim Smith and reproduced by kind permission of the Alphabet Business Concern.
33. Find out more about Cardiacs and their world at cardiacs.net. Their last guitarist, Kavus Torabi, teamed up with '80s snooker legend Steve 'Interesting' Davis to write the fascinating *Medical Grade Music* (White Rabbit Books, 2021) with Ben Thompson. As well as being a comprehensive guide to the outer reaches of the music cosmos the pair explore in their weekly radio show, this contains a lot more information about Cardiacs and Tim Smith. For a hit of their show, go to nts.live/ shows/fire-shuffle-with-steve-davis-kavus-torabi

Epilogue: The Black Mass

1. For a comprehensive list see what-song.com/Artist/136/The-Cure
2. '"A guitar hero when there were none", the fragile life of Rowland S. Howard', Daniel Dylan Wray, *The Guardian*, 20 April 2020.
3. Mute have subsequently released a remastered double CD of *Teenage Snuff Film* and *Pop Crimes*. Richard Lowenstein and Lynn-Maree Milburn's lyrical 2011 documentary tracing Rowland's life and times, *Autoluminescent*, is highly recommended. Catch up with Harry Howard's band NDE (Near Death Experience) at spookyrecords. com/NDE.html
4. 'Jeffrey Lee Pierce: Impurely an entertainer', Jack Barron, *Sounds*, 25 January 1986.
5. On 17 July 1988, the unfortunate Barron, now writing for *NME*, would catch the end of Nick Cave's fists after he asked the Bad Seed about his own drug problems during an interview the night before.
6. After Pierce's death, Cypress Grove invited friends of Jeffrey Lee to record songs they had worked on together, a project that has so far spawned three albums, *We Are Only Riders* (2009), *The Journey Is Long* (2012) and *Axels & Sockets* (2014), with contributions from Barry Adamson, Mick Harvey, Mark Lanegan, Lydia Lunch and

Jim Sclavunos among others. He has also made three albums with Lydia, *A Fistful of Desert Blues* (2010), *Twin Horses* (with Spiritual Front, 2015) and *Under the Covers with Lydia Lunch* (2017). For more, see rustblade.com/artist/cypress-grove

7. 'The Ballad of Jeffrey Lee Pierce', Sylvie Simmons, *Mojo*, March 2005.
8. 'Echo and the Bunnymen: Shooting from the Lip', David Burke, *Classic Pop*, January 2018.
9. *Good Night and Good Riddance*, David Cavanagh (Faber & Faber, 2015), p. 363.
10. Read the full story here: theguardian.com/football/2016/apr/26/hillsborough-disaster-deadly-mistakes-and-lies-that-lasted-decades
11. 'Spear of Destiny: World in Action', Martin Aston, *Melody Maker*, 6 July 1984.
12. 'Sad about the Boy', Emma Daly, *The Independent*, 29 April 1997, independent.co.uk/news/sad-about-the-boy-1270092.html, retrieved 23 August 2022.
13. See bbc.co.uk/programmes/m00165jb for the whole series.
14. Mitterrand is often quoted as having said Mrs Thatcher had the eyes of Caligula, but the President's former aide, Jacques Attali, insisted that the reference was to Stalin and it had subsequently been misquoted. See: theglobeandmail.com/community/inside-the-globe/thatcher-caligula-monroewait-did-i-hear-that-right-the-dangers-of-misquoting/article4101423
15. For the full story of what went on behind the scenes in the greatest powerplay of the '80s, Archie Brown's *The Human Factor: Gorbachev, Reagan and Thatcher and the End of the Cold War* (Oxford University Press, 2020) is highly recommended.
16. Heseltine had fallen out with the PM over her clandestine manoeuvres in the Westland Helicopters Affair, in January 1986. For further disclosure on the dark arts involved, see theguardian.com/politics/2015/oct/05/margaret-thatcher-could-have-been-brought-down-by-westland-affair
17. Recently released National Archives documents reveal the behind-the-scenes attempts to resolve the Poll Tax crisis. See bbc.co.uk/news/uk-38382416
18. Testimony from an Anti-Poll Tax Federation unpublished internal inquiry, July–September 1990, provided to author and investigative journalist Ian Hernon on condition of anonymity and published in his book *Riot!* (Pluto Press, 2006) in the Poll Tax Riot chapter, pp. 237–47.
19. Ibid.
20. 'No, no, no!' was what she had to say to European Commission President Jacques Delors, who wanted her to join the European Exchange Rate Mechanism. Both pro-Europe Foreign Secretary Howe and Chancellor Nigel Lawson had threatened to resign over this issue the previous year, for which Howe received a demotion. Lawson quit and was replaced by John Major.
21. The BBC series *The Borgias*, which followed the myriad intrigues of Lucrezia's family, gripped the nation in 1981. In 2011, the series was remade by Netflix.
22. The title *Vision Thing* comes from an article about Bush Sr written by *TIME* journalist Robert Ajemian, 'Where Is the Real George Bush?', in which he wrote: 'Colleagues say that while Bush understands thoroughly the complexities of issues, he does not easily fit them into larger themes. This has led to the charge that he lacks vision. It rankles him. Recently he asked a friend to help him identify some cutting

issues for next year's campaign. Instead, the friend suggested that Bush go alone to Camp David for a few days to figure out where he wanted to take the country. "Oh," said Bush in clear exasperation, "the vision thing." The friend's advice did not impress him.'

23. One of the greatest tributes to Ivy that I found is this article by Scott Rowley for *Guitar World* magazine, published 23 December 2021 and available here: guitarworld.com/features/poison-ivy-the-cramps

Further Down the Rabbit Hole . . .

As well as the books/journals/websites already mentioned in the text and notes, for more on all the bands, artists and historical figures/movements mentioned in this book, the following are recommended:

Marc Almond, *Tainted Life* (Pan, 2000); *Beautiful Twisted Night* (Ellipsis, 1999)

Paul Burston, *Gutterheart: Life According to Marc Almond* (Dunce Directive, 1997)

Jeremy Reed, *Marc Almond: The Last Star* (Lume Books, 2019); *Young Limbs Rise Again: The Story of the Batcave Nightclub 1982–85* boxed set

Nick Cave, *King Ink* (Black Spring Press, 1988)

Adrian Bell, *Aylesbury Bolton Wolverhampton Hove: A Little Man and 101 Cardiacs Gigs* (Iron Bell Publishing, 2011)

Robert Smith, *Songwords* 1978–89 (Omnibus Press, 1989)

Lol Tolhurst, *Cured: The Tale of Two Imaginary Boys* (Quercus, 2017)

Carol Clerk, *Light at the End of the Tunnel: The Damned Official Biography* (Omnibus Press, 1988)

Morgan Brown, *The Damned: Every Album, Every Song (On Track)* (Sonicbond Publishing, 2021)

Christian Paris, *A Pretty Smart Way to Catch a Lobster* (Magic Alice, 2011)

Will Sergeant, *Bunnymen: A Memoir* (Constable, 2021)

Tony Fletcher, *Never Stop: The Official Echo & The Bunnymen Biography* (Omnibus Press, 1987)

Jeffrey Lee Pierce, *Go Tell It to the Mountain* (2.13.61, 1999)
Ian Curtis, Deborah Curtis, Jon Savage, *So This Is Permanence: Joy Division Lyrics and Notebooks* (Faber & Faber, 2014)
Peter Hook, *Unknown Pleasures: Inside Joy Division* (Simon & Schuster, 2016)
Jon Savage, *The Searing Light, the Sun and Everything Else: Joy Division: The Oral History* (Faber & Faber, 2018); *England's Dreaming* (Faber and Faber, 1991)
Jyrki 'Spider' Hamalaien, *Killing Joke: Are You Receiving?* (New Haven, 2020)
Lydia Lunch, *Incriminating Evidence* (Last Gasp, 1992); *Paradoxia: A Predator's Diary* (Akashic, 2007); *The Gun Is Loaded* (Black Dog Publishing, 2008); *Will Work For Drugs* (Akashic, 2009); *So Real It Hurts* (Seven Stories Press, 2019)
Helen Chase, *Magazine: The Biography* (Northumbria Press, 2009)
Rory Sullivan-Burke, *The Light Pours Out of Me: The Authorised Biography of John McGeoch* (Omnibus Press, 2022)
Mark Paytress, *Siouxsie & The Banshees: The Authorised Biography* (Sanctuary, 2003)
Steven Severin & Catharyne Ward, *The Twelve Revelations* (Onerious Press, 2000)
Mark Andrews, *Paint My Name in Black and Gold: The Rise of the Sisters of Mercy* (Unbound, 2022)
Trevor Ristow, *Waiting For Another War: A History of the Sisters of Mercy Volume 1 1980–85* (GKW Press, 2021)
Dave Ball, *Electronic Boy: My Life In and Out of Soft Cell* (Omnibus Press, 2020)
Simon Tebbutt, *Soft Cell: The Authorised Biography* (Pan Macmillan, 1984)
Matt Sorum, *Double Talkin' Jive* (Awesome Books, 2022)
Rolf Vasellari, *Virgin Prunes: The Faculties of a Broken Heart* (Black Sheep Press, 1985)
Richard Cabut and Andrew Gallix, *Punk Is Dead: Modernity Killed Every Night* (Zero Books, 2017); Richard Cabut, *Dark Entries* (Cold Lips Press 2019); *Looking for a Kiss* (Sweat Drenched Press 2020); *Disorderly Magic and Other Disturbances* (Far West Press 2023)

Susan Compo, *Life After Death and Other Stories* (Visible Spectrum, 2020)
Tony Drayton, *Ripped & Torn* (Ecstatic Peace Library, 2018)
Roger K. Burton, *Rebel Threads* (The Horse Hospital/Laurence King, 2017)
Wesley Doyle, *Conform to Deform: The Weird Story of Some Bizzare* (Jawbone, 2023)
Ian Glasper, *The Day the Country Died: A History of Anarcho Punk 1980–84* (PM Press, 2014)
John Peel/Sheila Ravenscroft, *Margrave of the Marshes* (Corgi, 2006)
Simon Reynolds, *Rip It Up and Start Again* (Faber & Faber, 2005)
John Robb, *The Art of Darkness: The History of Goth* (Louder Than War, 2023)
Matthew Worley, *No Future: Punk, Politics and British Youth Culture 1976–84* (Cambridge University Press, 2017)
Peter York, *Style Wars* (Sidgwick & Jackson, 1980); *Peter York's Eighties* (BBC, 1996)
Rob Young, *Electric Eden: Unearthing Britain's Visionary Music* (Faber & Faber, 2011)
Francis Beckett and David Hencke, *Marching to the Fault Line: The 1984 Miners' Strike and the Death of Industrial Britain* (Constable, 2009)
Tony Benn, *End of an Era: Diaries 1980–89* (Penguin, 1994)
Nick Davies, *Flat Earth News* (Vintage, 2009); *Hack Attack* (Vintage, 2015)
Mark Garnett, *From Anger to Apathy: The British Experience Since 1975* (Jonathan Cape, 2007)
Martin Hickman and Tom Watson, *Dial M For Murdoch* (Allen Lane, 2012)
Peter Taylor, *Provos: The IRA & Sinn Féin* (Bloomsbury, 1998); *Loyalists* (Bloomsbury, 2000); *Brits: The War Against the IRA* (Bloomsbury, 2002)
Phil Baker, *The Devil Is a Gentleman: The Life and Times of Dennis Wheatley* (Dedalus, 2009); *City of the Beast* (Strange Attractor Press, 2022)

Jerry Hopkins and Danny Sugarman, *No One Here Gets Out Alive* (Plexus, 1980)
Kris Needs, *Dream Baby Dream: Suicide – A New York Story* (Omnibus, 2015)
Sandra Niemi, *Glamour Ghoul: The Passions and Pain of the Real Vampira* (Feral House, 2021)
Jennifer Otter Bickerdike, *You Are Beautiful and You Are Alone* (Faber & Faber, 2021)
Matthew Sturgis, *Beardsley: A Biography* (Overlook, 1999)
John Szwed, *Billie Holiday: The Musician and the Myth* (Viking, 2015)

Index